To Denise,
  May the Lord hold
you close to His
  heart of peace!
    Love In Christ,

WHAT THE BIBLE SAYS ABOUT PRAYER

WHAT THE BIBLE SAYS SERIES

WHAT THE
BIBLE SAYS
ABOUT
PRAYER

Mitchell Simpson

College Press Publishing Company, Joplin, Missouri

Copyright © 1987
College Press Publishing Company

Printed and bound in the
United States of America

Library of Congress Catalog Card Number: 87-070451
International Standard Book Number: 0-89900-255-2

DEDICATION

First and finally, this volume is dedicated to the glory of the Lord God Who answers prayer. May any truth therein be to His praise; may any error be known to be mine alone.

In addition, this volume is dedicated to my teachers in prayer. The first of these were my parents and grandparents. To the loving memory of Perry and Jimmy Simpson and Henry and Lavonne Durnbaugh I dedicate this volume for counsel and example. To their children and my parents, Ben and Doris Simpson, who took me to worship and showed me how to pray, I dedicate this volume. To my brother Ronald, who showed me courage and humor, I also dedicate this volume.

This volume is further dedicated to the faculties of Lincoln Christian College, Cincinnati Christian Seminary and Huntington College for patient instruction and modeling. To the congregation who taught us so much about the reality of prayer, we dedicate this volume: Central Church of Christ, Streator, Illinois; the Church of Christ, Alexandria, Kentucky; Spring Creek Christian Church, Logansport, Indiana; Black Oak Church of Christ, Gary, Indiana; and Milburn Boulevard Church of Christ, Mishawaka, Indiana.

I also dedicate this volume to Robert F. Yawberg who God used to spark my interest in the study and personal practice of prayer by his devotion to the Lord and to the discipline of daily petition.

And, especially, this volume is dedicated to the four who have taught me the most about the joys and pains of the reality of prayer: my wife, Debbie, whose prayers still frighten me a little, and my children, Christopher, Liberty and Megan. For your love, patience and help, I thank you.

Table of Contents

Prayer is a struggle for me. It always has been. I find in my communion with God the sweetest hours and the sharpest agonies of my life. I am told I am not alone in this. Many people have shared how important they know prayer to be and how easy it is to procrastinate their beginning to pray. Most Christians do not develop a private devotional habit of daily Bible reading and prayer. Some do not know how; some just need a push to get going. This book then is presented with twin purposes: to instruct in the Biblical facts of prayer and to encourage the increased practice of prayer.

The primary source of the information contained here is the Holy Bible. The secondary sources are the many wonderful works of great men and women of faith who took the time and effort to set down for us what they had learned about prayerlife with God. In addition, the personal experiences of those prayer warriors I have been allowed to know personally in my life have no doubt flavored my comments. Lastly, my own experiences before the throne of the Almighty Father have to be taken into account. I do not hold my own prayerlife up as any model.

You may well be far beyond me in the practice of this art. I am like the single Bible college student teaching a class on marriage; I speak of more than I know. But I am not worried. Neither my experience nor that of anyone on earth is to be our standard of truth; "Thy Word is truth."

This book will not be able to give you a mighty personal prayer ministry. Such a ministry only develops as one prays. Prayer is truly learned in praying. If this book can help motivate you to seek the Lord more regularly and thoughtfully, it will have served its purpose. May our Father use this book to help meet the individual spiritual needs of each of you who read any part of it. Amen.

Mitch Simpson
August, 1986

1

WHAT IS PRAYER?

A PARABLE OF PRAYER

The woman struggles through the crowd. Jostled on every side, she winces at each touch. "Unclean!" she screams in her heart, "Don't touch me. I'm unclean." But she pushes ahead in grim silence. Progress is difficult. The internal bleeding has left her constantly weak. Yet she clambers on toward the man at the center of the moving throng.

For many years, the woman has sought relief from the flow of blood from her body. Doctor after doctor has taken her money without helping until nothing is left. The priests tell her she is unclean,[1] unfit to worship. They hint she brought this agony upon herself by some unconfessed sin. Family and friends no longer visit. The loneliness gnaws at her each night as she huddles with her ceaseless aching and stench.

Now she has gathered the last vestiges of hope to break all the laws and seek out this new rabbi who was said to have the power of God to

---

1. Leviticus 15:25-30.

11

heal. Ugly memories of past encounters with religious men keep her from calling out to him directly. She has simply joined the crowd which follows him and is working to get close to the young man ahead of her.

Her goal approaches. Through tear-blurred eyes, she glimpses the young rabbi a few feet away from her. With her last energy, she stretches out her hand through the jumble of bodies finally just to touch His cloak. This instant, she knows; it is done. Her body is whole again; her life is saved.

The rabbi stops. Slowly turning, Jesus asks, "Who touched Me?" as His quiet eyes search the faces about Him. Hundreds had bumped Him or brushed by, but He sought the one who reached out in faith to touch His power.

The woman comes under His gaze and collapses at His feet. Her whole story rushes out of her lips amidst her sobs. With a gentle hand, Jesus lifts her up and says, "Daughter, your faith has saved you; go in peace, and be healed of your affliction."[2]

Apply this imagery to our prayers today. Like the throngs, many of us desire to get close to God, to talk with Him. Yet only those painfully aware of their need and confident in the Lord's grace actually touch Almighty God and His power. Prayer, then, is our effort to get in touch with God. From the feverish plea of a child in a darkened room to the wandering conversation of a little lady in a nursing home, prayer is our grasping for contact with Someone who cares about us and is able to help us as no man can.

While we desire this divine fellowship, we struggle against obstacles and inadequacies which hinder the development of our prayerlife. Our Father understands. He cares so deeply that we be able to share with Him that He has offered His Son to death. By Christ's sacrifice, God has torn apart both the physical and spiritual "veils" which kept us from Him. Jesus Christ did not stay in heaven but came down to bring God close enough to be touched. The Son then died for our sin to make us clean enough to approach the Father. This book unfolds God's invitation to us to communicate with Him through Jesus Christ.

---

2. See Matthew 9:20-22, Mark 5:25-34 and Luke 8:43-48. The translation, "has saved you," is a literal rendition of the text.

THE IMPORTANCE OF BEING IN TOUCH WITH GOD

Lest we waste time on a trivial subject, first we ought to ask, "Is prayer important? Why should we study prayer?" We recognize the central place of prayer in our lives through four evidences.

We study prayer because all peoples pray.

The universal practice of prayer suggests its importance. Men and women around the world in every age have sought God (or gods) in prayer. They each knew innately that their limited ability to handle life required supernatural intervention. Especially during wars, natural disasters, personal crises, illnesses and tragedies, mankind has turned to God with a desperate hope. As the "court of last appeal," prayer has offered the possibility of justice and mercy in a cruel world. Many echo the words of Abraham Lincoln, "I have been driven many times to my knees by the overwhelming conviction that I had nowhere else to go."[3]

Any activity which is practiced so universally deserves our interest and thoughtful study. If prayer has had such a widespread impact on human life, we need to understand its process, even if only to know ourselves better.

We study prayer because God changes
circumstances in answer to prayer.

The possibilities of prayer declare its importance. If a prayer may cause the Almighty God to act on one's behalf, what could be more important? In answer to prayer, God plagued Egypt until Israel was released from slavery. By prayer, Moses turned God's wrath from destroying His people. Prayer empowered the conquest of Canaan, the victories of the judges, the defense of Israel and Judah under their kings and the return of Israel from exile. Prayer preceded the opening of barren wombs, the provision of godly spouses, the healing of various diseases,

---

3. *The New Dictionary of Thoughts*, ed. Tryon Edwards, rev. ed. ([N.A.]: Standard Book Company, 1966), p. 504.

the protection of the helpless and the raising of the dead. Praying people have seen those lost in sin won to Jesus Christ and lives transformed for good; broken families have been reunited and forgiveness has joined those whom sin had separated. The church reaches around the world for Jesus Christ depending on the power of prayer. And God has not changed; He answers our prayers today as He answered those of Moses, Elijah and Paul.

In your congregation, do you not know of individuals or families who have seen God alter "impossible" situations in answer to believing prayers? Each of us can experience the Lord's gracious presence and receive the help we need when we are on our knees. In a world out of our control, our prayers become a center of strength and hope where we can deal with life as God empowers us. And that is a second reason for us to study prayer.

We study prayer because God desires us to pray.

God's own declaration of the importance of prayer makes it a mandatory habit of every Christian. While many activities are commanded for the Christian, prayer is specifically enjoined as a continual activity of the disciple's walk. Here are some sample passages:

a. "Seek the Lord and His strength; Seek His face continually" (I Chronicles 16:11 and Psalm 105:4).

b. "Call to Me, and I will answer you, and I will tell you great and mighty things, which you know not" (Jeremiah 33:3).

c. "Keep asking, and it shall be given to you; keep seeking, and you shall find; keep knocking, and it shall be opened to you" (Matthew 7:7).[4]

d. "With all prayer and petition pray at all times in the Spirit, and with this in view, be on the alert with all perseverance and petition for all the saints . . ." (Ephesians 6:18).

e. "Rejoice always; pray without ceasing; in everything give thanks; for this is God's will for you in Christ Jesus" (I Thessalonians 5:16-18).

---

4. The Greek verbs here are in the present tense, indicating repeated action. See H.P.V. Nunn, *A Short Syntax of New Testament Greek.* (Cambridge: Cambridge University Press, 1956), p. 66.

Why does the Bible command that we should pray? Consider the following line of Biblical logic:

1. Every good thing that any person has is a gift of God. (John 3:27; James 1:16-17)

2. Therefore, whatever we desire to receive for ourselves and for others, we are to seek from God in prayer. (Matthew 7:7-12; James 4:1-3)

3. Then when we have received, we are to thank God and praise Him in prayer for all His blessings. (Romans 1:18-21; I Thessalonians 5:16-18)

4. When we misuse what we have received, we confess our sin in prayer and God forgives us in Jesus Christ. (Psalm 32:5; I John 1:8-9)

5. When we receive the final gift of eternity with our Lord, our life in heaven will include praise and thanksgiving as a principal part of our ministry to Him. (Revelation 5:8-14; 7:9-12)

So God reveals prayer to be His chosen means for us to receive and to respond to His blessings, now and forever. Third, then, we study prayer because we owe it to God to do as He has commanded to the best of our ability. But, let us turn to a more personal reason to pray.

We study prayer because we desire to draw close to One we love.

As a child, I spoke to my parents for mostly selfish reasons. I asked for food or clothing or toys (later the car keys and gas money). I said I was sorry to avoid their wrath. I said thank you in the hopes of getting more. I discussed with them the people and events that interested me. I was bored by their interests. I was a child, speaking with the self-centered interests of a child. Young Christians can have a childish prayerlife if not led on to maturity in their relationship with Jesus Christ.

Now, when I go home, I desire to know Dad and Mom more than to get anything from them. I want to simply be with them, enjoy their company and share my life with them for a time. Our discussions become more intimate and heartfelt. Honesty tears at our masks and pretense is surrendered in favor of real fellowship. So it is with speaking to God. The importance of prayer for the mature Christian is the opportunity to get closer to God Himself, to touch His cloak, to begin to know Him. Prayer ceases to be a selfish necessity and it becomes a conversation of love, personal and warm. And, finally, that is why we should study prayer . . . for the love of God.

THE PURSUIT OF A BIBLICAL DEFINITION OF PRAYER

Accepting that prayer is vitally important to us, just what *is* prayer? It would be convenient if God had written a simple twelve word definition of prayer (and many other concepts) in the back of our Bibles. But He didn't. However, the Bible does indicate what prayer is in God's sight. But finding that definition will take a little time and work. So let's investigate together.

How do we use the word, "prayer," in daily speech?

Before searching for God's definition of prayer in His Word, think about what most of us mean when we talk about "prayer." What kind of communication are we describing? Are we using the word "prayer" in the same way God does?

Standard American dictionaries define "prayer" as: "the act of praying" (not overly helpful), "an entreaty; supplication," "a humble request, as to God,"[5] "an address (as a petition) to God or a god in word or thought," and "a set order of words used in praying."[6] Do you notice the stress on asking for something in these definitions; "entreaty," "supplication," "request," and "petition?"

In most situations, when we say we are "praying," we mean that we are appealing to God for some general or specific gift. A casual sampling of the prayers you hear in church services or at home will probably confirm this. So often, our prayers resemble shopping lists or self-centered letters to a cosmic Santa Claus.

True, asking God for something is an essential element of Biblical

---

5. David B. Guralnik, ed., *Webster's New World Dictionary of the American Language.* (New York: Warner Books, 1979), p. 469.
6. Henry Bosley Woolf, ed., *Webster's New Collegiate Dictionary.* (Springfield, Massachusetts: G. & C. Merriam Company, 1981), p. 896.

prayer. But is that all prayer is? Some have suggested so,[7] but the Biblical evidence implies a much wider field of communication for prayer as we shall see.

What words does the Bible use about praying?

In Appendix A, you will find two charts of the major Old and New Testament terms associated with prayer. Take a moment now to read through the lists and check some of the references. Then come back and join me to discuss some conclusions on the Biblical meaning of prayer.

What is the Old Testament concept of prayer?

Back so soon? Great! Let us begin with the Old Testament words. What were people doing when they prayed in ancient times? First, of all, they got emotional! They cried, they groaned, they roared, they sang! Can you imagine someone sleeping through a prayer meeting with all that going on? Joy and sorrow filled the Psalms from the living experiences of the people of God. Israel felt the desperate need for a God to help them, a desperation which modern people in their relative comfort may not share.

Imagine a world in which medicine could not suppress pain, where war was very personal and brutal (and frequent). Life was seen as a literal spiritual battle between the gods of nations, with the mightiest deities leading their city-state to the throne of empire (I Kings 20:22-30). In Peacetime, picture daily life which droned on with boring, bitter labor and slavery grew on every side. Nearby pagan worship included infant sacrifices and bestial orgies. Would not our prayers be a bit more vibrant if we had to literally struggle for each meal? The more a man realizes his need for God, the more honest and agonized his prayers can become.

---

7. John R. Rice, *Praying—Asking and Receiving.* (Wheaton, Illinois: Sword of the Lord Publishers, 1942).

But fear and sorrow are not the primary emotional themes of the prayers of Jacob's descendants. Celebration before the Lord is the norm. God had set five annual feast days, with only one annual fast for the nation (Leviticus 23). The Psalms consistently move on to end in joy and praise, regardless of the dark mood in which the author may begin his prayer (Psalm 22). Since the God of Israel was God indeed, His lovingkindness toward His people left them worshiping Him with exuberance and excitement (Psalm 100).

Yet, be reassured that there were also times of stillness and silence in the worship of Israel. So it seems likely that some tired shepherd might have nodded off when Moses prayed or David sang. Prayers were sometimes whispered and quiet meditation comforted many hearts.

Prayer in the Old Testament was a personal response to one's situation based on faith in the God of Israel. The Law did not have to command that the people pray; prayer was assumed to be a natural activity of a person conscious of both of his own needs and God's nature.

A distinctive emphasis of Old Testament prayer is its communal nature. One might speak to God with personal emotion, but the very nature of worship under the old covenant assumed that many personal prayers would be offered within a group setting. Crowds would bring their individual sacrifices to the tabernacle and later the temple. Men would stand by one another on the temple grounds to pray. Families would pray together. Cities and nations would repent and confess their sins as a unit. (At Nineveh in Jonah's time, even the animals were made to fast and wear sackcloth during their national repentance!) Victory songs of praise were taught to whole armies. Private prayers coexisted with collective prayers.

So, while it is true that God listened when a whole nation cried out to him, He also answered the requests of individuals which affected whole nations. In fact, the Old Testament contains the records of many great individual intercessors who changed history with their prayers. Moses' pleadings kept Israel from the wrath of God often; the people of Israel begged for Samuel to continue to pray for them; David taught his people how to pray and praise by his own example; the kings of Judah who sought God saw revivals in their time; Daniel and Esther saw God save His people from death in answer to their prayers even during their captivity. So both personal and group prayers were effective before the coming of Jesus.

Several components repeat themselves through all these prayers. Petitions, intercessions, confessions and praises (including thanksgiving) are directed to God again and again. These forms are often freely mixed in a single prayer or psalm (II Samuel 22; Daniel 9:1-21). Each of these was expressed verbally, that is, in words. These words may be openly expressed or whispered in the heart, but prayer clearly deals with words offered to God. Music and even dancing may have accompanied praise, but it was the words which were the praise offered (Psalms 149 and 150).

Special forms of prayer were developed for special circumstances. As agreements were made between men and God or between men, oaths began to be used, asking God to be a witness to the agreement. If those involved with these agreements or covenants acted as they had agreed, God would be invoked to bless them. If, however, one party broke the covenant, a curse demanded God to judge the offender and punish him. By New Testament times, an elaborate system of formal oaths had been developed to try to keep Israelites honest.

The person addressed in these and other prayers is normally a deity. Occasionally, men make requests from other men and words associated with prayer are used of these requests. But, this is not the religious use of the words. When the Bible simply says that a man or woman prayed, no one assumes he or she was addressing a human being; prayer is expected to be addressed to a god unless otherwise noted. And, if prayer is said to any other god but the God of Abraham, Isaac and Jacob, the Old Testament authors stated this was false and foolish prayer (Isaiah 42:8-10; 45:20-22). The only true prayer was directed to the only true God.

Prayer was also considered empty when not accompanied by faith and obedience in the person praying (Isaiah 29:13). Especially when viewed in the context of Israel's covenant with the Lord, the effectiveness of every prayer was conditioned by the completion by the petitioner of his commitments to God (Isaiah 1:14-20). Where the believer had failed to live up to his commitment, repentance and a right sacrifice were required to restore an open communication with God (Psalm 51).

In summary, the Old Testament definition of prayer could be stated as follows: prayer is personal and verbal communication from a loyal believer to the God of Israel. The New Testament adds to and modifies this definition as the fuller revelation in Jesus Christ is given.

What is the New Testament concept of prayer?

While the vocabulary of prayer in the New Testament is not as varied as the Old Testament, the meaning of prayer is clarified and deepened with the coming of Christ and the giving of the Holy Spirit in the new covenant. Let us look at the New Testament words associated with prayer by comparing and contrasting the concepts of the Old Testament with those of the New Testament.

1. Prayer remains an emotional practice in the New Testament. As in the Old Testament, words for crying, groaning, shouting and singing are used of praying people. The example of Jesus Christ is especially important here:

> In the days of His flesh, He offered up both prayers and supplications with loud crying and tears to the One able to save Him from death, and He was heard because of His piety. Although He was a Son, He learned obedience from the things which He suffered (Hebrews 5:7-8).

If prayer in agony was part of the "training" of the Son of God, how can we avoid its necessity in our lives? Those who would keep prayer dry and distant find no support in the Word of God.

2. The loud note of joy also rings through New Testament prayer. Paul insists several times in his letter to the Philippians that they should "rejoice in the Lord" (Philippians 1:18; 2:17-18, 28; 3:1; 4:4, 10). This happiness in our Savior balances the pain of our spiritual struggles in the prayer closet.

3. The "prayer closet" reminds us of shift in emphasis from the Old to the New Testament. In both, corporate prayer is encouraged by example and direct teaching. (See Acts 4:23-31 and James 5:13-18.) But, in the Gospels, Jesus emphasizes the personal dimension of prayer and underlines the danger of pride in public prayer (Matthew 6:5-6). So, personal prayer has come to be more central to our practice in many modern churches than congregational prayer.

4. The same components of prayer delineated in the Old Testa-

ment are repeated in the New. Petitions, intercessions, confessions and praises are again suggested. But now, thanksgiving, which was implicit in Old Testament praise, becomes explicit in New Testament teaching. While the Hebrew had no term to deal specifically with the concept of giving thanks, the New Testament Greek has several such terms.

5. The oaths of the Old Testament are discouraged in the New Testament; in fact, they are all but forbidden (Matthew 5:33-37; James 5:12). Rather than external motivations to honesty, internal commitment to truth by accepting Christ is encouraged.

6. Prayer in the New Testament is addressed to God as it is in the Old Testament. But, a new relationship is revealed for the believer and His God now. A new covenant based on God's grace in Jesus Christ has made us sons of God who pray to a heavenly Father, not just an awesome Deity Who lives on the far side of the universe. Intimacy could well describe this new union we have with God; He lives in us, we live in Him. No sacrifices are needed to atone for our sin and keep open the door to fellowship with God. The once-for-all sacrifice of Jesus Christ has opened the door permanently for all believers.

7. Prayer can still be hindered by the disobedience of the believer (I John 3:21-24). Yet, cleansing from sin is readily available in repentance and confession in prayer (I John 1:8-9). We no longer struggle to fulfill a covenant of law as the Old Testament believer did to maintain his fellowship with God. We can approach the Father due to the cleansing we receive in the blood of the Son. Indeed, no one can approach the Father in prayer, *except* through Jesus Christ (John 14:6). Furthermore, the New Testament informs us of two Intercessors Who constantly approach the Father on our behalf: the Son and the Spirit (Hebrews 7:25; Romans 8:26-27).

In summary, the New Testament definition of prayer could be stated as follows: prayer is the personal and verbal communication from a Christian to His Father, Almighty God, through Jesus Christ. This working definition will be used for the remainder of this book. This is what we will mean by "getting in touch with God."

Thought or Discussion Questions

1. Why do most people want to get in touch with God? Why do I desire

fellowship with Him? If I knew that I would not receive any material blessings from prayer, would I still pray? Why or why not?

2. What are some reasons to study prayer? Why am I interested in knowing more about prayer? What is the most that our church members could believe God would do in answer to their prayers this week? What answers to prayer have we seen in the past?

3. Do most people really believe God wants to hear from them in prayer? Why or why not? How can I encourage others to pray in my family and in my congregation? How many people I know want to know God better because they simply love Him? Why?

4. What do most people mean when they talk about "prayer?" What do I mean? Where do these ideas come from?

5. What is my summary of the Old Testament's concept of prayer? What is my summary of the New Testament's concept of prayer? How would I define prayer today? Does this describe what I do and how I see my own prayer life?

2

WHAT IS THE PURPOSE OF PRAYER?

Why pray? That is, what is the motivation to pray? Remember, your prayer essentially involves God and you. So, in this chapter, we will be answering these two questions: "Why does *God* want us to pray?" and "Why do *we* need to pray?"

WHY DOES GOD WANT US TO PRAY?

Certain myths have arisen to explain why God wants us to pray. For example, haven't you heard the following ideas: "I have to tell God what has happened to me and what I need so that He will know what to give me." "I think God is lonely; if we don't talk to Him, who will?" "I've got to pray. If I don't pray, God won't do anything." Let us lay these myths to rest and then get on to God's true reasons for commanding prayer.

23

The Myth of God's Ignorance

The first myth is an unspoken idea behind many of our prayers. The myth stated is: "The Lord needs our prayers to know what is going on." We often talk to God as if He had been "out of town" and needed to catch up on the latest news. We give a rambling description of recent events or a list of detailed petitions with explanations as if the Lord were ignorant about our lives. Yet, God does not need our prayers to inform Him of anything.

This myth seems to arise from our habit of thinking of God in human terms. When people talk to us, we learn new information. Erroneously, we often conclude that God also requires people to talk to Him so that He can acquire new information.

What does the Bible say? Jesus contrasted Christian prayer with pagan prayers in the sermon on the mount (Matthew 6:7-8). He noted the repetitive pagan prayers assume a "god" who can be aroused or impressed by an avalanche of words. But Christ reminds His disciples, "Therefore, do not be like them; for your Father *knows* what you need, before you ask Him." God is never surprised by anything we tell Him; He already knows what we will say before we ever pray.

"The eyes of the Lord are in every place, watching the evil and the good" (Proverbs 15:3). Our omniscient Lord does tell us to pray, but not in order to inform Him; He has seen and heard it all. Tossing that myth out, let's turn to a second.

The Myth of God's Loneliness

Another myth explaining God's command we pray is that God is all alone and desires some companionship. In the creation account of the poem *God's Trombones*, God is described in the following terms:

> He looked on His world with all its living things,
> And God said: I'm lonely still.
> Then God sat down—
> On the side of a hill where He could think,
> By a deep, wide river He sat down;

With His head in His hands, God thought and thought,
Till He thought: I'll make me a man![1]

The logic runs: since the Lord needed us to be with Him in the beginning of creation, He still needs our prayers to assuage His loneliness. God needs someone to talk with and we're it!

Again, this myth appears to be an attempt to understand God in human terms. People need other people; even God agrees to that.[2] So God must need someone else, too. We just cannot imagine that God was ever really happy in eternity past before He created the universe, the angelic host and us. We come perilously close to a pagan view of a "god" who needs his creation as much as his creation needs him.

What does the Bible say? Paul was addressing a pagan audience at Athens and confronting them with the truth about the true God:

The God who made the world and all things in it, since He is Lord of heaven and earth, does not dwell in temples made with hands; neither is He served by human hands, as though He needed anything, since He Himself gives to all life and breath and all things . . . (Acts 17:24-25).

It may be a blow to our human egos but God does not *need* either us or anything we can give Him. We are like children offering to make Dad a loan from the allowance He gives us. As Paul asked the Corinthians, "And what do you have that you did not receive?" (I Corinthians 4:7). If God is our ultimate source of every good thing,[3] how can we reverse the roles and believe He is dependent on us for the companionship we imagine He needs?

Remember, Jesus tells us that there was shared love and glory in the Godhead long before the world was ever founded (John 17:5, 24).

---

1. James Weldon Johnson, "The Creation," in *Poems To Read Aloud*, ed. Edward Hodnett (New York: W.W. Norton and Company, Inc., 1967), p. 177.

2. "Then the Lord God said, 'It is not good for the man to be alone; I will make him a helper suitable for him'" Genesis 2:18. Note that the word "good" is the same word used in Genesis 2:17 of the "tree of knowledge of *good* and evil." It seems God is saying that it is not morally right for man to be alone.

3. James 1:17.

Father, Son and Spirit have dwelt together in eternal joy in the past without need of men to complete their happiness. God may desire our prayers but He does not need them; He is not a cosmic Geppetto Who has created a race of Pinocchios to talk to Him. This purpose for prayer is not worthy of God; rejecting this, let's look at a last myth.

The Myth of God's Inability

A third myth traps God within the limitations of our prayers. While rarely directly stated, this myth is reflected in such sayings as, "God does nothing but in answer to prayer."[4] This myth makes prayer, not *a* means of God's grace, but *the* means through which God *must* work. Prayer becomes a virtual key to God's cage which releases Him to work for a time and then returns Him to the cage until we call Him again. This theory explains God's commands to pray as His setting up circuits to release His power (which would otherwise be unused).

Teaching that God is unable to act unless we pray is simply heresy. It makes the Lord Almighty a mere genie available at our rubbing of the magic lamp of prayer. The Scripture does not describe a God Who is simply responding to the initiatives of men but rather the Lord Who initiates what He wills, whether anyone asks or not. While it is true that God works through answering prayer, He is by no means bound by the limitations of our petitions. He acts as He wills, in perfect love and justice.

Consider the record of the acts of God: He created the universe (no one was around to pray for this); He created man (who did not ask to be created); He decided man needed a "helpmeet," woman (how could Adam have known to ask for?); when man fell, God set the hope of a Savior in the midst of His curse (Eve did not beg for this "seed"); God chose Noah and his family to live (Noah did not ask for this honor); the Lord frustrated the plans of men at Babel; God made a covenant with Abraham; God produced the son of promise, Isaac; God maintained the bloodline of the Messiah; God called Moses, sent plagues, split the

---

4. John Wesley as quoted in Paul E. Billheimer, *Destined For The Throne* (Fort Washington, Pennsylvania: Christian Literature Crusade, 1975), p. 17. See also p. 102 ff. for similar sentiments.

sea; God selected Joshua, separated the Jordan, knocked over city walls, defeated armies, gave lands, sent judgments by invasions, protected His ark, changed kings in Israel, sent His word in prophet's lips, removed His people into exile and brought them back, sent His Son to die for the sins of you and me and . . . *He* decided to do these things, not the prayers of men.

What does the Bible say? There was once a man who requested to contend with God in conversation. This man, Job, felt that God had acted unfairly and had not consulted him before allowing great pain in his life. Job demanded that God hear him and respond. After the Almighty had heard Job's cries and had shown a portion of His glory to the man, Job's humble response was:

I know that Thou canst do all things,
And that no purpose of Thine can be thwarted.
"Who is this that hides counsel without knowledge?"
Therefore I have declared that which I did not understand,
Things too wonderful for me, which I did not know.
"Hear, now, and I will speak; I will ask Thee, and do Thou instruct me"
I have heard of Thee by the hearing of the ear;
But now my eyes sees Thee;
Therefore I retract,
And I repent in dust and ashes (Job 42:2-6).

Many of our prayers are exactly declarations of that which we do not understand, like Job's. As we see God as He is revealed in Scripture, we are humbled and see how foolish it would be to make God dependent on our prayers. God does not request our prayers because He needs our advice on running the universe. He requires not our advice but our obedience.

If these three myths fail to explain God's interest in our prayers, what is the two-fold reason He commands that we pray?

Answer 1: God's love desires we receive all good.

God loves a world of free moral beings (us). And He mercifully wants to give us all we need, and, yet, allow us the privilege of having control of the major decisions of our lives. So, through prayer, the Lord gives us the right to ask for our needs and wants. He *could* lovingly meet our needs without requiring our prayers; but, as an additional gift, His love includes our ability to take part in the process of grace by praying.

Jesus invited His disciples to pray to God on the basis of the Almighty's love for them. In John 16:26-27, Jesus reassures the apostles of their right to prayer in His name after His resurrection.

In that day you will ask in My name, and I do not say to you that I will request the Father on your behalf; for the Father Himself loves you, because you have loved Me, and have believed that I come forth from the Father.

Did you catch that? God does not have to be persuaded by His Son to hear our prayers; He already loves those who love His Son and He desires to hear from us. After all, what did Jesus teach us to call God when we pray? Right you are! "Our Father!"[5] Why? So that we would realize that God cares for us as a loving Father and that we should pray accordingly. We pray knowing our Father knows what we need and wants to abundantly "give what is good to those who ask Him!"[6] Yet, there is another reason God's love desires our prayers beside His Father's joy in giving to us.

In order to learn to love someone, how do you get to know them? Would just watching what he or she does be enough? Well, I didn't get to know my wife by just watching her (though that was fun, too). We had to break the communication barrier; we had to talk. After you fall in love with that special person, how do you sustain and develop your relationship? Again, intentional communication is the basis of any intimate relationship. We have all seen marriages sinking in a sea of silence never to rise again. The families that "float" keep buoyant with loads of real conversation. Now what is true of physical families is also true of spiritual ones.

---

5. Matthew 6:9.
6. Matthew 6:8, 32-33; 7:7-11.

God loves us; we love Him; and people who love *talk*. God has sent us a bundle of "love letters" which are inexhaustible in their richness. In reply to His messages in the Bible, we respond with the "love language" of prayer. Like any father, God wants us to desire to know Him as much as we desire to receive anything from Him. And that's one reason He wants us to pray.

Answer 2: God's justice requires He receive all glory.

A second reason God commands us to pray to Him is this: the perfect justice of His nature demands that He (and He alone) should receive our praise, thanksgiving and petitions, and that He should reward those who seek Him. This reason can be further broken down into the three Biblical concepts underlined below.

The Lord deserves to receive our praise and thanksgiving. David sang in the eighteenth Psalm, "I call upon the Lord, who is worthy to be praised."[7] We are to render to all that which is due to them; unending praise is the Lord's due and our duty.[8] Who should receive our thanks but Him who is the source of every good and perfect gift? Praise and thanksgiving are simply the just responses of every individual to the Person and work of the Almighty God.

The Lord alone ought to receive our petitions. To what other person should we turn but the Lord when we seek aid beyond the power of man? The Lord answers in the prophecies of Isaiah:

Is it not I, the Lord?
And there is no other God besides Me,
A righteous God and a Savior;
There is none except Me.
Turn to Me, and be saved, all the ends of the earth;
For I am God, and there is no other.
I have sworn by Myself,
The word has gone forth from My mouth in righteousness

---

7. Psalm 18:3.
8. Romans 13:7.

And will not turn back,
That to Me every knee will bow, every tongue will swear
allegiance (Isaiah 45:21b-23).

We can rightly pray only to the only God Who is there to hear. Our prayers declare that the Lord, He is God, our unique Father and Savior. So God declares that we pray to Him so that we (and others) will recall that He IS God.

The Lord justly rewards those who seek Him. In order to differentiate between those who believe in the Lord and love Him and those who deny the Lord and reject Him, the Lord uses answered prayer to designate those who are His.[9] Both groups are sinners, but the believers have found forgiveness when they came to the Lord and He pronounced them righteous in Jesus Christ. So the Lord in justice hears the prayers of those who seek Him in faith.

And without faith it is impossible to please Him, for he who comes
to God must believe that He is, and that He is a rewarder of those
who seek Him (Hebrews 11:6).

In summary, God wants us to pray because He loves us and because He deserves our prayers. He wants to have us "get in touch" with Him for love and justice. Now what is the purpose *we* have for talking with God?

WHY DO WE NEED TO PRAY?

Trying to understand why God wants anything is difficult for mere mortals like you and me. So we have spent some space seeking to see why God wants us to pray. But understanding why we need to pray will not use much of our time. It's easy. We pray because we need that which only God can give. And what is it that only God can give? Ask John the Baptist. In John 3:27, John is responding to his disciples who

---

9. See the following sections from the Psalms: 4:3; 9:8-9; 10:3-4; 11:7; and 14:1-6.

expressed worries about the movements of the crowds away from John to follow Jesus. "John answered and said, 'A man can receive nothing, unless it has been given him from heaven.' " "Nothing," John? Do you mean that we wouldn't have *anything* if God had not given it to us? Yes, we need what only God can give — EVERYTHING!

Does opposition to this idea seem to automatically rise in your mind? Then you are normal. "But, God doesn't give me my salary; I earn it." "But, God didn't supply my needs when I was a child; my parents did." "But, God wasn't there to help me change that flat tire; my brother was." At this precise point, a great spiritual danger arises. We may mentally minimize our need for God's gracious gifts, given in answer to prayer.

Israel had the same problem. As they were about to enter the promised land, the Lord warned them through Moses through these words:

Beware lest you forget the Lord your God by not keeping His commandments and His ordinances and His statutes which I am commanding you today; lest, when you have eaten and are satisfied, and have built good houses and lived in them, and when your flocks multiply, and your silver and gold multiply, and all that you have multiplies, then your heart becomes proud, and you forget the Lord your God who brought you out from the land of Egypt, out of the house of slavery. . . . Otherwise, you may say in your heart, "My power and the strength of my hand made me this wealth." But you shall remember the Lord your God, for it is He who is giving you power to make wealth, that He may confirm His covenant which He swore to your fathers, as it is this day (Deuteronomy 8:11-14, 17-18).

God supplies us with everything, either directly or indirectly. So, when we realize our needs, we come to God in prayer. That's why we pray, to fill our many needs.

Our primary need is a continuing relationship with the Lord of the universe. The Lord is not merely the Giver of many gifts; He is the center of the Christian's life. We need God for Himself; He is our love, light, truth, peace and security. Like the Psalmist we cry,

As the deer pants for the water brooks,
So my soul pants for Thee, O God.
My soul thirsts for God, for the living God;
When shall I come and appear before God? (Psalm 42:1-2).

We need to praise Him and thank Him to express our convictions of joy and love. We confess sin in prayer in neediness for forgiveness and a clear conscience. We ask for ourselves and others to receive the necessities and gracious gifts He gives. All those needs are true of each of us as individuals, but it is also true that people as groups have needs which God meets in answer to their prayers.

Families pray together because families need God to bind them together. God joins together couples in marriage; God gives the gift of children; God sets into the family a structure derived from His own Fatherhood.[10] As a husband and father, I appreciate deeply not having the pressure of being the monarch of my home. I can gather my wife and children, and together we can bow in worship to the only Lord of our house. His wisdom is perfect, while mine is flawed; His provision is complete, while mine is partial; His love is endless, while mine is limited. Our family needs to pray to our Father.

Churches pray together because congregations exist only to do the will of God by His power to His glory.[11] The church which lives on the strength of its members will die; unless the Lord build His spiritual house, we labor in vain who try to build it. "For I am confident of this very thing," Paul said in explaining his prayers for the church, "that He who began a good work in you will perfect it until the day of Christ Jesus" (Philippians 1:6). Our congregations need to pray because we are helpless without our Father's blessings.

The needs expressed above should motivate us to pray. But, sadly, many Christian individuals, families and churches do not pray often or passionately because they have caught "Loadicean Languor."[12] This spiritual disease has very subtle symptoms: no body heat to speak of,

---

10. Matthew 18:6; Genesis 29:31-30:24 and Psalm 127:3-5; and Ephesians 3:14-15.

11. Ephesians 3:14-21.

12. For a full case study of this dread plague in the early church and its treatment by Jesus Christ, see His letter to Laodicea in Revelation 3:14-22.

blindness in self-examination and numbness to pain, poverty and nakedness. Those infected can be spotted by their smug grins of contentedness and self-satisfaction. They have made their own "peace" with their sinful habits; they do a little good and a little bad and are content. They have acquired enough worldly goods to attain a comfortable worldly life and are content. They remain blissfully ignorant of the Lord and His Word and are content. Simply, these people do not pray because they *feel* no need, though they are actually in desperate want. The Great Physician comes to those with the "Languor" with an excellent prescription:

> Those whom I love, I reprove and discipline; be zealous therefore, and repent. Behold, I stand at the door and knock; If anyone hears My voice and opens the door, I will come in to him, and dine with him, and he with Me (Revelation 3:19).

If the need of love to seek one's Creator and serve Him is insufficient, then sterner motivations must be used. To break through the numbness and contentedness, the Lord must bring in discipline, pain and testing. If they refuse the Lord's discipline, they become like victims of intense cold. Running from the pain until they are exhausted, they hide shivering in some rude shelter, growing completely numb, drifting into sleep and hardly recognizing when they cross over into spiritual death. But, if the Lord's discipline causes them to realize and accept their need, they can repent, throw open the door and welcome meeting with the Lord; then He can meet their every need. The "Languor" can be cured and the lukewarm set aflame.

To summarize our conclusions: Why does God want us to pray? God loves us and is just and so He wants us to pray. Why do we need to pray? We need the Lord and all He gives us and so we pray.

Thought or Discussion Questions

1. What three myths are suggested in this chapter to explain God's desire that men pray? Why would people think these were true? Which is most prevalent in my church? How would I lead someone to a more Biblical understanding of God's motives for requesting prayers?

2. What two motives are Biblically given for God's desire for us to pray? Which of these appeals to me the most? Why? How are each of these motives a direct reflection of the very nature of the Lord? Can we really say that God "enjoys" our prayers?

3. Though not discussed directly in this chapter, what are some improper reasons that people pray, either publicly or privately? (If you need some help getting started, look at Matthew 6:1-15.) Why are they improper? Why should we pray? Why do I pray?

4. Why do we have difficulty admitting our neediness for God? What are the benefits of admitting our neediness in prayer?

5. What countries of the world have the greatest outbreaks of "Laodicean Languor"? How does God discipline us to remind us how needy we are? Suggest some examples of people who have been turned back to God by His discipline and others who have refused to admit their dependency upon Him. Which am I?

3

WHAT PERSONS ARE INVOLVED IN PRAYER?

Your prayer closet is crowded. While many of us see prayer as a quite private affair, the Bible tells us that prayer involves a host of persons, struggling in a perilous warfare. In fact, the prayer process entails every conscious being of which we are aware. Briefly, we are going to look all these persons, classified into seven categories, and examine their relationship to our prayerlives.

GOD THE FATHER IS INVOLVED WITH OUR PRAYERS

When I answer the phone, one of the questions I ask at the very beginning is, "Whom am I speaking to please?" I want to know whom I am talking to so that I can respond properly. Prayer also requires we know Who is on the other end of the line.

The Proper Object of Prayer

Whom do we speak to in prayer? As Christians, we can discount men,[1] angels or other "gods" as the proper objects for prayer. But we are still left with the Father, Son and Holy Spirit; do we pray to one, two or all three of these divine Persons? The Biblical answer seems semi-clear; let me explain.

Except for a few verses, the Bible states that we are to pray to the Father. The Old Testament exclusively prescribes prayer to the Lord God; Jesus consistently taught His disciples to pray, "Our Father, who art in heaven"; the early church prayed to the Father; Paul's letters call for us to give all thanks to the Father.[2] So, the vast majority of verses point to the Father on the throne as the object for our petitions.

The relationship of the persons of the Godhead in prayer seems also well-defined in Scripture. Ephesians 2:18 clarifies this relationship beautifully; "For *through* [Jesus Christ] we both have access *in* one Spirit *to* the Father." In this passage, Paul describes Jesus as the One who brings both Jew and Gentile into the presence of His Father through His death for our sin. The indwelling Spirit is then the Person in whose very presence and empowering our prayers take place. And, clearly, the Father is the Person to whom we have access.

But, some "speed-bump" Scriptures keep us from rushing to the conclusion the Father is the *only* proper object of our prayers. The first comes from the teaching of Jesus in the upper room. John 14:13 and 14 reads:

And whatever you ask in My name, that will I do, that the Father may be glorified in the Son. If you ask Me anything in My name, I will do it.

Christ seems here to be inviting the disciples to pray directly to Him. Later, in the same discourse[3], Jesus specifically indicates that prayer should be addressed to the Father in His (Jesus') name. We may be fac-

---

1. The question of invoking saints in prayer will be dealt with later in this chapter.
2. Old Testament—Isaiah 45:21-23 and many others; Jesus—Matthew 6:5-14, 7:7-11; early church—Acts 4:23-30; and Paul—Ephesians 5:19-20, Colossians 3:16-17.
3. John 15:16; 16:23-24.

ing here another of the paradoxes of the Godhead, where the unity and diversity of the Father and Son are blurred. In some way we don't clearly understand, petitioning the Father in Jesus' name may also involve asking from the Son.

A second "speed-bump" is Stephen's petition to Jesus at his stoning recorded in Acts 7:55-60. This example is as uncertain as the verses above. Stephen has a vision in his dying moments of Jesus at the right hand of the Father in glory. Then, he speaks to Jesus, requesting that Jesus receive his spirit and forgive his executioners (in words reminiscent of Christ's sayings on the cross). Now, was this prayer or a supernatural conversation with Jesus similar to Paul's encounter with the risen Lord on the road to Damascus? The kindred words of Christ on the cross are thought of as prayers when addressed to the Father; the phrase "he called upon the Lord" is used to describe Stephen's activity and that phrase is normally associated with prayer. Is the question moot when few of us can claim to have a vision of the Son to accompany our petitions?

A third "speed-bump" is the selection of verses which ascribe praise, a form of prayer, directly to Jesus Christ. The clearest examples are in the book of Revelation.

> And I looked, and I heard the voice of many angels around the throne and the living creatures and the elders; and the number of them was myriads of myriads, and thousands and thousands, saying with a loud voice, "Worthy is the Lamb that was slain to receive power and riches and wisdom and might and honor and glory and blessing." And every created thing which is in heaven and on the earth and under the earth and on the sea, and all things in them, I heard saying, "To Him who sits on the throne, and to the Lamb, be blessing and honor and glory and dominion forever and ever." And the four living creatures kept saying, "Amen." And the elders fell down and worshipped (Revelation 5:11-14).

Here Jesus receives individually and with the Father the praises of all creation. Does that imply we should specifically include praises directly to Jesus in our prayers?

None of these "speed-bump" Scriptures seem definitive to me. The overwhelming voice of the Bible calls us to pray to the Father; no Scriptures indicate prayer may be offered to the Holy Spirit and the argument that prayer may be offered directly to Jesus seems to me to come more from a hyper-trinitarian theology than a clear teaching of the Word.[4] Except possibly for extraordinary circumstances, the normal object of our prayers is God the Father. Now, in order to properly respond to the One who listens to us, how is the Father described by the One who knows Him best, the Son? And how does His nature alter our prayers?

The God of All Places

In the sermon on the mount, Jesus devotes one section to prayer and the nature of the God who hears. He begins by denouncing self-serving, public, hypocritical prayers. Instead, He encourages us to pray in private to a God "who is unseen" and "who sees what is done in secret."[5] This refers to God's omnipresence, the fact that He is present at all places at all times.

Two consequences of this truth for our prayerlives concern the places we pray and the nakedness of sin. First, we can pray anywhere and know that God hears us. We do not need some public forum to be heard. Nor do we need to wait until we are in some "holy" location to talk to our Father; kneeling at a Lazyboy in your family room you can be as "close" to the Lord as seated in the "sanctuary" of your church.

Second, a God who is everywhere means that we cannot avoid the presence of the Almighty. Would you or I dare to lie, steal or lust before the very face of God? Yet we all do. Realizing this fact, our confessions become more meaningful when we accept that God was *there* when we sinned. And that's what it means to pray to an omnipresent Lord.

The God of All Knowledge

Jesus next spoke of pagans who tried to catch their "gods" atten-

---

4. One such argument is given in Wayne R. Spear's, *The Theology of Prayer* (Grand Rapids, Michigan: Baker Book House, 1979), pp. 18-30.

5. Matthew 6:5-6 (N. I. V.).

tion. If their idols weren't listening, they could not know the people's needs and meet them. So the pagans chanted and shouted in order to be heard. Jesus countered that our Father knows all about our needs before we even verbalize them.[6] This implies God's attribute of omniscience. As mentioned in the last chapter, our prayers do not inform the Lord or remind Him of unknown or forgotten information. Our needs, hopes and dreams are laid out before God in constant display.

God's omniscience denotes three ideas for praying. First, prayer must be honest. No one can lie to God and get away with it. How foolish to try to "con" God; yet, often I try to tell God that I *need* something which is actually just a *want*. He knows better. The only reasonable thing to tell an omniscient God is the truth.

Second, prayer should have no "empty" words. We do not impress the Lord by addressing Him as, "O magnificent and sublime Emperor of creation and our ultimate ground of being." The Lord is not reached by our eloquence; He knows exactly what we are really saying.

Third, prayers should be offered in faith that they are being heard. At times, my prayers *feel* like empty echoes. Even the Psalms reflect this common experience.[7] But I should know that He knows. Whether I sense His presence or not, He hears me when I call. Yes, sin can interfere with our prayer relationship with God (later we will spend a chapter discussing prayer problems). But, even then, emotions do not indicate accurately how open God is to any given request. Our faith in the God who knows everything insures His attention.

The God of All Holiness

In the first sentence of the model prayer, Jesus requests that God's name be held as holy, "Pray, then, in this way: 'Our Father who art in heaven, Hallowed be Thy Name' " (Matthew 6:9). He knew that holiness was essential to the nature of God. Holiness means to be set apart, especially morally.[8]

---

6. Matthew 6:5-6.
7. Psalm 22:1-2; 42:9-11.
8. See the definitions for "hagiazo" and "hagios" in F. Wilbur Gingrich's *Shorter Lexicon of the Greek New Testament* (Chicago: University of Chicago Press, 1965), pp. 2-3.

We should have three reactions to God's holiness. One, we should praise the Lord for His holiness. God is worthy to be exalted in our prayers, for He is perfect in righteousness and goodness.

Two, we should have an attitude of reverence in approaching the Exalted Lord. Our prayers cannot treat God as an equal of whom we are asking a favor. Only by His grace are we allowed into His presence; let us remember that fact as we address Him who is "Holy, holy, holy!" (Isaiah 6:3).

Three, we should realize the importance of continuing confession. As light allows no darkness in its presence, God will not abide sin. When we pray, we continue to be cleansed by the blood of Christ or we attempt to enter the throne room of the Almighty dragging a putrid bag of sin into His presence. No wonder the Psalmist says, "If I regard wickedness in my heart, the Lord will not hear" (Psalm 66:18). We cannot overlook our impurities as we realize His absolute purity.

The God of All Authority

"Thy kingdom come. Thy will be done, on earth as it is in heaven" (Matthew 6:10). In the second segment of the model prayer, Jesus declared the power and authority of His Father. The Lord is the absolute Sovereign of the universe. How does this affect our prayerlife?

Since He is the King of kings, we pray to a God whose power to help us is unlimited, save by His will. We often limit the Lord's ability to answer prayer to the limits of our concepts of His power. Paul reminds us of God's vast resources in one of his most lovely benedictions:

Now to Him who is able to do exceedingly abundantly beyond all that we ask or think, according to the power that works within us, to Him be the glory in the church and in Christ Jesus to all generations forever and ever. Amen (Ephesians 3:20-21).

In other words, we cannot even think of big enough requests to try the ability of God. But, because God *can* does not demand that God *will*.

God's sovereignty also implies that He has considered and evaluated every supplication before deciding whether and how to answer our prayers. Considering our limited and flawed view of life, we should be grateful that God sorts our requests instead of rubber-stamping them. We need to decide to follow Peter's admonition concerning our attitude in prayer.

> Humble yourselves, therefore, under the mighty hand of God, that He may exalt you at the proper time, casting all your anxiety upon Him, because He cares for you (I Peter 5:6-7).

The God of All Grace

Jesus included in His model prayer three petitions to meet our human needs of sustenance, forgiveness and deliverance.[9] As we noted last chapter, God does not meet these needs due to our worthiness. Specifically, forgiveness for sin cannot be earned. God is under no obligation to forgive or give us anything, yet He does. This reflects that segment of His nature which is called "grace." Consider your prayers in the light of the grace of God.

First, we do not have to harass our Father until we force Him to unwillingly help us. God loves to give to His children. Second, God is more willing to forgive than we are to repent. He "is patient toward you, not wishing for any to perish but for all to come to repentance" (II Peter 3:9). God's gracious will makes our confessions and prayers more relaxed as we realize He is on our side. And "if God is for us, who is against us?" (Romans 8:31).

The God of All Justice

Jesus' final statements in this section concern the justice of God. Somehow we might come to the erroneous idea that God can forgive sin through Jesus Christ because He doesn't really care that much about sin. Wrong! We even think that God gave His Son to bloody death so

---

9. Matthew 6:11-13, "Give us this day our daily bread. And forgive us our debts, as we also forgive our debtors. And do not lead us into temptation, but deliver us from evil."

that we can sin with a clear conscience. Wrong! Wrong! Jesus warns us:

> For if you forgive men for their transgressions, your heavenly Father will also forgive you. But if you do not forgive men, then your Father will not forgive your transgressions (Matthew 6:14-15).

Is the Lord saying we have to earn our forgiveness from God by forgiving others? Not at all. He is simply saying that God cannot justly forgive us when we are continuing in the sin of a critical and unforgiving spirit. Confession in prayer does not allow us to circumvent the justice of the Almighty.

How does God's justice affect our praying? Primarily, the moral purity of our lives can change the effectiveness of our prayers. God is not about to reward sinners given to their sin. Gentlemen, even the tactless way in which you handle your wife can hinder your petitions to a God of justice.[10] We cannot refuse to repent of known sin and expect the Father to eagerly fulfill our desires. God's mercy allows Him to bless the imperfect, but His justice demands that the Lord only reward those who seek Him and His kingdom.

While we do not have space here to develop a complete theology, the more we understand the Father revealed by the Son the more our prayers will be proper responses to Him. To come to the Father, we come through the Son, whose ministry we will study now.

JESUS CHRIST IS INVOLVED WITH PRAYER

Our Savior is central to our prayerlife. Jesus Christ is the mediator of our prayers, the high priest of our prayers and a great teacher of prayer. Examine with me each of these Biblical roles.

Jesus Our Mediator

Others have taught us about prayer in the Bible and throughout

---

10. I Peter 3:7.

history, but Christ is our *only* mediator with the Father.

> For there is one God, and one mediator also between God and men, the man Christ Jesus, who gave Himself as a ransom for all, the testimony borne at the proper time (I Timothy 2:5-6).

A mediator's task is to go between two parties and bring them together. Jesus Christ goes between God and men to bring them together. How does He accomplish this essential task? Jesus came to us on God's behalf to show us the Father's love by the costly demonstration of His own death and resurrection. Jesus now goes to the Father moment by moment on our behalf.

No one else has been given the pivotal position of mediator. The Catholic concepts of Mary as "mediatrix" or the "saints" in heaven invoked to mediate find no basis in Scripture. Yes, we may intercede for one another in our prayers. But, to be mediators, we would have to have a unique relationship with God whereby we can also represent God to men. Only Christ has these credentials.

We admit the mediatorial office of Jesus Christ as we are praying "in Jesus' name." Jesus told us that in His name we are to pray and in His name God will respond.[11] In fact, many occurrences in the New Testament are tied to the name of Jesus Christ. Consider the following list.

New Testament Occurrences	Scripture References
Demons are cast out in Jesus' name.	Luke 10:17; Acts 16:18, 19:13
The gospel is preached in Jesus' name.	Luke 24:47; Acts 8:12
The Holy Spirit is sent in Jesus' name.	John 14:26
Eternal life is made available in Jesus' name.	John 20:31
People are baptized in Jesus' name.	Acts 2:38; 8:16; 10:48; 19:5
A lame man is healed in Jesus' name.	Acts 3:6, 16
Salvation is only available in Jesus' name.	Acts 4:12
Signs and wonders were performed in Jesus' name.	Acts 4:30
Jesus' followers suffer for His name.	Acts 5:41, 15:26
Forgiveness of sin is received through Jesus' name.	Acts 10:43
Christians are washed, sanctified and justified in Jesus' name.	I Corinthians 6:11
Thanks are always given for all things in Jesus' name.	Ephesians 5:20
Every knee shall bow at Jesus' name.	Philippians 2:10
Christians are to do all that they do in word or deed in Jesus' name.	Colossians 3:17

---

11. John 16:23-24.

This astounding list indicates that the whole of the Christian life from beginning to end is to be done in the name of Jesus Christ. Now what does that mean? To act in Jesus' name is to act in accordance with His will and instruction. To act in Jesus' name is to act by accepting His work and power on our behalf to do what He desires.[12]

In practice, does praying in Jesus' name require actually using a *phrase* like "in Jesus' name"? The New Testament evidence seems to deny the use of a verbal formula. Verbatim prayers of Christ and the apostles consistently exclude the "Jesus' name" phrases (even our traditional "Amen" fails to appear in most cases). However, Paul does frequently ask that God act "through Jesus Christ" in his prayers and benedictions. Prayer in Jesus' name involves an attitude of submission to His authority and mediatorial office, rather than the use of a specific phrase. The latter smacks of "magical" words of power which make prayer "work"—a pagan concept of prayer. Our Mediator calls us to pray through His office in His name.

Jesus Our High Priest

In Jesus' day, some expected a Messiah who would also be a new and superior High Priest.[13] The work and office of the High Priest were central to the worship of Israel; the politically minded high priests of the New Testament era left the people wanting much more of their spiritual leaders. Jesus fulfilled that desire completely for them (and for us), though not as expected.

The High Priesthood of Christ for us is a central theme of the book of Hebrews.[14] As related to our prayers, Jesus' eternal and perfect High Priesthood means that we have assurance that our prayers can be heard. The work of the High Priest is to make it possible for the people

---

12. See Hans Bietenhard, "Name," *The New International Dictionary of New Testament Theology*, ed. Colin Brown (Grand Rapids, Michigan: Zondervan Publishing House, 1975), II, pp. 654-655.

13. Frank Stagg, *New Testament Theology* (Nashville, Tennessee: Broadman Press, 1962), p. 72.

14. One aspect of Christ's priesthood which we will not take space to discuss here deals with His relationship to two different priestly lines; Melchizadek and Aaron. Hebrews 7 deals specifically with this issue.

to "draw near to God" (Hebrews 7:25). This involves two essential actions by the Priest: to cleanse us from sin by making sacrifice and to intercede for us with God. Jesus provides both of these services for us perfectly.

First, Jesus presented the perfect sacrifice (Himself) as the perfectly pure High Priest (Hebrews 9:11-14; 7:26-28). By this sacrifice, we are cleansed once for all from sin and thus enabled to approach the Lord with loving boldness (Hebrews 10:19-22). Though only the ancient high priests could pass behind a heavy veil in the temple once a year on the day of atonement to approach God, through Jesus we are enabled to pass beyond through the veil of His flesh to come into the presence of the Lord Most High.[15] Why are we so honored? Because God has accepted the offering of Christ's death for our sin signified by His blood. We are clean because our High Priest has cleansed us. Let me share an illustration of our need for cleansing.

Willie Shoemaker remains one of the most famous jockeys in recent history. When Willie was dating his wife-to-be, Babs, they discovered that she was allergic to (of all things) horses! Now how could a jockey approach his wife who got hives from any contact with horses? The answer is that Willie has to scrub himself with surgical precision before he can go home from the track. And then, he showers again as soon as he gets home, just to make sure. *Then* he can approach Babs without causing her discomfort.[16] Perhaps the application is obvious; God cannot abide sin in His presence. We must be clean to come before Him. Willie Shoemaker could cleanse himself physically, but we cannot cleanse ourselves spiritually. Only the sacrifice of our High Priest cleanses us to approach our Father.

Second, in His role as our High Priest, Jesus acts as our eternal intercessor (Hebrews 7:25). This intercession includes His continuing loving requests for us before His Father to insure our spiritual victory in Him (Romans 8:33-37). He is uniquely suited to this office due to His two-fold nature. Since He is one with the Father, no closer intimacy

---

15. You may recall that the actual veil of the temple was torn open by the act of God in the moment of Christ's death (Matthew 27:51). This has been interpreted as both an act of grief (as people would tear their garments in sorrow) and an act of reconciliation in which God now accepts men openly into His presence due to Christ's sacrifice.

16. Jeanne Parr, *The Superwives* (New York: Coward, McCann and Geoghegan, Inc., 1976), p. 220.

could be imagined in which He seeks our best with the Father within His divine will. Since Jesus has also shared our humanity, He intercedes for us with deep sympathy and understanding of our weaknesses, needs and desires (Hebrews 4:14-16). Our Intercessor looks on us with mercy and faithfulness, always ready to aid us when we are tempted. (Hebrews 2:17-18) We have a divine "Prayer-partner" who goes to the Father with us to plead our case; therefore, our approach to God should be made with boldness.

> Since then we have a great high priest who has passed through the heavens, Jesus the Son of God, let us hold fast our confession. For we do not have a high priest who cannot sympathize with our weaknesses, but one who has been tempted in all things as we are, yet without sin. Let us therefore draw near with confidence to the throne of grace, that we may receive mercy and may find grace to help in time of need (Hebrews 4:14-16).

Jesus Our Teacher

Finally, while Jesus functions as our Mediator and High Priest, He is also a great Teacher concerning prayer. As all great teachers, Jesus both models the proper practice of prayer and instructs us in that practice.[17]

At every significant turn in His life, we find Jesus bowing in prayer to His Father. Isn't it comforting to know that Jesus in His strength needed His Father as we in our weakness need Him? (See John 5:19, 30; 14:10.) Consider the times in which the Gospels report that Jesus was in prayer.

Jesus lived a life of prayer. A model of the truth conveys its meaning more than many teachings. I can honestly say my own prayer life has been advanced more by sharing in prayer with great men and women of prayer than by the hundreds of books I may have read. Jesus provides

---

17. Note the excellent description of Ezra the scribe in Ezra 7:10: "For Ezra set his heart to study the law of the Lord, and to practice it, and to teach His statutes and ordinances in Israel." Here is a superb sequence for the preparation of a godly teacher: commitment, study, practice and THEN teaching. Too often we try to teach what we do not yet practice.

an example in His own life for us to absorb His methods.

As the great Rabbi, Jesus told us how to approach God in prayer (Luke 11:1). Many authors have written volumes attempting just to unfold Jesus' teachings on prayer. In fact, the model prayer (or "Lord's Prayer") has inspired many books by itself. So accurate and deep are Christ's teachings on prayer that no single author can mine all its treasures. Any Christian coming to the words of Jesus who asks, "Teach me to pray," will receive instructions in full. Throughout this book, I will attempt to share some of the wealth of Christ's teaching with you. While Jesus is our Mediator, High Priest and Teacher, the next Person we will examine is our Divine Intercessor.

Jesus Prayed:	Scripture
*At His baptism	Luke 3:21
Early in the morning, preparing to preach	Mark 1:35
Often alone	Luke 5:16
All night before calling apart His apostles	Luke 6:12
After being rejected by crowds and cities	Matthew 11:25-26
At the feeding of the 5,000	Luke 9:16
Before Peter's "Good Confession"	Luke 9:18
*At His transfiguration	Luke 9:28-29
At the return of the seventy	Luke 10:21
As His apostles asked Him to teach them to pray	Luke 11:1
When little children were brought to Him	Matthew 19:13
At the resurrection of Lazarus	John 11:41-42
*As He predicted His death on the cross	John 12:27-28
At the Last Supper	Luke 22:17, 19
For His disciples the night He was betrayed	John 17
For Peter's faith not to fail	Luke 22:32
In Gethsemane	Matthew 26:36-39
On the cross	Matthew 27:46; Luke 23:34, 41
At Emmaus, after His resurrection	Luke 24:30
At His ascension	Luke 24:50-51

*Occasions when His Father answered back from heaven.

THE HOLY SPIRIT IS INVOLVED WITH PRAYER

The third Person of the Godhead is a very controversial participant in prayer. Sadly, many Christians fear to speak of prayer in the Holy Spirit due to the rise of the charismatic movement. Images of swaying bodies with upraised hands fill our minds combined with sounds of emotional babbling and moaning, punctuated with outcrys of "Praise the Lord!" I neither hope nor attempt to please all sides in sharing the Biblical concept of the Spirit's place in our prayer life. I do desire to be true the Lord of truth. So let us begin. We will examine the Spirit's work in prayer in two divisions: His direct work and His indirect work.

The Direct Work of the Spirit in Prayer

The Holy Spirit affects us directly as we pray and He also intercedes with the Father for us. The Spirit's direct works in prayer include: access, adoption, adoration and intercession.

The Spirit of Access—Both Paul and Jude admonish us to "pray at all times in the Spirit."[18] What does that mean? Some would contend that prayer in the Spirit implies some supernatural experience where the mind relinquishes control to the Spirit. Yet Paul would hardly go on to give specific requests for his readers to "pray in the Spirit" if he did not expect them to direct their own prayers. And Jude sandwiches "praying in the Holy Spirit" between "building *yourselves* up on your most holy faith" and "keep *yourself* in the love of God." His accent is on self-discipline in godliness, not abandonment to a subjective episode or "speaking in tongues."

Then what *is* praying in the Spirit? In Ephesians, Paul uses the phrase "in the Spirit" of:

1. Our access to the Father (2:18).
2. Our building together as God's dwelling (2:22).
3. God's revelation to the apostles and prophets (3:5).
4. Our sealing for the day of redemption (4:30).
5. Our "filling," as opposed to getting drunk with wine (5:18).[19]
6. Our praying, standing firm in God's full armor (6:18).

In each of these passages, our condition "in the Spirit" appears to be a direct result of the Spirit dwelling in us, "a pledge of our inheritance" as Paul says in Ephesians 1:14. By His presence then, the Spirit gives: our

---

18. Ephesians 6:18-20; Jude 20.

19. In some translations, the Greek phrase, *en pneumati*, is translated "with the Spirit" in Ephesians 5:18.

right and ability to have access to the Father, revelation to the New Testament prophets, our sealing for redemption, our filling to share in mutual praise and service and finally our right and ability to pray for ourselves and one another. Praying in the Spirit is an objective spiritual state, not a subjective emotional experience. By being in Him (and He in us)[20], we acquire the right of access to God.

Additionally, prayer in the Spirit implies approaching God with a proper attitude and with proper requests. Jude 20 and 21 indicates these are proper when they are in keeping with the teachings of the Spirit in the Word (the "most holy faith") and are an appropriate response to the love of God.

The indwelling Spirit gives us access to the Father; but that access obligates us to prayer which acknowledges the Lordship of Christ in its humble attitude and Scripturally acceptable requests.

The Spirit of Adoption—The presence of the Holy Spirit in us underlines a change in our relationship with God. Before we accepted Christ, we were "without God in the world."[21] Now, in Christ, the Holy Spirit comes into our hearts doing two things: He comes into our hearts crying, "Abba! Father!" and by Him *we* cry out, "Abba! Father!"[22] The term "Abba" is Aramaic baby language for "Daddy."[23] Every spiritual child of the Lord is enabled by the Spirit to have the warm and intimate relationship with our Father in heaven of a baby on his daddy's lap. He does this in two ways.

First, the Spirit Himself comes into our hearts after we have become sons of God by adoption through the work of Jesus Christ. He cries, "Abba!"[24] Why? Is God the Holy Spirit's Father? Of course not! The Holy Spirit teaches us to call God our Father in the same way that any parent teaches a baby to say "Daddy." The parent keeps repeating the word to the child until the baby imitates the sound he hears. The Spirit applies the Word which He has inspired to our hearts wherein He has

---

20. In a similar way, we are "in Christ" as He is "in us." (See Ephesians 1:1-14 and 3:14-19.)

21. Ephesians 2:11-12.

22. Galatians 4:6; Romans 8:15.

23. See Otfried Hofius, "Father," *The New International Dictionary of New Testament Theology*, ed. Colin Brown (Grand Rapids, Michigan: Zondervan Publishing House, 1975), I, pp. 614-615.

24. Galatians 4:5-6.

said again and again that we are children of the Most High. He bears witness *with* our spirits through His Word that we are indeed children of God. (See Romans 8:16-17.)

Second, the Spirit of adoption encourages us to cry out, "Abba!" to God by His presence in us and His promises in Scripture. We know of the Spirit's presence in us because God has told us He is there and also because He enables us to put to death the deeds of the flesh and develop the fruit of righteousness.[25] When we believe the Spirit does indeed indwell us, we know that we are actually God's children since His Spirit in us is the seal and guarantee of our relationship with God.[26] We then realize that we have the right to approach God on the same intimate terms that Jesus Christ demonstrated during His life on earth. As Jesus called His Father, "Abba,"[27] so may we who are also His children.

Now does this mean that we should normally use the *words* "Abba" or "Daddy" to address God in our prayers? I think not. First, there is no example in Scripture or even early Christian writings where an apostle or any other Christian actually used such a title in speaking to the Father. Second, we must balance all the teachings of the Bible together in determining a proper pattern for prayer. In addition to this teaching concerning the intimacy of our prayer life, we must add the admonitions and examples to hold God in awe and reverence befitting His nature. Somehow "our Daddy who is in heaven" does not carry the tone of deference which our Lord deserves. So I understand the use of the term "Abba" to indicate an attitude of warmth and closeness to God without suggesting actual wording for our prayers.

The Spirit, then, leads us to understand and accept our adoption into God's family and the wondrous fellowship we are now allowed to have with our Father and God in prayer.

The Spirit of Adoration—Another function of the Holy Spirit in our prayerlife is the motivation of prayer and praise. What motivates your prayers? Fear? Duty? Sorrow? Joy? The Bible suggests that the Holy Spirit engenders a great love in our hearts which stimulates our prayers and praises to God. Examine the following three Scriptures with me:

---

25. Romans 8:12-13; Galatians 5:16-26; Ephesians 3:14-19.
26. II Corinthians 1:22, 5:5; Ephesians 1:12-14.
27. Mark 14:36.

At that very time He rejoiced greatly in the Holy Spirit, and said, "I praise Thee, O Father, Lord of heaven and earth, that Thou didst hide these things from the wise and intelligent and didst reveal them to babes. Yes, Father, for thus it was well-pleasing in Thy sight (Luke 10:21).

Here Jesus turns to the Father in praise after the seventy return and report that demons were being cast out in His name. Jesus taught that it was by the Spirit of God that demons were being cast out in His name (Matthew 12:28). So, motivated by the action of the Holy Spirit, Jesus lifts praise to the Father for choosing to work through His disciples. Moreover, the Spirit seems to encourage and support the exultation of Christ; that is, He rejoices "*in* the Holy Spirit." Whether this joy was caused by the Spirit's action in the disciples' ministry or in the heart of Jesus, causing Him to speak, is not clearly stated. But a connection between Christ being moved to praise and the work of the Spirit does seem clear. Next look at Romans 15:30.

Now I urge you, brethren, by our Lord Jesus Christ and by the love of the Spirit to strive together with me in your prayers to God for me. . . .

Paul seeks to motivate the Romans to pray on his behalf by bringing up the Lordship of Jesus Christ and the love created by the Spirit. This love which Paul speaks of seems to be the concern which the Spirit develops in Christians for God and for one another.[28] It is not by accident that heading the list of the fruit of the Spirit in Galatians 5 is love. Love can powerfully motivate us to communicate. Most of us remember a time in our lives when love drove us to seek out that one special person as often as possible. We may have written notes or songs of adoration for him or her. Every moment of conversation with that person was precious. And love can also powerfully motivate us to seek out God in prayer, both because we love Him and want to share our lives with Him and because we love those for whom we pray. Again, the Spirit encourages our prayers and adoration by the stimulation of godly love. Finally, consider I Thessalonians 1:6-7.

---

28. See Romans 5:3-5; Colossians 1:8.

You also became imitators of us and of the Lord, having received the word in much tribulation with the joy of the Holy Spirit, so that you became an example to all the believers in Macedonia and in Achaia.

The Bible names the Holy Spirit as a source of joy in several passages.[29] And joy can find its expression in praise to God and thanksgiving for His gracious gifts. In fact, the Spirit encourages our whole life of worship.[30]

In Galatians 5:22, Paul notes that love and joy are the first two fruit which the Spirit produces in us. As we learn to love the Lord and to rejoice in Him always, our prayer life explodes with excitement. We no longer struggle to force ourselves into the prayer closet; we desire to pray and seek the opportunity day by day. Now that may not be your experience; some days it certainly isn't mine. For we can oppose the work of the Spirit within us. But we can also choose to cooperate with Him by exposing ourselves to His Word and asking God in prayer to be filled anew with His love and joy. Then, we can and will adore our Father in the love and joy engendered in us through the work of the Holy Spirit.

The Spirit of Intercession—The Holy Spirit goes beyond helping us to pray; He actively intercedes with God the Father for us. Paul has a wonderful promise for us in Romans 8:26-27.

And in the same way the Spirit also helps our weakness, for we do not know how to pray as we should, but the Spirit Himself intercedes for us with groanings too deep for words; and He who searches the hearts knows what the mind of the Spirit is, because He intercedes for the saints according to the will of God.

Paul describes three groanings in this chapter: the groaning of creation in its corruption, the groaning of Christians in our sufferings and the groaning of the Spirit in prayer for us. In response, Paul first reminds us that, even in our groaning, we have hope to encourage us. Then, in these verses, Paul gives a second reason for us to be encouraged in the

---

29. See Acts 13:52; Romans 14:17; and Galatians 5:22.
30. Philippians 3:3.

midst of our groaning: the Spirit is helping our weakness, especially in prayer.

One indication of our weakness is our inability to know what we should be asking for at any specific moment.[31] For example, we are hurting with a broken relationship. Should we ask God to change the other person's heart or to change us or both? Should we request for God to save the relationship or give us strength to let it go? Should we just ask for patience to wait? Frankly, we just don't know what to ask God for with any certainty. We know generally what we want, but often not how to get it or even if what we want is what God desires. When we experience this helplessness in our prayer life, we can come to these verses for reassurance.

The Holy Spirit always helps us in our weakness, but especially in our praying in ignorance. Unlike you and I, the Holy Spirit knows *both* exactly what we actually need and exactly what the Lord's will is for us. Then, upon the basis of that knowledge, the Spirit speaks on our behalf to the Father with unspoken groanings (noting the depth of His feeling for our problems).[32] The text here is not referring to "speaking in tongues" or any other human prayer, but the intercession of the "Spirit Himself" "for [on behalf of] the saints." It is the Spirit Himself who is our Intercessor.[33]

In summary, the Holy Spirit directly affects our prayers by:
1. providing access to the Father.
2. maintaining our relationship as children of God.
3. encouraging praise by filling us with love and joy.

---

31. The phrase "how to pray" refers to the content of prayer rather than the method of prayer. See Wayne R. Spear, *The Theology of Prayer* (Grand Rapids, Michigan: Baker Book House, 1979), pp. 45, 83.

32. William Hendriksen, *New Testament Commentary, Exposition of Paul's Epistle to the Romans* (Grand Rapids, Michigan: Baker Book House, 1980). I, pp. 274-276.

33. This great chapter of Romans actually tells of two intercessors for us with the Father; the Spirit and the Son (in Romans 8:26 and 34). How do these two intercessors differ? I put some major differences in the following chart:

Difference in Intercession	Holy Spirit	Jesus Christ
Location of Intercessor	On earth	In heaven
Place of Intercession	In our hearts	At God's right hand
Emphasis of Intercession	Meeting our present real needs	Redemptive work in us

4. interceding for us with the Father.

But the Spirit also has an indirect influence on our prayers.

The Indirect Work of the Spirit in Prayer

The Holy Spirit changes our prayers indirectly by His activity in inspiring the Scriptures, sealing us in Christ and sanctifying us to become like Christ.

The Spirit of Scripture—Unquestionably, Christians are to be led by the Spirit of God. How do we know? Romans 8:14 states: "For all who are being led by the Spirit of God, these are sons of God." That seems obvious. But this concept has been a rock of stumbling for the prayerlife of many.

Many have prayed to God, "Lead me by Your Spirit," and then sat back to await some supernatural feeling, voice or vision to guide them. If the supernatural direction came, those so directed are encouraged to seek further supernatural experiences of guidance. If no feeling is felt, no voice heard or no vision seen, the seekers feel rejected by God (and are often told they are lacking in faith). How does the Spirit actually lead us?[34] Another way of asking the question is "How can I know the will of God for me?" We are going to take time to answer this.

If we are experiencing the leading of the Holy Spirit, we would think that we know what and how we should pray in a living relationship with God. And then we hear other believers relate how the Lord "told" them to ask this or do that and we feel very unspiritual and neglected. We haven't heard any inward voices (at least we're not sure) or had any miraculous signs to show us the perfect path God has designed for our specific lives. We sometimes feel, "How can we even know we're saved if God isn't speaking to us?" How can we pray aright if the Spirit doesn't supernaturally lead the prayer?

Since there are several basic misconceptions in this thought pattern, we have a lot to study. When we're through, you may feel better about your relationship with God and the leading of His Spirit.

---

34. Much of what follows comes from two major sources: Garry Friesen, *Decision Making and the Will of God* (Portland, Oregon: Multnomah Press, 1980) and Knofel Staton, *How to Know the Will of God* (Cincinnati, Ohio: Standard Publishing, 1976).

First, we need to sort out the categories many people impose on God's will. One popular way of looking at God's will suggests three categories as listed in the chart below.

Suggested Categories of God's Will

Type of Will	Definition	Scriptures
God's Sovereign Will	God's predetermined plan for everything that happens in the universe	Daniel 4:35 Romans 9:19; 11:33-36 Ephesians 1:1
God's Moral Will	God's moral commands that are revealed in the Bible teaching men how they ought to believe and live	I Thessalonians 4:3; 5:18 And all other commands in Scripture
God's Individual Will	God's ideal, detailed life-plan uniquely designed for each believer	Colossians 1:9; 4:12 Romans 12:2 Ephesians 5:17; 6:6 Proverbs 3:5-6; 16:9

To further clarify these three categories, let's consider a second chart comparing the categories.[35]

Comparing and Contrasting
the Suggested Categories of God's Will

God's Sovereign Will	God's Moral Will	God's Individual Will
1. A detailed plan for all events in the universe.	1. A body of general commands and principles for life.	1. A detailed plan for all decisions in a believer's life.
2. Hidden—the believer cannot find and know it.	2. Believers are expected to find, know and do it.	2. Believers are expected to find, know and do it.
3. Believers cannot miss it because it always comes to pass.	3. Believers can miss it by failure to discover or obey it.	3. Believers can miss it by failure to discover or obey it.
4. It can only be discovered after it has come to pass.	4. It was revealed to apostles and prophets and can be found completely in the Bible.	4. It is being revealed to the hearts of believers and cannot be found at all in the Bible.

---

35. From Gary Friesen, *Decision Making and the Will of God* (Portland, Oregon: Multnomah Press, 1980), pp. 38-39.

5. It is not revealed by the Holy Spirit to us in any way.	5. It was revealed by the Holy Spirit through supernatural revelation.	5. It is revealed by the Holy Spirit through inward impressions using many means.
6. It has no known directives, either general or specific.	6. Its directives are general for all believers. ("Marry only a believer.")	6. Its directives are specific for one specific believer. ("Marry Jane next month in Omaha.")

Looking at the chart above, you can see that God's individual will is the category we usually mean when we say we are "seeking the will of God." This is also the one we normally mean when we seek "the leading of the Holy Spirit."

God's universal will allows (but does not approve) many events which are not in His moral will; that is, for example, He allows us to choose to disobey Him in His universal will while condemning our disobedience in His moral will. Within His moral will, we are told, God has established a specific plan for each of us concerning every decision of life (His individual will). This is the "bull's eye" which we are trying to hit by figuring out exactly what that individual will is for us.

How do people go about finding God's individual will for their lives? Here are seven "road signs" often used to find the leading of the Holy Spirit.

1. The Word of God. Since God's individual will for us must be within the limits of His moral will defined in His Scriptures, we study the Bible to find the borders of His will.

2. Circumstances. We look at the situation in which we find ourselves and recognize that God is in control of all things. Therefore, He may maneuver events to provide guidance for us through our circumstances. This is often called the concept of open and closed doors. (See Colossians 4:3.) Also in this category is the concept of putting out a fleece (providing God a set of circumstances to fulfill which will indicate His directions for us). (See Judges 6:36-40.)

3. The Inner Witness of the Holy Spirit. Many people expect the Spirit to directly lead them through a subjective experience often called a "still small voice" in our hearts (Romans 8:14; I Kings 19:11-13).

4. Mature Counsel. Since the Spirit inhabits every Christian and has gifted some to be leaders and teachers, the thoughtful counsel of mature Christian leaders is also a means through which God has been

said to indicate His individual will for us (Proverbs 24:6).

5. Personal Desires. The Holy Spirit is sanctifying us and remaking us to become like the character of Jesus Christ. Therefore, the desires of our renewed nature might be a way God is leading us.

6. Common Sense. Our minds are also being renewed by the Spirit, so our common sense should not be ignored (I Timothy 3:2).

7. Special Supernatural Guidance. Throughout Scripture, men and women have been informed of God's will through supernatural means; visions, angelic visits, signs, dreams, voices, etc. Some Christians expect such direct guidance to continue today for all Christians (Acts 9:3-6).

But with all these signposts, what if they don't all agree? Or what if some of them are unclear? The answers to those questions vary according to the teacher who is answering. Yet, this process is still the most common way taught on how to determine God's will. You might wonder why this would be so. So do I. Here may be an answer.

Do you have the three basic categories straight? God's sovereign, moral and individual wills? Great! Now think about any Christian books and magazines you've read lately, Christian television or radio programs you've heard or Christian speakers or tapes you've listened to recently. Which area of God's will is getting the most exposure in the major Christian media? I believe we often find God's individual will, miraculously revealed, to be the current favorite. After all, it fits with the egocentric bent of our "me-generation." God's universal will is not open to us; God's moral will (in the Bible) is objective and considered "cold and intellectual" by many. But God's individual will paints a picture of God caring for *me* with a personalized plan for *me* which will be personally revealed by the Lord directly to *me*. As we began this book, we noted all of us want to get in touch with God. And this theory makes personal contact with God its hallmark. I believe that is its appeal.

Now here's the problem; one of those three categories of God's will is NOT taught in the Holy Bible. Can you choose the non-Biblical category? That's right! The Bible does NOT teach that God has an individual will for each person's life. That is, God has no preference on what we decide in non-moral issues as long as we act wisely (in line with His Biblical principles). The so-called Biblical support for God's individual will can be faulted in the following three areas.

1. In every Biblical *example* used, the means of communication is

supernatural revelation, which is an *exception* to the way the Lord normally deals with us. The heroes of the Old and New Testament were exceptional in their place in God's plans. There was only one Adam or Noah or Abraham or Moses or David or Peter or Paul. We should not take their unique experiences and make them normative for all Christians for all time. The revelations and signs which occurred in their lives had a specific purpose; to provide an authoritative Word from God.[36] Constant new revelations would require a constantly expanding Bible, whereas the Scriptures are complete for all needs until Christ comes again.[37] We are not in the same position as these early pioneers of the faith; we do not require the supernatural direction they needed for the propagation of the gospel.

2. In every *doctrinal* passage used, God's *moral* will is being taught; NO passage indicates communication of God's will via inner impressions. Simply nowhere in Scripture do we find anyone being led by an inner impression of the Holy Spirit. When the Spirit speaks, it is in clear declarative statements, not feelings or a "sense of inner peace." When God informs us to follow His will, He is speaking of His revealed will as first spoken by His prophets and apostles and written for us in His Word, the Holy Bible.

3. In every attempt to *apply* the sign posts used to determine God's individual will, the typical Christians find four major difficulties.

a. In ordinary daily life, the decision-making process must be abandoned in the "minor" decisions of life. If one follows the logic out that God has a detailed plan for every person's life, then you would not want to move, even to brush your teeth, until you knew God wanted you to move. In fact, no Christian I am aware of expects God to direct them outside of the Bible except on what they consider major life issues (i.e. whom should I marry, where should I live, what should my career be, etc.). Yet, if God has made the master plan for each of us, then how do *we* know what is major and what is minor? We don't know. No one practically has the time to seek God's individual will in even the majority of daily decisions. It just doesn't work.

b. In facing two or more equal options, insistence upon only one "correct" choice generates anxiety over "missing THE will of God for

---

36. See Hebrews 2:1-4.
37. II Timothy 3:16-17; Jude 3: Revelation 22:18-19.

me" rather than gratitude for more than one fine opportunity. Say that I am looking for a different place of ministry. Here are several alternative locations; each has certain points which commend them. I should be thankful for the many areas in which I can serve rather than stay up nights trying to find God's guidance to the "right" place. God wants me to serve Him; where I serve Him can be determined by following the Biblical principles for making a wise (godly) decision and, if there are two or more "good" choices, choosing the one I desire.

c. In Christians of every age, the logic of the existence of an individual will for each person tends to promote immature approaches to decision making. Waiting for a revealed choice can be simply avoiding the responsibility of making our own decisions as God desires us to do. Again, some Christians claim to have been "led by the Spirit" in a given area and then refuse to listen to a mature counsel, even when they are breaking Biblical injunctions. I have heard people claim the Spirit told them to: have an affair, not be baptized, renounce godly leaders, interrupt worship services with meaningless announcements, file bankruptcy and do other things which only bring disgrace to the name of Christ.

d. In using subjective means to find God's will, certainty is impossible when no objective source of knowledge is the base for our choices. Does a "closed door" mean "Not this way," "Wait a while and try again," or "Your faith is being tested; go ahead anyway"? Does a feeling of peace mean God approves of your decision or that YOU are happy with the decision? Certainty can only be claimed by another subjective feeling of certainty when feelings are the basis of decisions.

So, what IS God's will for you? God's will for you (and all people) is revealed in the Holy Bible. His personal version of His moral will for you is to obey His principles of life in your given circumstances. How? I'm glad you asked.

The Holy Spirit leads us primarily through the revealed Word. But what is the real daily process of making decisions in which we are led by the Spirit? Here is a suggested plan from the Word. For, the Bible says we can cooperate in being led by the Spirit.

1. We can study and memorize the Holy Bible which the Holy Spirit inspired (Psalm 119). If we have studied God's Word and find ourselves with two or more equally good choices according to God's moral will, then what?

2. Ask the Lord for wisdom (James 1:5-8). Wisdom is not the same

thing as specific information. James describes the wisdom which he is talking about in James 3:17 where it is described as an attitude toward a decision which is "first pure, then peaceable, gentle, reasonable, full of mercy and good fruits, unwavering, without hypocrisy."

3. In areas specifically addressed by the Bible, obey Biblical commands and principles (John 14:15).

4. In areas where the Bible does not speak (non-moral decisions), you are free to choose your own course of action under the umbrella of God's universal and moral will (Genesis 2:16-17).

a. Make your objective to please God in whatever you do (II Corinthians 5:9; I Thessalonians 4:1). So choose whatever will work best for His kingdom which is in His moral will.

b. Select godly goals (Romans 1:11-15).

c. Set your goals in priorities (Romans 15:20-29).

d. Pray and submit your plans to the sovereign will of God (James 4:13-17). God can still prevent those actions which would bring only harm to us when we ask Him to not lead us into temptation.

e. Don't lavish time on little decisions.

f. Thank God for multiple "open doors" and your right to choose the step you desire. In II Corinthians 2:12, Paul shares about an "open door" the Lord had provided. In verse 13, Paul notes that he was too upset over another concern to walk through that door! No guilt or anguish, he just chose to go another direction which was *also* open to him.

g. Use common sense on every decision as a facet of godly wisdom (Titus 1:8; 2:2, 5-6).

h. Use mature counsel in the given area of your decision (Proverbs 11:14).

i. Consider your circumstances as the context of your decision and weigh them in your decision making process (Romans 8:28-30).

j. Persevere in your choice (Luke 9:62).

k. Weigh impressions; they may come from a wide variety of sources, not all of them godly. And don't lay out fleece to determine God's will. Originally,[38] Gideon did not lay out fleece to determine God's will; God had already told him what to do. Gideon was just afraid

---

38. See Judges 6:11-24, 36-40.

to do it and wanted reassurance. So, laying out fleece is simply a sign of weak faith, not of seeking God's will.

The Holy Spirit is leading us today. He leads us as He has done the vast majority of God's people throughout history: through the principles and examples of the Holy Bible. In some very special times, God has given supernatural guidance. But don't count on your problems to be God's very special times. Open your Bible; use your mind; pray for godly wisdom; have the courage to take the responsibility to make decisions as you pray within the Spirit's leading in the Scriptures.[39]

The Spirit of Sealing — Earlier, we mentioned the sealing work of the Holy Spirit. Our prayers are "certified" by the presence of the Holy Spirit in our hearts. As a result, we pray with New Testament hope; that is, a real certainty that God hears us. We also hope (expect) that God will fulfill His promises which are noted in the Bible and pledged to us by the Holy Spirit in us.[40] So, indirectly, the Spirit provides a firm foundation of hope for our prayers by His sealing ministry.

The Spirit of Sanctification — The process of sanctification can be defined as a progressive "separation to God" and "separation of the believer from evil things and ways."[41] Note that there are two sides to becoming holy: growing closer to God in relationship and character and putting to death the deeds of the flesh.[42] This process is overseen by the Holy Spirit according to several Scriptures.[43] How does this Spirit-led process alter our prayer lives?

First, the sanctification process encourages the prayer activity of confession. Before we can admit sinful patterns, we need to know that our activities or thoughts are wrong. Then we must be convinced that we ought to change and we must choose to desire to change. This is the convicting work of the Holy Spirit described in John 16:7-11. In practice, we are convicted of sin through hearing, reading and studying the

---

39. Interestingly, Paul seems to equate being "filled with the Spirit" with letting "the word of Christ richly dwell within you." See the parallel passages in his letters to the Ephesians (5:17-20) and the Colossians (3:15-17).

40. See II Corinthians 1:22 and Ephesians 1:13-14, 4:30.

41. W.E. Vine, *An Expository Dictionary of New Testament Words* (Old Tappan, New Jersey: Fleming H. Revell Company, 1966), p. 317. See also Romans 6:15-23, especially verse 22.

42. Romans 8:12-13; Ephesians 4:17-24; James 4:7-10.

43. Romans 15:15-16; I Corinthians 6:11; I Thessalonians 4:1-8; II Thessalonians 2:13; and I Peter 1:1-2.

Holy Bible, which is the Holy Spirit's tool (Ephesians 6:17). Paul wrote that the Scriptures act on us in five ways:[44]

1. The Scriptures can give us "the wisdom that lead to salvation through faith which is in Christ Jesus."

2. The Scriptures can teach us the basic facts of life which we are to believe and the moral standards of God which we are to follow.

3. The Scriptures can reprove us; that is, rebuke erring Christians so as to bring about conviction of wrong.

4. The Scriptures can correct us; that is, show us the path back to righteousness, the process of healing and rebuilding after sin has wounded and broken down.

5. The Scriptures can discipline us or train us in how to live a godly life in imitation of Jesus Christ.

You can see how the Spirit encourages confession and repentance through the Scriptures by showing: God's grace, which brings us to salvation (providing hope in confession for forgiveness); God's standards, which we may have failed to follow; God's reproof which convicts us of the sinfulness of our sins; God's correction, which shows us how to turn around (always including the confession of sin); and God's instructions for mature godly living, which show us we can live as we ought.

Second, the sanctification process involves an internal strengthening by the Holy Spirit to enable us to do what the Scriptures teach us we should do. One of Paul's prayers in Ephesians says:

> For this reason, I bow my knees before the Father, from whom every family in heaven and on earth derives its name, that He would grant you, according to the riches of His glory, to be strengthened with power through His Spirit in the inner man; so that Christ may dwell in your hearts through faith; and that you, being rooted and grounded in love, may be able to comprehend with all the saints what is the breadth and length and height and depth, and to know the love of Christ which surpasses knowledge, that you may be filled up to all the fullness of God (Ephesians 3:14-19).

---

44. II Timothy 3:14-16 with comments adapted from Jay Adams, *The Christian Counselor's Manual* (Grand Rapids, Michigan: Baker Book House, 1973), pp. 94-95.

The Spirit's power to change allows us to keep Christ in our hearts, understand Him and His love, and be filled with God's character. It is not enough to know what we should be or even how to go about change; we need the internal strength to follow through on the godly steps of change. A person addicted to some substance or lifestyle may understand exactly what he or she ought to do; but that person still has no hope if the power to change is not provided. Here is where prayer becomes involved in two ways; like Paul, we can request the strength which the Spirit gives and, then, as we receive this strength, we respond to God's gracious gift with thanksgiving and praise, as indeed Paul does after stating this request (Ephesians 3:20-21). So, the sanctifying Spirit affects our prayers.

We have spent some time examining the Holy Spirit's involvement with our prayers, directly and indirectly. While not every problem has been thoroughly discussed, at least we can summarize the Spirit's ministry in prayer as follows: without any specific subjective experience in us, the Holy Spirit enables and motivates us to pray, interceding for us and directing us through His inspired Word.

EACH CHRISTIAN IS INVOLVED WITH PRAYER

We had better be involved in regular prayer. For, not only has God commanded us to pray, but, as we said in the second chapter, we need to pray. Christians can do *nothing* without the help and strength which God supplies.[45] And God supplies that help and strength in answer to prayer.[46]

Prayer is the individual responsibility of each Christian. While some Christians may be more proficient in prayer than others, we cannot default on our personal obligation by allowing others to pray in our place. The Lord commands through Paul:

Rejoice always; pray without ceasing; in everything give thanks; for this is God's will for *you* in Christ Jesus (I Thessalonians 5:16-18).

---

45. John 3:27; 15:4-5; II Corinthians 12:7-10; Philippians 4:10-13.
46. Matthew 7:7-11; James 4:1-3.

It is God's will for us to rejoice, pray and give thanks; each of us. We cannot hire a professional to be religious on our behalf. As we cannot be saved by another's faith, we cannot live our Christian lives on the prayers of the preacher or the elders or a godly mother or spouse or anyone else. Prayer is the individual duty of the individual Christian.

When a Christian kneels in prayer, he becomes a focal point of spiritual activity. God the Father graciously attends to him; Jesus Christ mediates for him at the throne; the Holy Spirit strengthens and intercedes for him from within his heart; other Christians struggle in prayer with him and are the loving subjects of his intercession; the world is also a target for his supplication that they might be saved; the prince of darkness and his legions oppose the work of prayer as the Savior and His angels defend the praying Christian. While he is not alone, every Christian is involved with prayer.

EACH NON-CHRISTIAN IS INVOLVED WITH PRAYER

Most men and women pray, even though they may not be believers in Jesus Christ. We will be examining in a later chapter how God reacts to the prayers of non-Christians. But, while non-Christians may or may not pray, they should always be the object of our prayers. Paul has written:

> First of all, then, I urge that entreaties and prayers, petitions and thanksgivings, be made on behalf of all men, for kings and all who are in authority, in order that we may lead a tranquil and quiet life in all godliness and dignity. This is good and acceptable in the sight of God our Savior, who desires all men to be saved and to come to the knowledge of the truth (I Timothy 2:1-4).

Paul is speaking here about at least four types of intercession which a Christian is expected to pray on the behalf of the non-believers: general prayer for their needs, thanksgiving for God working in them, specific prayer for those in authority and evangelistic prayer for the salvation of those who are lost.

First, general intercession for non-believers covers the whole world of needs they may experience. We pray for the victims of natural disasters, for the constant needs of the poor, for the sorrows of broken families, for those struggling with disease, for those grieving, all regardless of their faith or lack of it. As we see people around us, near and far, we should develop our "eyes of compassion" to see what we should seek from God for them. But, what if these unbelievers are attacking us? Can we be expected to intercede for those who hate us? Jesus answered this with powerful words in His "sermon on the mount":

> You have heard that it was said, "You shall love your neighbor, and hate your enemy." But I say to you, love your enemies, and *pray* for those who persecute you in order that you may be sons of your Father who is in heaven; for He causes His sun to rise on the evil and the good, and sends rain on the righteous and the unrighteous (Matthew 5:43-45).

We may not be able to like or enjoy the unbelievers God has brought into our lives, but that does not prevent us from loving them and praying for them according to the will of the Lord.

Second, thanksgiving is to be offered to God for unbelievers. I appreciate God's gifts of public officials, policemen, firemen, doctors and nurses, and even lawyers. Not all of these are Christians, but I am still grateful for them. I meet individuals in restaurants, banks, malls or barber shops who are sometimes considerate and sometimes hostile. I thank God for the opportunity to meet them all.

Third, we are to pray for those in authority. Paul wrote during the ascendancy of the Roman Empire. While this government had much to commend it, we would hardly call it a "model democracy." Yet, it was of *this* government that Paul said, "it is a minister of God to you for good." (See Romans 13:1-7.) Now, if that bureaucratic empire served God, so does our federal system. The leaders of the world's nations need and deserve our prayers, if only to insure our own domestic tranquility.

Finally, we pray for the salvation of the lost. In fact, Paul points out that God Himself desires all men to be saved and He calls us to pray for all men. These evangelistic prayers have two target groups: those who share the gospel and those who hear the gospel.

Those who share the good news of salvation in Jesus Christ can only be effective when they are supported by the prayers of Christ's body.

R. A. Torrey has said, "There have been revivals without much preaching; but there has never been a mighty revival without mighty praying."[47] Biblically, we are to pray four requests for evangelistic workers.

1. We are to pray for workers to be sent out. Jesus said:

The harvest is plentiful, but the workers are few. Therefore beseech the Lord of the harvest to send out workers into His harvest (Matthew 9:37-38).

What a strange saying! Here is the Lord of the harvest at harvest time. What is the desire of the Lord of the harvest at harvest time? To bring in the harvest, of course. Yet, He will not send out workers to bring in the harvest until we plead with Him to do so. Our prayers encourage God to do what He desires to do: send out evangelists to bring men and women into the church.

2. We are to pray for workers to have boldness in their proclamation. Paul requests his readers to:

. . . pray on my behalf, that utterance may be given to me in the opening of my mouth, to make known with boldness the mystery of the gospel, for which I am an ambassador in chains; that in proclaiming it I may speak boldly, as I ought to speak (Ephesians 6:18-20).

"Boldness is the absence of fear in speaking with confidence and cheerful courage."[48] If I am trying to persuade you of a certain truth, any show of fear or hesitancy on my part may tell you I am not sure of the matter I am trying to communicate. As I speak with confidence, looking you straight in the eye, you may be more open to accept the ideas I am presenting. God can supply us with this holy boldness in evangelism.

3. We are to pray for workers to have an opportunity to share and to be clear. Again, Paul again asked his reader to be:

---

47. *The Power of Prayer* (Grand Rapids, Michigan: Zondervan Publishing Company, 1974), p. 43.
48. From W.E. Vine, *An Expository Dictionary of New Testament Words* (Old Tappan, New Jersey: Fleming H. Revell Company, 1966), pp. 137-138.

. . . praying at the same time for us as well, that God may open up to us a door for the word, so we may speak forth the mystery of Christ, for which I have been imprisoned; in order that I may make it clear in the way I ought to speak (Colossians 4:3-4).

In answer to prayer, I have heard of God bringing people right to the front door of Christians who desired to share the gospel. The Lord delights in opening doors for the proclamation of Jesus Christ. But, even if I have the opportunity to share, I will misuse that moment if I am disorganized or unclear in my presentation. A muddled gospel proclamation has little power to convict or convince. So we pray to be crystal clear as to our message.

4. We are to pray for workers to have success and be protected from evil men. Paul asked the Thessalonians:

Finally, brethren, pray for us that the word of the Lord may spread rapidly and be glorified, just as it did also with you; and that we may be delivered from perverse and evil men; for not all have faith (II Thessalonians 3:1-2).

The success of our evangelistic endeavors rests in the work of God, not just in human labor. So we pray that the Word may spread and bear fruit. As the Word spreads, those who carry it will be opposed by those working for the kingdom of darkness. When Christians are attacked by these faithless men, we cry out to God for protection as they preach.

But our prayers are not raised simply for those who will preach the gospel; we also approach the Almighty on behalf of those who need to accept the Christ as their Lord and Savior. Paul speaks with deep emotion in Romans 10:1 about his hopes for his people, Israel. "Brethren, my heart's desire and my prayer to God for them is for their salvation."

Do we still have this kind of burden in us? How few have been the prayers which were fervent pleas for the souls of men, women and children (at least that I have heard in our churches through the years). While we bemoan churches both stagnant and impotent, perhaps we have not because we ask not.

And these evangelistic prayers need to be more specific than our generic, "Lord, save all those outside of Christ." We must pray for specific people and groups, both near and afar. Sadly, we often exclude whole nations from our intercessions because our faith is too small to believe that God can convert them. Can God win the Moslem world to Christ? Can the officially atheistic Albania be penetrated with the gospel? What of Russia, China or Vietnam? Can the Lord triumph there? The answer to each of these questions is, "Yes! God can." The question is, "Will we pray and will we go?"

SATAN IS INVOLVED WITH PRAYER

All life may be viewed as a great spiritual battle. Opposed to all the works of the Lord stands the enemy of God. He is known by many names: the accuser of our brethren, the adversary, Beelzebul, Belial, the devil, the evil one, the father of lies, the god of this world, the great dragon, a murderer, the prince of darkness, the prince of the power of the air, the ruler of demons, Satan, the serpent of old and the tempter.[49] Though powerful, he is doomed to defeat and damnation. Christ came to destroy his evil work and He did destroy it. (I John 3:8; Hebrews 2:14) But we are still in conflict with this dark power:

> Finally, be strong in the Lord, and in the strength of His might. Put on the full armor of God, that you may be able to stand firm against the schemes of the devil. For our struggle is not against the flesh and blood, but against the rulers, against the powers, against the world forces of this darkness, against the spiritual forces of wickedness in the heavenly places (Ephesians 6:10-12).

Paul goes on to describe each piece of our godly armor, ending with the *two* great offensive weapons in the Christian's arsenal: the word of God and prayer (Ephesians 6:17-20). Such weapons Paul described as "divinely powerful for the destruction of fortresses" (II Corinthians 10:4). But we have to use them if they are to be effective. The Bible never studied and the prayer never prayed will not challenge Satan in

---

49. See Revelation 12:10; I Peter 5:8; Matthew 12:24; II Corinthians 6:15; Matthew 4:1; Matthew 13:19; John 8:44; II Corinthians 4:4; Revelation 12:9; John 8:44; Ephesians 6:12; Ephesians 2:2; Matthew 12:24; Matthew 4:10; Revelation 12:9; and Matthew 4:3.

the least.

The devil would love to keep us from using the weapon of prayer against him. Hope MacDonald has speculated:[50]

> Have you ever stopped to wonder what the devil's favorite word might be? I've thought a lot about this and have come to the conclusion that his favorite word is *tomorrow*. He is always trying to keep us from praying today. In fact, that must be one of his main jobs — to keep all Christians off their knees.

Regretfully, Satan has succeeded with many of us in keeping us essentially prayerless and powerless. In fact, one of the dangers in reading (or writing) a book about prayer is the temptation to replace the practice of prayer with the mere study of it.

The attacks of Satan are basically temptations to sin.[51] Prayer opposes these attacks by asking God to help us to:

1. Avoid Satan's temptations.
2. Overcome Satan's temptations.
3. Recover from Satan's temptations.

Prayer helps us to avoid Satan's temptations. In the model prayer which Jesus taught us, the last requests are, "And do not lead us into temptation, but deliver us from evil" (Matthew 6:13). In at least seven modern translations, the last phrase reads, "deliver us from the evil one," that is, from Satan.[52] Jesus is telling us that we may ask God to avoid the traps which Satan lays out for us. And, in fact, our very prayers themselves may be a means of keeping our minds centered on the Lord and eluding temptations (Matthew 26:41). But what if we cannot avoid being tempted?

Then prayer helps us to overcome Satan's temptations. One of the great promises of the Word of God reads:

No temptation has overtaken you but such as is common to man;

---

50. *Discovering How To Pray* (New York: Pillar Books, 1977), p. 28.
51. Matthew 4:3; I Corinthians 7:5; I Thessalonians 3:5.
52. The translations are the Amplified Bible, the Good News Bible, the Jerusalem Bible, the Living Bible, the New English Bible, the New International Version and the New King James Bible.

and God is faithful, who will not allow you to be tempted beyond what you are able, but with the temptation will provide the way of escape also, that you may be able to endure it (I Corinthians 10:13).

Two of the ways of escape which allow us to endure temptations is praying for ourselves and for others. We pray in the midst of our own spiritual battles. For, we can:

. . . draw near with confidence to the throne of grace, that we may receive mercy and may find grace to help in time of need (Hebrews 4:16).

Not only can we find strength for ourselves to overcome Satan's temptations; we are to pray for one another. Like Aaron and Hur, we must uphold our brother lest he weaken and the battle be lost (Exodus 17:8-13). Like Paul, we need to pray for our fellow Christians not to falter when tempted by the evil one.[53] But what happens if Satan momentarily triumphs and we fall into temptation and sin? How can prayer help us then?

Then, prayer helps us to recover from Satan's temptations. When Jesus foresaw that Peter would deny Him, He gave Peter these words of hope:

Simon, Simon, behold, Satan had demanded permission to sift you like wheat; but I have prayed for you, that your faith may not fail; and you, when once you have turned again, strengthen your brothers (Luke 22:31-32).

When we do sin, our faith indeed may be in danger of failing. We may doubt our ability to serve God as He desires or perhaps His ability to sustain us to the end. Then, prayer can dress the wounds to our spirits and strengthen the faith that is weakened, not only for future tests but for aiding our brethren in their trials as well. Satan will only find us stronger in the Lord after we have prayed in the very midst of our

---

53. See II Corinthians 13:7 and I Thessalonians 3:1-13, 5:23.

weakness.

Christian leaders seem to be special targets of Satan's attacks. Anne J. Townsend, a missionary doctor in Thailand, writes that a church may send out a missionary and that is good.

> But does his church know what it is sending him to? I know from experience that he is being sent straight into the front line of the battle between God and the devil.

Therefore, she says, the church which financially supports a missionary has the responsibility to uphold him in consistent prayer.[54] The same could be said for our ministers at home, our elders, our deacons and our teachers. If Satan can turn the leaders, he can sway the followers into sin as well. If you love your leaders and your church, pray for those over you.

During the writing of this book, I may say that our family has passed through some of the most trying months of our years in ministry. The tempter has thrown a barrel of failures and disappointments at us with very little time for recovery. Yet, the Lord has kept us from giving up on each other, on the church or on writing this book. I believe our strength came in answer to all those desperate prayers we sent before God's throne. Satan has been beaten again and you are holding another proof of the Lord's victory.

The secret of overcoming Satan is given in James 4:7-8. "Submit therefore to God. Resist the devil and he will flee from you. Draw near to God and He will draw near to you." Satan cannot withstand anyone who is in submission to the Father and who lives under His wings. And it is through prayer that we draw near to the Almighty.

ANGELS AND DEMONS ARE INVOLVED IN PRAYER

The final group of beings involved with our prayers are the spiritual messengers of both the armies of God and the legions of Satan. These messengers, angels and demons, had a common origin: both were be-

---

54. *Prayer Without Pretending* (Chicago: Moody Press, 1973), pp. 45-46.

ings created by God to serve Him. But some vast group of the created angels rebelled against His rule before the creation of the first man and became the "fallen angels" (Biblically called, "unclean" or "evil spirits" and "demons").[55] Since that great rebellion, these two spiritual armies have been involved with us in spiritual warfare, often centering around prayer.

Angels: Ministers to Those Who Pray

Angels are described by the following rhetorical question from the book of Hebrews:

Are they not all ministering spirits, sent out to render service for the sake of those who will inherit salvation? (Hebrews 1:14).

They minister in a variety of ways. Some angels stand in God's very presence to worship Him with us (Revelation 5:11). Some have acted as His messengers (as the meaning of their name implies) and brought God's replies to the prayers of Old and New Testament saints.[56]

In addition to communication duties, angels are involved in actively serving God and His saints. God can send His angels to provide the aid which we request in prayer. Angels can provide protection for those threatened, physical strength for those weakened, freedom for those imprisoned and also judgment against those who oppose the Lord and His work through His people.[57] The primary ministry of angels for believers today appears to be through meeting our needs in unseen

---

55. The term "fallen angel" does not appear in Scripture, although Satan's messengers are clearly labeled "angels" in Matthew 25:41; II Peter 2:4; Jude 6 and Revelation 12:9. Examples of the use of the other terms can be seen in Matthew 10:1; Acts 19:11-17 and Matthew 9:34.

56. Angels brought messages (revelations) to Hagar (Genesis 16:7-11), Jacob (Genesis 31:11-13), Moses (Exodus 3:1-2), Zechariah (Zechariah 1:9), Mary Magdalene (Matthew 28:1-5), the shepherds of Bethlehem (Luke 2:9-11), Philip (Acts 8:26), Paul (Acts 28:22-25) and John (Revelation 1:1) among others. Angels brought responses to prayers to Manoah (Judges 13:8-9), Daniel (Daniel 8:15-17, 9:1-27), Zachariah (Luke 1:8-13) and Cornelius (Acts 10:1-4) among others.

57. See Daniel 6:21-22; Luke 22:43; Acts 12:5-17 and Acts 12:23. Angels are channels of God's judgment repeatedly throughout the book of Revelation.

ways. We may know by the evidence of Scripture that angels are at work on our behalf, but we will be unable to point to any given event and say with certainty, "God sent His angel to do that for us."

One of the angels' unseen services for us appears to be warfare against demonic forces which oppose us, even in connection with our prayers. In Daniel, we get a glimpse of this struggle when Daniel had been mourning for three weeks (with a partial fast) apparently over the sins of Israel and their captivity. The angel Gabriel appears to Daniel at the end of these twenty-one days and explains to him the delay in God's answer to Daniel's sad prayers.

> Do not be afraid, Daniel, for from the first day that you set your heart on understanding this and on humbling yourself before your God, your words were heard, and I have come in response to your words. But the prince of the kingdom of Persia was withstanding me for twenty-one days; then behold, Michael, one of the chief princes, came to help me, for I had been left there with the kings of Persia (Daniel 10:13-14).

The "prince" and "kings of Persia" seem to refer to powers of darkness which obstructed Gabriel's mission. Then, Michael the archangel[58] appears to help Gabriel escape the demons and complete his mission. After strengthening Daniel, Gabriel says that he must return to continue the battle against the "prince of Persia" with the continuing aid of Michael (Daniel 10:20-21). The exact nature and manner of such struggles are beyond our comprehension, but we are assured that the angels are united with us in the warfare of the Lord against the forces of evil.

Demons: Opposers of Those Who Pray

On the opposing side of our spiritual warfare, we face the angels of Satan, the demons. Some years ago, C. S. Lewis wrote a warning to all

---

58. Jude 9.

Christians concerning the devils.[59]

> There are two equal and opposite errors into which our race can fall about the devils. One is to disbelieve in their existence. The other is to believe, and to feel an excessive and unhealthy interest in them. They themselves are equally pleased by both errors and hail a materialist or a magician with the same delight.

To take Mr. Lewis' warning seriously, we shall seriously but briefly consider the demonic influence on prayer. You do not have to be afraid of studying these beings, for Jesus' disciples noted long ago that, "even the demons are subject to us in [Jesus'] name" (Luke 10:17). But to discount the devil and his demonic hoards is dangerously stupid. For Satan still sways the world against the awesome might of the gospel. Only in great folly could we ignore this very real source of malignity.

The fallen angels can be divided into two groups; those presently bound in the abyss and those free to roam the earth and the air.[60] Both groups shall end up in the lake of fire which is the second death (Matthew 25:41). They are both also intricately bound to their leader, Satan, and his work is their work.

Now what is the work of the fallen ones? They seek to defeat the plans of the Almighty (our salvation) and to oppress mankind. Indeed, Jesus came with the purpose to relieve demonic oppression (Acts 10:38). The primary means the demons seem to use include deception, temptation and physical or mental assaults. In our materialistic world, such spiritual onslaughts may seen fanciful, but the testimony of the Scriptures and many modern Christians consistently contend that this is reality.

The demons use deception to corrupt our understanding of the truth, especially the gospel. Satan's forces attack truth because it is by knowing and following the truth in Jesus Christ that men may become free from sin and the domination of Satan (John 8:31-36, 42-47). Demonic deception can come through false religion or false doctrine in

---

59. *The Screwtape Letters* (Charlotte, North Carolina: Commission Press, Inc., 1976), p. 17.

60. See Jude 6 and II Peter 2:4 for the bound demons and Ephesians 2:2; 6:11-12 along with all the Gospel accounts for the free demons.

the church.[61] John urged his readers to discern which "spirits" were the source of their beliefs, especially concerning Jesus Christ (I John 4:1-6). We combat this devilish activity by our study of the Word of God and by our prayers for wisdom and understanding (Colossians 1:9-14; James 1:5-8).

The demons also use temptation to corrupt our morality. Paul notes that the men who teach the "doctrines of demons" are also those who are "seared in their own conscience" (I Timothy 4:1-3). The loss of theological truth demands the loss of ethical truth, for the standards of life are changed from the reality of God's nature to the errors of Satan. Following the example of their master Satan, the demons tempt us to sin with subtle and devious thoughts and twisted logic.[62] Paul again indicates that our chief weapons against the "world forces of this darkness" are the Bible and prayer, consistent and comprehensive prayer (Ephesians 6:10-20).

Finally, the demons use mental and physical assault to demoralize and terrorize men. Especially during the earthly life of Christ, demons possessed people and caused a variety of ailments.[63] While the disciples of Christ were given authority over the unclean spirits, once only Christ could cast out a demon, though the apostles had tried but could not. Jesus indicated their failure lay in two directions: first, their faith was not sufficiently strong and, second, their prayerlife was lacking (Matthew 17:19-20; Mark 9:29). Again, the power of seeking God in prayer is seen when faced with demonic powers.

Demon possession does not appear to have been common before or after the life of Christ. Perhaps the coming of the Son of God brought out an expansion of the powers of darkness to oppose Him. Yet the ac-

---

61. Paul said in I Corinthians 10:19-21 that the idols of the pagans were in fact demons. These false gods could even produce signs and wonders to further lead people from the true God (Exodus 7:11, 22; 8:7; II Thessalonians 2:9-12). Paul also warned of demonic doctrines which would attempt to infiltrate the church (and have all too often succeeded) in I Timothy 4:1-3.

62. For an interesting discussion of the pseudo-logic of Satan in temptation (especially in his encounter with Christ in the wilderness), see D.G. Kehl, "Discerning the Devil's Deductions," *Christianity Today*, XVI (November 10, 1972), 10-12.

63. The ailments included mental delusion (twice, Luke 8:26-35; Acts 19:13-16), epilepsy (once, Matthew 17:15), blindness (Matthew 12:22), dumbness (Matthew 9:32-33) and others. The Bible differentiates between naturally occurring diseases and those caused by demons (Matthew 4:24).

tivity of the demonic armies has not ceased. We still deal with unchained unclean spirits in our day. We need to remember Jesus' admonition. "This kind cannot come out by anything but prayer" (Mark 9:29).

Summary

Our survey of the persons involved with our prayers has taken us from the divine to the demonic, including all men and angels. Maybe as you pray today, you will realize that your "solitude" with the Lord is only an illusion. Every person in heaven and earth is within your reach as you bow before the King of kings.

THOUGHT OR DISCUSSION QUESTIONS

1. To whom do you address your prayers? What do you think about praying to the Son or the Spirit of God? How does a person's understanding of God's nature expand or limit his prayers?

2. Where do you *feel* closest to God? Why? What past experiences might make such locations seem holier than others? Where do you *feel* farthest from God? Why? How does the fact of God's omnipresence alter your "feelings" about "holy" or "unholy" places to pray?

3. Since God is omniscient, honesty is the only logical course in prayer. In what ways are our prayers sometimes dishonest? How is it possible to be most honest with God? How would you counsel someone who complained, "I just don't *feel* like God is listening to me"?

4. Does the thought of God's holiness draw you closer to Him or drive you farther away? Why? How should His holiness affect our prayers?

5. You address the absolute Sovereign of the universe when you pray; what then limits what you can ask from Him? How do we earn the Father's gracious gifts? Can God be just and still answer the prayers of the imperfect, such as ourselves? If so, how? If not, why not?

6. What are some rights and privileges we are entitled to receive in Jesus' name? Choose three of the following Scriptures which deal with the blood of Jesus Christ and describe in your own words what the blood does for us.

[ ]Luke 22:20   [ ]Ephesians 1:7-8   [ ]I Peter 1:17-19
[ ]John 6:53-56   [ ]Ephesians 2:11-13   [ ]I John 1:7
[ ]Romans 5:9   [ ]Colossians 1:19-20 [ ]Revelation 1:5

If Jesus Christ had never come, what truths about prayer would we not know?

7. Describe in your own words the meaning of the phrase, "praying in the Spirit." How does the Holy Spirit motivate your prayers? What does the Spirit's intercession for us mean to you? If a friend asked, "How can I be led by the Holy Spirit?" how would you answer? How has the Spirit convicted you of sin in the past? Why do we need the inner strengthening of the Holy Spirit in prayer?

8. What responsibility do you feel as a Christian to pray regularly? How are we to pray for unbelievers? How do we balance praying for the conversion of the lost and accepting the free will of the lost?

9. Describe your understanding of the ministry of angels for Christians today. How do the angelic hosts affect our prayers? How active do you believe demons are in your family and church today? In what ways might the angels of Satan be misleading us concerning the teaching and practice of prayer?

4

WHAT ARE THE PARTS OF PRAYER?
I — PRAISE

Two preachers were friendly rivals in the game of golf. John was the admitted better player, but Peter was right behind him. In an effort to even their matches, Peter gave John a book on "How to Play Better Golf." For Peter had a plan.

Sure enough, the first game after he had read the book, John stood frozen at the tee. He was trying desperately to remember which "helpful hint" from the book he should use. He concentrated, bent, straightened, pulled, shifted and flowed, but the result was only to send his ball dribbling into the weedy rough. The rest of the John's game was a well-studied disaster; Peter won with ease. There is nothing like a list of rules to empty enjoyment and power from an activity. I hope *this* book will not be as disturbing to your prayer life as the golf book was to John's golf game.

This chapter, we begin discussing the basic parts of prayer. Realize that this listing contains the danger of becoming a recipe for proper prayer. "Oops, not enough praise and too much intercession!" While balance is important, artificial symmetry in prayer can become an awkward "set of rules" instead of a freeing principle. In fact, the prayers of the Bible are remarkably "uneven" in the use of prayer's five parts. Some Psalms are ninety-seven percent praise, while Samson's prayers were pure petition. The prayers of Israel during the time of the judges tended to be confessions of their sin with petitions for aid included. Even the "Lord's Prayer" is comprised of six petitions (although the other parts of prayer are implied in these six). So, the proper balance in prayer is not a legalistic "equal time" provision, but a prayerlife in which all parts of prayer are equally represented through a day, week or year.

As your situation alters, different areas of prayer may become more important to you for certain periods. Should your child become ill, obviously your stress might fall on intercession. When the child returns to health, thanksgiving and praise would be the proper response. When you feel the crush of a burden of guilt, repentant confession may be the order of the day. Circumstances will require different prayer responses, with some kinds of prayer dominating for each moment.

But a word of caution should be stated. At no time should one form of prayer drown out the other forms completely. Even in times of fear and anguish, praise and thanksgiving may lift your hurting soul as petition or intercession cannot. James indicates that confession should accompany prayers for healing. And, in times of great joy, we are still dependent on the Lord for daily bread, and we need the humility of petition to remember that, even in the midst of our rejoicing before Him. Consistent use of all five parts of prayer determines the well-rounded prayerlife, but not necessarily by using a chart with allotted minutes for each kind of prayer.

Now, what are the "proper" divisions of prayer? The answers from Christian authors vary widely. The chart on the following page contrasts five representative views.

These systems of prayer division use an amalgamation of Biblical and non-Biblical terms, and that can be dangerous. Non-Biblical terms may be describing non-Biblical categories, unless clearly defined and defended. The Scriptures do not contain the terms "adoration," "contrition," "Scripture praying" or any of Rosalind Rinker's terms, according to my concordance studies.[1] Also the terms "meditation," "dedication,"

---

1. I do not include the Living Bible since I have found that Mr. Taylor uses a variety of terms which are not warranted by the original text.

The Parts of Prayer
As Seen by Five Christian Authors[2]

Rice	Rinker	Lindsell	Ogilvie	Eastman
1. Asking	1. Help Me, Lord	1. Petition	1. Supplication	1. Petition
	2. Help My Brother	2. Intercession	2. Intercession	2. Intercession
	3. Jesus Is Here	3. Adoration	3. Adoration	3. Praise
	4. Thank You, Lord	4. Thanksgiving	4. Thanksgiving	4. Thanksgiving
		5. Confession	5. Contrition	5. Confession
			6. Meditation	6. Meditation
			7. Dedication	7. Listening
			8. Commitment	8. "Scripture Praying"
				9. Waiting
				10. Watching
				11. Singing
				12. Praise Again

---

2. The order given may differ from that of the authors; the chart is made to set parallel terms next to each other as much as is possible. The authors represented are: John R. Rice, *Prayer—Asking and Receiving* (Cleveland, Ohio: Union Gospel Press, 1942); Rosalind Rinker, *Conversational Prayer* (Waco, Texas: Word Books, Publisher, 1970); Harold Lindsell, *When You Pray* (Grand Rapids, Michigan: Baker Book House, 1969); Lloyd John Ogilvie, *Praying with Power* (Ventura, California: Regal Books, 1983); and Dick Eastman, *The Hour That Changes the World* (Grand Rapids, Michigan: Baker Book House, 1978).

"listening," "commitment," "waiting," "watching," and "singing" do not appear to be used in the Bible as classifications of types of prayer.

So, removing non-Biblical and misused classifications, the following five parts of prayer remain as Biblical divisions: praise, thanksgiving, petition, intercession and confession. Understand that these five categories are not listed by Jesus or Paul (or anyone else in the Bible) as the *only* proper divisions for prayer. Yet, these five Biblical divisions seem to cover all the prayer activities of the Scriptures; meanwhile, reducing this list by using wider categories needlessly blurs the clear distinctions between these five areas.[3] For the sake of clarity and simplicity, we will use these five categories to examine the parts of prayer in this chapter.

One last point on these divisions; did you see that they divide prayer according to the content of the words? One could divide prayer by the means used (singing, spoken, written or silent), the position assumed (standing, sitting, kneeling or reclining) or the people praying (congregation, small group, family, couple or individual) among other methods. But the essence of prayer is in the message communicated to God, not in how that message is delivered. So we will begin with the first part of prayer: praise.

PRAISE: TALKING TO GOD ABOUT HIMSELF

When Jesus began the Lord's Prayer, His opening words were all centered on God. God is our Father; His name should be held up as holy; He should reign and all who are in rebellion should bow in obedience to Him. Christ began His prayer by lifting up God, by praying on behalf of God. Shouldn't our prayers be prayed in like manner: God first (not our problems or desires)? Praise is our way to put God first in our prayers.

---

3. For example, one could combine praise and thanksgiving under the title, "speaking of God to God," and then combine petition, intercession and confession under the title, "speaking of man to God." Then both could be further combined to read simply, "speaking to God." We arrive finally at a definition with no distinctions. But, what good purpose would be served by this reduction? Has prayer's process been clarified? From trying to determine the essential elements of prayer, we would only come to say prayer has no elements, only essence.

Praise can be defined as the act of relating to our Father (and secondarily to ourselves and to others) the wonder, delight and gratitude which His character and acts generate in us. God is wonderful and we respond with wonder; He is delightful and we delight in Him; He is generous and we are grateful. It is the word, "Praises!" which is written across the top of the book of Psalms; God revealed Himself to Israel and those who loved Him burst into song![4]

This praise is difficult to confine to a prayer closet. Indeed, praise in the Old and New Testament has two distinctive elements: praise is vocal and praise is public.[5] To praise God biblically implies to publicly announce His glorious nature and marvelous acts. We become God's publicists, encouraging the household of faith with reminders of His faithfulness and evangelizing the world with proclamations of His deity. At least, that is God's plan.

Dearly beloved in Christ, when was the last worship service you have attended where the whole body made central to their gathering the praise of God? Our hymns tend more and more to center in our subjective experiences (personal joys or sorrows) rather than to uphold the objective glory of God revealed supremely in Jesus Christ. Soloists are applauded while prayers are shortened and the service is polished to a professional sheen. Many of our sermons have become spiritual self-help lectures. Sin is down-played and the holiness of the Almighty is swallowed up in proclaiming His love. Competing with television, we strive for "good shows" more than for lifting up the Father. Our bulletins become full while our people leave empty.

During your prayer period in worship (if your church has such any longer), does the leader simply list the current sick and grieving for the congregation to hear how they are? Or does he lead you in praising the name of the Holy One, Creator and Redeemer? If pressed, could you worship God in praise for five minutes without repeating trite phrases? If we outlawed the words "Praise the Lord," "Hallelujah," "Hosanna" and "Glory" from our prayers, the majority of our praise vocabulary could

---

4. The standard Hebrew title for the book of Psalms is *Tehillim, "praises."*

5. See Ronald Barclay Allen, *Praise! A Matter of Life and Breath* (Nashville: Thomas Nelson Publishers, 1980), pp. 57-72. A concordance study of the words of praise will show you that Allen's excellent analysis of the Psalms can be expanded to the whole Old and New Testament; i.e. praise by nature is vocal and public.

be stripped from us in an instant. Perhaps our poverty of praise comes from ignorance, not disobedience. Let's examine the purposes and practice of praise.

The Purposes of Praise

Praise prizes its object as worthy of the price of honor (indeed, the English word "praise" comes the French word *presier* meaning "to prize" which comes from the Latin word *pretium* which means "worth" or "price").[6] There is a price for praising God, for we are called not merely to utter words but to worship in "spirit and truth" by serving Him.[7] Why should we pay this price to honor God with our praise? The answer to that question can be presented from God's viewpoint and from ours.

God's Purposes for Praise — God designed praise in order that He might receive glory. Mary lifts her voice in praise to God with these words, "My soul exalts the Lord, and my spirit has rejoiced in God my Savior" (Luke 1:46-47). The word "exalt" is a translation of a Greek term meaning "to magnify, to make or manifest as great." While our praises does not *make* the Lord great, it does *proclaim* that He is great. That is the purpose for our praise which God desires.

Don't be misled here; God does not need our praise in any way. His ego is not flagging nor does He enjoy demanding compliments from us. God does not need anything from us, least of all our puny praise. As the Lord reminds us in Psalm 50:12, "If I were hungry, I would not tell you; for the world is Mine, and all it contains." We are but His creatures; our evaluation of His nature and works does not add or detract from who He is at all. Lloyd John Ogilvie puts the emphasis in the right place when he says, "God does not need our praise as much as we need to give it."[8] God commands us to praise Him *for our own good*. We shall see how this benefits us in a moment.

---

6. "Praise," *Webster's New World Dictionary of the American Language* (Cleveland: The World Publishing Company, 1958), p. 1146.
7. See John 4:24 and Matthew 4:10 where worshiping God is shown by exclusively serving Him.
8. *Praying with Power* (Ventura, California: Regal Books, 1983), p. 25.

Praise is God's desire because it is His proper due as we consider who He is and what He has done. We react to God who has already acted. God reveals Himself and our right response is adoration. The Psalmist admonishes God's people to, "Ascribe to the Lord the glory due His name" (Psalm 96:8). We consider the character of God and praise Him because He deserves it. Praise is not all God is due, but it is a real part of obligation to our Creator. In fact, A. S. Herbert defines the very act of worship as "the recognition and acknowledgment at every level of human nature of the absolute worth of God."[9] The very hymns of heaven resound with the theme of the Lord's worthiness to be praised (Revelation 4:8-11). C.S. Lewis writes:[10]

Admiration is the correct, adequate or appropriate response to [Him], that, if paid, admiration will not be "thrown away", and that if we do not admire we shall be stupid, insensible, and great losers, we shall have missed something.

Praise is God's desire because it is the truth about Him. Praise can be thought of as a string of truths about God strung together with the joy of the beholder. These truths seem to center around certain themes. These include:
a. The attributes of His character.
b. The holiness of His name.
c. The incomparability of His majesty.
d. The might of His work in creating and sustaining all things.
e. The grace of His work for His people.
Finally, praise is God's desire because He knows what good praise does in us. Ultimately, God desires every man, woman and child on planet earth to be drawn to Him through His Son Jesus Christ. Praise is another means He uses to promote the truth of His love and justice to all men to call them to His kingdom.[11] Just how does praise do us good?

---

9. *Worship in Ancient Israel* (Richmond, Virginia: John Knox Press, 1959, p. 47.
10. *Reflections on the Psalms* (New York: Harcourt, Brace and World, 1958), p. 92.
11. See Psalm 145:3-4, 10-13, and 20-21.

Man's Purposes For Praise — We *need* to praise the Lord in order to have a healthy life; spiritually, emotionally and mentally. The morning when God is not applauded is a darkness in our hearts regardless of the sunshine.

We need praise to alter our perspectives. When you and I stumble through our days without a firm realization of who God is and what He has done and is doing, we are living in Fantasyland. To avoid praise is simply foolish. "The fool has said in his heart, 'There is no God' " (Psalm 53:1). So praise is like a splash in the face with the cold water of reality. It awakens in us a true view of life. Of God, C.S. Lewis says:[12]

> He is that Object to admire which (or, if you like, to appreciate which) is simply to be awake, to have entered the real world; not to appreciate which is to have lost the greatest experience, and in the end to have lost all.

Praise awakens us to who God really is. The making of idols has not ceased. We all tend to remold our image of God into some form more pleasing to our particular preferences.[13] We can easily become guilty of the charge leveled by the Lord in Psalm 50:21b: "You thought that I was just like you." By drawing our concepts for praise from the Bible, we hold in our minds the true image of the Almighty, especially as revealed in Jesus Christ. Although we can never know all there is to know of God, we should base the truth about Him on what we do know. And this is important; for we must know God truly in order to love Him as He deserves. Many of us have had the sad experience of misjudging a person for good or ill and thereby creating a crippling relationship with him or her based on our misinformation. Praise keeps our relationship with God centered on truth about Him.

Praise awakens us to see ourselves more clearly. By looking steadfastly at the Lord's perfect love and holiness, our own imperfections become more obvious by contrast. Have you recently opened a curtain in a darkened room to allow light to stream in? In the gloom

---

12. Lewis, p. 92.
13. A sample listing of eighteen "unreal gods" worshipped by modern man is explained by J.B. Phillips in his classic, *Your God Is Too Small* (New York: Macmillan Publishing Co., Inc., 1977).

beforehand, the rug and furniture seemed clean enough. But under the bright beams of sunlight, the dust and subtle stains become obvious and we scurry off for the cleaning equipment. Likewise, praise of the Lord's perfection leaves us dissatisfied with our own imperfections. Yet praise balances our shame for sin with hope for renewal. As we recall the Lord's faithfulness and compassion in the past, we are encouraged to trust His mercy and grace in the present and future. The Psalms are filled with passages linking praise and hope.[14]

> For Thou art my hope; O Lord God, Thou art my confidence from my youth. By Thee I have been sustained from my birth; Thou art He who took me from my mother's womb; My praise is continually of Thee. . . . Let those who are adversaries of my soul be ashamed and consumed; Let them be covered with reproach and dishonor, who seek to injure me. But as for me, I will hope continually, And will praise Thee yet more and more (Psalm 71:5-6, 13-14).

Associated with our hope in praise is a new boldness and conquest of fear. Like David we proclaim, "The Lord is my light and my salvation; Whom shall I fear? The Lord is the defense of my life; Whom shall I dread?" (Psalm 27:1). By praise, we remind ourselves of the might and goodness of the One whom we are privileged to call, "Father."

Praise awakens us to re-evaluate our troubles. Praise changes our focus from our problems to the God who can overcome them in us. Let's say you get up and recall a difficult job you have to do today. But you begin your morning prayer time with a concentrated period of praise and adoration. You restate God's righteousness, omnipotence, omniscience, omnipresence, justice, mercy and grace; you recall incidents of His loving support and protection in your own life. Now you face again your present task, and somehow, while you praised, it shrank. Now it fits neatly in the hand of your Father. Praise reminds us of the vast resources available in our King. Even in great trials praise reassures our hearts.

---

14. See also Psalms 33:21-22; 42:5, 11; 43:5; 146:5-7 and 147:10-12 on the relationship between praise and hope.

This does not mean that you ignore tragedy and suffering. Instead, it means that you lift your eyes above the tragedy to the One who knows the end from the beginning, to the One who made this world and all that is in it.[15]

When Jude faced a church infiltrated with apostasy, he did not give in to useless fury or utter despair. He concluded his general epistle with a benediction of reassuring praise.

Now to Him who is able to keep you from stumbling, and to make you stand in the presence of His glory blameless with great joy, to the only God our Savior, through Jesus Christ our Lord, be glory, majesty, dominion and authority, before all time and now and forever. Amen (Jude 24-25).

Then, praise awakens our proper dependence upon and faith in the Lord God. In the reign of Jehoshaphat over Judah, a great confederacy of surrounding nations prepared to attack Jerusalem. Read carefully the condensed account below of how praise was used as a weapon of faith against God's enemies as Jehoshaphat depended upon the Lord alone to save them.

And Jehoshaphat was afraid and turned his attention to seek the Lord; and proclaimed a fast throughout all Judah...and he said, "O Lord, the God of our fathers, art Thou not God in the heavens? And art Thou not ruler over all the kingdoms of the nations? *Power and might are in Thy hand so that no one can stand against Thee.* Didst Thou not, O our God, drive out the inhabitants of this land before Thy people Israel, and give it to the descendants of Abraham Thy friend forever? And they lived in it, and have built Thee a sanctuary there for Thy name, saying, 'Should evil come upon us, the sword, or judgment, or pestilence, or famine, we will stand before this house and before Thee (for Thy name is in this house) and cry to Thee in our

---

15. Bobb Biehl and James W. Hagelganz, *Praying How to Start and Keep Going* (Glendale, California: G/L Publications, 1976), p. 11.

distress, and Thou wilt hear and deliver us.' And now behold, the sons of Ammon and Moab and Mount Seir . . . [are] coming to drive us out from Thy possession which Thou hast given us as an inheritance. O our God, wilt Thou not judge them? For *we are powerless* before this great multitude who are coming against us; nor do we know what to do, *but our eyes are upon Thee.* . . . [Jahaziel said] "Do not fear or be dismayed because of this great multitude, for *the battle is not yours but God's.*" . . . and all Judah . . . fell down before the Lord, worshipping the Lord. And the Levites . . . stood up to praise the Lord God of Israel, with a very loud voice. . . . And when they began singing and praising, the Lord set ambushes against the sons of Ammon, Moab and Mount Seir, who had come against Jerusalem; so they were routed (II Chronicles 20:3-4, 6-12, 15, 18-19, 22).

Jehoshaphat knew two things: he and Judah had no power but their God had all power. So the only logical expression of these praise thoughts was to faithfully depend on the Lord for victory. Praise both expresses our faith and encourages our faith in God. Who would waste their time in praise to a god in whom they did not believe? And who would not be encouraged in their faith by the truths expressed in joyful praise? Jehoshaphat was, and the result was victory!

However, a caution is required here. Praise is not a specialized form of magic spell which forces God to help us do what we desire. God later carried into slavery the same nation of Judah which He saved in Jehoshaphat's day, and praise had not ceased before the coming of the captivity. Praise did not save them, for praise without humble obedience is worse than a meaningless exercise; it is a blasphemy. Praise without obedience is an attempt to manipulate God into becoming a mere means for our personal ends. Such a person seems to be saying, "Here, God; here is some praise. Now, You've been paid so here is what I want. No, I do not want to do what You want." It makes me shudder even to type such words; but it really horrifies me to think I may have praised God with just such thoughts behind my "adoration."

No, humble obedience makes praise meaningful. And praise makes humble obedience easier as it reinforces the perfect role Model for us; God Himself. Paul says;

But we all, with unveiled face beholding as in a mirror the glory of the Lord, are being transformed into the same image from glory to glory, just as from the Lord, the Spirit (II Corinthians 3:18).

Praise centers our gaze upon the Lord and hastens the transformation process. How? The more strongly we care about someone, the more that life becomes a standard to us, a model to which we compare ourselves. Whether our parents or some hero from history or sports, we all tend to pick someone to follow. That's why praise alters our perspective of life; it awakens in us a desire to imitate the perfect beauty of the Lord we concentrate upon in adoration.

Furthermore, praise awakens in us a greater desire for the life offered in Christ; eternal life in heaven in the presence of God. Having seen a lot of teen-age lovers, I cannot recall one pair who demonstrated their affection by wanting to get farther apart. (Some couples look welded to each other.) When we come to realize just how wonderful our Father is, we too want to get closer to Him. And so heaven becomes more desirable; not for fluffy clouds or insipid cherubim, but for drawing closer to Him. We don't mean a physical closeness; we mean to know Him more perfectly than is possible in the sin swamp of earth. "Now I know in part," Paul lamented, "but then I shall know fully just as I also have been fully known" (I Corinthians 13:12b). To know Him fully — that is the joy of heaven! No wonder the occupation of the saints in eternity seems centered in praise. The more we know of the Lord, the more there is to praise. So let us begin now to tune the instruments of our hearts for the eternal symphony. Middle C is "Praise the Lord!"

Aside from altering our perspective, a second purpose for us to praise God is to aid our victory in spiritual warfare. We struggle amidst the unseen forces described in the last chapter. How do we bring the power of the presence of God into the daily skirmishes of our personal lives? Praise does that.

In Psalm 22:3, David speaks to God to say, "Thou art holy, O Thou who art enthroned upon [or who dost inhabit] the praises of Israel." Whichever translation you choose, man's praises and God's presence are clearly connected. And how does that help our spiritual battle? James sandwiches the call to "resist the devil and he will flee from you" between "Submit therefore to God" and "Draw near to God and He will draw near to you" (James 4:7-8). As we draw near to God and humbly submit to lift Him in praise, then the devil indeed can be resisted. "Praise is the devil's death knell." It is the proclamation of our ultimate and immediate victory in Jesus Christ.

Recently, the Lord has been providing some real spiritual victories in our congregation: people won to Christ, financial giving increased and spiritual unity growing. As I am writing, in the last three days, our family car has "died", our taxes are coming back from the preparer to be paid, one of our children developed problems at school, a crown fell off my tooth and a committee just completed rewriting the by-laws of the church. At such critical points, I would like to go immediately ("do not pass 'Go' ") to petition in my prayers. But I have discovered praising my Lord gives me more peace and joy than talking to Him about the problems (though I do that, too).

Another area where praise gives us victory is in evangelism. We noted earlier the public nature of Biblical praise. By praising God before unbelievers, we may be channels for the Holy Spirit to contact them and convict them of sin and their need for a Savior. The angels sing "Glory to God" and a band of shepherds runs to find the Christ child. Paul and Silas sing praises at midnight from the depths of a prison and a jailer is prepared to hear the good news (with a little help from an earthquake). "Faith comes by hearing and hearing by the word of Christ" and that word is not restricted to didactic teaching or expository preaching; the simple praise of a once-lame man leaping in the temple may bring together a crowd ready to hear the gospel. Here is the promise: "He put a new song in my mouth, a song of praise to our God; Many will see and fear, and will trust in the Lord" (Psalm 40:3).

This evangelistic power of praise is not limited to the world "out there." Praise can help us win the most precious of converts (to our hearts): our own children and grandchildren. How many kids have been "turned off" to Jesus Christ and His church by the carping of their religious parents? We can understand the emotions of one young man who was listening to his dad's tirade after a church board meeting. After hearing twenty minutes of complaints and accusations, the boy suddenly jumped up and cried, "Let's get the elders! I'll hold'm and you hang'm. Can I light the match to the church?" The story may be fictitious but the emotions are real. How many young men and women have been lost to Christ because they never heard any positive remarks from their parents concerning Him or His people?

The Psalmist says that when Israel finally believed the words of God through Moses, "they sang His praise" (Psalm 106:12). Praise demonstrates our faith; murmuring and complaining demonstrate our doubts. And our children absorb our words like literary sponges. That is the reason the Psalms mention specifically the task of praise in educating future generations.[16]

> But tell to the generation to come the praises of the Lord, and His strength and His wondrous works that He has done. For He established a testimony in Jacob, and appointed a law in Israel, which He commanded our fathers, that they should teach them to their children, that the generation to come might know, even the children yet to be born, that they may arise and tell them to their children, that they should put their confidence in God, and not forget the works of God, but keep His commandments . . . (Psalm 78:4b-7).

How's that for a victory? You would know that the next generation had a positive view of God to motivate them to serve Him as it has motivated you to do so. Next Sunday, after services, why not spend the ride home sharing with your family why you praise God for the fellowship that morning? You might make it a topic for your grace at the noon meal. Feed your children positive thoughts about the Lord God, His Son, His Spirit and His church, and do not be surprised if the result may not be a child's faith in the God Whom Mom and Dad have proclaimed as faithful.

A third purpose for our choice to praise God is to promote our own spiritual growth. Praise changes our self-concept by promoting self-dethronement. The hymns of adoration are to be sung to lift up God alone, not the worshiper or any other.[17] As the praise psalm begins, the worshiper focuses his attention upon the glorious, holy, immortal Father Who has intervened time and again for the salvation of men. As the praise crescendos, the worshiper may become so involved with the vision of the loving majesty of the great Author that "no thought of self

---

16. See also Psalm 71:18; 79:13; 102:18 and 145:4.
17. Clause Westermann, *The Praise of God in the Psalm* (Richmond, Virginia: John Knox Press, 1965), p. 9, n. 1.

remains."[18] If thoughts of self enter the heart, they are thrown into contrast with the reality of eternal Love and Justice. To a selfish man, the result of comparison with God is a total humbling and a cry for grace. (I Peter 5:5-11) With the Psalmist the worshiper cries:

> Not to us, O Lord, not to us, but to Thy name give glory because of Thy lovingkindness, because of Thy truth (Psalm 115:1). O Lord, our Lord, how majestic is Thy name in all the earth, Who hast displayed Thy splendor above the heavens! . . . When I consider Thy heavens, the work of Thy fingers, the moon and the stars, which Thou hast ordained; what is man, that Thou dost take thought of him? And the son of man, that Thou dost care for him? (Psalm 8:1, 3-4)

Praise brings man to see himself as he is, and, for this world of proud sinners, that means an experience in humility. And we need that. "The worship and praise of God demands a shift of center from self to God."[19]

What good does this humbling do for us? Simply, a humble spirit is our source of inner peace and purity. Paul Billheimer explains this in these words.[20]

> The quintessence of all our mental and nervous disorders is overoccupation with the personal ego; namely, self-centeredness. When the personality becomes centripetal, that is, ego-center, it disintegrates. Out of extreme self-centeredness arises defensiveness, hostility, and aggressive antisocial behavior. . . . To make one's self his center is self-destructive. Jesus affirmed this principle when He said, "Whosoever would save his life shall lose it, but whosoever will lose his life for my sake, the same shall save it" (Luke 9:24). Here is one of the greatest values of praise: it decentralizes self.

---

18. James Hastings, ed., *The Christian Doctrine of Prayer, The Great Christian Doctrines Series* (New York: Scribner's, 1915), p. 58.

19. Paul E. Billheimer, *Destined for the Throne* (Ft. Washington, Pennsylvania: Christian Literature Crusade, 1975), p. 118.

20. Ibid, p. 117.

As we bow to God on the throne of our lives, the power of greed, covetousness, lusts and desires to sway our lives is loosened. Sin arose when "even though [men] knew God, they did not honor Him as God, or give thanks; but they become futile in their speculations, and their foolish heart was darkened" (Romans 1:21). But when we do honor God as God and give Him thanks, we return to wisdom and our minds are cleared, filled with light. And then the deeds of darkness cannot dwell at ease in the light of God's presence. Lives are cleansed and transformed.

Spiritually healthy people find much to praise everywhere; unhealthy people are often critical, finding fault everywhere. Praise is both the sign of and the medicine for good mental health. By praise, we may focus on our Deliverer rather than our traumas and so find peace. "The steadfast of mind Thou wilt keep in perfect peace, because he trusts in Thee" (Isaiah 26:3).

A fourth human purpose for practicing praise is that praise sets all prayer in its proper perspective so that we speak to God as we ought. Are your prayers not "blessing" you as you had expected? Had you ever considered applying the following principle of Christ to your prayers? "It is more blessed to give than to receive" (Acts 20:35). When our prayer focus shifts from *receiving* from God to *giving* praise to God, He blesses us with great joy and peace.

In addition, praise motivates us to pray (and obey) when we otherwise just don't feel like it.[21] Prayer takes effort; we tend to be lazy. So what can push us to put forth the effort? Well, what motivates us to put forth the effort to do anything? We look at our objective; we ask the question, "What are we trying to do?" Then, *if* we consider the objective worthy to us, we will put forth the effort. If we do not think the objective worth our while, we abandon the effort to reach it. Praise points out to us the worthiness of speaking to God. We hear ourselves saying how wonderful and glorious our Lord is and how much He has done for us. Obviously, then, prayer to such a Divine Father is profitable for us; praise makes a profoundly compelling argument that any reasonable person *must* pray.

---

21. This argument is found in Ken Poure and Bob Phillips, *Praise Is a Three-Letter Word* (Glendale, California: G/L Publications, 1975), pp. 31-37.

Praise also affects the other parts of prayer. When I began praising in earnest, my petitions got a little less selfish and silly. My thanksgiving became more concrete and detailed. My confessions grew fervent and humble. And my intercessions came out with a bold joy before this great Father of mine. By examining God in praise, I even came closer to fully asking the Lord the ultimate petition, "I trust You, Lord, with all I am and all those I know; whatever Your will, Thy will be done."

Now, can you understand why the Psalmist wrote, "Praise the Lord! For it is good to sing praises to our God; for it is pleasant and praise is becoming" (Psalm 147:1)? Praise is good, good for us and good for God. Praise is pleasant, pleasant for us and for God. Praise is becoming for you and me and God.

Now why have I taken so much time to present the reasons why we ought to praise God? Because we are not praising God often enough, in our private devotions or our public celebrations. Perhaps we have just not grasped the importance of praise. Perhaps we have been afraid we might be identified with a particular spiritual movement who are known to praise God more than the rest of us. Perhaps we simply have not learned how. But the time has come for us to learn, and to make praise the hallmark of our prayers.

Praise is not natural for fallen creatures like us, but it is necessary for us to master it. Therefore, God has given us clear instructions on how to approach Him in praise.

The Practice of Praise

How do we go about praising God? The Bible has many helpful directions for us. Try some or all of these this week.

1. Praise God *for* something. (See Psalm 150; Revelation 19:6) Don't deceive yourself that merely inserting "Praise the Lord!" into your prayer vocabulary has fulfilled your obligation of adoration. The "hallelujahs" of the Bible are all attached to specific reasons for praise.[22] These reasons fall into two broad areas with three subdivisions each.

a. Praise God for His nature.

---

22. Juan Carlos Ortiz, *Disciple* (Carol Stream, Illinois: Creation House, 1975), pp. 66-68.

i. Praise Him for His attributes (love, justice, truth, omniscience, omnipotence, omnipresence, kindness, etc.).

ii. Praise Him through His glorious names (the Almighty, Father of Lights, our Fortress, the Holy One of Israel, our heavenly Father, etc.).

iii. Praise Him as incomparable (above any man, any angel, any so-called "god," etc.).

b. Praise God for His works.

i. Praise Him for His works in and through His creation.

ii. Praise Him for His works in and for His people in history and in the present.

iii. Praise Him for His works in and for you in the past and present.

2. Try praising God with open eyes. (I realize the thought alone sounds like heresy, but it is Biblical. See Psalm 121:1 and John 17:1.) By opening your eyes, you connect your praise with reality. You find immediately a multitude of reasons to praise God. Just scan from your left to your right (or vice versa) and find reason to praise God in each thing you see. A picture of your family? Praise God as your eternal Father. A plant? Praise God as the Creator of all green things. A Bible? Praise God as the Unimaginable One who reveals Himself to you and me in Jesus Christ. A dust ball? Praise God as the Cleanser of our hearts and minds. Get the idea? You have heard of "Show and Tell"; let your praise time be a "See and Say" time with God.

3. If you are a methodical person, develop a notebook for prayer including a section on praise. The page might include columns such as the following:

Date	Lord, I praise You for...	Scripture Passage

Make it a personal contest to find something new each week for which to adore your God.

4. Learn to praise by using the book of Psalms. Martin Luther said of the Psalms:

> Whoever has begun to pray the Psalter seriously and regularly will soon give a vacation to other little devotional prayers and say, "Ah, there is not the juice, the strength, the passion, the fire which I find in the Psalter. It tastes too cold and too hard."[23]

In the early church, it was not unusual to memorize all the Psalms. I know; that sounds like a tremendous challenge to me, too. But the Psalms are the master patterns for praises and prayers in all kinds of situations. Here are some ideas on how to use them.

a. Read the Psalms daily. If you read five Psalms a day, you will complete all one hundred and fifty in one month (reserve Psalm 119 for a day all by itself, the thirty-first if your month has one). Try reading them out loud to God.[24]

b. Pray through the Psalm. Personalize the Psalm with your name and first person pronouns. For example, Psalm 115:1-3, 9-10 reads:

> Not to us, O Lord, not to us, but to Thy name give glory because of Thy lovingkindness, because of Thy truth. Why should the nations say, "Where, now, is their God?" But our God is in the heavens; He does whatever He pleases. . . . O Israel, trust in the Lord; He is their help and their shield. O house of Aaron, trust in the Lord; He is their help and their shield.

Personalized, it would read:

> Not to me, my Lord, not to me, but to Thy name give glory because of Thy lovingkindness, because of Thy truth. Why should I say, "Where, now, is my God?" But my God is in the heavens; He does whatever He pleases (and so, I am pleased). . . . O Mitch, trust in the Lord; He is your help and your shield. O house of Simpson, trust in the Lord; He is our help and our shield.

---

23. Quoted by Dietrich Bonhoeffer in *Psalms: the Prayer Book of the Bible* (Oxford, Oxfordshire: SLG Press, 1982).

24. For a similar plan for wisdom development, read one chapter of Proverbs each day with your Psalms.

After personalizing the Psalm, offer it to God as a personal prayer and praise. See Acts 4:24-31 where the church at Jerusalem used a portion of Psalm 2 in their praise to God. Try this as a family and perhaps you can make a scrapbook of personalized Psalms for each member's use. (Incidentally, when you use "my" or "our" referring to the Lord, you might remind yourself that you are not saying that you possess God but that you are possessed by Him.)

c. Set the Psalms to music (or learn psalms already in song form). Then use these hymns of praise in your public and private worship (Ephesians 5:19).

5. Meditate on one specific attribute or action of God each day. "If there is . . . anything worthy of praise, let your mind dwell on these things" (Philippians 4:8). Meditation has developed a questionable reputation after it has been confined in the popular mind to the Eastern mystical variety. Biblical meditation is the rumination of the mind on specific revelations of God in Scripture (not a pagan "mantra" or meaningless "oom!"). For example, John tells us that "God is light" (I John 1:5b). What does that mean? What does light do? Well, light discloses that which hides in darkness. How does God do this? Light shows forth beauty. Where has God revealed something beautiful? Light can also blind and burn. How might God's presence blind or burn certain people? How is John using this idea of God as light in this passage? As you explore this idea about the Lord, stop to praise Him for the additional facets of His character which you discover. See how it works? Meditation is recommended throughout the Psalms. Why don't you accept David's recommendation?

6. Look at Christ in the gospels or the prophets. God "in these last days has spoken to us in His Son . . . " (Hebrews 1:2). So when we see Jesus more clearly, we see the Lord more clearly as well. If you can meander the Gospels for a few minutes and not find causes to praise God, you probably aren't listening to what you hear.

7. To vary your praise time, try using an instrument or dance in praise to the Lord of the Dance (Psalm 150). Try some phase of art or poetry to express your joy in Him. Or put yourself in the place of Moses before the burning bush and remove your shoes in recognition that you are in God's presence and, hence, on holy ground (Exodus 3:5; Joshua 5:15). Or try changing your body position; stand, kneel or lie prostrate. Kneeling is not necessarily a more holy position to address God, but its

humble pose can help you praise God meekly, especially when you are not in the "proper" mood to begin (Psalm 95:6; 134:20).

Begin with phrases like, "I, [your name], am about to talk with the Almighty, the Lord God of the universe," or "I love You, my Lord. Let me tell You why." Incorporate prewritten prayers into your devotions. Modern or medieval, these godly prayers of other saints introduce us to new ways of expressing our delight in the Lord. Great hymns may be used in a similar way. Hymnals are integral tools for many Christians' praise hours.

When I have just been with someone who has accepted Christ or seen God change a heart or heal a broken family, I easily fall into the Biblical form praise called "shouting" (Psalm 47:1)! In fact, I've gotten some strange looks driving home from a spiritual success. After all, why should "Yaahoo!" be limited to football games? If Paul and Silas could sing praises in prison at midnight, I feel free to "get excited" about the great God I serve, too. Try it (privately, at first, to get used to the noise).

8. Balance your private and public praises. As we noted earlier, praise is normally public in the Scriptures. Yet, private praise is not unknown. David recalls private sessions of adoration in Psalm 63:6-8.

When I remember Thee on my bed, I meditate on Thee in the night watches, for Thou hast been my help, and in the shadow of Thy wings I sing for joy. My soul clings to Thee; Thy right hand upholds me.

To your private praises, actively add public acknowledgment of God's greatness. I know getting started may not be easy; and you don't have to start by standing up in the middle of your local mall and singing "A Mighty Fortress Is Our God" (unless you so desire, of course). Begin by sharing with a friend some way in which you have come to love God more. Bring up a "praise request" in your Sunday School class instead of a prayer request. Dare to speak of God's goodness in a conversation with an unbelieving friend. Share God's praise around the dinner table with your family. Soon praise will feel more natural; it can even get to be a good habit.

Praise can arise spontaneously in any situation where you see God working. Remember when you last saw a beautiful deer along the road (we do in Indiana), or spied a rainbow, or heard a good joke?

Remember how you could hardly wait to share the experience with someone else? Or at least I hope you could hardly wait. There is something mean and small about a heart that wants to hoard all the beauty it beholds within itself. An imperative of joy should be praise: "How lovely!" "Glorious!" "Neat!" "Far out!" (whatever that means.) No wonder Paul called us to, "rejoice in the Lord always; again I will say, rejoice!" (Philippians 4:4) Start today to praise the Lord! Give God the glory; great things He has done.

Praise sets the foundation for all approaches to God. From this base, we can build a sound life of worship, a prayer life which lifts up God and lifts us up as well. Then, in praising God, we will find ourselves slipping into its companion piece; thanksgiving, the next part of prayer.

Thought or Discussion Questions

1. How would you define praise? How well does your church praise the Lord in its worship services? Are there changes you could suggest which could improve the praise in your congregation? What about your personal praise life? How might you improve your patterns of praise?

2. What most easily moves you to praise? Why do you think that is so? Have you developed a sufficient vocabulary of adoration so that you could verbally offer praise to God for five minutes without repetition? Read through Psalms 144-150 and underline each phrase which praises the Lord. Check each phrase which you could use directly or paraphrased in your own prayers.

3. Have you ever felt the *need* to praise God? If so, what were the circumstances? What do you understand to be the reasons we *do* need to present praise to the Lord? Do we have a clear image of what God is really like? Is our concept accurate enough to stop us from creating our own mental "idol" and calling it "God?" How can we develop a more mature view of Who God really is?

4. How would you describe the relationship of praise to evangelism? Does your family major more in praise or in criticism? Why is that? How

can you increase the praise and decrease the criticism? For a moment, try to objectively look at yourself and ask, "Am I centered primarily in myself or in God?" Think of how you have used the last twenty-four hours. What percentage went to God and His kingdom? What percentage went to your interests and pleasures? Are there any changes you would like to make in your use of the next twenty-four hours?

5. Look around you. Can you list at least twenty reasons to praise God which come to your mind as you examine your surroundings? Try it. Using Psalm 113, paraphrase the Psalm and personalize it to be used in your prayers this week. Flip through a hymnal and find a hymn of praise which you enjoy. Incorporate it in your devotions and in your heart-songs this week.

6. Below are listed a few of the attributes of the Lord God. Choose one to meditate upon and develop it into a praise subject as one of your quiet times. Repeat this with another attribute later and continue until you have completed the list.

[ ]Omniscience: my Lord knows all the truth about everything in the past present and future.

[ ]Omnipotence: my Lord is the source of all power and can do any good thing and handle any problem.

[ ]Omnipresence: my Lord is present everywhere at any one moment.

[ ]Holiness: my Lord is set apart from all evil and sin to goodness and virtue.

[ ]Justice: my Lord requires and will establish that good is rewarded and evil is punished.

[ ]Grace: my Lord offers to forgive me and give me all I need for fullness of life due to no worthiness in me, but due to His great love.

5

WHAT ARE THE PARTS OF PRAYER?
II — THANKSGIVING

A second part of prayer is the offering of gratitude to God for His gifts to us; thanksgiving. There is a special joy for the Christian who has learned to receive every moment of life with real appreciation before the Lord and who takes the time to tell Him so.

Too often in our lives, we emulate the nine lepers who were cleansed by Christ's power, but went on about their renewed lives without returning to their Savior with thanks (Luke 17:1-19). Indeed, like Israel, we not only forget the many benefits we have received, we grumble over the supposed necessities we have *not* received from the beloved Father. How tragic for us to so deceive ourselves. We need to give the thanksgiving so much more than God needs to receive it. Too often, our prayers are as self-centered as the little girl who prayed:

Now I lay me down to sleep, I pray the Lord my soul to keep, And if I die before I wake, I pray the Lord my toys to break So none of the other kids can use 'em . . . Amen.[1]

1. Shel Silverstein quoted by Terry Muck, *Liberating the Leader's Prayer Life* (Waco, Texas: Word Books, 1985), p. 79.

Hearts so turned within to self have left no room for gratitude to enjoy any gift they have received.

Rather, our attitude should follow the heart of a German preacher named Martin Rinkart. The Thirty Years' War had brought horrors of death, disease and poverty into his community in 1636. It is said Martin buried an average of fourteen of his church members each *day*; five thousand in one year. And each day the minister's children would repeat the table grace he had written for them.

> Now thank we all our God
>   With heart and hands and voices;
> Who wondrous things hath done,
>   In whom his world rejoices.
> Who, from our mother's arms,
>   Hath led us on our way
> With countless gifts of love,
>   And still is ours today.[2]

Did Martin Rinkart simply ignore the tragic war surrounding him? No, he had learned the essential lesson of seeing the action of God in the very midst of anguish and sorrow, and, then, of thanking the Lord in whatever state life might find him.

THANKSGIVING: TALKING TO GOD ABOUT HIS GIFTS

It would be a mistake to box thanksgiving exclusively into a word of prayer. Gratitude is an attitude which should permeate life. Consider these two Scriptures:

> Let the word of Christ richly dwell within you, with all wisdom teaching and admonishing one another with psalms and hymns and spiritual songs, singing *with thanksgiving* in your hearts to God. And whatever you do in word or deed, do all in the name of

---

2. Richard D. Dinwiddle, "The Sacrifice of Praise," *Christianity Today*, XXV (November 20, 1981), 40-41.

the Lord Jesus, *giving thanks* through Him to God the Father (Colossians 3:16-17).

. . . in everything *give thanks*; for this is God's will for you in Christ Jesus (I Thessalonians 5:18).

Throughout each day, if I could pry open the lid on your heart, I would hope to hear echoes of hymns of gratitude inside. You and I know that this is no easy habitual practice to develop. We seem to grumble more easily than we sing. And the explanation for this aversion to thanksgiving is sin. But it is possible to fill our hearts with gratitude if we use God's power to do so.

The Purposes of Thanksgiving

According to the Bible, thanksgiving fulfills at least three purposes in our lives: fulfilling obedience, altering perception and promoting prayer.

Thanksgiving Fulfills Obedience. — Thanksgiving is not an option for the Christian; it is a matter of obedience. Since the Scriptures make abundantly clear that thanksgiving is commanded, ingratitude is not only gauche; it is sin (See Psalm 136:1-3; Ephesians 5:18-21; and I Thessalonians 5:16-18).

A miracle of Christ previously noted demonstrates that God expects our gratitude. Ten lepers come begging mercy from Jesus (and healing, we assume). Jesus commands them to go show themselves to the priests to fulfill the law concerning being legally pronounced clean of leprosy. In the act of going to the priests, the lepers are healed. One (and only one) of the ten runs back to thank the Lord. One can almost hear the pain and wonder in the voice of Jesus as He asks,

Were there not ten cleansed? But the nine—where are they? Was no one found who turned back to give glory to God, except this foreigner? (Luke 17:17-18).

Aside from commands, we have godly examples of godly men giving thanks. Jesus Himself provides us a model of a grateful heart. Though He is the Son of God, He often is recorded to have openly stated His appreciation for the works of the Father. (See Matthew 11:25; 26:27; Mark 8:6; and John 11:41.) Then, Paul's letters regularly include a prayer of thanksgiving for God's work in the churches or individuals addressed. In fact, of all Paul's epistles, only the letters to the Galatians and to Titus do *not* include a passage of thanksgiving.[3] Whether by model or command, the Scriptures make it clear that God desires His children to express their gratitude for His blessings.

Thanksgiving Alters Our Perceptions. — A second reason to give God thanks for His goodness toward us is the power which thanksgiving has to transform our irritations. William Law put it beautifully:

> If anyone would tell you the shortest, surest way to all happiness and all perfection, he must tell you to make a rule to yourself to thank and praise God for everything that happens to you. It is certain that whatever seeming calamity happens to you, if you thank and praise God for it, you turn it into a blessing. If you could work miracles, therefore, you could not do more for yourself than by this thankful spirit. It heals and turns all that it touches into happiness.[4]

Thanking God in all that happens to you is really an affirmation of your faith that He indeed "causes all things to work together for good to those who love" Him (Romans 8:28). This is simply to see that, though the forces of darkness meant our situation for evil against us, "God meant it for good" (Genesis 50:20). God can work through the most agonizing days of our lives if we allow Him to do so through our faith. Then, we will come to realize how we grow through the "valleys" and not on the "mountaintops" of life. And we can always be thankful that the bad was not the worse.

And yet, this is not to take sin lightly or rejoice in the anguish of humanity in its lostness and pain. While we obey the Word to "*in* everything give thanks," we are not commanded to give thanks specifically *for* every single thing in our lives. For, if we did, we would then find ourselves appreciating the sin which damns the lost, the pain

---

3. And you also might add Hebrews, though see 13:15.
4. William Law, *A Serious Call to a Devout and Holy Life* (New York: Paulist Press, 1978), p. 218.

of the innocent, the death of the young and the condemnation to hell of a seeming majority of mankind. The fact that we perceive light in the deep black of tragedy does not mean we accept the darkness or rejoice for the sorrow.

Another way thanksgiving changes our perceptions during a crisis is to remind us of Who our God is and how He treats us. We are called to echo the cry of David:

Bless the Lord, O my soul; and all that is within me, bless His holy name. Bless the Lord, O my soul, and *forget none of His benefits*; Who pardons all your iniquities; Who heals all your diseases; Who redeems your life from the pit; Who crowns you with lovingkindness and compassion; Who satisfies your years with good things, so that your youth is renewed like the eagle (Psalm 103:1-5).

If this sounds like the old song, "Count your blessings, name them one by one," it is the same concept. We prevent ourselves from dwelling on our trouble (and weakening our faith) and, instead, we rejoice in the generosity of the Lord for us (and strengthen our faith) as we thank Him for His manifold blessings. In remembering God's benefits, I am also reminding myself that the Lord who has blessed me in the recent past is One whom I can trust with my immediate (and long range) future.

Thanksgiving also changes our perception of those things we receive from God. Sometimes we have difficulty receiving gifts, from men or God. We mumble something about being unworthy and a perfunctory "thanks." Then, every time we see the object we were given, we feel, not joy or gratitude, but uneasiness and even guilt. "He shouldn't have," we keep saying to ourselves. And the gift becomes a curse instead of the blessing intended. Paul had men in his day who said that God's great gifts of marriage and food should be avoided to develop "self-control." But Paul replied,

God has created [them] to be gratefully shared in by those who believe and know the truth. For everything created by God is good, and nothing is to be rejected, if it is received with gratitude; for it is sanctified by means of the word of God and prayer (I Timothy 4:3b-5).

107

Our grateful spirits receive God's gifts and consecrate them or set them aside to the purpose God intended. If that purpose is that we should enjoy them, then the holiest thing we can do is to delight in them and relish them with great gratitude. I had a couple of grandmothers who both used to say, "It's a pleasure to cook for a man who loves to eat." I believe God finds it a pleasure to give to people who are excited to receive His gifts and really appreciate them. So, celebrate whatever God gives you today!

Our attitude of gratitude also reminds us that God does give specific gifts to us for His own purposes. Thanksgiving should include the realization that what we get is to be used as God intended. Essentially, God retains ownership of all He gives and our thanks admit that He gives for His own good purposes and not just for our convenience or enjoyment. So be grateful for that television (or two) that God has allowed you to obtain, but also tune in only the programs God would approve to fill your mind. Remember God's priorities in using the powerful tool of television and be grateful to have it to turn on, but also give thanks to be able to turn it *off* and share with your family in real conversations, work, worship and fun. Godly thanksgiving allows us to enjoy God's gifts without becoming enslaved to them.

Thanksgiving Encourages the Other Parts of Prayer. All five parts of prayer are interrelated and using one affects the use of all the others. Thanksgiving should be the Christian's natural response to God's answers to petitions and intercessions and to the forgiveness we receive in confession. Then, we find it easy to move back and forth from praising God for Who He is to thanking Him for what He has done. But let us examine these relationships in a bit more detail.

Thanksgiving makes petition and intercession effective. The fact is we often approach the Lord with considerable anxiety. Are our petitions really proper? Does He care to hear us? Intellectually, we may know the answers, but our hearts still quiver within us. So Paul recommends the following procedure:

> Be anxious for nothing, but in everything by prayer and supplication *with thanksgiving* let your requests be made known to God (Philippians 4:6).

Do you see that? We should mix thanksgiving in with all our requests.

Why? One reason is to enhance our faith by the recalling of past benefits. Another is to paint a background of gratitude behind our supplications, helping us come to God with humble hope rather than demanding pride. Again, thanksgiving in everything also helps us submit our wills to His will in the answers of our prayers. Finally, the size of our problems tends to shrink when compared to God's faithfulness in past blessings. Try to make a promise to yourself and God to never utter a request without the accompaniment of a thanksgiving.

Thanksgiving also aids our confessions to the Lord. An essential question behind confession is, "Did the Lord accept me back into His fellowship?" "Is my sin really covered by the blood of Jesus Christ?" Here thanksgiving can provide a great service. After confession as we thank the Lord for the forgiveness we have in Christ and the vastness of His grace toward us, we begin to *feel* what we *know*. Just as He has promised, He DOES forgive our loathsome sins and empower us to overcome even the most maddening habit. Oddly enough, we find it easier to believe the testimony of our own thanksgiving that God is "faithful and righteous to forgive our sins and to cleanse us from all unrighteousness" (I John 1:8). After all, thanksgiving is itself a confession; a confession of God's blessings back to Him, agreeing how He has generously given to us.

Finally, thanksgiving and praise are intimately related. As we experience God's delight in giving to both our needs and our desires, we should respond just like a little child. "Wow, Mom, a real Captain Whizbang Decoder Ring! Thanks! You're the greatest!" The natural response to undeserved gifts is BOTH thanks for the gift and praise for the giver. The Psalmist said three truths about our response to our gracious God:

> I love the Lord, because He hears my voice and my supplications. . . . What shall I render to the Lord for all His benefits toward me? . . . To Thee I shall offer a sacrifice of thanksgiving, and call upon the name of the Lord (Psalm 116:1, 12, 17).

What has the Psalmist said? One, since God gives so much to me, I love Him. Two, since God gives so much to me, I need to return something to God. Three, since God gives so much to me, I give the Lord "the sacrifice of thanksgiving." Now, I remind you that the Old Testament words for "thanksgiving" have the basic meaning of "praise": public acknowledgment of God. In other words, praise and thanksgiving are not two separate concepts in the Old Testament; they are combined as being the proper return which a man should offer God for His lovingkindness.

The New Testament reinforces the close connection between thanksgiving and praise. When the Samaritan leper returned to Christ after his healing, the Scripture says he gave glory to God giving thanks to Jesus (Luke 17:16-18). Giving thanks praises God. So thanksgiving encourages praise and praise encourages thanksgiving. George Herbert put it beautifully in this prayer:

Thou hast given so much to me,
Give one thing more,—a grateful heart;
Not thankful when it pleaseth me,
As if Thy blessings had spare days,
But such a heart whose pulse may be Thy praise.[5]

To review, our thanks to God fulfills three purposes: it completes part of our obedience to God, it alters our perception of our situation and it encourages us to use the other parts of prayer. Now, let's suggest how we should go about this wonderful process of giving gratitude to our God.

The Practice of Thanksgiving

You can make practical thanksgiving a habit in your spiritual disciplines by:

1. Developing proper *Attitudes* for thanksgiving.
2. Learning the *Basics* for thanksgiving.
3. Observing our *Causes* for thanksgiving.

Attitudes For Thanksgiving — Two attitudes underlie a vibrant life of thanksgiving; gratitude and humility. Let's look at each in turn.

We often omit thanksgiving because we are not grateful. "But I don't

---

5. Donald T. Kauffman, ed., *A Treasury of Great Prayers* (Westwood, New Jersey: Fleming H. Revell Company, 1964), p. 41.

feel like giving thanks," you say. "Wouldn't it be hypocritical to say 'Thank you, Lord,' when I don't mean it?" No, it would not be hypocrisy but obedience. We need to move away from "feeling-centered" prayer. Feelings are constantly in flux; now I'm up, now I'm down. Attaching our prayers to our feelings simply *guarantees* an inconsistent prayerlife. Instead, we need to *choose* to make a habit of ac-consistent prayerlife. Instead, we need to *choose* to make a habit of acting in a grateful manner (giving thanks) which will develop into an at-

Gratitude develops through choosing to be grateful. A good pattern to use to develop gratitude involves regular daily reviews each night. For one month, spend five minutes at the end of each day going over that day, looking for ways God has blessed you, your family, your friends, your church, and your world. As we specifically thank Him for each of these blessings day after day, gratitude begins to stir in our hearts.

Another way to develop gratitude is to give generously of yourself to others. "Give to get grateful?" you ask. "How does that work?" This connects with an underlying circular law of human nature. Jesus defined it this way; "Give, and it shall be given to you" (Luke 6:38), and "Freely you received, freely give" (Matthew 10:8). As we give, we receive and the more we receive the more we give. Now one of the benefits we receive when we give is the gratitude of others. And the more gratitude we receive, the more gratitude we are able to give (back to God). Here's how it works. I give some time and concern to visit Molly in the nursing home. She is so pleased to see me come in and, after we pray, she squeezes my hand and says, "You don't know what your visit means to me." I walk out to my car with a warm heart, having received her gratitude. But now I want to thank Someone for how good I feel, to pass the gratitude on. And God is only a prayer away. Giving begets gratitude.

A second underlying attitude for proper thanksgiving is humility. The New Testament records a prayer of thanksgiving which God would not acknowledge. In Luke 17:9-14, the Scripture reads:

And [Jesus] also told this parable to certain ones who trusted in themselves that they were righteous, and viewed others with contempt: "Two men went up to the temple to pray, one a Pharisee, and the other a tax gatherer. *The Pharisee stood and was praying*

thus to himself, 'God, I thank Thee that I am not like other peo-
ple: swindlers, unjust, adulterers, or even like this tax-gatherer. I
fast twice a week; I pay tithes of all that I get.' But the tax-
gatherer, standing some distance away, was even unwilling to lift
up his eyes to heaven, but was beating his breast, saying, 'God, be
merciful to me, the sinner!' I tell you, this man went down to his
house justified rather than the other; for everyone who exalts
himself shall be humbled, but he who humbles himself shall be exalted."

Thanksgiving presented in pride is only prayer to ourselves, not to
God. When we give thanks, we should not even hint that we have
deserved these gracious gifts, earned them by our righteousness. Such
claims are always lies against God. Rather we should come humbly admitting that we are not worthy of any of the blessings which fill our lives.
Confession of sin is an excellent way to make sure our thanksgiving remains humble before God. When you see yourself as the tax-gatherer
saw himself, "the sinner," your prayers will rise from an attitude of
humility.

Basics For Thanksgiving — Once our attitudes are right before God,
we need to understand the basic procedures of thanksgiving. They include the following concepts:

1. Specific and general thanks.
2. Giving and giving thanks.
3. Spoken and silent thanks.
4. "Saying grace."

First, thanksgiving can be either general or specific. Specific thanks
takes more work and is of greater value in developing a true spirit of
gratitude. Rote memorized phrases, like "Lord, we thank You for all
You have given unto us," tend to be thoughtless fillers. If you had spent
time and effort to pick out just the right wedding gift for your niece, what
kind of thank you note would you expect?

Note A	Note B
Dear Uncle Al and Aunt Pat,	Dear Uncle Al and Aunt Pat,
Thanks for your gift and your at-tendance at our wedding. Come see us sometime.	Thank you for your thoughtfulness to select the basket of kitchen utensils, all color coordinated to fit our new kit-

Yours Truly,
Frank and Jane

chen counters! After the five (5!) toasters, your loving, carefully chosen gift reminded us how much we love you two. Please plan to join us for our housewarming on June 14th at 7 p.m.

All our love,
Frank and Jane

Note A could be mass produced without thought, while Note B is a sincere and personal note of gratitude and love. I think God expects our thanksgiving to be more like Note B than A. Our prayers to the Father should be as specific in thanking Him as our petitions should be in asking from Him. There is a place for an honest general thanksgiving for what God has done, especially since we often do not even realize all His specific acts on our behalf or, if we do realize what He has done, we forget in our human weakness. But the bulk of our thanksgiving should be intentionally specific.

Second, one Biblical means of thanking God is giving to others some of what He has graciously given to us. In the Old Testament era, when an Israelite was thankful to God, he would bring an offering to be sacrificed to the Lord (Leviticus 7:11-14). When Israel finally settled in the promised land, each man was to bring an offering of his firstfruits, publicly announcing how God had given him the land and brought him out of Egypt with His mighty hand, and worshipping the Lord in joy for all the good which He had given (Deuteronomy 26:1-11).

In the present era, we can offer thanks to God by giving to the church and to others in their need. In II Corinthians 8 and 9, Paul suggests that God supplies us with more than sufficiency to meet our own needs so that we can give to others as well. And what is the result of our giving?

For the ministry of this service is not only fully supplying the needs of the saints, but is also overflowing through many thanksgivings to God (II Corinthians 9:12).

Our thanks produces giving and our giving produces more thanks. In fact, the efforts we give to God in praise are also our sacrifices of thanks to Him when accompanied by doing good for others and sharing what

113

we have received (Hebrews 13:15-16). In summary, then, if you are grateful, give!

Third, thanksgiving can be spoken or silent, in thought or writing. The Scripture mentions thanks being given by public prayers, by songs of thanksgiving, by private prayers and by writing. Each mode of expressing gratitude helps us in specific ways.

The worship of Israel assumed public audible thanksgiving. David assumed that answered prayers would surely be followed by thanksgiving, the public acknowledgment of what the Lord had done.[6] We can use this same means of both glorifying God and evangelizing the lost. From time to time, I see ads in "Personals" column of the newspaper like the following:

> Many gracious thanks to St. Jude
> for favors granted.
> A. R. and G. R.

Someone has promised to publicly thank their "patron saint" if a certain request is answered. The Bible knows nothing of "patron saints" but it does indicate that the Lord who answers prayers deserves the public thanks of His people.

Giving God thanks in our daily conversation gives us a special benefit. It helps us to cleanse our speech of filthy talk and coarse jesting (Ephesians 5:4). James suggests the two possibilities of the tongue with these words:

> With it we bless our Lord and Father; and with it we curse men, who have been made in the likeness of God; from the same mouth come both blessing and cursing. My brethren, these things ought not to be this way (James 3:9-10).

It certainly should not; but too often it is "this way." Start today to replace your rougher language with the sweet words of thanksgiving to God as you talk with others.

---

6. See Psalms 6, 9, 18, 26, 28, 30, 35, 52, 54, 57, 69, 86, 108, 109, 138, 139, 142 and 145.

114

Songs may also be used to lift thanks to the Almighty. The Psalmist suggests this:

> O come, let us sing for joy to the Lord; let us shout joyfully to the rock of our salvation. Let us come before His presence with thanksgiving; let us shout joyfully to Him with psalms (Psalm 95:1-2).

Music can reinforce the emotional elements of thanksgiving, especially joy. Unfortunately, finding hymns of thanks in a modern hymnal can can be like mining for diamonds; the "finds" very rare indeed. "Now Thank We All Our God" and the chorus "Thank You, Lord, For Saving My Soul" come to mind, but after that songs of gratitude seem few to be found. Maybe you would write us a few new songs of thanksgiving . . . please?

Thanksgiving can also be lifted in private prayers. Actually, to fulfill the command to "in everything give thanks," we would have to include thanks in our private prayer life (I Thessalonians 5:18). But, Paul states that thanks is to be intermingled with all our petitions and intercessions (Philippians 4:6; Colossians 4:2). As we ask, we also thank God for His answer, *whatever* that answer may be. We thank Him just to know that He hears us, as Jesus did (John 11:41-42). Fill your prayers with the repeated chord of thanks.

Finally, thanksgiving may be stated in writing. All of the thanksgiving prayers in the Bible were obviously set down in writing by the human authors of each book. Paul had a special way of using written thanks. In all of his letters but four,[7] Paul writes somewhere in the opening paragraphs how he thanked God for the person or persons receiving the letter. This gentle compliment both communicated that Paul thought his readers worthy of thanks and that he saw them as God's gifts. You can continue this practice in your life by notes to your brothers and sisters in Christ which include your thanks to God for them. You can even obtain "Prayer-A-Gams," "Praise-A-Grams" and "Thank-U-Grams," specially printed forms and envelopes on which to

---

7. The letters which lack the opening thanksgiving are II Corinthians, Galatians, I Timothy and Titus (and Hebrews, if you include this book in Paul's letters).

write your petitions, praises and thanksgivings to be sent to others.[8]

Another way to keep your thanksgivings in written form is to begin a "Book of Remembrance" section in your prayer notebook. On these pages, you would write down the many blessings which you thank God for day by day. Then, on some particularly gray afternoon, pull out your notebook and lift your spirit by reviewing all the blessings God has provided in your life to this point. Headings such as those below might be used.

Date	Lord, I thank You for . . .

As was mentioned earlier, the evening is a good time to review the day and find those blessings which God has given to us and those around us. How often have you gone to bed with a grateful heart? Or are your last thoughts before sleep often of fear, worry or discontent? Try that old habit of "counting your blessings; name them one by one" and soon it will *not* "surprise you what the Lord has done." So, whether it is aloud or silent or singing or written, close the day with thanks to the Lord Who loves to give.

Fourth, every meal presents us an opportunity to give thanks as we "say grace." Jesus gives us His example in this area. See the occasions on the following page when Jesus paused to offer gratitude to God for food given.

You may notice that two different terms are used: "gave thanks" and "blessed." "Give thanks" we understand, but what does it mean to "bless" food? The word translated "to bless" here is the Greek term *eulogeo*, which means, literally, to "speak well of." But more than this,

---

8. Available from Prayer-A-Gram Foundation, P.O. Box 8127, Sta. D, Fort Wayne, Indiana 46898.

"to bless" is to "call down God's gracious power."[9] When called upon an inanimate object, this blessing consecrates that object; sets it apart to the service of God. Does that apply to food? Can we give the lima beans the Lord has given us back to Him? (I know some kids who would *love* to give back *all* the lima beans!) Read what Paul says to Timothy concerning those who wanted to limit a Christian's enjoyment of life.

Occasion	Description	Scripture
Feeding of the 5,000	". . . He took the five loaves and two fish, and looking up toward heaven, He blessed the food. . . ."	Matthew 14:19
Feeding of the 4,000	". . . taking the seven loaves, He gave thanks and broke them, . . . They also had a few small fish; and after He had blessed them, He ordered these to be served as well."	Mark 8:6-7
The Last Supper	"And when He had taken some bread and given thanks, He broke it, and gave it to them, saying, 'This is My body which is given for you; do this in remembrance of Me.' And in the same way He took the cup after they had eaten, saying, 'This cup which is poured out for you is the new covenant in My blood.' "	Luke 22:19-20
Dinner at Emmaus after the Resurrection	"And it came about that when He had reclined at the table with them, He took the bread and blessed it, and breaking it, He began giving it to them."	Luke 24:30

But the Spirit explicitly says that in later times some will fall away from the faith, paying attention to deceitful spirits and doctrines of demons, by means of the hypocrisy of liars seared in their own conscience as with a branding iron, men who forbid marriage and advocate abstaining from foods, which God created to be *grateful-ly* shared in by those who believe and know the truth. For everything created by God is good, and *nothing is to be rejected, if it is received with gratitude; for it is sanctified by means of the Word of God and prayer* (I Timothy 4:1-5).

---

9. William F. Arndt and F. Wilbur Gingrich, trans. and ed. *A Greek-English Lexicon of the New Testament and Other Early Christian Literature,* by *Walter Bauer* (Chicago: The University of Chicago Press, 1957), p. 322.

Think of it: we make our meals holy (sanctify them) when we receive them from God with thanksgiving (gratitude). And what is the holy task for which God uses the meals we give back to Him? We get to eat them with grateful joy and be physically strengthened to serve Him.

How do mealtime prayers work at your house? Do you get a hurried "God-is-great-God-is-good-and-we-thank-Him-for-our-food-Amen?" Or has some other cliche replaced this sing- song "grace"? Since prayers for meals tend to be our most common spoken prayers, they have the greatest tendency to become repetitious and humdrum. How can we keep this consecration fresh and real? Here are some suggestions:

1. Try having someone write out a brief prayer for each evening meal. Writing gives us time to think and be creative in our prayers.

2. If only one person has been doing all the praying in your family, begin taking turns around the table. The prayers of a five-year-old can be very instructive to any older folks.

3. Try taking a simple chorus and fitting in new words to make a prayer you can sing together. For example, take "Michael Row the Boat Ashore" and use these words:

Lord, we thank you for this food. Allelujah!
You are great and wise and good. Allelujah!

Now you can certainly do better than that. If you have a budding composer around the house, have them write a whole new prayer song. Just remind him or her to keep it short and simple.

4. Make it a game in your family to thank Him for something new (not previously mentioned) at each meal. Since the world is filled with God's blessings, you need not worry about running out of thanks to give.

5. Give thanks *specifically* for this meal by listing each dish God has provided. How do you remember them? You don't. You simply pray with your eyes open.

6. Make this a time of sharing love by holding hands around the table. We have rarely had problems doing this, even in restaurants. Strangers have even stopped by our table to say, "Thank you for praying together like that. Keep it up!"

7. If you are dieting or fasting, go right ahead and pray at mealtime. The Bible suggests this.

. . . he who eats, does so for the Lord, for he gives thanks to God; and he who eats not, for the Lord he does not eat, and gives thanks to God. (Romans 14:6)

And if you stay on your diet, give God all the more thanks! You can consecrate lettuce to the Lord with just as much holiness as a prime rib dinner with strawberry pie for dessert. (If you are overweight, there may be considerably more holiness in eating the lettuce!)

So much for the basics of thanksgiving. Now, what are we going to thank God for?

Causes For Thanksgiving — Every day and every situation contains many reasons to be grateful to God. We often do not notice because we are not thinking about God being involved with our lives at all. Lehman Strauss reminds us:

The words *think* and *thank* come from a common root. If we would take the time to *think* more, we would undoubtedly *thank* more.[10]

So *think* together with me about the following three general causes to bring thanks to the Almighty.

1. Thank Him for all He is and all He has done.
2. Thank Him for other people and His actions through them and for them.
3. Thank Him for His control in every situation.

Thank Him for all He is and all He has done. — Have you thanked God for Himself lately? Doesn't He deserve it? Asaph has thought about God in Psalm 77 and he comes down to a question.

I shall remember the deeds of the Lord; surely I will remember Thy wonders of old. I will meditate on all Thy work, and muse on Thy deeds. Thy way, O God, is holy; what god is great like our God? (Psalm 77:11-13).

The answer is "there is no god like our God, for He *is* God." If you have any kind of imagination, you can conjure up how God *might* have been

---

10. *Sense and Nonsense about Prayer* (Chicago: Moody Press, 1974), p. 58.

if He were not the God disclosed in the Bible. The Greeks imagined gods with every human frailty, except the lack of raw power. The gods were lusty, greedy, envious, childish beings without self-control or holiness. The ancient gods of Canaan were bloodthirsty for the bodies of sacrificed children and the masters of priests and priestesses who were prostitutes. The Hindu gods are sensuous and horrible, amoral and easily angered. The gods of Mormonism are glorified men who keep their many wives eternally pregnant and have to have a council to join forces to create a world. Aren't you thankful that our God Who is God is not even remotely like those demonic heresies?

In the first three verses of Psalm 107, we are told a proper response to the Lord who is the Lord of hosts:

> Oh give thanks to the Lord, for He is good; for His lovingkindness is everlasting. Let the redeemed of the Lord say so, whom He has redeemed from the hand of the adversary, and gathered from the lands, from the east and from the west, from the north and from the south.

Isn't He good? Haven't you found His lovingkindness to be consistent and sure? Hasn't He redeemed you from your enemies of sin and death? Say so! Thank Him for who He is daily.

Add to these thanks your gratitude for what God has done. Every speck of dust is a tiny world; any microscope will tell you that. Every snowflake is a delicate and unique geometric design, even though its form may melt into nothingness in a moment. Every drop in a stagnant pond is crowded with life, moving and multiplying. Perhaps you are not a person who is impressed by the complex intricacies of the minutiae of creation. Look an elephant eye to eye. Examine the devastating power released in the breaking of a single atom. Study the sun, a fission/fusion furnace vast enough to contain a multitude of earths — in one of its sunspots. Or try to mentally stand off and watch the Milky Way spin and realize that our sun is a second-rate star lost and unnoticed in one of the two great arms of the spiral. And, then fling your mind out into space where the uncounted galaxies majestically sail through a universe huge beyond our knowing. Now combine these two visions, from the infinitesimal to the immense, and fit them into this sentence: "In the beginning God created the heavens and the earth" (Genesis 1:1). This is creation; it surrounds you; and God has done it. Thank Him.

Every page of history is covered with the "fingerprints" of God. He has dealt with Adam, Abel, Abraham, Aaron, Ahab, Ahasuerus, Aristides, Amos, Aristotle, Alexander the Great, Mark Anthony, Caesar Augustus, Andrew, Ananias, Augustine, Alfred the Great, King Arthur, Pope Adrian I, Mogul Emperor Akbar, John Alden, Queen Anne of England, John Adams, Ethan Allen, John Jacob Astor, Louisa May Alcott, Chester A. Arthur, Susan B. Anthony, Alfonso XIII of Spain, Marion Anderson and Dear Abby. And that is just a tiny portion of the "A's." The Lord works in every life of every man, woman and child who ever lived anywhere. Wherever you look in history, recent or distant, if there was kindness, loyalty, love, justice or mercy, God was there. In the blackest hours, He was the light of hope. In the brightest victories, He was the Commander in triumph. Whatever moves you to joy or courage or peace, thank God for being in that moment in that place. Every result of democracy, peace and freedom you enjoy is a heaven-sent gift; give the Lord of heaven an offering of thanks. Your family background, your community, your home and your life are God-given; return gratitude for His grace.

Thank Him for other people and His actions through them and for them. — People are the most precious things on earth. If God has His will done here, a person will be involved. For even the most evil of us, God received the atonement of blood of His own Son to enable anyone at all to come to Him in peace. The Lord has sent you your friends and family (and your enemies). Thank Him.

Today and tomorrow you will meet people. Had you ever thought that each meeting could be a "divine appointment?" While each of us acts in his own freewill, God weaves our acts together according to His will. You meet the people you meet because the Father is guiding your path. Do you shoot up little quick prayers to Him saying, "Thank you, Father, for bringing me together with this person. May I be used in Your will in this moment"? Try it today.

Our families are our special focus in prayer. We would not expect someone else to provide for them as we do or care about them as we care. Frankly, I cannot imagine anyone else being as thankful for my wife as I am. It is no task for me to regularly tell my God how grateful I am for Debbie. Then there are three "whirlwinds" which keep me far from boredom. Yet, I still believe that Christopher, Liberty and Megan

121

are special and wonderful gifts of God and I thank Him for the privilege of being their father.

Yes, enemies can be godly gifts as well. When we suffer at the hands of others, Jesus tells us to "rejoice, and be glad" (Matthew 5:12). Their persecution on account of Christ tells us we are on the right spiritual track. We are becoming enough like Christ that men are beginning to treat us as they treated Him. Thank the Lord! Enemies also keep us sharp and growing; a friend might let me relax and slide back. My opposition won't fail to challenge me . . . daily. Some of the best of Christ's teachings came out His clashes with the Pharisees and Sadducees who had early decided on the necessity of His death. Spiritually, the trials we face through men can be our spiritual training ground where we burn off the fat of sin and put on the muscle of faith. So thank the Lord for your hard people to love.

Thank Him for His control in every situation. — There is a command which as we think about it seems more and more impossible to fulfill. I Thessalonians 5:18 reads, " . . . in *everything* give thanks; for this is God's will for you in Christ Jesus." Our reply might run something like this, "Uh . . . well, Lord, I know you want us to be grateful daily, but . . . not *everything*, Lord! Not my wife leaving me. Not the death of my grandfather. Not the job I lost. Not the 'F' on the quiz. Not the accident or the surgery or the cancer or the death I am so close to I think I can touch it. Not in everything, Lord."

If God was actually telling us to be thankful *for* everything, this command would be foolish indeed. Would our Father have us thankful for the death of the lost? Should any rational believer be grateful for the holocaust of the Nazi concentration camps? I do not believe it. We do not thank God for sin. I understand the Lord God to be telling us to find His hand in every situation, no matter how horrid. It is for His grace in the midst of pain for which we give Him our thanks. We thank the Almighty *in* everything, not *for* everything.

One of the most precious promises in all the Scriptures is found in Paul's first letter to the church at Corinth. It reads:

No temptation has overtaken you but such as is common to man; and God is faithful, who will not allow you to be tempted beyond what you are able, but with the temptation will provide the way of escape also, that you may be able to endure it (I Corinthians 10:13).

Regardless of the temptation you may face (even right now), this wonderful verse says:

1. Thank God, for you are not alone. Your temptation may be in a unique situation, but men and women have faced similar stresses from the beginning of the world.

2. Thank God, for no matter how unfaithful others (including you) may have been, God is faithful. He will not forget you or His promises to you.

3. Thank God, for He has limited your temptation to stay within your God-given ability to handle the test. Obviously, we can always be grateful that the bad times aren't worse. Then, we can thank the Father for the trials He has protected us from having to face. Matthew Henry, who wrote a noted set of devotional Bible commentaries, was once robbed of his entire life's savings. His prayer that night reads as follows:

I thank Thee first because I was never robbed before; second, because although they took my purse, they did not take my life; third, although they took my all, it was not much; and fourth, because it was I who was robbed and not I who robbed.[11]

4. Thank God, for He has planned an escape route for every trial. No trap of the enemy can hold you, even if death is His chosen way out for you. Ask for wisdom to see His way of escape and take it with gratitude and joy.

5. Thank God, for He has promised you will be able to endure your temptations. That does not mean there will be no pain or struggles. But, in the midst of those sorrowful struggles, thank the Lord for His promise which holds out sure hope for deliverance.

And even in the face of death, thank the Lord. Paul had discovered the reality of being able to welcome death at the proper time. He didn't care if God gave him another hour or another decade of life. He simply said:

---

11. Source unknown.

For to me, to live is Christ, and to die is gain. But if I am to live on in the flesh, this will mean fruitful labor for me; and I do not know which to choose. But I am hard-pressed from both directions, having the desire to depart and be with Christ, for that is very much better; yet to remain on in the flesh is more necessary for your sake (Philippians 1:21-24).

When it is God's timing, we can indeed say, "Precious in the sight of the Lord is the death of His godly ones" (Psalm 116:15). We cannot know God's timing, but, as we trust Him, we can thank Him that *He* knows the proper time for all things.

The second part of prayer is thanksgiving. It never will go out of style because our generous God will never stop supplying our needs. Learn thanksgiving for eternal use.

Thought or Discussion Questions

1. With which of the following three types of people is your church presently filled? Why?
[ ] The grateful: frequently thank God and others for the many gifts they see themselves receiving.
[ ] The ingrates: not moved to thank God or man for much of anything; figure they have earned the little they have gathered.
[ ] The grumblers: assume they have been short-changed by God and man and thank no one as they feel no gratitude.

Which describes your family best? Why?

[ ] The grateful   [ ] The ingrates   [ ] The grumblers

Which describes you best? Why?

[ ] The grateful   [ ] The ingrates   [ ] The grumblers

2. How would you explain our need to express our gratitude to the Lord? How well do we express our enjoyment of God's gifts? Do "glee" and "celebration" fit into our understanding of living with Christ? What

makes some people hesitate about rejoicing in their Christian life? Which view of Christianity pervades your family: grateful joy or solemn reverence?

3. Which determines the average Christian's thanksgivings: his feelings of gratitude or the gifts God gives? To ask it another way: is our gratitude determined by our feelings or our recognition of God's generosity? How can we make our thanks less dependent on our feelings? How does giving to others stimulate our gratitude to God?

4. List twenty-four specific gifts you have received from the Lord in the last twenty-four hours. How easy was that to do? Why? Which of these gifts could you in turn pass on to others? Check five items you intend to share with someone else within this week in the name of Jesus Christ.

5. Think of the five people in your life for whom you are most grateful. Have you thanked God for each of these individuals? Have you told them how grateful you are for their influence? Consider writing a letter of thanks to each of these people whom God has given you.

6. How monotonous have your mealtime prayers become? Check one.
[ ] We don't "say grace."
[ ] We say, "let's just be thankful in our hearts."
[ ] Only one person prays and repeats him/herself often.
[ ] We take turns and try to keep our prayers original.
    How could you improve your mealtime prayers? When will you start these improvements?

6

WHAT ARE THE PARTS OF PRAYER?
III — PETITION

If prayer could ultimately be simplified to a single word, perhaps that word would be, "Help." Dietrich Bonhoeffer has said, "The essence of Christian prayer is not general adoration, but definite, concrete petition."[1] We come in prayer primarily to ask. Why? Because, as fallen creatures in a fallen world, we need the grace of God every moment of every day.

Only a fool would fail to realize how dependent we are on our Father. Yet each of us would have to admit to often being foolish when we attempt the warfare of life without the armor and provision of God. God's supplies are imminently available, but they are only available for the asking.

The average Sunday morning service prayer is not intended to be answered, since it rarely really asks for anything. The bulletin says it's time to pray and so we do. The lips may then utter requests but the heart remains satisfied and indifferent. Many of those who pray in our

---

1. *The Cost of Discipleship* (New York: Macmillan Publishing, 1963), p. 183.

services remind me of the man described by C. S. Lewis as one who prayed faintly "lest God might really hear him, which he, poor man, never intended."[2] It is time to return petitions to God to the the heart of our prayers.

The third part of prayer is petition, which may be defined as an act of requesting our needs to be met and our desires to be sorted by the Lord. As before, this part of prayer is related to all the other parts in its own way.

Praise acknowledges God as the ultimate Source of every good and perfect gift.[3] But my prayers would be inconsistent if I praise God for His generosity but do not ask to receive anything from Him. If I praise the Lord as the true God Who answers the prayers of men, I seem to deny the same truth if I refuse to offer requests to Him to be answered. Rather, as He does answer my petitions, I will respond with hearty praise. Petition is related to praise.

Thanksgiving should also be a natural Christian response to receiving whatever I have asked from the Lord. Yet I also need to thank the Lord when He wisely denies my requests. Paul speaks of being thankful for food which we eat and *also* being thankful for food we do not eat (Romans 14:6). When I consider my more foolish prayers of my past, I am profoundly grateful that my Father was kindly enough to say "No" regardless of how much I hounded Him. As a parent, I have learned that often the best thing to offer a child demanding sweets is a simple denial and then silence, while he tries himself in whining and threatening. More experienced parents tell me that occasionally the more sensitive of their children one day did thank them for the discipline of their denials. Petition is related to thanksgiving (whether the petition is granted or not).

Intercession and petition are difficult to separate in a mature Christian's prayer. Like the Lord's Prayer, the prayer of a man or woman of God is often framed in petitions for "us" ("Give *us* this day *our* daily bread. And forgive *us our* debts, as *we* also have forgiven *our* debtors. And lead *us* not into temptation, but deliver *us* from evil" Matthew 6:11-13). We should desire the same kinds of blessings for others which

---

2. *Letters To Malcolm: Chiefly On Prayer* (New York: Harcourt Brace Jovanovich, Inc., 1964), p. 114.
3. See James 1:17.

we request for ourselves. Intercession and petition are further inter-mingled when we pray about that most difficult of areas, human relation-ships. We can ask for ourselves that a broken friendship be restored, yet this is at the same time an intercession for the friend we seek to regain. Likewise, I have found that praying for my wife is also praying for myself, for her joy gives me joy. Petition often relates to intercession.

Confession can make petition effective. Psalm 66:18-20 reads:

> If I regard wickedness in my heart, the Lord will not hear; but cer-tainly God has heard; He has given heed to the voice of my prayer. Blessed be God, Who has not turned away my prayer, nor His lovingkindness from me.

No one would want his prayers to God "turned away." But, our prayers may be blocked by sin which remains in our hearts. Confession deals with the sin within us and acts as cleansing agent for our personalities. Confession then prepares us to approach the Lord with our requests. Confession and petition are also related in that confession may be seen as a specialized form of petition. We will discuss this in a later chapter.

After seeing that petition fits into the unified whole of prayer with each of its parts, we are going to study petition by answering four ques-tions:

1. Why do we ask?
2. What do we ask?
3. How do we ask?
4. How does God answer?

WHY DO WE ASK?

When we consider why we bring petitions to God, we discover that some of our motivations for petitioning God do not have Scriptural sup-port. For example, petition has sometimes been viewed as "spiritual leverage," a way to pressure God into coming over to your point of view and obeying your will. Petition can even be imagined to "twist God's arm," if properly applied. Such thoughts are not only unworthy of a Christian's love for His Lord, they are ludicrous when compared to the teaching and example of the Word of God. Look at God's challenge in the prophecy of Isaiah.

"I, even I, am the Lord; and there is no savior besides me. It is I who have declared and saved and proclaimed, and there was no strange god among you; so you are My witnesses," declares the Lord, "And I am God. Even from eternity I am He; and there is none who can deliver out of My hand; I act and who can reverse it?" (Isaiah 43:11-13).

"Who can reverse it?" Not you or I with some meager prayer. Our Lord cannot be "pushed around" by our petitions and it is foolish to even try to "bend Him to our will."

A similar (and equally poor) motive for petitioning our Father is the attempt to use prayer as an "Aladdin's lamp" which will grant our wishes if properly " rubbed." This magical view of prayer is widespread, as childish as it seems. Again, the attempt in this motivation is to manipulate God to obey us. This stands utterly opposed to the Biblical view of petition. The great Japanese Christian Kagawa was asked to define Christian prayer. He replied with one word: "Surrender."[4] This is the Biblical view. In both the model prayer of the Sermon on the Mount and the prayer of Christ in Gethsemane, the phrase repeated is not "MY will be done" but "Thy will be done."

A final misrepresentation of the proper motives for approaching God with a request might be labeled "Christian whining." We go to God to share our worries and fears with Him and complain about the "needs" He has not filled for us. Such whining is as annoying to the ears of God as similar grumbling is to the humans who have to put up with it from others.[5] Jesus taught His disciples to surrender all their worries and concerns and trust their heavenly Father to provide for them what was needed (Matthew 6:19-34). Not only is anxious pleading not a Biblical concept of petition, but Paul actually contrasts the two:

Be anxious for nothing, *but* [instead] in everything by prayer and

---

4. Quoted in E. Stanley Jones' pamphlet, *How to Pray* (n.p.: Abingdon Press, 1943), p. 6.
5. See the Lord's reactions to the grumblings of Israel during their wilderness wanderings. A good summary is found in Psalm 106:7-27.

supplication with thanksgiving let your requests be made known
to God. And the peace of God, which surpasses all comprehension, shall guard your hearts and your minds in Christ Jesus
(Philippians 4:6-7).

So our petitions are to be offered out of more than just fear or worry,
but what are the Biblical reasons to bring our requests to the Lord?

We ask because God commanded it and Jesus modeled it.

When someone offers to help us, we risk offending him if we should
refuse his aid. Now God has commanded us to call on Him for aid in
times of need, daily needs or extraordinary assistance.

Ask, and it shall be given to you; seek, and you shall find; knock,
and it shall be opened. For everyone who asks receives, and he
who seeks finds, and to him who knocks it shall be opened. Or
what man is there among you, when his son shall ask him for a
loaf, will give him a stone? Or if he shall ask for a fish, he will not
give him a snake, will he? If you then, being evil, know how to
give good gifts to your children, how much more shall your Father
who is in heaven give what is good to those who ask Him! (Matthew 7:7-11).

Jesus here calls on the disciples and the crowds to seek out God and ask
Him for the good gifts He offers. Even earthly fathers will not substitute
a dangerous look-alike for the request of their sons; how likely is it,
Jesus insists, that our heavenly Father would refuse us that which we
ask which would do us good? So the command to ask is tied to our trust
in the loving nature of God, our Father in Christ Jesus.

Jesus often showed His own dependence on the Father as a Son of
man through His many petitions. Our Lord is described in Hebrews 5:7
with these words:

In the days of His flesh, He offered up both prayers and supplications with loud crying and tears to the One able to save Him from
death, and He was heard because of His piety.

131

The prayers here referred to include His prayers in the upper room (John 17:1-26; especially 1-5), in Gethsemane (Matthew 26:36-44) and on the cross (Luke 23:44-46). Since Jesus is our model in all things, His prayerlife also is a reflection of God's will for us, including that we should offer petitions to the Father. The fact Christ Himself made requests of the Father reassures us that asking help from God is not an inferior or worldly level of prayer. God commands that we offer petitions and Jesus serves as our example in His own petitions.

We ask because we need.

We need what only God can give: _____.
How would you fill in that blank? In several prayer seminars I have held through the midwest, I asked that question: "What is it we need that on-ly God can give?" The normal responses went something like this:

A long silence.

"Grace," one woman suggests timidly.

"Yes, that's right. What else?" I encourage the group.

Another nervous empty space.

"Salvation from our sins," one of the deacons states loudly.

"Good. And what else can only God give us?" I urge.

After a pause, "The Holy Spirit?" someone in the back says hesitantly.

"Right you are. Can you think of other gifts only God can give us?" I say and lean forward.

"'Our daily bread?'" the young man quotes.

"Healing," a older woman says quietly.

"Help . . . like when we're in trouble," the deacon again.

"Excellent! Tell me more," I begin to smile as I know they are getting close to the best answer.

"Well, God gives us our crops . . . and good weather," a farmer's wife contributes.

"He gives us our families," a teen-age girl says with a grin.

"Love," one man says.

"Peace," chimes in another.

"Joy and hope . . . the fruit of the Spirit?"

"All creation!"

'My wife."

"Yes! Yes! You're all right on top of it! Now, what is it that we need that only God can give?" I ask one last time.

[Now you, dear reader, should know the answer, since I told you in chapter two.]

There is a moment more of silence as the group mentally moves back to take in all the items mentioned. Then, someone says with a sheepish grin (afraid the answer will sound silly), "Well, everything . . . He gives us everything."

"Fantastic! You got it! 'He who did not spare His own Son, but delivered Him up for us, how will He not also with Him freely give us *all things?*'[6] We need what only God can give—EVERYTHING!" I conclude and we all sit back, smiling, catching a glimpse of the vastness of God's loving care for us.

Since we need the provision of God in every area of our lives, we come to see that our greatest need is a proper relationship with our Father Who supplies everything else. John Chrysostom, one of the greatest preachers of the church in its early centuries, has written:

> God gave to some animals the speed of flight; to others, claws or wings; but He has so disposed man that He, God Himself, is his strength.[7]

Our petitions are an admission of our need for God and His gifts.

We ask because we believe God can answer.

In order to approach God with petitions in faith, we "must believe that He is, and that He is a rewarder of those who seek Him" (Hebrews 11:6). That is, we would not be asking God for anything if we seriously doubted that He was willing or able to give what we requested.

I haven't asked my parents for a million dollars lately. Why? They don't have a million, either to keep or to give. I also have not asked God

---

6. Romans 8:32.

7. Quoted in "Confidence In Prayer," *Christopher News Notes* (New York: The Christophers, November, 1984),

for a million dollars lately. Why? Not because I question His *ability* to furnish the cash; but, I do suspect that it is not His will for me to have enough money to squander in luxury and indulgence.

Every earnest request to God is a statement of our belief that the Lord is a prayer-hearing and a prayer-answering God. We believe (often in error) that our individual requests are within His will for us and therefore will be fulfilled for us. Otherwise, why would we ask at all?

We ask because we need the humility of asking.

God is omniscient; He knows everything, including our every need and desire. Then what is the point of asking Him for that which He already knows we need? Let me answer this with a quote from Ray Stedman:[8]

Of course [God] knows what we have need of, for he knows everything about us. But prayer is something *we* need. God does not need to be told; we need to tell him, that is the point.

To understand why this is true, ask yourself what happens when you neglect to pray for, and thank God for, your daily needs. I think if you are honest and examine your life over an extended period of time, you will see that, inevitably, a slow and subtle change occurs in your heart. What happens is that we begin to take these things for granted and gradually succumb to the foolish delusion that we actually can provide these necessities ourselves . . . that we *can* supply them quite apart from God.

The resulting pride from such an attitude puts us in opposition to God and makes it impossible to receive His grace. (II Peter 5:6-7) We need to be humbled through the process of petition.

Asking for everything we need humbles us by reminding us both of our dependency on the Lord and our servant status. Like small children, we cannot just open the refrigerator and take out whatever we want (unless we are willing to pay the consequences for such an act of

---

8. *Jesus Teaches on Prayer* (Waco, Texas: Word Books, Publisher, 1975), p. 70.

rebellion). First, we must ask and then we can legitimately receive, humbly.

We ask because God is pleased with our asking.

I am not against my children borrowing one of my tools in principle. But I am pleased when they ask me before taking one. Similarly, God has furnished so much for us to enjoy and use in His service that He is obviously not opposed to our use of His gifts. But He, too, is pleased when we pause to ask Him first. The apostle John wrote us:

Beloved, if our heart does not condemn us, we have confidence before God; and whatever we ask we receive from Him, because we keep His commandments and do the things that are pleasing in His sight (I John 3:21-22).

God is not only pleased when we ask; he also is pleased when that which we request is to be used to further please Him in obedience to His will. As parents, we appreciate our children asking when they want a Twinkie snack cake, but we are more pleased when they ask if they could have an apple. So, not only our act of asking but the very content of what we ask may be pleasing to God.

In summary, then, we first petition God in obedience to His commands and in imitation of the example of Jesus Christ. Second, we also ask of God because only He can supply all that we need. Third, our requests demonstrate our faith that God can hear and answer our prayers. Fourth, the act of seeking God and His gracious gifts humbles us and, in doing so, overthrows our pride and helps us realize our dependence upon the Lord. And, fifth and last, our petitions please the heavenly Father Who desires us to call upon Him.

In the last point, we mentioned that the content of our petitions *may* be pleasing to the Lord God Who hears us. But how do we know what we ought to ask?

WHAT DO WE ASK?

By taking isolated verses out of context and ignoring the rest of the

135

teachings of the Scriptures, some people have taught that *any* request may be brought before God and, with sufficient faith, it will be delivered as requested. Some of the verses so misused include the following (with emphasis added):

> Ask, and it *shall* be given to you; . . . . For *everyone* who asks receives . . . (Matthew 7:7-8). Again, I tell you that if two of you on earth agree about *anything* you ask for, it *will* be done for you by my Father in heaven (Matthew 18:19). And *all* things you ask in prayer, believing, you *shall* receive (Matthew 21:22). *All things* are possible to him who believes (Mark 9:23). Therefore I say to you, *all things* for which you pray and ask, believe that you have received them, and they *shall* be granted you (Mark 11:24). The things impossible with men are *possible* with God (Luke 18:27). Even now I know that *whatever* You ask of God, God will give You (John 11:22). If you ask Me *anything* in My name, I *will* do it (John 14:14). *Whatever* you ask of the Father in My name, He may give to you (John 15:16b). Truly, truly, I say to you, if you shall ask the Father for *anything*, He *will* give it to you in My name (John 16:23).

While this list is impressive, I repeat that these Scriptures cannot be correctly understood when removed from the context of their surrounding passages and when not correlated with the rest of the teachings of Scripture.

James clearly states that there are two reasons why we may not receive that which we need or desire.

1. "You do not have because you do not ask" (James 4:2). We may not ask for the very things God knows that we need. Indeed, we may know that God desires us to have certain gifts but refuse to seek them because *we* do not desire them. For example, a couple going through a marital crisis may avoid praying for the self-discipline to make personal changes which would improve their relationship. Why? The discipline is painful and does not allow them to pamper their pet resentments and sins. Instead, they ask for "wisdom to make a good divorce for themselves and the kids," which leads us to the second reason why prayers are ignored by God according to James.

2. "You ask and do not receive, because you ask with wrong motives, so that you may spend it on your pleasures" (James 4:3). Some prayers cannot be granted by the Lord because they are selfish requests to fulfill some fleshly or worldly craving. A whole school of theology has sprung up recently to encourage such prayers. These teachers proclaim that God's desire for every Christian is health, wealth and happiness without stint. This essentially pagan concept of prayer has us using God to our own ends of present happiness and peace. Herein is the crux of what we ask in prayer.

We ask within the Will of God as we understand it.

The difference between Christian and non-Christian petitions to God can be stated in this question: am I trying to bend God's will to fulfill my desires or am I trying to transform my desires to fulfill God's will? Non-Christian petitions seek to fulfill our desires; Christian petitions seek to fulfill the will of God.

Since God's will *cannot* be bent to our desires, non-Christian petitions always fail in the end. Since our petitions to fulfill His will are prayers God delights to answer, Christian petitions always succeed in the end. Self-centered prayers consistently fail; God-centered prayers consistently succeed.

One Biblical passage seems to explain this principle very well. John writes the following in his first general epistle:

And this is the confidence which we have before Him, that, if we ask anything according to His will, He hears us. And if we know that He hears us in whatever we ask, we know that we have the requests which we have asked from Him (I John 5:14-15).

John begins by saying that we have confidence or boldness before God. The Greek word used for "boldness" literally means "freedom of speech."[9] We can freely speak to our Lord without fear or reserve. John also says that God is listening to us. He wants to hear from us and

---

9. William Barclay, *The Letters of John and Jude* (Philadelphia: The Westminster Press, 1960), p. 136.

does not have to be compelled to hear our prayers.

But there is a basic condition set on our requests. In order for our requests to be heard favorably by the Lord (and granted),[10] we must ask "according to His will." The essence of our prayer is "Thy will be done," not, "Thy will be changed."[11] We come to this conclusion: "I trust my Father in all that He does, whether I understand His reasons or not. All that I desire is that His will be enforced over the sin and rebellion of this world. This is my prayer. So every petition I lay before Him will be circumscribed by His will. If something I ask is outside of His will, my greater prayer is that His will prevail and my flawed request be ignored."

If we ask "according to His will," we know that He hears us and we further know and are confident that, when He hears us, our petitions will be granted. All of the promises cited earlier concerning God granting whatever we ask come into focus right at this point. We may have anything we request which is in line with God's will.

To put it another way, we should only desire and ask that which lies within the will of God. Outside of the will of God would be sinful requests, when we know they are not what God requires. But we are free to seek boldly anything within His will.

Does this not imply a limitation on what we can ask of God? Well, yes and no. Yes; it is true we cannot thoughtlessly approach God and just demand whatever happens to come to mind and expect Him to grant every idle wish. But, no; to any thoughtful Christian, keeping our petitions within the will of God is not a limitation but a statement of exactly what we desire most: to please Him in all we ask.

If then our desire is to make our petitions strictly within the will of God, we will encounter two kinds of requests. First, there are requests which are based on a specific Biblical promise and are therefore clearly the will of God. For example, we may request wisdom when confronting trials and expect God to give generously according to James 1:2-5. Second, there are requests which have no prohibition in Scripture but

---

10. To say that God does not hear our flawed prayers at all, that He does not know that they took place or take note of them, would be to deny the omniscience of the Lord. The "hearing" here is effectual hearing which results in granting of the petitions heard. See John R. W. Stott, *The Epistles of John* (Grand Rapids, Michigan: Wm. B. Eerdmans Publishing Company, 1975), p. 186.

11. Barclay, p. 136.

are not specifically stated as the will of God. We don't know if these are within God's universal will.[12] The requests may be compatible with the revealed will of God in the Bible but not connected to a specific promise. A typical example is a request for physical healing of oneself or another. The Scriptures indicate that God can heal and is often willing to do so but that He also withholds healing for various reasons.[13] Therefore, we cannot pray with any absolute assurance that any healing is what God desires.

How do we handle these two different types of requests? Let's express how to pray for each type as a simple formula.

IF GOD'S WILL + OUR REQUEST IS PROMISED ⟶ WE PRAY "THY
IS KNOWN   WITHIN HIS WILL   WILL BE DONE"

IF GOD'S WILL + OUR REQUEST IS COMPATIBLE ⟶ WE PRAY "IF IT
IS UNKNOWN   WITH GOD'S REVEALED WILL   BE THY WILL"

When we know our request is in God's will, we can pray with confidence and simply ask that His will be done in granting our request. Jesus made us this promise in John 15:7, "If you abide in Me, and My words abide in you, ask whatever you wish and it shall be done for you." We abide in Christ by obeying Him and the words we have heard from Him through the New Testament (John 15:10). When His words root in us and we understand His will, our prayers will be empowered by plugging our requests into specific promises of the Word. Of course, in saying "Thy will be done," we also commit ourselves to DO His will in cooperation with His actions on our behalf.

On the other hand, when our request has no specific promise attached to it from Scripture, we must not in arrogance demand it be granted. Instead, we use the approach of Jesus Christ in the garden of Gethsemane: "Father, if it is Your will, [state your request]; never-

---

12. See the discussion of being led by the Holy Spirit in Chapter 3 for the various dimensions of the Will of God.

13. Bill Gothard has discerned at least three different Scriptural reasons for illness: 1. Sickness unto death (Psalm 90:10); 2. Sickness unto chastisement (I Corinthians 11:28-33); and 3. Sickness to manifest the work of God and to glorify Him (II Corinthians 12:6; John 9:2-3). *Institute in Basic Youth Conflicts/Research in Principles of Life* (n.p.: Institute in Basic Youth Conflicts, 1981), p. 17.

theless not [my] will, but Yours, be done" (Luke 22:42).[14] The specific words you use are not the important point here; the point is submission of your will to His will. Implied in "not my will" is the assumption that we will accept whatever we receive with thanksgiving.

For either type of request, can you see the importance of combining our regular Bible study with our prayers? We want to ask of God, believing He will answer; otherwise, without faith, we should not expect to receive anything from Him (James 1:6-8). But, faith is not a blind leap in the dark; faith is based upon the firm foundation of the Word of God. "So faith comes from hearing, and hearing by the word of Christ" (Romans 10:17). As we read, memorize and meditate on the Word, our petitions will ever draw closer to consistently being asked within the will of God. So, a daily "quiet time" of Scripture reading and prayer is a basic necessity for every Christian's life.

We ask what we really want that is in God's will.

We waste our petitions if they are not honest in stating what we truly desire from the Lord. We are to seek the Lord with *all* our heart and *all* our soul (Deuteronomy 4:29). But often we do not. Part of us wants God's will, but part of us wants our will, too. James calls that being "double-minded," doubting God's goodness, and leaving us with uncertain prayers which the Lord will not grant (James 1:6-8).

To the "double-minded," Jesus comes to ask a simple but troubling question: "What do you want Me to do for you?" (Luke 18:41). Stop right now! Think. Since you are in the presence of Jesus Christ if you are His, what is the primary request you have for Him this very moment? May I suggest you take some time to just ask yourself what you really want in your life? Now?

Ready to go on yet? Are you sure? These words will be here to read later if you need to finish thinking through your real priorities before the Lord. So take your time and only continue reading when you are actually ready. OK.?

---

14. Translation from *The New King James Bible/New Testament* (Nashville, Tennessee: Thomas Nelson Publishers, 1979).

Let me add now a second question from Jesus Christ. He found a lame man lying by the pool of Bethesda who had been ill for thirty-eight years. Jesus asked this man a question which was either very profound or very cruel. My Lord was never cruel. He asked, "Do you wish to get well?" (John 5:6).

Do we? Do we want to healed of the deadly diseases of sin which have infected us? Or have we become comfortable in our iniquity? Do we want Jesus to take away only the symptoms of our disease? The guilt, the broken relationships, the sleeplessness, the physical stresses? Or do we want to be cured, the sins themselves replaced by the virtues of Christ? Do you just want to feel better or "do you wish to get well?" Think about it. Now. What do you want?

Our various petitions can be divided into three types: petitions for our daily needs, petitions for our special needs and petitions for our desires. Let's look at each in turn.

Petitions for our daily needs. — "Give us this day our daily bread" (Matthew 6:11). We have perhaps heard that so often that we do not wonder at it anymore. Jesus is teaching us that we need to ask God each day for the needs to be supplied for that day alone. "Therefore do not be anxious for tomorrow; for tomorrow will care for itself" (Matthew 6:34a). Alcoholics Anonymous has rediscovered this principle to help its members deal with life here and now. One of their slogans is :"One day at a time."[15] In prayer, this slogan also fits well.

What is our "daily bread"? Beside our food, "daily bread" represents all our needs for each day. Among these would be physical necessities (food and clothing: see I Timothy 6:8), health, courage, strength, wisdom and protection from the powers of darkness. The last need is specifically mentioned in the Lord's Prayer; "And do not lead us into temptation, but deliver us from evil" (Matthew 6:13). I have come to see the foolishness of ignoring my spiritual opposition or, worse, trying to handle the warfares in my own strength. Daily I need the deliverance of God from the evil in its ceaseless assaults and I am no longer too proud to ask for that protection.

Petitions for our special needs. — Our needs change day by day.

---

15. *One Day at a Time in Al-Anon* (New York: Al-Anon Family Groups, 1978).

Beyond our normal daily requirements, each day has special demands which require special petitions. Tonight is Bible Study and I am praying about that now, that I may have a clear mind to share the truth accurately and enthusiastically with those who will attend. Tomorrow I will be praying about the counseling session and evangelistic call set up for tomorrow evening. And the next day I will ask for travel mercies to pick up my daughter from a Christian camp. And so our prayer lives go. Each day comes with its unique needs and supplications.

Also unique to each day are our trials and temptations during that twenty-four hour period. I don't know what I will be tempted by tomorrow, but I am sure what I am fighting today. I turn back to Hebrews 4:14-16 for reassurance.

Since then we have a great high priest who has passed through the heavens, Jesus the Son of God, let us hold fast our confession. For we do not have a high priest who cannot sympathize with our weaknesses, but one who has been tempted in all things as we are, yet without sin. *Let us therefore draw near with confidence to the throne of grace, that we may receive mercy and may find grace to help in time of need.*

Jesus understands our struggles and stands ready, not only to sympathize, but to help us in our temptations.

Similar to this are our periodic spiritual growth spurts. We are convicted by the Holy Spirit to put off some old sinful habit and replace it with some godly virtue. Prayer is an integral part of this growth process. Over the days and weeks required for the change to normally become permanent, our petitions will focus on this special spiritual project. We will then celebrate our victory in Christ and turn to the next area needing improvement, watchful in prayer that we not fall back and lose what He has gained for us.

Personal crises naturally become special prayer requests. The range for such problems is wide: from sickness to sudden success, from getting hired for a new job to getting fired from an old one, from facing a wedding to facing a divorce, from the birth of a baby to the death of a parent. Whatever happens, God is still God and we still need Him, day by day, to meet our special needs.

Petitions for our desires. — Can we ask God for something which is just something we want (assuming it does not oppose the stated will of God)? Sure. In the first chapter of Romans, Paul mentions that he had often asked the Lord to be allowed to go to Rome to share the gospel there (Romans 1:8-15). He adds at the end of the same letter that his desired trip to Rome was only a part of a longer projected trip to Spain (Romans 15:22-33). Now could Paul have not served the Lord where he was? Was this trip necessary? Or was it simply a goal which Paul had in his own mind? We see that he made this personal desire a petition which he submitted to God's will (Romans 1:10; 15:32). So it is with our desires.

First, we evaluate our desires in light of the revelation of the will of God in the Word. Some desires are simply unworthy of the child of God. So God must reject petitions which ask that an illicit affair might develop with a given person or that a crooked business deal might succeed or that I might get a promotion to "show those others how good I am." Generally, requests which are aimed at immediate gratification of our sensual desires would be better left unstated to God.[16]

In fact, the desire for immediate gratification, for happiness, is a self-defeating aspiration. When we reach out for happiness, we are acting in a self-centered fashion. But,

> self-centeredness and happiness are mutually exclusive. God Himself cannot make them jibe. We destroy happiness when we reach out to possess it for ourselves. *We can have it only as a by-product of better things.* We shall not, then, pray directly for our own happiness.[17]

Blaise Pascal said it so well, "Always looking forward to being happy, it is inevitable that we should never be so."[18] To seek happiness first is to choose the lesser good and miss the greater good. I am reminded of the

---

16. The sensual desires would fall under the three categories of I John 2:16: "the lust of the flesh and the lust of the eyes and the boastful pride of life." These are also the "pleasures" which motivate empty prayers in James 4:3.

17. Donald J. Campbell, *The Adventure of Prayer* (Nashville, Tennessee: Abingdon Press, 1949), p. 46; emphasis added.

18. Quoted in William R. Parker and Elaine St. Johns, *Prayer Can Change Your Life* (Englewood Cliffs, New Jersey: Prentice-Hall, Inc., 1957), p. 2.

prayer of the young Augustine before his conversion to Christ, "O God, make me pure, but not now."[19] He thought to become pure he would have to give up all the practices that gave him momentary pleasure. He had not yet learned that in purity before God was a spring of happiness unquenchable (Matthew 5:8). So as we pray for growth in Christlikeness, we receive as a side benefit true joy and happiness.

Our desires fall into the category of "wants" instead of "needs." As such, God does not promise to fulfill every desire as if He were some waiter trying to make sure we are well taken care of and pleased at any given moment. Some teachers have pointed to Psalm 37:4 to say God *does* promise us all our desires. The passage reads: "Delight yourself in the Lord; and He will give you the desires of your heart."

But two responses are necessary here. First, this verse is not saying that any worldly or sinful desire will be fulfilled by God. The first clause, "Delight yourself in the Lord," indicates that the "desires of your heart" are desires to please the Lord and live in obedience to Him. Second, this verse is not speaking about prayer. It is explaining a spiritual law which Christ stated as, "seek first [God's] kingdom and His righteousness; and all these things shall be added to you" (Matthew 6:33). When we delight in the Lord and seek His kingdom, He will fulfill all our deep desires by adding to us all the blessings we need, either now or in the world to come. But we do not have the right to badger Him for our idle wants.

How then should we sort out our desires? After all, we rarely have any desires which arise totally and absolutely from unselfish and altruistic motives. Normally there is a good bit of selfishness mixed into any of our desires, making it more difficult to judge them objectively. For example, I may want to get a book on Bible study. Now this sounds like a good request: "Lord, let us have enough extra money this month to allow me to buy this book without breaking our budget." I want to study the Bible better and help others to do so and I want to be financially responsible at the same time. But, mixed in with those good motives may be these:

* full shelves of books impress some people and I want to be impressive.
* I want to have a new book to suggest to others at the next

---

19. Jones, p. 13.

ministers' meeting so they will respect my scholarship.

* I like to own books; I don't want to just borrow this book and read it, I want it to be *mine*, with *my* name written inside the cover.

* my "ego" would like to think I am a great Bible teacher and having this book will help me prove that to others.

Such reasons as these make me more than a little repulsed as I see them in me. Yet they exist side by side the excellent reasons I spoke of above. So how should we approach God with these "questionable" requests? I believe we should go ahead and ask with the understanding that we want His will to be done. I then believe that it is at this point when the Holy Spirit intercedes for us.

> And in the same way the Spirit also helps our weakness; for we do not know how to pray as we should, but the Spirit intercedes for us with groanings too deep for words; and He who searches the hearts knows what the mind of the Spirit is, because He intercedes for the saints according to the will of God (Romans 8:26-27).

The picture which comes to my mind is that of a translator at the United Nations. The Holy Spirit hears what we pray and then He "translates" our words to the Father; that is, He puts our requests in a form which is in line with the will of God. This may involve altering certain requests, adding unspoken needs or dropping entirely requests which are not acceptable.

To summarize, then, petitions should be within the will of God to the best of our understanding and they should reflect what we really want, whether daily needs, special needs or simply personal desires. May I say that our problem with petitions seems to be that we so often ask too little of God. Teresa of Avila once said, "You pay God a compliment by asking great things of Him."[20] What about your petitions? Is God complimented by the faith you place in Him, revealed by the wide scope of your requests? Or perhaps is the Lord occasionally insulted by the puny favors we ask of Him? And are we even asking in the best ways and means in our petitions? That is where we turn next.

---

20. Quoted in [Dick Eastman,] *Change the World! School of Prayer* (Studio City, California: World Literature Crusade, 1976), p. C-13.

HOW DO WE ASK?

Before looking at eight attributes of effective petitions, remember that our greatest temptation is not to ask in error but *not to ask at all*. We have not because we ask not (James 4:2). We are like a young boy whom his father found trying to turn over a large rock. As the boy pulled and groaned, the rock stayed put.

"Son, are you using all your strength?" the father asked.

"I sure am, Dad," the boy panted.

"No, you're not," replied the father with a smile, "You haven't asked me to help you."

Our Father's strength is ours for the asking, *if* we ask. Now here are eight attributes for effective petitions.

1. *Ask specifically.* — Regretfully, most of the prayers I hear these days are filled with wandering generalities. "Bless everybody real good," could be a summary of many public petitions in our churches. We use generalities to avoid at least two problems in praying. First, we do not want to take the time to think through and spell out exactly what we really do desire from God. Second, we are afraid that if we are too specific that our faith will be bruised if God does not grant the request. We can always comfort ourselves that God did indeed "bless" someone we prayed for even if we don't see any change in them at all (especially since we have only the vaguest idea what it means for God to "bless" anyone anyway). But, if we ask God to cure Aunt Minnie's lumbago by Thursday so that she can attend Thelma Lou's wedding, we will know God's answer by Thursday evening.

The consistent pattern of prayer in the Old and New Testament calls for specific petitions by which one could clearly see if and when God granted the requests. Consider the following chart of specific prayers and their answers. Obviously the Lord enjoys answering our petitions with answers that are just as specific as the requests.

Specific Petitions of the Bible

Person Praying	Specific Petition	Specific Answer
Abram	A son for an heir Genesis 15:2	A son for an heir Genesis 21:1-3
Abraham's servant	A specific sign to show the Lord's choice for Isaac's wife Genesis 24:12-14	A specific sign to show the Lord's choice for Isaac's wife Genesis 24:15-27

Isaac	A barren wife to have a child Genesis 25:21	A barren wife to have Twins(!) Genesis 25:21-26
Jacob	Deliverance from his brother, Esau Genesis 32:9-12	Deliverance from his brother, Esau Genesis 33:1-17
Israel	Release from Egyptian bondage Exodus 2:23-25	Release from Egyptian bondage Exodus 12:29-51
Israel	A deliverer from the hand of Cushan-risha-thiam Judges 3:9	A deliverer from the hand of Cushan-risha-thiam Judges 3:9-11
Israel	A deliverer from the king of Moab Judges 3:12-15	A deliverer from the king of Moab Judges 3:15-30
Israel	A deliverer from the king of Canaan Judges 4:1-3	A deliverer from the king of Canaan Judges 4:3-24
Israel	A deliverer from the Midianites Judges 6:1-6	A deliverer from the Midianites Judges 6:7-8:35
Gideon	Two signs that Israel would have victory Judges 6:36-37, 39	Two signs that Israel would have victory Judges 6:38, 40
Israel	A deliverer from the Ammonites Judges 10:10-16	A deliverer from the Ammonites Judges 11:1-33
Samson	Water to quench his thirst Judges 15:18	Water to quench his thirst Judges 15:19
Samson	Strength to destroy his enemies and himself Judges 16:28-30	Strength to destroy his enemies and himself Judges 16:30-31
Hannah	A son in her barrenness I Samuel 1:9-11	A son in her barrenness I Samuel 1:19-20
David	His house (lineage) continue forever II Samuel 7:29	His house (lineage) continue forever II Timothy 2:8-10
Solomon	Wisdom in judgment I Kings 3:5-9	Wisdom in judgment I Kings 3:10-28
Hezekiah	Deliverance from Sennacherib II Kings 19:14-19	Deliverance from Sennacherib II Kings 19:20-37
Hezekiah	Healing and longer life II Kings 20:1-3	Healing and longer life II Kings 20:4-7

Reubenites	Victory against the Hagrites I Chronicles 5:18-20	Victory against the Hagrites I Chronicles 5:20-22
Abijah's army	Rescue and victory over Jeroboam's army II Chronicles 13:13-14	Rescue and victory over Jeroboam's army II Chronicles 13:15-20
Asa	Victory over the Ethiopians II Chronicles 14:9-11	Victory over the Ethiopians II Chronicles 14:12-15
Jehoshaphat	Rescue from Aramites II Chronicles 18:31	Rescue from Aramites II Chronicles 18:31
Nehemiah	Overcome opposition and complete the wall Nehemiah 4:1-9	Overcome opposition and complete the wall Nehemiah 6:15-16
Jonah	Salvation from a great fish Jonah 2:1-9	Salvation from a great fish Jonah 2:10
Zacharias	A son in their old age Luke 1:1-13	A son in their old age Luke 1:57-58
Apostles	Direction in choosing a replacement for Judas Acts 1:24-25	Direction in choosing a replacement for Judas Acts 1:26
Jerusalem Church	Boldness and power to speak the Word Acts 4:23-30	Boldness and power to speak the Word Acts 4:31-35

One of the best ways to make our petitions specific is to simply write our requests down on a prayer list, in a prayer notebook or in a letter to the Lord. Writing gives us time to think through what we are really asking. We can see sweeping generalities easier in print than when they are just silent thoughts speeding through our minds. So try praying with your pen or pencil in hand, specifically. For a prayer notebook, one layout often used is illustrated below.

Request Date	Request	Date Needed/Received	Answer

2. *Ask positively.* — Our prayers influence us directly as we hear ourselves speaking to God. If we only speak to God of our problems, we convince ourselves of the hopelessness of our situation. Negative prayers reflect our own negative thoughts and even reinforce them. Further, negative prayers produce negative results. If all we tell God is how bad things are, we are giving greater commitment to the pains than to the Great Physician. It is well possible that the Lord will give us the negatives we are convinced we will receive. It is true on many levels that "You are what you pray."[21] We are often the makers of our own misery.

On the positive side, we should ask without anxiety but with thanksgiving, assuming that the Lord *will* do the best for us (Philippians 4:6-7). The result will be peace. Paul suggests we let our minds dwell on thoughts which fall into one or more of eight areas: (Philippians 4:8)

   a. Whatever is true.
   b. Whatever is honorable.
   c. Whatever is right.
   d. Whatever is pure.
   e. Whatever is lovely.
   f. Whatever is of good repute.
   g. Any excellence.
   h. Anything worthy of praise.

Such suggestions sound Pollyanna-like in their optimism. While our problems and the power of the Lord are both reality, remember that our problems are only momentary and fleeting when compared to our eternal Savior who is *the* Truth. Our faith can be shipwrecked by constant harping on the sorrows which afflict us. Instead, focus your petitions on what the Lord *can* and has *promised* to do for you.

Practically, when we are emotionally down, it is hard to start our prayers without a little "bleeding" before the Lord. Christ in Gethsemane is our model here. The burden of the coming cross had so hurt Him that He felt that death was already upon Him. (Matthew 26:38) He fell on His face before His Father and prayed in such agony that His blood vessels began to collapse under the strain and He began to bleed through His skin (Luke 22:44). Yet, as He set His heart to accept the Father's will as His own, He was strengthened by an angel.

---

21. Parker and St. Johns, pp. 128-130.

Jesus came away from His prayers with such power that the crowd who came to arrest Him drew back and fell to the ground at the mere sound of His voice (John 18:6). We should come away from our prayers strengthened and empowered, not further depressed.

Here are some examples of negative and positive petitions for you to compare with your requests.

Negative Petitions	Positive Petitions
"Lord, my child is so sick. He hasn't gotten any better. Can't You do anything? Don't you care? Jim has been sick so much lately. Help him, Lord. I beg You. Please."	"Father, You hold Jim in Your hand and love him even more than I do. I ask You to bring him sleep and healing tonight. May Your perfect will be done in his life. Grant us your comfort and peace. Thank You."
"Dear God, my husband left me. What am I going to do? He did not even let me know where he was going. What am I going to tell the kids? Or my mother? The bills aren't going to get paid and we'll probably lose the house. God, why didn't You stop him? I can't take this!"	"Dear Lord, My world seems to be falling apart; only You can hold it . . . and me . . . together. Wherever he is, be with him now; bring him home in Your good time. Until then, give me Your patience and wisdom. Especially help me talk to the children. Thank You for never leaving me alone."
"God, nobody likes me. Why did you make me this way? If I were only taller and better at sports and stuff, . . . but I'm not and I never will be. It's not fair. All the rest of the people have friends. Why not me? What's wrong with me anyway? I'm just terrible. No wonder everyone hates me."	"My Lord and King, I feel down today and kind of lonely. But You're still here and I thank You for caring. Is there some sin or attitude in me which turns people off? Show me, Lord. Help the love of Your Son to flow through me to all I meet. Help me to care more about them than about myself. Thanks for listening; I feel better, knowing You're working with me."
"Lord, I feel spiritually empty and useless. I guess I'm losing my faith. And I'll go to hell. Might as well give up."	"Father, thank You for the stirrings of Your Spirit in me. Help me begin to grow; with You I know I can."

You can see some hallmarks of the negative and positive petitions. Negative petitions tend to contain the following features: overstatement of problems, "me-centered" sentences, affirmations of failure, "why me" questions, few real requests for help, subtle or open doubt that

God can do anything, and emotionally charged words. Positive petitions have such features as these: recognition of God's power over our situation, frequent gratitude and praise to God, affirmations of success, willingness to accept the will of the Father without reservation, recognition of personal responsibility for problems and willingness to change, faith in the ability and amenability of God to act for us and a true statement of feelings without abandonment to them. Ask in that most positive of attitudes, faith, and God will be ready to listen.

3. *Ask visually.* — In Hebrews 11, the author describes faith through the Old Testament saints. One concept often recurs here. Read the sections below and see if you see it. (Some words are highlighted to give you another clue.)

Now faith is the assurance of things hoped for, the conviction of things not *seen* . . . (Hebrews 11:1).

By faith we understand that the worlds were prepared by the word of God, so that what is *seen* was not made out of the things which are *visible* . . . (Hebrews 11:3).

And without faith it is impossible to please Him, for he who comes to God must believe that He is, and that He is a rewarder of those who *seek* Him (Hebrews 11:6).

By faith Noah, being warned by God about things not yet *seen*, in reverence prepared an ark for the salvation of his household, by which he condemned the world, and became an heir of the righteousness which is according to faith (Hebrews 11:7).

By faith Abraham, when he was called, obeyed by going out to a place which he was to receive for an inheritance; and he went out, *not knowing where he was going.* By faith he lived as an alien in the land of promise, as in a foreign land, dwelling in tents with Isaac and Jacob, fellow heirs of the same promise; for he was *looking* for the city which has foundations, whose architect and builder is God . . . (Hebrews 11:8-10).

151

All these died in faith, without receiving the promises, but having *seen* them and having *welcomed* them from a distance, and having *confessed* that they were strangers and exiles on the earth. For those who say such things make it clear that they are *seeking* a country of their own. And indeed if they had been thinking of that country from which they went out, they would have had opportunity to return. But as it is, they desire a better country, that is a heavenly one. Therefore God is not ashamed to be called their God; for He has prepared a city for them . . . (Hebrews 11:13-16).

By faith Moses . . . [considered] the reproach of Christ greater riches than the treasures of Egypt; for he was *looking* to the reward. By faith he left Egypt, not fearing the wrath of the king; for he endured, as *seeing Him Who is unseen* . . . (Hebrews 11:24, 26-27).

Therefore, since we have so great a cloud of *witnesses* surrounding us, let us also lay aside every encumbrance, and the sin which so easily entangles us, and let us run with endurance the race that is set before us, *fixing our eyes* on Jesus, the author and perfecter of faith, who *for the joy set before Him* endured the cross, despising the shame, and has sat down as the right hand of the throne of God (Hebrews 12:1-2).

Did you *see* the principle of faith in these passages? The great men and women of faith *visualized* what God had promised. As they looked for them to come to pass, these saints welcomed God's gifts even before they arrived. Each man or woman of God confessed to himself and to others that that which he was convinced would come was indeed a fact.

By faith we can witness the worlds we see being created out of the unseen by God's word. By faith, we seek the Lord Who cannot be seen by mortal men. By faith Noah pictured a flood, even though he had never seen one. By faith Abraham envisioned a heavenly city in which he and his descendants would dwell. By faith Moses saw the value of giving up all the wealth of Egypt as he viewed in his mind what God would do for him and all Israel, even imagining what the very presence of the Almighty would be like. By faith we "look" intently to Jesus Christ with the eyes of our heart.

In prayer, visualization helps us in two ways. One, visualization makes clear to us what we are asking from the Father. Going back to the all-purpose prayer word, "bless," what do you picture when you ask the Lord to "bless" you? Do you glow with a momentary halo? Are you standing in the midst of piles of money and expensive gifts (like the winner on some TV game show)? Are you surrounded by a loving family at a warm fireplace? What does being "blessed" mean to you? Because what you *see* is what you *mean* by your petition. So, as you ask, visualize what you are seeking and you will better understand what you are actually after.

Two, visualization strengthens our faith. "We walk by faith, not by sight" (II Corinthians 5:7). That is, what we believe is not determined by what our physical eyes behold. We are not materialists, accepting only the evidence of the physical senses. We have, however, a second set of "eyes." Hear this lovely prayer of Paul for the Ephesian believers:

I pray that *the eyes of your heart* may be enlightened, so that you may *know* what is the *hope* of His calling, what are the *riches* of the glory of His inheritance in the saints, and what is the surpassing greatness of His *power* toward us who believe (Ephesians 1:18-19a).

Paul asks the Lord to enable the Ephesians' "spiritual eyes" to *know* the hope, riches and power that are ours in Jesus Christ. This knowing is the "conviction of things not seen" of Hebrews 11:1; that is, faith. As we envision what we believe, it becomes more real to us and more "believable." Haven't you heard someone who disbelieved that something was possible say, "I just can't picture it"? When we believe on the solid foundation of the Word of God that a given event is possible, we *can* picture it with the eyes of our heart. Visualize your petitions.

4. *Ask confidently.* — Asking when you are in doubt whether God can or would grant your request is useless. James sets down the following law of petition concerning any man seeking something from God.

But let him ask in faith without doubting, for the one who doubts is like the surf of the sea driven and tossed by the wind. For let not that man expect that he will receive anything from the Lord, being a double-minded man, unstable in all his ways (James 1:6-8).

Note that this is our problem, not the Lord's. James had just said that God "gives to all men generously and without reproach" (James 1:5). The Lord is more willing and able to give to us than we are willing and able to receive (Ephesians 3:20-21). We need confidence in Him (another word for trust or faith). That confidence comes as we meditate on His word and find Him trustworthy by living in faith in Him.

The Lord has given us an excellent passage to meditate upon in Peter's writings. In II Peter 1:2-4, He told us:

> Grace and peace be multiplied to you in the knowledge of God and of Jesus our Lord; seeing that *His divine power has granted us everything pertaining to life and godliness*, through the true knowledge of Him who called us by His own glory and excellence. For by these *He has granted to us His precious and magnificent promises*, in order that *by them you might become partakers of the divine nature*, having escaped the corruption that is in the world by lust.

Peter says that God has promised that all we need to live godly lives has already been granted to us by His divine power. Why, then, don't we have godly lives? We have not confidently asked to receive according to His precious promises. We are like the little congregation who had gathered to pray for a break in a tragic drought. The old preacher stood behind his pulpit and eyed his flock for a minute with his steely eyes. Suddenly he asked, "Do you truly believe the Lord will break open the sky and send down His showers on us?"

"Yes, Brother Jones," the church replied with one voice.

"Do you believe He could send His showers *today?*" the old preacher shouted back.

"Yes, Brother Jones, He could," responded the church.

"Well, brothers and sisters, if we came to church today with such great faith to pray to the Lord for rain, where are your umbrellas?" the old preacher thundered.

If we have confidence that God can and is willing to transform our lives into the image of His beloved Son, where are our virtues? Where is our fruit? Where are our good works? Where is our faith? Do our prayers reflect confidence in the Lord or doubt?

One form of petition which encourages confidence has become scarce in modern prayers. We normally offer petitions by invocation: "Lord, please give . . . ." "Father, I ask for . . . ." "Dear God, may You in Your mercy help me . . . ." But the Scriptures also give many examples of petitions by affirmation. A petition by affirmation is not a request but a statement of what God has done, is doing and will do on our behalf. Often affirmations and invocations are mixed together in a single prayer. Below is the twentieth Psalm; can you check the affirmations and leave the invocations unmarked? Try it.

[ ] May the Lord answer you in the day of trouble!

[ ] May the name of the God of Jacob set you securely on high!

[ ] May He send you help from the sanctuary, and support you from Zion!

[ ] May He remember all your meal offerings, and find your burnt offering acceptable.

[ ] May He grant you your heart's desire, and fulfill all your counsel!

[ ] We will sing for joy over your victory, and in the name of our God we will set up our banners.

[ ] May the Lord fulfill all your petitions.

[ ] Now I know that the Lord saves His anointed;

[ ] He will answer him from His holy heaven, with the saving strength of His right hand.

[ ] Some boast in chariots, and some in horses; but we will boast in the name of the Lord, our God.

[ ] They have bowed down and fallen; but we have risen and stood upright.

[ ] Save, O Lord; may the King answer us in the day we call.

That was probably a little too easy for you; especially when all the invocations began "May" (except the last one). If you would like a little stiffer challenge, turn to the seventeenth chapter of John and read through Jesus' so-called "High Priestly Prayer." Then go back through and underline every affirmation He makes in His great prayer. Jesus often used affirmations in His prayers.[22] And, as we have already seen,

---

22. See Matthew 11:25-27; John 11:41-42; Luke 22:31-32; and Luke 23:44-46.

155

the Psalms contain many petitions by affirmation. Interestingly, the book of Revelation is filled with prayers of affirmation, especially around the throne of God in heaven.[23] If you would like to try adding affirmations to your petitions by invocation, below are some examples of turning invocations into affirmations. (Note: we only affirm what God has promised in His word to do.)

Invocation	Affirmation
"Father, help me be wise when I share Jesus with John."	"Father, You will be with me as I share Your Son with John and You will help me to be wise in my words and actions with Him."
"Be with me now, Lord, and give me peace as I wait for the results of these medical tests."	"Lord, You are always with me according to Your promise and Your peace surrounds me as You already know what the tests will show me. You are preparing my heart for whatever comes."
"God, may Your Spirit help me to keep my temper as I change this stupid flat tire and may I get to my meeting without any further delays. Please?"	"Father, You know I am late and my anger is ready to explode. Your Spirit has been with me since I accepted You and is giving me Your self-control. You will get me to my meeting when You want me to get there."
"God! Help me out of this terrible mess . . . now!"	"My Lord, I am now and always safe in the hollow of Your hand. You will not drop me."

If prayers of affirmation sound a bit presumptuous, remember that confidence in God means that we do presume He will be true to His word. There is not to be an attitude of arrogance but of complete trust in our affirmations of faith. Be confident in the Lord and try petitions by affirmation.

5. *Ask consistently.* — ". . . Pray without ceasing; . . ." (I Thessalonians 5:17). Paul's words here have left many people with the

---

23. See Revelation 4:8-11; 5:8-15; 7:9-12; 11:15-18; 12:10-12; 14:6-13; 15:3-4; and 19:1-9. Many of these are praise by affirmation mixed with petition or intercession by affirmation.

picture of all good Christians on their knees, praying for twenty-four hours a day. That idea is hardly practical and even less Biblical. Paul is simply calling for us never to give up prayer, but to pray consistently and habitually.[24] The prayer in view here is petition.

Why ask God consistently for His specific gifts? First, the logic of our situation is rather obvious: we are in constant need of God's provision, and God is constantly willing to grant us what we ask; so we need to pray consistently to receive as we need and as God gives. Second, Peter tells us to "cast all your anxiety upon Him, because He cares for you" (I Peter 5:6-7). So our choice is to carry the burden of all our anxieties personally or to keep placing our worries in the hand of the Almighty to deal with them.

In fact, Luke describes Jesus putting it in stronger terms. Luke introduces a parable with the words, "Now He was telling them a parable to show that at all times they ought to pray and not lose heart" (Luke 18:1). Here the alternatives are to pray consistently or lose heart. One of the symptoms that we are not praying consistently is an inner struggle with discouragement, anxiety, fear, guilt and despair. In specific terms, the New Testament uses the term "lose heart" in four distinct situations.

a. We can lose heart when the job is hard (II Corinthians 4:1, 16-18). In this passage Paul describes the glory and the cost of being an apostle of Christ. We already know that Paul's prayerlife supported him through those rough times by God's mercy. Though we are not apostles, our tasks in Christ's kingdom can drain us if we are not consistently "recharging our batteries" in the prayer closet.

b. We can lose heart when the harvest is delayed (Galatians 6:9-10). When we have obediently labored for the Lord for weeks and months and years and nothing seems to be happening, we can burn out. Paul warns the Galatians against weariness in doing good before the harvest arrives. The harvest will surely come, but the weary laborers need the consistent cool cups of prayer to refresh them as they work.

c. We can lose heart when others suffer (Ephesians 3:13-14). Paul was reassuring the churches that his tribulations were no cause to give up, but that he was praying for them. Often we get upset when our minister has to leave under pressure from others in the church. We can

---

24. Charles R. Swindoll, *Contagious Christianity/A Study of First Thessalonians* (Fullerton, California: Insight For Living, 1985), p. 63.

be more sensitive for others we care for than for many things which happen to us. But Paul is saying that the best thing to do when others suffer is not to get angry but all the more give yourself to prayer.

d. We can lose heart when others do not work (II Thessalonians 3:13). Some of the Thessalonian believers were so sure that the second coming of the Lord was imminent that they stopped working and became meddling moochers, leeches on the rest of the body of Christ. Those who remained at work were getting discouraged and tired of doing their own tasks and pulling along the dead weight of the moochers as well. Paul tells them to hold on and keep going; he also tells the sluggards to get back to work.

Often some of us feel as if we are the only ones who do anything in the church. It has been said that every church is composed of pillars and caterpillars: the pillars hold up the weight of the churches while the caterpillars just crawl in and out. Some of us pillars get tired (and a little angry). We need the consistent cleansing release of prayer to remind us that we are empowered by Christ to hold up our positions and that He will complete what He starts in us.

6. *Ask Generously.* — To ask generously means to enter into the divine cycle of giving. The cycle is built out of the truth in three Scriptures: "Ask, and it shall be given to you; . . . For everyone who asks receives, . . ." (Matthew 7:7-8). "Freely you received, freely give" (Matthew 10:8). And "Give, and it will be given to you; . . ." (Luke 6:38a).

There are four strokes to the cycle:

a. *Stroke # 1: We freely ask.* We reach out to God for what we need, not only for ourselves, but enough to have to share with others (II Corinthians 9:6-15). To ask in order merely to keep for your own purposes is, by Biblical definition, a futile prayer (James 4:1-3). What God has given you out of His grace is intended to bless not only you but all those around you with whom you freely share it.

b. *Stroke # 2: God freely gives.* God gives to us without a cause in us. That is, we have not earned what He gives us by any good deeds. However, we can block His generosity by our own stinginess in dealing with others in need.[25] Not only does God give freely, He also gives

---

25. "If a man shuts his ears to the cry of the poor, he too will cry out and not be answered" (Proverbs 21:13).

generously to those who ask with a generous heart. "For by your standard of measure it will measured to you in return" (Luke 6:38c).

c. *Stroke # 3: We freely receive.* As we open our hands and hearts to receive the Lord's gifts, we will be inundated: "good measure, pressed down, shaken together, running over, they will pour into your lap" (Luke 6:38b).

d. *Stroke # 4: We freely give.* The motivation for our giving should imitate the motives of God Himself: "For God so loved the world, that He *gave* . . ." (John 3:16). As the Father loved and gave, so the Son "loved me and gave Himself for me" (Galatians 2:20c, NKJV). And the "apostle of love" wrote this summary to us:

> We know love by this, that He laid down His life for us; and we ought to lay down our lives for the brethren. But whoever has the world's goods, and beholds his brother in need and closes his heart against him, how does the love of God abide in him? Little children, let us not love with word or with tongue, but in deed and truth (I John 3:16-18).

And, as we give freely, we are free to ask freely of God, Who gives freely to us who receive freely in order to freely give again. And so the cycle rolls forward, empowered by the love of God and to a lesser extent by our own love for God and others. Asking generously can be the start of an exciting adventure of giving and receiving beyond all you can imagine.

7. *Ask Obediently.* — The best time for my children to ask me for a favor is *not* right after they rebel and break the rules which my wife and I have laid down for their protection. At the same time, my children are less likely to ask for anything from us then. Their guilt temporarily makes them shy away from us. Something like this also takes place in our prayerlife. When we sin, our relationship with God is bruised in two ways: He may withhold blessings to aid our repentance and we may lose our confidence in asking Him for something. Like Adam, our sin often drives us to hide from God, even to lie to him (Genesis 3:7-12). So disobedience does affect our petitions, both in how they are received from God and in how we do or do not offer them.

On the other hand, obedience can have a positive effect on our petitions. John describes this with these words:

Beloved, if our heart does not condemn us, we have confidence before God; and whatever we ask we receive from Him, because we keep His commandments and do things that are pleasing in His sight (I John 3:21-22).

John had just described how we may reassure ourselves that we are indeed of the truth, by loving others with Christ's selfless love. Then, when our conscience makes us feel guilty, John says to rely on the fact that God has shown us we are His by this Christlike love. So we come before God with another kind of confidence than we spoke of in the last section. This confidence is not faith in Christ, but rather trusting God's word about *us*.

Confident that we are accepted by the Lord, we can ask Him for anything and He will give it, because we have fulfilled the condition of being in His will (obedient) and only wanting to please Him. We don't earn this by being good; we are just showing that we are asking in His will because we *do* His will and would not try to ask something which would displease Him.

Suppose a child has shown himself to agree with his parents' standards by following their wishes and going beyond this to try to please them in all he does. Soon, his parents would have little fear that he is going to ask them for something which would anger them or hurt himself or others (except in ignorance). So God begins to trust our petitions as we seek to obey Him.

8. *Ask persistently.* — How often should we ask the same petition of our Father? Once? Twice? Seven times? Seventy times seven? A recent school of thought has said that a request should only be stated once to the Lord. These teachers argue that to ask again would betray a lack of faith that God has given us what we have requested. Instead, they tell us, we should ask once and then begin thanking the Lord for granting our request until it comes true. This is an unrealistic "positive thinking" principle of prayer. In fact, this *does* cross the line into presumption before God, deciding for Him which requests He will answer.

Should we repeat a request? After all, Jesus Himself warned us, "do not use meaningless repetitions, as the Gentiles do, for they suppose they will be heard for their many words" (Matthew 6:7). Doesn't that mean we should not persist in "hounding" the Lord about any given

160

desire? No, it doesn't. Jesus teaches by word and example that we are to be persistent in petition.

The same Lord Jesus Who told us to avoid "*meaningless repetitions*" also gave a parable to show that we should continue to approach God with proper requests until we are answered. Both teachings are true. The "meaningless repetitions" referred to the chanting and shouting of pagan religions which taught that it is hard to get the attention of the gods. The prayers of the prophets of Baal on Mount Carmel would be a good example, for they "called on the name of Baal from morning until noon saying, O Baal, answer us" (I Kings 18:26). The Scripture adds simply, "But there was no voice and no one answered."

A modern "meaningless repetition" might be the prayer wheels of Tibet. Written prayers on slips of paper are put into a hollow drum to which a crank is attached. The contraption is then set by a busy trail. As passers-by approach, they can give the drum a few turns with the crank and so "offer" thousands of prayers at once. In some places, to save human labor, the drum has been attached to water wheels. As the water turns the drum, anyone passing through then is credited with the prayers. Prayers without effort . . . or meaning.

Current Christian prayers can also become regretfully meaningless repetitions. Our petitions become trite formalized formulas constructed of well-worn phrases which can be "offered" with as little thought as repeating our address or Social Security number. No thought equals no prayer.

But Jesus told of a poor widow who kept pestering an unjust judge to get the legal protection she deserved. Finally the judge wearies and gives her what she asks because of her persistence. Jesus explained the parable with these words:

Now shall not God bring about justice for His elect, who cry to Him day and night, and will He delay long over them? I tell you that He will bring about justice for them speedily (Luke 18:7-8a).

Jesus here *contrasts* our Father with the unjust judge. If even a crooked politician can be pushed until he finally grants a good request, how much more will not a loving Father come quickly to vindicate the cries of His chosen children? Of course, we recall that the "speedily" is in the terms of God's view of time, wherein "one day is as a thousand years"

161

(II Peter 3:8).[26] But the point for us is to persist in faithful prayer, since we know that we have no where else to go to seek justice or blessing.

Jesus also modeled what He taught. In His agonized prayer in Gethsemane, Jesus is reported to have "prayed a third time, saying the same thing once more" (Matthew 26:44). Christ had no qualms about approaching His Father more than once with the same petition (and neither should we). Paul followed this example in his prayers. He wrote how he had prayed three different times for his "thorn in the flesh" to be removed (II Corinthians 12:8). The three requests were probably three specific seasons of prayer of an indeterminate length.[27] Persistence in prayer was the practice of the Lord and His followers. And *we* are to be His followers, too.

If then you have lifted up earnest petitions to the Lord, what can you expect to happen? Will you ever be able to point to anything and say, "See? There is the Lord's answer to my prayer"? That is the topic of the last section of this chapter.

HOW DOES GOD ANSWER?

Is "yes" the only real answer to our prayers? If God does not grant what we have asked when we want it, has the Lord ignored our petition? What should we expect from prayer? Such questions trouble many sincere Christians. However, the Bible illustrates four types of answers God has given to the petitions of men.

God's answer may be a Direct Granting.

More often than not, God gives His children what we request. Like Eve in the garden of Eden, we tend to only focus on the one thing (tree) we cannot have. But, in fact, Jesus tells us essentially to expect to receive in His famous words from the sermon on the mount.

---

26. Leon Morris, *The Gospel According to Luke* (Grand Rapids, Michigan: William B. Eerdmans Publishing Company, 1974), pp. 263-264.

27. J. Massie, *Corinthians* (Edinburgh: T. C. & E. C. Jack, Ltd., n.d.), p. 327.

162

Ask, and it shall be given to you; seek, and you shall find; knock, and it shall be opened to you. For everyone who asks receives, and he who seeks finds, and to him who knocks it shall be opened. Or what man is there among you, when his son shall ask him for a loaf, will give him a stone? Or if he shall ask for a fish, he will not give him a snake, will he? If you then, being evil, know how to give good gifts to your children, how much more shall your Father who is in heaven give what is good to those who ask Him! (Matthew 7:7-11).

Two great truths stand out in this glorious promise: we must desire enough to ask persistently and we must know God as our good Father. The persistence is seen in the verbs Jesus uses: ask, seek and knock; all in the present (continuous) tense. The most accurate translation could be, "Keep asking and it shall be given to you; keep seeking and you shall find; keep knocking and it shall be opened to you."[28] As we implied in the last section, persistence lets God know we really mean that we desire what we ask. I have learned as a father not to add every toy my children mention to their Christmas or birthday list. The ones I get tired of hearing about are the ones on which I check the prices. So God will normally say, "Yes," to the requests for those things we truly desire in His will.

Second, we must know God as our good Father. The Scriptures do not teach the universal Fatherhood of God, that God is the spiritual Father of every person.[29] John states that we gain "the right to become children of God" by faith in Jesus Christ (John 1:12-13). We then begin to see that God *is* good to us and rewards those who seek Him (Hebrews 11:6). So this general promise that God normally responds to our petitions by granting them is fenced by two conditions: asking with persistence and asking with faith in the Father and Son.[30]

---

28. D. Martyn Lloyd-Jones, *Studies in the Sermon on the Mount* (Grand Rapids, Michigan: Wm. B. Eerdmans Publishing Company, 1960), II, pp. 201-202.

29. See John 8:31-47, where Christ describes those Jews who rejected Him as of their father the devil. He specifically denies their contention that their father is God in verses 41 and 42.

30. Note that this fulfills the two conditions I mentioned earlier for what we are to ask: we ask within the will of God (asking with faith), and we ask what we really desire (asking with persistence).

Direct granting of our petitions has as its primary obstacle our acceptance of the granting. If it seems too easy to us to simply pray and receive, we add in mentally how God *ought* to answer if He were like us. We would have to deliberate and weigh the arguments before deciding to help; but God knew what we were going to ask before we were born. His answer was predetermined in eternity; He has no need to think about it. If we let Him, He can supply us now with the wisdom or courage or moral strength or peace or comfort or daily needs or special needs we request. The need to wait comes from our lack of faith, not God's inaction. He wants to say, "Yes," more often than we let Him.

We need to remember here that just getting things is not the point of prayer. We want most of all to get to know our Father well. When God continues to give us things, we tend to focus more on the gifts than on the Giver. We can be like greedy children at Christmas, ripping open presents without even looking at the tag to thank the givers. The Lord brings us to the place where we can begin to understand Him when we stop looking at Him as a "blessing machine." But, even then, we will still need His gifts and He will still enjoy giving to us. We just will keep growing in gratitude and focus more and more on the Source of our every blessing and not on the blessings themselves.

What is the proper response to God's direct granting of our petitions? The response He desires from us is our gratitude and praise.

God's answer may be a Different Granting.

By a "different granting" I mean that we receive what we want but not in the way we expected it. How requests are to be granted is a decision that God has reserved to Himself. We often run into spiritual problems when we try to usurp this right to decide from God. Not only do our prayers state our desires, they also often state or assume how these desires are to be met. For example, when I have a headache, I ask the Lord to heal the headache. What I may envision is God touching me mystically and — poof! — the headache disappears. What God may have in mind is something more prosaic, like two aspirin and a nap.

Naaman, the valiant warrior and leper, came to be healed by the prophet Elisha. When Naaman and his retinue approached the house of the prophet, Elisha sent out his servant with instructions for Naaman to wash seven times in the Jordan River. The leper became furious and said,

> Behold, I thought, "He will surely come out to me, and stand and call on the name of the Lord his God, and wave his hand over the place, and cure the leper" (II Kings 5:11).

Naaman's anger was the result of his own presuppositions about how Elisha would go about helping him. Likewise, our grumblings against God often have at their roots our presuppositions of how the Lord *ought* to answer us.

We ought to be prepared to be equally grateful for the Father's gifts regardless how they are delivered. Especially we should be on guard against either demanding God must use supernatural means to answer us or denying that He can use supernatural means. God usually does not do miraculously what can be done by normal means. Our daily bread tends to come to us through the grocery rather than floating down from heaven.

We also need to realize that God does not have to answer similar prayers in the same way. The Lord Who can design a billion snowflakes without repeating Himself is surely creative enough to think of more than one way to answer a prayer. The gospels detail Jesus healing blind people on four different occasions: in two cases He touched the blind person's eyes and they were healed immediately; another time He spit on the eyes and touched the eyes twice before the healing was complete; and in the last case He spit and made clay which He applied to the eyes and then instructed the blind man to wash in the pool of Siloam where he was healed.[31] Now was there one "right" way for Jesus to heal blindness? Of course not.

In the same way, the Lord enjoys answering similar prayers in divergent ways. Moses had a hard time understanding that. In two separate cases, the people of Israel grumbled to Moses that they were thirsty. Moses turned and then cried out to God. The first time God answered, He told Moses to take His staff and *strike* the rock God in-

---

31. See Matthew 9:27-31; 20:30-34, Mark 8:22-26 and John 9.

165

dicated (Exodus 17:1-7). Moses obeyed the Lord and water flowed out. The second time God answered Moses' cry for water, He told Moses to take his staff and *speak* to the rock God indicated (Numbers 20:2-13). Guess what Moses did. You're right! He struck the rock just like he did the first time. (In fact, he hit it twice for good measure!) This combined with the fact that Moses did not give God the glory resulted in Moses being prohibited by God from entering the promised land. What was Moses' problem? He thought that God would answer both prayers the same way; he was wrong.

One of the tragedies associated with some Christian television and radio shows is the number of Christians who get depressed listening to them. Guests after guests come on and tell about their fantastic "answers to prayer," complete with "visions" and "miracles." Then the listeners mumble to themselves, "I wonder why God never does that stuff for me? I guess I just don't have enough faith." It is sad that the guests do not admit the possibility that equally faithful Christians may have a different answer from God.

God's answer may be different in two ways: the surface request may be answered in unexpected ways or the deeper need may be met while the surface request is denied. What do I mean by "surface request" and "deeper need"? The surface request is our petition taken literally and at face value. "Lord, let me marry Joan," is taken to mean, "Joan is the only girl for me, Lord, and You can get her to accept my proposal of marriage." The deeper need is the essential desire built into us by God which the surface request tries to meet. The deeper need beneath, "Lord, let me marry Joan," could be: the desire to be married, the desire to marry a Christian in God's will, the desire for physical intimacy or the desire of companionship, among others. Of course, the deeper need may be a combination of desires. Now do you understand the difference between a "surface request" and a "deeper need"? Good! Then let us look at the two ways God may grant our requests differently.

First, the surface request may be answered in unexpected ways. We have already discussed how God may answer a request contrary to our expectations. Another way God may answer our surface request in unexpected ways is to act on us rather than on our situation or vice versa. When Israel called to God for help in battle, His answers fell into two different types. Sometimes He changed the situation around Israel; He caused the enemy armies to run away or to fight among themselves.

Other times, He changed the people who prayed; He empowered the Israelites to defeat the enemies personally. Sometimes He combined both approaches; He held the sun still (changed the situation) while Israel fought the battle and won the victory (changed those who prayed). So, say you have prayed for help on a test. The Lord has two directions to go to aid you: one, He can work through the teacher, having him ask questions to which you know the answers, or He may enable you to remember all the information you studied (or to stay up until you learn some information). Both are equally a granting of your petition (surface request) but each is distinct from the other (unexpected ways).

Sometimes the Lord will tell us, in essence, "I will take care of your request; watch and wait." Sometimes He will say, "Get to work on your request; I will empower you." Normally, He calls, "Let's get going, you do your part and I'll do Mine." So, one way or another, your surface requests may be answered by the Lord in wonderful, but different ways.

Second, the deeper need may be met while the surface request is denied. When I was dating, I must have asked the Lord to make sure that each of the eighteen girls I dated would be the girl for me. He denied all those surface requests because He knew my deeper need was for a woman who would be my wife for life. Saying "Yes" to any of those surface requests would have said "No" to my deeper needs. Since this also involves the fourth general answer to petitions, denial, we will wait until then for a fuller discussion of this reply of God to our requests. But presently we will look at the third general answer, the delayed granting.

God's answer may be a Delayed Granting.

A delayed granting of our prayer is when God says, "Yes, but not now." An old prayer saying reassures us that "God's delays are not God's denials." But, to impatient Christians like me, God's delays sure *look* like God's denials! When Israel was groaning in Egyptian bondage, God did hear their cry and was going to help them . . . in about eighty years, after He got Moses trained for the job (Exodus 2:23-25). Two generations came and went in slavery while God prepared His man, and for those generations delay looked like denial. "Year after year" Hannah went up to the house of the Lord to ask for a child, as her husband's fertile wife tormented her (I Samuel 1:7-11). How often do you think did Hannah wonder if God had not rejected her forever? For hundreds of years men called for the Messiah to come and free them from their sins. Two men from Emmaus "had hoped" this Jesus of Nazareth was the Anointed One; but now He was dead (Luke 24:21). Maybe God changed His mind.

Delayed granting to our prayers may be caused by our need to grow spiritually. Why do we have to face trials? Aren't we told to pray, "Lead us not into temptation, but deliver us from evil"? James explains it this way:

> Consider it all joy, my brethren, when you encounter various trials, knowing that the testing of your faith produces endurance. And let endurance have its perfect result, that you may be perfect and complete, lacking in nothing (James 1:2-4).

Endurance perfects. And endurance is not possible without pressure. For pressure tests our faith. Like putting gold in a fire to burn off the dross, God allows us to pass through the flames to come out purer and stronger (I Peter 1:6-9). We cry for release and, when we have been burned clean, our Father takes us out of the heat and cools us in His blessing. The delay is over and the granting comes.

Often also there is delay in God's full granting as He uses natural processes to supply our requests. Our marriages gradually go sour over the years until the pain comes in a crisis. Then, instead of an instant restoration, we find we have grown back together in the places we were torn apart, slowly and with difficulty. So we complain. Like a little child, we take our broken toy to Daddy to fix. Then, we run off and come running back two minutes later crying, "Is it done yet?"

"No, not yet. Be patient," Dad says with a smile.

We frown and watch awhile. But, Dad isn't *doing* anything; he's just looking at the toy, long and hard. "Hurry up, Dad! I want to play," we whine.

"Soon, my child, soon. Just let me work on it a bit and it will be better than new," says Dad patiently.

We walk off with a little pout. We wait four and a half minutes this time. Surely that's enough time to build the toy all over again. We run back to be disappointed by the sight of Dad just beginning to carefully unscrew the first tiny screw on the bottom.

"Aren't you done yet?" we ask.

"Just getting started," Dad says calmly.

And, if we are especially impatient that day, we just go over and grab the toy and stalk out of the room, muttering, "I knew he couldn't fix it."

But how can we ever develop patience without waiting for things? Patience, the first attribute of love, the fourth fruit of the Spirit, an attribute of God Himself, is purified in the kiln of waiting. We stand under the pressure and heat, until God says, "Enough. You have been refined enough for now. Here is your desire granted more wonderfully than you can imagine." And somehow the waiting was worth the pain.

Aside from delay as a refining tool, delayed granting of a petition may also result from spiritual opposition. Daniel had a vision which left him in mourning for three weeks without refreshment as he begged God for an explanation of what he saw. Finally, an angel appears to interpret the vision but begins with this explanation of the twenty-one day wait:

> Do not be afraid, Daniel, for from the first day that you set your heart on understanding this and on humbling yourself before God, your words were heard, and I have come in response to your words. But the prince of the kingdom of Persia was withstanding me for twenty-one days; then behold, Michael, one of the chief princes, came to help me, for I had been left there with the kings of Persia. Now I have come . . . (Daniel 10:12-14).

Now I do not hope to fully explain what this spiritual opposition entails, other than to say that apparently the "prince of the kingdom of Persia" and "the kings of Persia" represent some of the "world forces of this darkness" Paul later mentions (Ephesians 6:12). Against such we struggle. We arm ourselves with God's armor and fight under these orders: (Ephesians 6:18)

> With all prayer and petition pray at all times in the Spirit, and with this in view, be on the alert with all perseverance and petition for all the saints . . . .

While we wait the long hours of spiritual struggle, we do not abandon prayer, we cling to it all the more. For even the courage and strength to wait are the gifts fo God, sought in supplication. And though the granting of triumph is delayed, that only makes the victory sweeter. Unless the answer of the Lord is not delay, but denial.

God's answer may be a Denial.

If our prayers include the concept, "If it be Thy will," then "No" is not only a proper but a necessary answer from our Lord to our requests. Denial does not mean that our prayers have been disregarded by our Father. Denial means that God has chosen the best for us in this case, and the best here is for us not to have what we have requested.

The possibilities of petition demand that God retains the right to deny the granting of some of our prayers. When prayers are granted, they are unlimited by space or time. The whole power of God is available to us when we ask Him to use it. It is as if we have been given a nuclear reactor which we control by our wish, to gain power or to destroy ourselves and others. That is why God has kept to Himself a discretionary power of granting or refusing our requests; otherwise, prayer could crush us.[32] Any parent knows that you do not give a razor to a toddler just because he keeps asking for it. We should praise God when He tells us, "No"; it is a sign of His love.

What are the reasons for which God might deny our petitions? We are going to look at seven of them briefly.

1. *Our petitions may be denied because they hindered by sin.* We are going to spend a whole chapter at the end of this book discussing problems in prayer, including prayer hindrances. So, if you can't wait, turn there now for the discussion of sin as a hindrance to prayer. Otherwise, let's go on.

2. *Our petitions may be denied because the result would be spiritual pride.* The Lord may not be able to grant your requests if He knows the results are going to be a spiritual arrogance which would

---

32. C.S. Lewis, "Work and Prayer," *God in the Dock/Essays on Theology and Ethics*, ed. Walter Hooper, (Grand Rapids, Michigan: William B. Eerdmans Publishing Company, 1970), p. 107.

harm your relationships with others and with Him. Any time we begin to think or say, "See what *my* prayers did?" we are in danger of losing the virtue of humility. The other side of this is that, if God denies our requests, we are in danger of losing our confidence in Him. So, either to receive our petition or to have it denied, we stand in danger of attacks of pride on the one hand or doubt on the other. God supports our confidence by normally granting our petitions; He supports our humility by denying some prayers, often those we desire for secret motives of pride or envy.

3. *Our petitions may be denied because our desires are self-centered and worldly* (James 4:3). God is under no obligation to support our natural man in its habits of sin. In fact, as a holy God, He is obligated to oppose all that which is utterly destructive to us. Unfortunately, petitions for meeting our fleshly desires are often some of our most passionate prayers. "Lord, please make her love me." "Help me beat him tomorrow." "God, send the money to get this car and I promise to . . . ." But, God does not judge our prayer simply on how passionate we are. When our petitions oppose His will, we should expect Him to deny our prayers. Sometimes, however, the most terrible judgment that God can send against us is to give us what we ask in the flesh.[33] When Israel demanded that Samuel anoint a king for them, the Lord told Samuel to first warn them of the sad results of rejecting God as their ruler in return for a mere mortal. Then, when the people persisted, the Almighty told Samuel to go ahead (I Samuel 8:4-22). The results were the rise, division and fall of Israel as a nation, ending in captivity and ruin. If we persist in our sin, we may also be given the terrible judgment of receiving what we want.

4. *Our petitions may be denied because we do not consider the welfare of others.* Paul was faced with the possibility of his own death as he sat in prison. Frankly, he was not opposed to that departure; he was more than ready, he was willing. Indeed, he longed to be home in heaven in the very presence of his beloved Lord, Jesus Christ. So he wrote:

> For to me to live is Christ, and to die is gain. But if I am to live on in the flesh, this will mean fruitful labor for me; and I do not know

---

33. See the three "God gave them over to's" in Romans 1:18-32.

which to choose. But I am hard-pressed from both directions, having the desire to depart and be with Christ, for that is very much better . . . (Philippians 1:21-23).

If we stopped right there, we would assume that Paul's request to God would be for a speedy death, if it was His will. But Paul had a wider view than his own needs and desires. He continued:

. . . yet to remain on in the flesh is more necessary for your sake. And convinced of this, I know that I shall remain and continue with you all for your progress and joy in the faith, so that your proud confidence in me may abound in Christ Jesus through my coming to you again (Philippians 1:24-26).

Paul saw the needs of others to be more important than his own desires. Likewise, our petitions may be denied by the Lord because answering our prayer might hurt someone else.

A classic example of the clash of needs is the farmer and the painter who were neighbors. The farmer prays for rain which his crops desperately need. The painter prays for sunshine so that he can paint houses and earn his living. Whose prayer should be answered? Let the Lord decide, since He alone knows all the options and all the possible results and He *knows* the right decision. But it may well be true that granting one petition may involve denying another.

5. *Our petitions may be denied because God is more interested in our character development than our comfort.* Paul's famous "thorn in the flesh" illustrates this reason for God's denial of some requests. Whatever the "thorn" was, Paul wanted it removed and asked the Lord for just that. But God said, "No." Why? Look with me at the verse which describes Paul's "thorn" and see what phrase is repeated twice in the verse to tell why the "thorn" was given.

And because of the surpassing greatness of the revelations, for this reason, to keep me from exalting myself, there was given me a thorn in the flesh, a messenger of Satan to buffet me—to keep me from exalting myself! (II Corinthians 12:7).

Did you see it? "To keep me from exalting myself," right? Paul had just told about a vision he had had some fourteen years before when he was taken into the "third heaven" or "Paradise" and heard marvelous things. He added that he could boast about such visions, but, to prevent his boasting, the "thorn" from Satan struck him. So he had to stop exalting or lifting himself up. And God was continuing to protect his humility by refusing to grant Paul's requests for release from the "thorn." God even was willing to do for Paul that which often He does not do for us; God explained His refusal directly. Then, based on God's explanation, Paul reconciled himself to accept his "thorn."

> And He said to me, "My strength is sufficient for you, for my power is perfected in weakness." Most gladly, therefore, I will rather boast about my weaknesses, that the power of Christ may dwell in me. Therefore I am well content with weaknesses, with insults, with distresses, with persecutions, with difficulties, for Christ's sake; for when I am weak, then I am strong (II Corinthians 12:9-10).

What does Paul's experience say to us? When God denies a request, He often does so that we may grow through the endurance of the person or situation which we face. We are like a starting guitar student. We don't like to practice because it makes our fingers hurt. So we ask our teacher if we could practice less. Instead of cutting our practices, he encourages us to be sure to play at least twice each day. Why? Because he loves to see us in pain? No, of course not. The teacher simply knows that our fingertips will not harden into calluses unless we keep practicing. Then we will be able to play better and without pain. But the pain *must* come before the playing better.

In the spiritual realm, the same rule applies. How can we learn patience, for example, if there is nothing to *try* our patience? Something has to keep us waiting or we have nothing for which to use our longsuffering skills. So the Lord gives us long stoplights, people who hog bathrooms, immovable check-out lines and repetitive, long-winded sermons. Thank you, Lord (I think). The pain *must* come before the living better. So, if God must deny our requests for comfort to encourage our growth in Christlikeness, we should learn to accept and eventually rejoice in our trials (James 1:2-4).

6. *Our petitions may be denied because God does not normally intervene in the natural order.* God has created an orderly universe work-

173

ing in harmony with certain physical and spiritual laws. One is the law that each person must die (unless they are alive at the moment of Christ's return). "It is appointed for men to die once and after this comes judgment" (Hebrews 9:27). So, when we pray that a seriously ill person not die, he may recover for some time, maybe for years; but, at some time, that prayer must be denied. Why? Because everyone must die. That is God's law for this world.

Another law, this time in the spiritual realm, is "whatever a man sows, this he will also reap" (Galatians 6:7). If I have overeaten for twenty years, God may forgive my sin, but He will not miraculously "heal" me of obesity no matter how earnestly I pray. He can give me the self-control and patience to start exercising and eating less, because this falls under His natural laws. If I sow overeating, I reap fat. If I sow self-control, I reap a slimmer body and health.

Our petitions for the overturning of these God-given laws will be denied in the vast majority of the time. Otherwise, the world would be a very undependable place where no law is really a law if any prayer could undo it. Should the law of gravity be repealed every time we trip and start to fall? How then (and why) would we ever learn how to walk? No, we need a world with consistent laws and consistent results when those laws are broken. Only on relatively rare occasions does God temporarily suspend a law (perform a miracle) on behalf of His children; those occasions are for Him to choose, not us.[34]

7. *Our petitions may be denied because God has a better answer to our deeper needs.* We come now to perhaps the most famous petition ever denied by the Father. The place is a quiet garden on the Mount of Olives, just across the Kidron Valley from the city of Jerusalem. The garden or grove of olive trees is called, "Gethsemane," which means, "an oil press."[35] And here, under the pressure of an ultimate choice, the Son of God bleeds. He begs of the Father two requests.

Abba! Father! All things are possible for Thee; [1.] remove this cup from Me; [2.] yet not what I will, but what Thou wilt (Mark 14:36).

---

34. For an excellent discussion of miracles, see C.S. Lewis, *Miracles: A Preliminary Study* (New York: Macmillan, 1963).

35. D.H. Tongue, "Gethsemane," *The New Bible Dictionary*, ed. J.D. Douglas (Grand Rapids, Michigan: Wm. B. Eerdmans Publishing Co., 1962), p. 465.

What cup was Jesus speaking of? Earlier in the evening, Jesus had instituted the communion service with the words, "This cup which is poured out for you is the new covenant in My blood" (Luke 22:20). The cup was the symbol of His blood poured out as He would die, nailed to a cross timber outside the gates of Jerusalem. Between the prayer and the death, Peter tried to prevent His master from being arrested by using violence. Jesus stopped him, saying: "Put the sword into the sheath; the cup which the Father has given Me, shall I not drink it?" (John 18:11). Obviously, Jesus understood by the end of His prayer how the Father had answered Him. Here is a simple chart of Jesus' two requests and the Father's two responses:

Jesus' Requests	The Father's Response
"Remove this cup from Me."	[No, You must drink it.]
"Yet not what I will, but what Thou wilt."	[Yes, what I will will be done.]

One could say that Jesus' asked, not two requests, but one conditional request; "Remove this cup from Me if that can be Your will." Regardless of how you divide the prayer, God said, "No," to the surface request to avoid the cup of sin and death, but said, "Yes," to the deeper need that the will of the Father and Son be one.

The modern Christian may have similar experiences in his prayerlife today. God may have to deny a surface request in order to grant a deeper need. This may take extreme lengths: it may sometimes seem as though the world is united against us and the ear of God deaf to our pleas. It is then, in anguish, a simple question is formed; will you still trust the Lord's will? The question came to Job and at least his first answer was, "The Lord gave and the Lord has taken away. Blessed be the name of the Lord" (Job 1:21). Hananiah, Mishael and Azariah (also known as Shadrach, Meshach and Abed-nego) were also faced with the clear prospect of the loss of everything for their faith. As they faced King Nebuchadnezzar, he threatened them with death in the furnace of blazing fire. They replied,

If it be so, our God whom we serve is able to deliver us from the furnace of blazing fire; and He will deliver us out of your hand, O

king. But *even if He does not*, let it be known to you, O king, that
we are not going to serve your gods or worship the golden image
that you have set up (Daniel 3:17-18).

Their surface request might have been for their lives to be spared, but
their deeper need was that they should remain true to the Lord, even if
it took their lives.

Today, we may plead that the cancer within us be cured or abated.
We may ask our job at the plant be saved. We may cry for our marriage
to be restored. But beneath these understandable requests should be a
more wondrous request that God be glorified in us whatever happens.
One of the most lovely and simple of modern prayers came from Bobby
Richardson at a meeting of the Fellowship of Christian Athletes. He asked, "Dear Lord, Your will, nothing more, nothing less, nothing else.
Amen." That prayer is on a plaque on my desk now to remind me what
should be under all my other petitions.

However God may answer our requests, either grantings or denials,
we must then actively receive what comes from His hand. Let me illustrate: let's say you asked me for a pencil. I reach into my pocket and
take out a pencil and say, "Here you are." Do you have the pencil at
that moment? Why not? First, *you* must reach out and take the pencil I
have offered in order to have it. So it is with God's gifts (including His
greatest gift of salvation). Christ put it like this, "Therefore I say to you,
whatever things you ask when you pray, *believe that you receive them*,
and you will have them" (Mark 11:24, NKJV). Our faith reaches out to
gratefully receive from God's hand and whatever He gives is ours.
Simply stated, "His giving is my taking."[36]

How do we reach out? If we ask for inner strength or wisdom, we
act and make decisions to the best of our ability assuming God is empowering our life. If we ask for daily bread and He supplies, we should
share it with gratitude, not hoard it for fear He will not supply tomorrow.
If we ask for self-control to bridle our anger or a cutting tongue, we
should speak calmly and with grace knowing that He deserves the
glory. If we really believe that we have received, we will act as though
His gifts were indeed ours. If we doubt that He has granted us anything,

---

36. Meister Johannes Eckhart (1260-1327) quoted by Parker and St. Johns, p.
246.

we will continue to live as we always have. A change in action is the sign of true faith that we have received from God what He promised.[37]

As we close this chapter on petition, read carefully the wise words below which were said to have been found in the pocket of a Confederate soldier after a battle during our Civil War.

He was a Christian and he prayed.
He asked for strength that he might do greater things; but he was
    given infirmity that he might do better things.
He asked for riches that he might be happy; he was given poverty
    that he might be wise.
He asked for power that he might have the praise of men; he was
    given weakness that he might feel the need of God.
He asked for all things that he might enjoy life; he was given life
    that he might have all things.
He had received nothing that he asked for; all that he hoped for.
His prayer is answered, he is most blessed.[38]

THOUGHT OR DISCUSSION QUESTIONS

1. Do petitions do any good? How so? Explain how you would paraphrase the saying, "Prayer changes things." What are some false views of offering petitions to God with which you are familiar? How do you think the Lord responds to "Christian whining," complaining and worrying in prayer? What reasons would you give if a nonbeliever asked, "Why do you ask God for things in prayer?"

2. What two general reasons does James give why we may not receive that which we need or desire from the Lord? How do Christians try to bend the will of God to fulfill their desires? Is this right or wrong? Explain. Does "asking within the will of God" limit your prayers? Explain. How can we pray within God's will if we don't know God's will? What should the relationship be between our petitions and regular study of

---

37. See James 2:14-26 and all the examples in Hebrews 11.
38. Quoted by James DeForest Murch, *Teach Me to Pray* Restoration Reprint Library (1958; rpt. [Joplin, Missouri:] College Press, n.d.), p. 161.

God's Word? In what three areas do we ask our desires from our Father?

3. How specific are most of your prayers? Why? At this moment, could you sit down and write out five specific requests which you desire from the Lord? Try it. Look at your requests. How positive do you feel about asking God for these? Why? How could you make these petitions more positively? Look at your list again. Can you picture how your life would be different if you received each of them? Are your pictures realistic? Try to visualize each petition in a positive way. How does visualization help us in our making requests to the Father?

4. How does doubting affect our petitions? What about confidence; how does trust affect our requests? How do you choose between a false confidence that God will do what you ask because you feel like He will and a Biblical confidence that God will act because He has promised to do so in the Scriptures? Look back at your list of petitions from the last question. Can you make affirmations out of each of your invocations (if they are not in that form now)? What is the difference between prayers of affirmation versus prayers of invocation?

5. How does inconsistent praying lead to losing heart? Which of the four reasons for losing heart given in the Bible do you have the most trouble handling? How does giving affect our receiving? How many Christians are convinced this is true? In what ways does our obedience or disobedience affect the offering and granting of petitions? How often should we pray about the same request? How do we know when to stop? Try this: make a tape recording of your "normal" meal and bed-time prayer. Now play it back and listen for the "meaningless repetition" phrases which have slipped in over the years. Try to pray again, but without using any of those trite phrases. It may slow you down, but who should be in a hurry while talking with God anyway?

6. What are the four possible answers God may give to our petitions according to the author? Do you agree? Explain. Do you agree that "more often than not, God gives His children what we request?" Explain your answer. As you ask do you normally expect "it shall be given to you?" Why or why not? How easily do we accept that God has really

granted what we have asked? Why? When God's granting comes in a different form than we were expecting, how do we often respond? Why are we so intrigued with "supernatural" answers to our requests? Does the Lord have to answer similar requests in the same way? Explain, please. What are some unexpected ways God has answered your prayers or the prayers of other people you know?

7. What is so difficult about a delayed granting to one of our petitions? What are some causes for delayed grantings? How can we handle our own impatience with the Lord God? How does the unseen spiritual struggle affect the granting of our prayers? How can the denial of the granting of a petition be a sign of the Almighty's love for us? Which of the reasons God may deny our requests are related to our need to grow as Christians? Do we always know why our prayers are not granted? In which are we normally more interested: our comfort or our character development? Which is God's higher priority? How is it that, when we are weak, then we are strong?

8. How would you change the "natural order" if you could? Can we avoid reaping what we sow by praying? Explain. What request should be "underneath" all other requests? Why this request? How do we actively receive what God grants to us? What changes in action would indicate that you believe that you have received the five requests you wrote down earlier? Have you made those actions? Will you?

7

WHAT ARE THE PARTS OF PRAYER?
IV. INTERCESSION

What could astonish Almighty God? Hard to imagine anything which could amaze Him, isn't it? Yet the Bible says the Lord is astounded by something.

> Now the Lord saw, and it was displeasing in His sight that there was no man, and was *astonished* that there was no one to intercede; then His own arm brought salvation to Him; and His righteousness upheld Him (Isaiah 59:15a-16).

Israel had abandoned God's standards of justice. Then, God looked for a man — a man who would come to the Lord in prayer for the nation; an intercessor. It is as if the Lord thought, "How could it be that there is no single person who cares enough about My people to ask Me to withhold My judgment? Or is there not even one to ask that I *send* judgment as a chastisement to turn Israel back to Me? If no man will seek My righteousness, I will Myself uphold justice and save My honor." The Lord repeated such a sentiment in Ezekiel 22:30-31.

"And I searched for a man among them who should build up the wall and stand in the gap before Me for the land, that I should not destroy it; but I found no one. Thus I have poured out My indignation on them; I have consumed them with the fire of My wrath; their way I have brought upon their heads," declares the Lord God.

Again God looked in Ezekiel's day for one man to stand in the "gap" of the wall and turn away His fierce wrath, as Moses had done so often in the past.[1] The Lord found no one.

If we heard the Lord's concern today, would He again be wondering who was interceding for your church, your community, your state, your nation and your world? Let us not astonish God again, but let us learn and practice the fourth part of prayer, intercession.

INTERCESSION: TALKING TO GOD ABOUT OTHERS

How shall we define "intercession"? Intercession is the act of carrying another person (or persons) before your Father to be blessed in His will. More simply, Dr. Harry Emerson Fosdick described intercession as "love on its knees."[2] While praise and thanksgiving express love toward God and petition and confession express love toward ourselves, intercession expresses love toward other people. We pray for others because we care for them and we believe they need the help which God can and will give them.

How does the Bible illustrate intercession? In the Old Testament, two good examples are Aaron and Samuel. Aaron was the first high priest of Israel. Intercession was a central part of his work. This work is visualized for us in at least two ways. First, in describing Aaron's special priestly clothing, the breastplate visualizes the work of intercession. The breastplate was primarily of gold with twelve stones embedded in it and the stones were to have the names of the twelve tribes engraved on them. Why?

---

1. Exodus 32:7-14; Deuteronomy 9:7-10:11 and Psalm 106:21-23.
2. Quoted by Stephen Winward, *How to Talk with God/the Dynamics of Prayer* (Wheaton, Illinois: Harold Shaw Publisher, 1961), p. 85.

> . . . Aaron shall carry the names of the sons of Israel in the breastplate of judgment over his heart when he enters the holy place, for a memorial before the Lord continually (Exodus 28:29).

Like the breastplate, intercession is the carrying the names of those we pray for as a burden on our hearts before the presence of the Lord as a memorial continually.

A second way that Aaron visualizes the process of intercession occurs at the time of the rebellion of Korah. God had opened the earth to swallow some rebels and had sent a consuming fire to destroy the rest. The remaining Israelites blamed Moses and Aaron for this judgment, which aroused the wrath of God anew. The text tells the rest of the story.

> . . . and the Lord spoke to Moses, saying, "Get away from among this congregation, that I may consume them instantly." Then they fell on their faces. And Moses said to Aaron, "Take the censer and put in it fire from the altar, and lay incense on it; then bring it quickly to the congregation and make atonement for them, for wrath has gone forth from the Lord, the plague has begun!" Then Aaron took it as Moses had spoken, and ran into the midst of the assembly, for behold, the plague had begun among the people. So he put on the incense and made atonement for the people. And *he took his stand between the dead and the living*, so that the plagues was checked (Numbers 16:44-48).

Like Aaron, our intercession leaves us standing between the dead and the living lifting the incense of prayer to God on behalf of His imperfect people by the atonement of Jesus Christ.

Samuel also was a model intercessor for Israel. (See I Samuel 7:5-11.) When Saul had been anointed king, Samuel gave a farewell address as he stepped down from leading the people. In this speech, Samuel told what he saw as his continuing work for Israel.

> Moreover, as for me, far be it from me that I should sin against the Lord by ceasing to pray for you; but I will instruct you in the good and the right way (I Samuel 12:23).

Samuel saw himself in the critical role of providing two-way communication between Israel and the Lord God. He would teach Israel the way of the Lord and he would intercede for Israel with God. In fact, Samuel stated that he would be sinning if he *stopped* praying for the people. Intercession, then, is more than a "good work" for us; it is a moral obligation which God expects us to fulfill.

Among the many examples of intercessory prayer in the New Testament, the pre-eminent model is Jesus Christ. His longest recorded prayer is predominantly an intercession for His apostles and for those of us who trust Him through the apostles' testimony (John 17:1-26). The content of the prayer may be summarized by the following outline:

I. May all glory go to the Father. (Verses 1-5)

II. May the apostles be protected in unity from the evil one by the power of Your name and the truth of Your Word. (Verses 6-19)

III. May the church be united in Christ and in His love as a testimony to the world concerning the coming of Christ. (Verses 20-26)

Jesus implies that which He openly states elsewhere; the result of the Lord helping people should be that the Lord receives the glory for His actions for us. We need to remember that the Father delights in caring for His children. In fact, the Lord cares more about those we pray for than we do. We are not pressuring a reluctant miser for gifts to those we love; we are asking a Father to help His children Who is more eager to answer than we are to ask. The testimony of the Bible is united that the Lord awaits our intercession for one another. Let's not keep Him waiting.

WHY DO WE INTERCEDE FOR OTHERS?

In this section, we will be examining the reasons why we should include intercession in our prayerlife.

Intercession is commanded by the Father.

As in each of the other parts of prayer, intercession is not a human invention concocted to placate an angry god. Rather, our loving Father has given us intercession as a command for our own benefit.

184

Through the pen of Paul the Lord told us:

> First of all, then. I urge that entreaties and prayers, petitions and
> thanksgivings, be made on behalf of all men, for kings and all who
> are in authority . . . (I Timothy 2:1-3).

The primary reason we pray for others then becomes that it pleases our
Father to care for our fellow human beings in this way.

Intercession invites God to act in the lives of others.

At first glance, it seems absurd to assume that God uses our intercession to act on behalf of others. After all, the Lord does not need
our requests to allow Him to do good, does He? Well, in some strange
way, the Bible does seem to indicate that our God somehow limits
Himself within our requests. For example, look at Jesus' call for His
disciples to entreat the Father for harvest workers.

> The harvest is plentiful, but the workers are few. Therefore
> beseech the Lord of the harvest to send workers into His harvest
> (Matthew 9:37-38).

Now answer a few questions with me. Whose harvest is this? The
Lord's, right? And so Who has the greatest interest in seeing that the
harvest is gathered in? That's right; the Lord of the harvest. So Who has
the authority and ability to send out workers to gather in the harvest? Of
course, the Lord does. Then, *why does He need us to ask Him?* The
answer is humbling to us. The Lord does *not* need us; but our God has
chosen to exalt us as His fellow workers in the ministry of prayer as well
as harvesting. And He has bound Himself by the structure He has
created. He will not send unless we ask. As Augustine put it, "Without
God, we cannot . . . without us, God will not."

It follows then that we need the intercession of one another as a
means to receive the grace God desires to give us. The Scriptures support this. James indicates that, to acquire healing and forgiveness in
some cases, we must call on our fellow Christians to intercede with the
Lord on our behalf (James 5:13-20).

But this spiritual partnership with the Lord in intercession is not to be abused. God is now and always the Senior fellow worker with us and the Designer of our work. As in petition, we ask primarily that the Lord's will be done in this person's life for whom we pray. Intercession is not a means for us to play at godhood by directing the lives of other people with our prayers.

Intercession opens our hearts to others.

Another purpose for intercession is the way our entreaties for others change *our* attitudes. In the Sermon on the Mount, Jesus presents us with a difficult challenge and a means to conquer the challenge in the same sentence. He told the disciples,

> But I say to you, love your enemies, and pray for those who persecute you in order that you may be sons of your Father who is in heaven; for He causes His sun to rise on the evil and the good, and sends rain on the righteous and the unrighteous (Matthew 5:44-45).

In order to fulfill the amazing command to love our enemies, we must detach our behavior from the actions of others. As long as we simply respond to what others do toward us, we will return good for good and evil for evil. We will not be able to act in love toward our enemies. But, when we release ourselves from being mere reactors to others' actions, we are free to return good for evil.

Now how do we detach from the actions of others? We must first detach from ourselves. We react to those who hurt us because we focus on our hurt. When we focus on the needs of the other people instead of our feelings, we are free to act in love.[3]

But how do we focus on them rather than ourselves? Jesus said it; "pray for those who persecute you." As we intercede for the very people who bring us pain, we begin to change in our attitudes towards both them and ourselves. To pray for them I must try to understand what

---

3. See D. Martyn Lloyd-Jones, *Studies In The Sermon On The Mount,* I (Grand Rapids, Michigan: Wm. B. Eerdmans Publishing Company, 1959), pp. 304-305.

their needs are, their problems and sorrows. I begin to see what life might look like through their eyes. I may not agree with their view of life, but I begin to understand them, and, perhaps, to care.

If intercession can build our concern for our enemies, think how much more our prayers can positively alter our care for our family and friends. We begin seeing them with new eyes, caring eyes. William Law summarizes this power of intercession.

> Intercession is the best arbitration of differences, the best promoter of true friendship, the best cure and preservative agent against unkind tongues, all anger and haughty passion.[4]

Intercession empowers the church.

The commonest of all methods of bringing a dead church back to life is to form a prayer group which prays earnestly for the members AND the lost. The prayer meeting that renews goes far beyond praying for the sick and the families of the dead. Paul wrote of his prayers for the church:

> To this end also we pray for you always that our God may count you worthy of your calling, and fulfill every desire for goodness and the work of faith with power; in order that the name of our Lord Jesus may be glorified in you, and you in Him, according to the grace of our God and the Lord Jesus Christ (II Thessalonians 1:11-12).

Did you hear him? Paul said, "I know you desire to live good lives and do the works God has called you to do to glorify Him. I just pray that the Lord gives you the power to fulfill your desires." That is what we need: the power to do the works of faith in goodness! Let me focus on three "works of faith" which intercession empowers us to do.

The first work of faith intercession empowers is unity among the brethren. In His great prayer of intercession, Jesus Christ prayed for the

---

4. Quoted by Lloyd John Ogilvie, *Praying With Power* (Ventura, California: Regal Books, 1983), p. 69.

unity of His disciples (John 17:20-23). We need such prayers today for every church in every location. We see splintered churches multiplying in our splintered brotherhood. And the world grows deaf to our message as they see our infighting and power struggles. We need to be praying for unity in Christ between the leaders of our congregations, the leaders and the people, the family members, the new Christians and the "old timers," the races and economic classes in our churches and between the sexes, too. Christ told us of the inevitable failure of a house divided against itself (Mark 3:25). How we need to pray with Paul:

> Now may the God who gives perseverance and encouragement grant you to be of the same mind with another according to Christ Jesus; that with one accord you may with one voice glorify the God and Father of our Lord Jesus Christ (Romans 15:5-6).

The second work of faith intercession empowers is evangelism. Dwight L. Moody said, "Every revival recorded in history can be traced to a single kneeling figure." We multiply programs of "soul-winning" which are ingenious but powerless without solid prayer support. Paul, an inspired apostle of Jesus Christ, wrote to an ordinary group of Christians with this request:

> Finally, brethren, pray for us that the word of the Lord may spread rapidly and glorified, just as it did also with you; and that we may be delivered from perverse and evil men; for not all have faith (II Thessalonians 3:1-2).

If Paul the apostle needed the prayer support of other Christians to proclaim the gospel effectively, how much more the average Christian today; member, deacon, elder or preacher!

The third work of faith intercession empowers is Christian growth. Many of Paul's prayers in his letters are intercessions on behalf of the members of the churches asking for them to be enabled to live as God desired them to live. One good example is Paul's prayer for the Colossian Christians.

> . . . we have not ceased to pray for you and to ask that you may be filled with the knowledge of His will in all spiritual wisdom and

188

understanding, so that you may walk in a manner worthy of the Lord, to please Him in all respects, bearing fruit in every good work and increasing in the knowledge of God; strengthened with all power, according to His glorious might, for the attaining of all steadfastness and patience; joyously giving thanks to the Father, who has qualified us to share in the inheritance of the saints in light (Colossians 1:9-12).

Such growth is not possible without God's gracious gifts extended in response to our prayers for one another.

Intercession empowers others for spiritual battle.

One of the clear perspectives on the Christian life in the New Testament is that we are daily involved in a desperate warfare with spiritual forces, whether we are aware of it or not (Ephesians 6:10-20). Paul's response to this struggle is to command us to "be on the alert with all perseverance and petition for all the saints" (Ephesians 6:18). Here are three areas our intercession for battle will help.

First, our intercession helps others avoid falling into sin. Why is it I haven't heard anyone lately pray this prayer: "Now we pray to God that you will not do anything wrong . . . but that you would do what is right?" (II Corinthians 13:7) Could it be we don't believe that is possible? The Lord's Prayer includes the petition/intercession, "do not lead us into temptation" (Matthew 6:13b). I know how much I need the prayer support of others to fight my way through each day. Don't you? One of the most challenging little written prayers I have ever read says: "Dear Lord, grant that no person may fail in his hour of temptation or trial because I have not prayed for him. Amen."[5] We need to pray for others to avoid the sin in their path.

Second, our intercession helps others find deliverance from evil. Again, the Lord's Prayer says, "deliver us from evil [or the evil one]" (Matthew 6:11b). This snare of evil primarily takes the form of human or demonic opposition. Paul asked the Roman Christians to "strive

---

5. Paul D. Lowder, comp., *Let Us Pray/A Minister's Prayer Book* (Nashville, Tennessee: The Upper Room, 1963), p. 42.

together with" him in prayer to God to deliver him "from those who are disobedient" (Romans 15:30-31). Paul also asked the Thessalonians to pray that he might be delivered from "perverse and evil men" (II Thessalonians 3:1-2). Speaking of his own approaching death, Paul reassures Timothy that God "will deliver me from every evil deed, and will bring me safely to His heavenly kingdom" (II Timothy 4:18). We also face those who do not wish the cause of Christ well; in the battle with the world, pray that your fellow Christians will be delivered from the snares of the forces of darkness.

Third, our intercession helps others recover from trials. The sad fact is that the spiritual warfare leaves many of us wounded. One of the most encouraging verses in the Bible for those of us who stumble in the battle is a statement from Jesus Christ. He is speaking to Peter in the upper room only a short time before the fisherman would fold under pressure and deny his Lord. Here are the reassuring words of Jesus.

Simon, Simon, behold, Satan has demanded permission to sift you like wheat; but I have prayed for you, that your faith may not fail; and you, when once you have turned again, strengthen your brethren (Luke 22:31-32).

What a prayer! Peter was reassured that, even though he was going to be tested by Satan (and fail!), when the trial was past, his faith would still be intact and he would still have a ministry to do. Mentally look around in your congregation right now. Do you "see" any wounded soldiers of the cross? A man who failed in a marriage? A teen-ager who faltered in purity? A woman who fell victim to the domination of "diet pills?" A couple who messed up the job of parenting? A leader who fell prey to pride? Is their faith still intact? How many have been reclaimed for positions of service in the kingdom of God? Or have they been abandoned to bleed to death, isolated and forgotten? Or have they been pampered in soft arms of acceptance without being given the strong (but essential) medicine of repentance? We can pray for such "walking wounded" and see them returned to a healthy ministry in Christ as we reach out to them with tough-minded compassion.

Intercession improves our society.

Our prayers for those around us have the capability to be used by

190

our God to literally change the world. Here are three ways intercession can change our society for the better.

First, we ask God to direct governmental leaders to keep society stable. Paul specifically commanded that we pray for "kings and all who are in authority, in order that we may lead a tranquil and quiet life in all godliness and dignity" (I Timothy 2:1-2). Who can change the minds of those who sit in the seats of power? God can (Proverbs 21:1). We need to pray regularly for the leaders of our cities, counties, states and nations. Such concern will also tend to make us better and more involved citizens.

Second, we ask God to withhold His judgment on society. One look at the headlines of our day will give you many reasons why God should bring His just punishment against our world. One of the most detailed intercessory prayer sessions in the Bible involves Abraham's verbal struggle with himself as he pleads for mercy from the Lord for the evil cities of the plain, apparently out of fear that righteous men might be destroyed in the wrath of God (Genesis 18:22-33). Note that his prayer for mercy failed because the Lord could not find ten good people for whose sake He could save the cities. So righteous living must accompany an intercession for our society if it is to be effective.

Third, we ask God to change society to conform to His will. Like Esther, we ask for God's people to fast and pray to ask God to move the hearts of the leaders of nations (Esther 4:13-17). We cannot continue to stand back and shake our heads sadly at the moral decline around us. To stand back is to miss the very nature of prayer.

> It is, in essence, rebellion—rebellion against the world in its fallenness, the absolute and undying refusal to accept as normal what is pervasively abnormal.[6]

We must realize that "to pray declares that God and his world are at cross-purposes."[7] We are here as a fifth column to alter this society, not to accept it. We believe that God can overwhelm the organizations of men (even the A.C.L.U.). We are not to come to an uncomfortable

---

6. David F. Wells, "Prayer: Rebelling Against the Status Quo," *Christianity Today*, November 2, 1979, p. 33.
7. Ibid., p. 34.

peace with a world at odds with our Lord; this would be treason to the kingdom of heaven. Our prayers must keep a prophetic edge as we ask God to bring our nation under His control (even if He must chastise us to change us).

Intercession joins us in ministry with
Jesus Christ and the Holy Spirit.

We are called to be intercessors. The importance of this task can best be underlined by looking at those who share this office. The first fellow intercessor we see is the Son of God, Jesus Christ.

> . . . He is able to save forever those who draw near to God
> through Him, since He always lives to make intercession for them
> (Hebrews 7:25).

The second fellow intercessor who shares this ministry with us is the Holy Spirit of God.

> . . . the Spirit Himself intercedes for us with groanings too deep
> for words; and He who searches the hearts knows what the mind
> of the Spirit is, because He intercedes for the saints according to
> the will of God (Romans 8:26-27).

How is that for a prayer group? The Son of God, the Spirit of God and you! Since Christ is our example and the Spirit is living within us, intercession becomes (hopefully) a natural occupation for the Christian. The calling to be an intercessor is an invitation to privileged ranks of soldiers in the inner guard of Almighty God.

We have now examined seven reasons to intercede for others in our prayers. Assuming we are convinced, what do we say in intercession?

WHAT DO WE ASK FOR OTHERS?

What are the areas into which our intercessions for others should fall? We have already seen in the previous chapter that all our requests should first fall within God's will. In intercession, we are also seeking God's will for those for whom we pray and not our own. Our requests are complicated by the fact that those we pray for have the power to choose for themselves. We may ask for their spiritual growth, for example, but they must cooperate with God for this prayer to be fully answered.[8] Whatever we ask, they may oppose.

But we may still ask and God will still answer, whether those for whom we pray accept, reject or ignore God's working. We can divide the types of blessing we may request by the areas suggested in Luke 2:52. In this passage, the young Jesus is described as increasing in four areas: "in wisdom and stature, and in favor with God and man." We request that others are blessed in these same four areas: intellectual, physical, spiritual and social.

We pray for others' intellectual blessing.

The area of wisdom includes both the ability to understand truth and to apply that truth to our life situation. Every person needs God's blessing of wisdom and He is willing to give it to us (James 1:5). There are two groups who especially need wisdom to function.

Governmental leaders need godly wisdom to rule as they should (Proverbs 20:28; 29:14; Ecclesiastes 4:13). As we have already seen, this group is to be a special target for our intercession (I Timothy 2:1-2). Dick Eastman suggests using the three requirements of God in Micah 6:8 as an outline to pray for governmental officials:[9]

1. "Do justice"—make decisions fairly and impartially.

2. "Love kindness"—have humane compassion for those you govern.

3. "Walk humbly"—serve the people with modesty and meekness.

Our fellow Christians also need godly wisdom to function in the body of Christ as they should. Paul's prayer in Colossians 1:9-11 requests their intellectual growth through three areas of knowledge

---

8. Harold Lindsell, *When You Pray* (Grand Rapids, Michigan: Baker Book House, 1969), p. 50.

9. *The Advanced Intercessor's Institute* (Studio City, California: World Literature Crusade, 1979), p. AII-10.

resulting in seven additional blessings.[10]

1. Knowledge of the Lord's will.
2. Knowledge in all spiritual wisdom (how to apply His will).
3. Knowledge in all spiritual understanding (how to see each situation from God's point of view).

Resulting in:

1. Walking worthy of God.
2. Pleasing Him in all respects.
3. Bearing fruit in every good work.
4. Increasing in the real knowledge of God Himself.
5. Being strengthened with all power according to God's glorious might.
6. Attaining all steadfastness and patience.
7. Giving thanks to the Father joyously.

Church leaders could especially use such wisdom as they minister in the body.

We pray for others' physical blessing.

I know; asking for physical blessings doesn't sound very, well . . . spiritual. But it is still God's will for our intercessions. The beloved apostle, John, prays for Gaius, "that in all respects you may prosper and be in good health, just as your soul prospers" (III John 2). Prosperity and good health both seem to refer to physical blessings since they are compared to Gaius' soul prospering. We have an apostolic example then of praying for the physical health and well-being of men and women.

Specific physical requests might include: protection in travel, healing in injury or sickness and provision in need. Ezra was transporting a large amount of treasure from Babylon to Jerusalem through dangerous territory. He proclaimed a fast and entreated God for safe travel. The result was a safe journey for all his company (Ezra 8:21-23, 31-32). Asking for "travel mercies" seems to be Biblical (even if the phrase is not).

---

10. Adapted from Eastman, p. AII-12.

194

He who has been injured or becomes ill is instructed by James to:

> call for the elders of the church, and let them pray over him,
> anointing him with oil in the name of the Lord and the prayer of-
> fered in faith will restore the one who is sick, and the Lord will
> raise him . . . (James 5:14-15).

Clearly, proper intercession would include praying for the sick to
become well.[11]

We also intercede for the physical lack of the needy to be filled.
"Give us this day our daily bread" (Matthew 6:11). As we shall explore
later in this chapter, we are also obligated to meet the needs of the
needy ourselves as God enables us.

> If a brother or sister is without clothing and in need of daily food,
> and one of you says to them, "Go in peace, be warmed and be
> filled," and yet you do not give them what is necessary for their
> body, what use is that? Even so faith, if it has no works, is dead,
> being by itself (James 2:15-17).

So we are called to pray for the needs of others and to meet those needs
as we are able (due to God's blessings).

We pray for others' spiritual blessing.

The previous two blessings, intellectual and physical, are important
and really needed. But spiritual blessing deals with the highest priorities
of this life and the destiny of all men in the world to come. Yet, if we
analyzed our average intercession, my hunch is that we focus almost exclusively on the physical and social areas. For many mature Christians,
however, the spiritual requests for others tend to dominate their
prayers. Let's head this direction, too. Here are three directions to pray
for the spiritual growth of others: confessional intercession, evangelistic
intercession and perfection intercession.

---

11. I realize there are many questions about this area in the minds of many people.
I will deal with some of these questions in Appendix B.

Confessional intercession is a paradox. We confess sins which are not ours and ask God to forgive them. That does not seem fair that one who may not even be repentant should yet be forgiven for sins they have committed. Yet, no less an authority than Jesus Christ supports such intercession. His famous words from the cross echo back: "Father, forgive them; for they do not know what they are doing" (Luke 23:34). Later the early church leader Stephen asked the same thing for those who were unjustly stoning him to death (Acts 7:60). Then the apostle John includes the following passage in his first general letter.

If anyone sees his brother committing a sin not leading to death, he shall ask and God will for him give life to those who commit sin not leading to death. There is a sin leading to death; I do not say that he should make request for this. All unrighteousness is sin, and there is a sin not leading to death (I John 5:16-17).

First, we need to define some of the phrases in this passage to understand it. What are a "sin not leading to death" and a "sin leading to death"? A "sin leading to death" is a continued rejection of any witness to Jesus Christ and a continued habit of sin without shame.[12] A "sin leading not to death" is any other sin which leaves one open to repent and follow Christ. The "death" spoken of in both phrases is spiritual death, not physical death (since all will die physically because of sin — Romans 8:10). Now what is promised here?

John is saying that we can pray for the various sins we may see in the lives of those around us and God will forgive those sins in Jesus Christ. Nonetheless, if the people we pray for continue to sin and reject Jesus Christ, the Lord pronounces them to be spiritually dead and tells us not to ask Him to forgive that sin, for it cannot be forgiven.

---

12. Compare the exegesis of the following authors: William Barclay, *The Letters of John and Jude* (Philadelphia: the Westminster Press, 1960), pp. 139-143; Leon Morris, "I John," *The New Bible Commentary Revised*, ed. D[onald] Guthrie and J. A[lec] Motyer (Grand Rapids, Michigan: Wm. B. Eerdmans Publishing Co., 1970), pp. 1269-1270; and John R. W. Stott, *The Epistles of John/An Introduction and Commentary* (Grand Rapids, Michigan: Wm. B. Eerdmans Publishing Company, 1975), pp. 186-191. Also compare this passage to Matthew 12:31-32; Mark 3:29; Luke 12:10 and Hebrews 6:4-6 and 10:26-29. The "sin leading to death" seems to be comparable to the "blasphemy against the Holy Spirit" and to have "fallen away" and to "go on sinning willfully."

One of the most complete confessional intercessions in the Scriptures is the prayer of Daniel in Daniel 9:3-21. There are at least five sections to this confessional prayer for Israel.

1. *Identify with the sin.* Daniel identifies himself with the sin of Israel (Verses 4-6). Daniel perhaps understood the principle which James would later teach: "For whoever keeps the whole law and yet stumbles in one point, he has become guilty of all" (James 2:10). Even though Daniel had not personally rebelled against God's commandments or rejected the message of the prophets as Israel had, he had sinned in other ways, making him no better than the Jews in captivity with him. We also need to be able to identify with those we pray for, whether we have done the sin which they have or not. "We have sinned" (Daniel 9:5).

2. *Accept the shame.* Daniel accepts that Israel's sin is shameful (Verses 7-8). Some have so seared their consciences that they no longer feel or acknowledge the shame of what they had done. But the intercessor must have a conscience which is still tender to the chagrin of being found guilty of sinning against the Lord. He must accept the shame which the one he prays for has earned. Even though the person himself may not be contrite before God, we who pray must be.

3. *Admit the sin and the rightness of its condemnation.* Daniel does not dispute the judgment which has already come against his people; indeed, Daniel proclaims God's righteousness in His condemnation of their sin (Verses 9-15). Pity for the sinner does not make us easy on the sin. We have to state the truth: sin is always wrong and worthy of judgment.

4. *Ask for forgiveness.* Daniel then boldly asks that the sins of his people be forgiven and their relationship with Him restored (Verses 16-19). The purpose Daniel gives for the forgiveness is important. He does not ask for forgiveness due to the essential goodness of the people (they weren't), or due to his own righteousness (he wasn't), or due to the sorrow of the Jews in their captivity. Daniel asks God to forgive for God's sake! Listen to his words.

. . . we are not presenting our supplications before Thee on account of any merits of our own, but on account of Thy great compassion. O Lord, hear! O Lord, forgive! O Lord, listen and take action! For Thine own sake, O my God, do not delay, because

Thy city and Thy people are called by Thy name (Daniel 9:18b-19).

Daniel is saying, "Lord, Your compassion and Your name are on the line here. If You forgive, Your name will receive praise for Your compassion to the people who bear the honor of being identified with Your Name." We should also approach God for others with lifting the Lord's glory as our primary purpose, not just obtaining forgiveness for some sinner who is dear to us. We are asking that God act in accordance with the mercy and grace He has disclosed in Jesus Christ.

5. *Confess your own sin.* Though the exact words are not recorded, a postscript informs us that Daniel confessed his own sin as he prayed for Israel (Verses 20-21). We should come as clean channels through which the grace of God may flow to others. In actual order of prayer, we should first confess our own sins before interceding for the sins of others; first, we remove the log in our eye, then the speck in theirs (Matthew 7:3-5).

Confessional intercession is then the first of three ways we pray for the spiritual blessing of others.

The second spiritual petition we pray for others is evangelistic intercession. Billy Graham has said often, when asked why his campaigns have been so successful, "It was the people who prayed who made the difference." R. A. Torrey added, "There have been revivals without much preaching; but there has never been a mighty revival without mighty praying."[13] Preaching the gospel without praying is like broadcasting seed without breaking up the topsoil. The seed somehow does not get into the soil where it can grow. So we need to be praying for the evangelization of those around us in two directions: we pray for the Christians reaching out and we pray for the lost to be saved.

For the workers, the Christians reaching out, we need to intercede in four areas:

1. *We pray for workers to be sent out* (Matthew 9:37-38). If next Tuesday was named "Calling Night" at your church, how many people would show up to make evangelistic calls? If your church were doing really great, perhaps five to ten per cent of the adults in your member-

---

13. *The Power of Prayer* (Grand Rapids, Michigan: Zondervan Publishing Company, 1974), p. 43.

ship would come to reach out. Most churches would probably have the preacher and two or three others (this week; in three weeks, just the preacher). How can we reach the world with so few workers? We can't. So we must pray for the Lord of the harvest to send out workers into the field.

2. *We pray for workers to be bold in sharing the gospel* (Ephesians 6:18-20). Paul twice asks the Ephesians believers to pray that he might speak with boldness the gospel. Having a prepared worker meet a receptive prospect does no good if the worker is afraid to open his or her mouth. Boldness implies confidence in my message and in my (God-given) ability to communicate it well so that I can share freely and openly. Such boldness is the result of having the backing of others in prayer so that I am trusting in the blessing and presence of God and not in my own ability.

3. *We pray for workers to have opportunities and to be clear in their sharing* (Colossians 4:2-4). Paul asks the Colossians to pray for the Lord to "open up to us a door for the word." Sometimes we offend those we seek to reach by "battering down" the doors of their lives instead of seeking the Lord to arrange an opening. His openings work so much better than our batterings. But once we have an "open door," we can stand there, stammering and sputtering, unable to communicate the good news we know. So Paul adds a request for prayer to "make [the mystery of Christ] clear in the way [he] ought to speak." Pray that the Lord's workers may communicate with clarity and honesty.

4. *We pray for workers to spread the word unimpeded* (II Thessalonians 3:1-2). Satan is not going to sit back and simply watch as we win person after person out of the kingdom of darkness. His opposition often appears in the form of people who try to derail our ministry. Paul asks for prayer that he "may be delivered from perverse and evil men" so "the word of the Lord may spread rapidly and be glorified." Wrap your workers in prayers of protection. These are four areas of requests for the workers; now to pray for the lost.

For the lost, we need to be praying regularly and zealously. Some have questioned whether it is Biblical to pray for the lost. "Doesn't that violate their free will?" they ask. No; no more than praying for a diabetic means the person will not be able to eat some sugary goody and send their blood sugar level wild. We are asking for the Lord to work within the boundaries of His own will and man's free will.

199

Paul describes his zeal for evangelizing the Jewish people in these terms: "Brethren, my heart's desire and *my prayer to God* for them is for their salvation" (Romans 10:1). The apostle prayed for the salvation of the Jews. He later writes to Timothy the following instructions:

First of all, then, I urge that entreaties and prayers, petitions and thanksgivings, be made on behalf of *all men*, for kings and all who are in authority, in order that we may lead a tranquil and quiet life in all godliness and dignity. This is good and acceptable in the sight of God our Savior, who desires *all men* to be saved and to come to the knowledge of the truth (I Timothy 2:1-4).

Notice that Paul commands that Christians pray for all men in the first verse and then he states what God's will is for all men in verse four; that they all be saved. It seems obvious that we should pray for men what God desires for them; salvation. And what we pray for mankind as a whole we should pray for each individual God brings us into our lives. I know many of you have been praying for certain individuals to accept Christ for years. Don't give up. Though there is no guarantee that each person we intercede for will decide to accept Christ, I personally believe that most persons (if not all) who do accept Jesus have someone praying for them. Someone was praying for you, weren't they? They were for me.

The third spiritual petition we pray for others is perfection intercession. By this phrase, I mean praying that Christians come to maturity in Christ. As fervently as we often pray for someone to become a Christian, we need to pray with equal zeal for that person to grow in Christ.

My personal experience lately has been that Christians are under a massive attack by Satan's forces in every area of life: finances, marriages, health, jobs, self-control, unity of the church, material possessions and so on. Especially I see congregational leaders being beaten upon from every side. The other side of this is the remarkable growth in faith and joy and ministry in the lives of many of those who have had the greatest burdens. I believe this is explainable only by the number of prayers focused on these precious individuals. The sad opposite may be said: we have lost some wonderful brothers and sisters to kingdom service by not supporting them with real, consistent prayer. To finish this section, listen in on this beautiful intercession of Paul for the Ephesians:

For this reason, I bow my knees before the Father, from whom every family in heaven and on earth derives its name, that He would grant you, according to the riches of His glory, to be strengthened with power through His Spirit in the inner man; so that Christ may dwell in your hearts through faith; and that you, being rooted and grounded in love, may be able to comprehend with all the saints what is the breadth and length and height and depth and to know the love of Christ which surpasses knowledge, *that you may be filled up to all the fullness of God* (Ephesians 3:14-19).

We pray for others' social blessing.

The last of the four categories for our intercession covers all of our relationship with others. These prayers can get very personal; prayers for spouses out of contact, for children in rebellion, for neighbors with sharp tongues, for church members at odds, for church leaders caught in power struggles, for friends who have become enemies. While the specifics of these prayers may vary widely, they seem to center around two themes: unity and love.

Unity is the theme of intercession when relationships are drifting apart or are breaking up or never were connected at all. For families and congregations, unity is God's design (Ephesians 5:31-6:4; John 17:20-23). But, given human tendencies to sin, tensions seem constant on most relationships to pull people apart. Any time two or more people commit themselves to each other, we need to remember that unity that lasts is "what God has joined together" (Matthew 19:6). We need to ask the great Unifier to conjoin us. We have already seen how Jesus prayed for our unity in John 17:20-23. We read also how Paul prayed for unity in his letter to the church at Rome (Romans 15:5-6). Our intercessions should mimic theirs.

But what produces this unity? Paul wrote, "And beyond all these things put on love, which is the perfect bond of unity" (Colossians 3:14). And this binding love is one of the fruit which the Spirit produces in us, and so must be sought from the Lord in prayer, at least in part. For we also have the responsibility to cooperate in the development of the fruit of love in our lives.

We need love. We need it in every relationship. For love "does no wrong to a neighbor," "is the fulfillment of the law" and "covers a multitude of sins" (Romans 13:10; I Peter 4:8). Love motivates all that we each must do to keep our relationships going. Without the commitment of love, why would we pay for the price of the pain, boredom, insanity, misunderstanding and silliness involved in so many friendships? (Remember that the "love" we are considering is not a passing emotion but a sacrificial commitment.)

Is it any wonder that Paul prays for the churches as in these passages?

And this I pray, that your love may abound still more and more in real knowledge and in all discernment, so that you may approve the things that are excellent, in order to be sincere and blameless until the day of Christ; having been filled with the fruit of righteousness which comes through Jesus Christ, to the glory and praise of God (Philippians 1:9-10).

Now may our God and Father Himself and Jesus our Lord direct our way to you; and may the Lord cause you to increase and abound in love for one another, and for all men, just as we also do for you; so that He may establish your hearts unblamable in holiness before our God and Father at the coming of our Lord Jesus with all His saints (I Thessalonians 3:11-13).

We also need to be praying for one another that our social relationships may be motivated and directed by God's love in us.

At this point you might ask, "I know now the four areas in which I can intercede for others; but which others? I can't pray for all four billion plus people alive today (except in a very general way). Who are my special prayer targets as an intercessor?" Good questions! And I think you know the answers as well.

First, since you cannot pray specifically for those you have never met or heard of, you can only pray specifically for people you know exist as individuals. Second, the better you know someone, the better you will be able to intercede for them. Third, since people have greater specific needs at certain times in their lives than at other times, we should pray for those whom we are aware are under specific pressures right now. So we have at least three qualifications to determine who are our special prayer targets: acquaintance ("Do I know them?"), closeness ("How well do I know them?") and urgency ("What current needs do I know they have?")

These three qualifications point to five groups that each of us have as our special targets. First, we should be praying specifically for our family and friends. Our primary requests should center on those who are lost as well as those with current special needs. Second, we should be praying specifically *for* our enemies(!) (Matthew 5:44). We do take special notice of this group anyway; now we know why—to pray for them. Third, we should be praying specifically for our local congregation; its members, leaders, workers, programs, missions and missionaries, prospects and new converts. Fourth, we should be praying specifically for our city, county, state and country, especially for their leaders. Every crisis is a prayer cue. Fifth, we should be praying specifically for our world, its nations and peoples, and the church universal. If that sounds contradictory, to pray specifically for the world, yet we are commanded to pray "on behalf of all men" (I Timothy 2:1). So we do, reaching around this troubled globe for Jesus Christ on the wings of intercession. Now how do we go about our task?

HOW DO WE INTERCEDE AS INDIVIDUALS?

The process of intercession is neither complex nor easy. Like threading a needle, the procedure is clear but requires concentration and effort. There are four steps involved in intercession.

Step One: See another's needs.

To know what to pray for others, we must be aware of their needs. To be aware, we must have eyes that see and ears that hear. Jesus models for us the seeing eye and hearing ear (Proverbs 20:12). Others saw crowds; Christ saw the multitude and evaluated their condition and their needs, "and He felt compassion for them because they were like sheep without a shepherd" (Mark 6:34). It is one thing to see people; it is quite another to care for them enough to recognize their needs.

When Christ encountered a prejudiced Pharisee, He asked him a strange question concerning an immoral woman. The woman had timorously entered the Pharisee's house to anoint the feet of Jesus who was a guest at the dinner taking place. Jesus perceived that Simon, the Pharisee, resented her presence and He asked Simon, "Do you see this woman?" Now, of course, Simon had a visual perception of the woman; but he was blinded by his arrogance to the woman's wants and possibilities. The Proverbs warn such a man, "He who gives to the poor will never want, but he who shuts his eyes will have many curses" (Proverbs 28:27). How open are our eyes to the anguish of others?

Then, Christ reminded His followers as He taught, "He who has ears to hear, let him hear." Our ears are intended for hearing, that is, understanding the meaning of the sounds around us, but often we do not put forth the effort to evaluate and comprehend. The wistfulness and pain in voices around us go unheeded far too often. Worse, at times we intentionally shut our ears so that we do not have to get involved with the problems of others. Again, the Proverbs warn us, "He who shuts his ear to the cry of the poor will also cry himself and not be answered" (Proverbs 21:13). We threaten our own petitions by not listening with concern to the needs of others.

So we consciously begin to see and hear the exigencies of those we encounter. In fact, we begin to see that the Lord in His providence allows us to become aware of the troubles of others in order to allow us to help them. That help may take the form of our intercession and/or direct aid.

Once we know another's need we are regretfully not certain to remember that need. A Chinese proverb says, "The weakest ink lasts longer than the strongest memory." So written lists are a great aid to an intercessor's task. Some possible aids of this kind are:

1. A permanent prayer list of people who are your own special targets for prayer. Their needs may vary but our responsibility to pray for them does not (I Samuel 12:23).

2. A temporary list for those short term needs for which you agree to intercede. Incidentally, we should try to avoid the common broken vow of saying, "I'll pray about it," when in fact we are in the very process of forgetting the person's need.

3. A prayer map of locations of individuals or areas we desire to

remember in our prayer time.

4. A list of political leaders who are particular prayer burdens for us.

5. A picture album of items to bring before God. Photos can bring people to life more than a plain list.[14]

Such care to remember the requests we need to bring before the Lord is but a function of our love for those for whom we pray. But first we have to see the needs.

Step 2: Lift up his needs.

This step is simply to identify personally with the pain of our prayer targets. We lift up their needs, feel the weight of them in some degree. We "weep with those who weep" (Romans 12:15). Paul understood this identification. After enumerating the many physical woes he had endured in the service of Christ, Paul comes at length to the end of his list with this closing statement.

Apart from such external things, there is the daily pressure upon me of concern for all the churches. Who is weak without my being weak? Who is led into sin without my intense concern? (II Corinthians 11:28-29).

When Christ agonized in prayer on the Mount of Olives, the result was blood. Such a price for prayer is uncommon but still an example to disquiet those of us who address God in comfortable ease. J. H. Jowett asks us:[15]

Do our prayers bleed? Have we felt the painful fellowship of the pierced hand? I am often ashamed of my prayers. They so frequently cost me nothing; they shed no blood.

The gospels give a lovely illustration of this empathetic aspect of in-

---

14. See Marion Duckworth, "The Picture Way to Pray," *Christian Standard*, January 19, 1986, p. 7.

15. Quoted by Edwin and Lillian Harvey, comp., *Kneeling We Triumph* (Chicago: Moody Press, 1971), p. 88.

tercession. A father had brought his demon-possessed son to Jesus hoping for healing. The spirit threw the boy into a convulsion in Christ's presence.

> And [Jesus] asked his father, "How long has this been happening to him?" And he said, "From childhood. And it has often thrown him both into the fire and into the water to destroy him. But if You can do anything, take pity on *us* and help *us!*" (Mark 9:21-22).

The father links himself with his son. To take pity on the son and help him was to take pity on the father and help him as well. Identifying with the frenzy of his son, the father lifted up the burden of the boy and brought the weight to Christ for relief.

Step 3: Carry his needs to God in prayer.

"Bear one another's burdens, and thus fulfill the law of Christ," Paul wrote (Galatians 6:2). While we can put out shoulder under our brother's burden, we can only rest him for a time. Only God can finally lift burdens. And so we carry our brother with his needs before the Lord in prayer. We need to realize that, if we try to carry his burdens ourselves, they will only crush us, too. God invites us to give Him our burdens (Matthew 11:28-30).

As we pray for another, we should not have the audacity of telling the Lord what to do. Rather, we bear to Him our brother in need and and ask that the Lord meet that need *as He wills.* As Evelyn Christenson puts it, "We do not pray answers, we pray requests."[16] So, we ask not as we will or the target person wills, but what God wills.

Two dangers in intercession are to make our prayers too general or too narrow. Generalized intercession sounds like this: "Bless the church and all the missionaries. Amen." Such an "unfocused" prayer is a blur in our minds as well as a meaningless repetition to the Lord. On the other hand, our intercession can be focused so sharply on such a small group that it excludes many important prayer concerns. We can be as

---

16. *What Happens When Women Pray* (Wheaton, Illinois: Victor Books, 1976), p. 67.

parochial as the man who prayed: "God bless me and my wife, My son John and his wife, Us four—no more—Amen."[17] Broadening our scope and specifying our requests will keep our intercession balanced.

Finally, we only carry another to God in prayer if we believe God cares to help and that He alone truly can help (Ephesians 3:20-21). We need to take on the attitude of the centurion who came to Christ concerning his servant who was paralyzed and in pain. After Jesus indicated His willingness to come and heal the servant, the centurion replied, "just say the word, and my servant will be healed" (Matthew 8:5-10). Jesus "marveled" and told His disciples, "Truly I say to you, I have not found such great faith with anyone in Israel." This "great faith" was simply to believe that Jesus cared and could help if He would.

Step 4: Offer yourself as God's tool.

Intercession does not imply that our responsibility for another's need is fulfilled. Do not think that prayer relieves us of the call to service. Understand what we mean by intercession.

It does not mean leaving everything to God and doing nothing; it means bringing everything to God and being ready to do whatever He may want us to do in that situation.[18]

Keith Miller in one of his books tells of a time he was riding the subway to work. As he made a few notes on a manuscript, someone bumped the briefcase on his lap on which he was writing. He looked up to see an obviously pregnant young lady standing in the crowded car and hanging onto a ceiling strap. As he went back to work, Keith thought, "Lord, help this young lady to find a seat soon." A minute or two passed and the thought came clearly into Keith's mind, "Keith, you are sitting on the answer to your prayer." I have asked myself more often lately after some time of fervent intercession, "Very moving, Mitch. Now, are you sitting on the answer to your prayer?" Paul combined his prayer for

---

17. Winward, p. 91.
18. Frederick J. Tritton quoted by Osborne T. Miller, comp., *The Path of Prayer* (New York: Harper and Brothers, 1954), p. 55.

others with a prayer that God would allow him to come to them to help fulfill the prayer (Romans 1:8-13; I Thessalonians 3:9-13).

As we pray for others, we should assume that we are also offering ourselves *without reserve* to answer those prayers. We see in the cases of Moses and Paul a commitment so strong that they were willing to give up their own salvation to save those for whom they prayed (Exodus 32:32; Romans 9:1-5, 10:1). Christ asked His Father to forgive those who crucified Him while He died to make that forgiveness possible. Meeting the needs of others can be dangerous. We may have to endanger a friendship to share the gospel with a friend. We may be misunderstood if we offer aid to a needy brother or sister. Not everyone accepted what Jesus did for them either. But that does not keep us from offering ourselves to God for service.

At the same time, we must also realize that there are times when we need to stand back and let God work through other channels. A wife who has badgered her unbelieving husband for years to go to church may need to seek the Lord *in silence* concerning the salvation of her spouse. Hers may be the worst voice to share the gospel with him at this time. Here we need godly wisdom to discern when God wants us involved with answering our intercessory prayers and when we should back away. We can ask for that wisdom and God has promised to respond.

In summary, the four steps of individual intercession are:
1. See another's needs.
2. Lift up his needs.
3. Carry his needs to God in prayer.
4. Offer yourself as God's tool.

But intercession can be an even stronger tool when we experience it as a group, praying together in God's presence. So next we look at how to intercede as a family group.

HOW DO WE INTERCEDE AS FAMILIES?

This section deals specifically with learning to intercede together as families. But as we start, let me say that much of what follows is equally true of any small group of believers gathered for prayer. So, if you do not have a family group to meet with, seek out (or start!) a small group in the church to join in regular intercession.

The family is a place of spiritual training by God's design (Deuteronomy 6:6-7; Proverbs 6:20-23 and Ephesians 6:4). Where do most of us learn our style of personal prayer? Usually at the knees of a parent who showed us the need and joy of seeking the Lord. But others had to wait for years to learn the art of supplication because their parents either did not have or would not share their experience of prayer. Without a consistent model it is difficult to mold a personal prayerlife.

Intercession is also best learned in a family group (of two or more). Learning to pray for others is better caught than only taught. First someone in the home must know how to pray and intercede. How does one prepare for this task of leading others into a real prayerlife? The great priest Ezra showed us the method from his own life.

> For Ezra had set his heart to study the law of the Lord, and to practice it, and to teach His statutes and ordinances in Israel (Ezra 7:10).

Here are the four steps of preparation for teaching the way of the Lord to others:

1. Set your heart; decide that you desire primarily to know and obey the Lord.

2. Study the word of God; search His Scriptures for how to please the Lord.

3. Practice the word of God; do what you find the Bible instructs you to do.

4. THEN teach the word of the Lord to others by modeling and instruction; like Paul, be able to say, "Be imitators of me, just as I also am of Christ" (I Corinthians 11:1).

So, first, one person in the family has to understand in their mind and in their experience how to touch the Lord in prayer and intercession. Then that person can gently lead others to pray together. There are many benefits to sharing together as a family. Here is a short listing.

1. Group prayer invites the presence of Christ. "For where two or three have gathered together in My name, there I am in their midst" (Matthew 18:20).

2. Group prayer unifies individuals. As we pray together, there is a

harmonizing effect which arises out of the fellowship of the Spirit and a common experience of sharing.

3. Group prayer keeps us motivated. A single ember will quickly cool set apart, but an ember set in the midst of many coals will be kept hot. The Christian in a group is continually inspired and challenged by the others with whom he discloses himself to God.

4. Group prayer builds excitement, especially as answers to their prayers are experienced. When something wonderful happens, the joy we feel is multiplied as it is shared. As you fill in an answer to a prayer in a family prayer diary, your children get excited about a God who really hears and acts.

5. Group prayer helps individuals learn to pray aloud. Properly directed, a family prayer *circle* is the most comfortable place to share you first "public" prayer.

6. Group prayer helps members of the family understand each other. It opens a parent's heart to hear a child pray, "God, I'm sorry I shouted at Jimmy this morning. Help me be nicer to him, even when he calls me names." It draws a child closer to a parent to hear an admission like, "Lord, forgive me for losing my temper with my children today. Give me the patience to love and direct them as You would desire" (James 5:16).

7. Group prayer somehow adds power to our intercession. Harold Lindsell calls this fact the "law of geometric progression."[19] He notes that in Leviticus 26:7-8 the Lord promises, "five of you will chase a hundred, and a hundred of you will chase ten thousand." Now simple math would tell us that, if five chases a hundred, then a hundred would chase two thousand, not ten. But the Lord says the one of the five would only chase twenty, but one of the hundred would chase a hundred! There is no direct mathematical relationship implied here, but a principle; the more of God's people who struggle together, the greater the results God will provide. Jesus promised us this:

Again I say to you, that if two of you agree on earth about anything that they may ask, it shall be done for them by My Father who is in heaven (Matthew 18:19).

---

19. Lindsell, pp. 109-110.

210

The context of this promise is the difficult area of church discipline; how to decide as a congregation or a group of leaders how to handle the sin of a brother or sister in Christ. Yet the promise says that group prayer can be God's channel of power to choose and do what is right. Of course, God can and will help the individual Christian who prays, yet a family group opens a greater channel to receive even greater blessings.

8. Group prayer provides an arena for healing hurting relationships. Abraham had brought judgment against the whole family of Abimelech by lying about his relationship to Sarah. At God's command, the only way for judgment to be removed from Abimelech's house was for Abraham to pray for him (Genesis 20:1-17). The one who caused the hurt should pray for the healing of the hurt. In families this principle can result in almost magical reunions.

Likewise, when the people of Israel grumbled against Moses and decided to find another leader, it was the prayer of Moses which caused the Lord to pardon their sin (Numbers 14:1-21). Here the one hurt prays for forgiveness for the ones who hurt him. God honors such prayers. In fact, He commands that we forgive all others who have hurt us as we approach Him in prayer (Mark 11:24-25). Therefore, make your family prayer circles forgiving and healing times.

Seeing the benefits of praying together, how do we go about it? Most prayer meetings may be defined as gatherings where one person gets eloquent while everybody else gets bored. Frankly, even great spiritual fervor can be chilled by long-winded petitions. But the long prayers of the pious may often be a response to the fact that only the same tiny corps of prayer warriors pray aloud at any gathering. And these warriors then feel responsible for making up for the silence of the rest of the group. But there is a far better way to pray together. The method I suggest is simple conversational prayer.[20]

Conversational prayer is a style of praying together which resembles a conversation in that no one person dominates but prayer goes back and forth among the group members. Evelyn Christenson has suggested six "S's" as a framework for praying conversationally.[21]

---

20. This term was popularized in the writings of Rosalind Rinker including *Conversational Prayer* (Waco, Texas: Word Books, Publisher, 1970). Many of the concepts in this discussion come from her work.
21. Christenson, pp. 40-51.

1. Subject by Subject — Instead of bringing up a whole series of varied petitions, we pray about one subject at a time. Concentrate on that one area until there is a mutual feeling it is time to move to another.

2. Short Prayers — Each person is to pray only one simple sentence or so on each subject, giving others opportunity to pray also if they desire.

3. Simple Prayers — No "churchy" language is needed or encouraged in group prayer. Leave out the "redeemest," "sanctificational," "Thee" and "Thou." God understands, accepts and prefers our ordinary way of speaking as we share with Him.

4. Specific Requests — Replace generalities with specific requests. Go from "bless them" to "help John and Mary to find a suitable apartment close to the church in a price range they can afford within the next two weeks." Keep a dated, written record of both requests and answers to refer to later for praise and thanksgiving.

5. Silent Periods — Do not be afraid of periods of silence between sentence prayers. Group members will soon find that these quiet pauses do not increase but decrease tension. We seem to grow in the quiet times. In our hearts we continue to be in contact with the Lord. Also do not be embarrassed when (inevitably) two people start to pray at once. Simply expect one of the two to go ahead and the other to pray next.

6. Small Groups — Keep the group size under seven people. Four or five seems to work best. If you have more people, break them into smaller groups. Then there is more opportunity for each one to participate and less of an "audience" to put pressure on the shy person in the group.

Perhaps an example would help you visualize what happens in conversational prayer. Here is a family consisting of five members: John (father), Mary (mother), Dave (brother, 14), Rick (brother, 12) and Susan (sister, 9). When John calls, "Prayer time, everyone," the family gathers in the living room. They are standing in a circle with their hands joined and heads bowed.

John begins, "Father, I thank You that our family can gather again in Your presence."

Susan: "Thank You, Lord."

Mary: "Thank You for being here right now."

Boys: "Thank You."

John: "Lord, You have blessed our home with so much this week. I thank you for getting the car fixed . . . finally."

Dave: "Yes, Father, thank You, so I can finally get to ball practice on time." Someone giggles. A short pause.

Susan: "And thank You for Grandma Jones getting better."

Mary: "Yes, Lord, You are so kind to us . . . and loving."

A short pause, then, Rick: "Yea, thanks for Grandma feeling better . . . and for me getting a hit in the game yesterday."

Another silence, then, Susan: "Thank You for Jesus."

Mary: "Always, Lord."

John: "Lord, I have a long shift at the plant tomorrow. Give strength to make it and stay awake."

Dave: "I agree, Lord; help Dad do a good job tomorrow."

Susan: "And I have a English test tomorrow, too. Help me remember what I know . . . what I need to know for the test."

John: "Yes, Father. Help Sue study well."

Rick: "Yes, Lord."

A long pause, then, Mary: "Dear God, Janie Smith has her surgery this week. I know she is afraid. Please give her Your peace as she prepares to go to the hospital."

John: "I agree. Help Max [Janie's husband] know what to say to help her relax."

A quiet time, then, Rick: "Jim is thinking about becoming a Christian. I don't know how to . . . what to say. Help me help'm decide right."

Dave: "Yea, help me to help him, too."

Mary: "Lord, give the boys Your wisdom as they share with Jim and we thank You for working through them."

A long silence, then, John: "Thank You for this time together with You, Lord. May Your will be done. In Jesus' name, Amen."

This shortened summary gives you an idea of how it works. It really is easy to learn and enjoy this style of prayer. Here are some additional suggestions:

a. Be supportive to the prayers of others by short words of agreement ("yes, Lord," "I agree") or rephrasing the request.

b. Pray "I" when you mean "I" and "we" when you mean "we." If you mean "I ask Your forgiveness for being selfish today," do not say "We ask Your forgiveness for selfish feelings."

c. Someone should be selected to begin and end a session, but no one (but the Holy Spirit) needs to direct the flow of prayers ("Greg, it's your turn."). If someone does not want to pray, do not force them.

d. Concentrate on getting to know God, who He is and what He does. Do not have a long preliminary period before starting to pray; you do not have to list who to pray for as this will come out naturally in the conversation.

e. You may want to begin with an affirmation of the presence of God in your midst. This sets a tone of expectancy and reverence for your time in prayer.

f. Who prays next? Rosalind Rinker suggests that, if your heart starts pounding, you are next.[22] I admit that is a pretty subjective way to pray, yet it does not change the objective content of the prayers.

g. Standing together in a circle is a good way to get started because it signals everybody, "This isn't going to go on too long." But sitting or kneeling is fine, too. The holding of hands is an important way to demonstrate unity physically. With younger children, the only difficulty is trying to get them to hold hands with a brother or sister without acting up.

When do you gather to pray as a family? Naturally, your family schedule determines the time. Daily prayer together at the beginning or end of the day would be great. Prayer after one meal each day can become an exciting family meeting. Once a week (or more often) your prayertime can be lengthened to include a sharing time when personal problems and discoveries can be discussed. Also a short practical Bible study can be added regularly. Obviously, your times together should be supported by each person's private prayers and devotions.

Praying conversationally with the whole family is not the only way to intercede together. Prayers with your spouse and/or children at mealtime and bedtime are a normal practice in many Christian homes. Parents often pray together regularly with their children. And many families also become involved with their local congregational prayer programs.

One hard time to pray together is when one or more of the family members is away from home for a time. Some ideas to continue the habit of praying together include: praying over the phone together, praying at the same time daily even when separated, leaving prayer

---

22. Rinker, p. 59.

notes in luggage or lunchboxes and keeping up an exchange of prayer requests and praises by mail. So, the family that wants to pray together can stay together, even across the miles.

When the families of your church become prayer centers, the church will itself experience dynamic change and growth. But the local congregation is responsible to have its own organized programs of intercession. What kinds of programs? Our next section will discuss that very question.

HOW DO WE INTERCEDE AS CONGREGATIONS?

A church without a backbone of praying Christians is "Silly Putty" in the hands of Satan. No programs or lesson series can replace a group of Christians on their knees before God. For with prayer, our churches are open to God's power and influence; without prayer, our churches are open to Satan's power and influence. If your congregation wants to avoid becoming a religious treadmill, the way to a living relationship with the Lord God lies down the path of prayer ministry.

The church in the New Testament met on two levels; the large gathering of all believers in a city (in the temple for the Jerusalem church) and the small gatherings of believers (the "house to house" groups) (Acts 2:46-47). Both sizes devoted themselves to prayer (along with the apostles' doctrine, fellowship and the breaking of bread) (Acts 2:42). Today we also need prayer ministries on two levels: congregational gatherings and small group gatherings. Here are some intercession ideas for both size groups. This list does not even remotely claim to be an exhaustive list of the ways a church may minister in prayer. But perhaps these will be springboards for you to see possibilities for your local congregation's needs.

What are some intercession ideas for small groups?

I hope the previous section on family intercession gave you several ideas about incorporating conversational prayer into new or established groups in your church. We need to learn to pray aloud together. One estimate suggests that over half of the members of most churches have

215

never prayed aloud with anyone at anytime in their lives.[23] The point is simply not praying aloud but praying together in *agreement*. How can I agree together with you in prayer if those prayers are not verbalized? I cannot read your mind (nor, thankfully, you read mine).

Why is it important that we agree upon our petitions and intercessions? Jesus told us:

> Again I say to you, that if two of you *agree* on earth about anything that they may ask, it shall be done for them by My Father who is in heaven (Matthew 18:19).

Obviously, the Father would find it difficult to faithfully answer the request of a prayer group if the participants were divided over what they were asking Him to do. When our desires are in harmony as we pray, the Lord listens both to the prayers and the unity in which they are expressed.

Small united prayer groups are very important to the spiritual life of the church. It has been said that, "No revival of religion has come in all the history of Christianity without group prayer."[24] That makes sense. Here you have a group of Christians committed to each other in unity and to God in faith that He is able to do what they ask and a group willing to do what He asks. Is not that group exactly what any church needs to experience a new movement of the Spirit of God? W.E. Sangster concludes:

> The gates of hell prevail against us for lack of prayer, the Kingdom is impeded in its coming for lack of prayer. You could be of service to God, to the nation, and to the world, if you would form, or help form, a prayer cell. It might be the most useful thing you have done in your life.[25]

How do you go about starting a prayer group or cell? First, pray about this project, that God support you and use you to His glory. Se-

---

23. Christenson, p. 39.
24. Donald E. Demaray, *Alive To God Through Prayer* (Grand Rapids, Michigan: Baker Book House, 1965), p. 24.
25. Quoted in [Dick Eastman], *Change the World! School of Prayer* (Studio City, California: World Literature Crusade, 1976), p. D-31.

cond, pray for other members for the group whom God would choose. Third, seek those members by looking for those who express a desire for service and spiritual growth and invite them individually to join you for a single time of prayer. Your home might be a good location to meet.

Fourth, at this prayer time, introduce the group to conversational prayer. Guide them through a simple time of praise, thanksgiving, petition and intercession (save confession for later meetings). If you feel totally unable to lead the session, invite someone from your church who is experienced in conversational prayer to lead the session. But I would suggest you would do better yourself, even if it is your first time. After praying, invite discussion of this kind of prayer. Look at the possibilities of what such a group as yours could do for the church and the kingdom of God. Ask if those present would like to commit themselves to a ten week period of regular weekly prayer cells. If even two or three are interested, set the date for your next meeting then.

Fifth, tell your minister or elders that there is a group of Christians who would like to meet for ten weeks to pray together for personal concerns and for the church. Ask for their support and ask to be informed of any special prayer needs the group could take to the Lord. If the group seems to be effective, suggest that, after the ten weeks, the group could be split and others invited to join. Let the leadership know they are invited to come and observe the group and join in, if they desire.

Sixth, keep the group alive. Pray for members between meetings. Call them occasionally just to keep in touch and let them know you care. Let go of leadership of the group and encourage others to begin and end sessions. Have those who desire to bring a special passage of Scripture to share with the group at the beginning of your sessions. But remember that intercession is the primary reason you are meeting, not fellowship, Bible study or discussion of current events. See your small group as the litter bearers who broke through all obstacles to bring the sick for Jesus to heal; bear those around you to God for Him to touch and make whole (Mark 4:1-12).

Seventh, at the end of the ten weeks, evaluate your progress with the group. Have we grown in unity? Have others been blessed by God? Have our prayers been balanced between praise and thanksgiving on one hand, and petition, intercession and confession on the other? Would the members be willing to recommit themselves for another ten

217

weeks? Then talk about the need to involve others. You have probably grown close over the early development of your prayer cell; but, remember that cells grow by dividing. Branch off a new group and encourage each member to pray for and find one *new* prayer partner to bring to the first meeting of the next ten week period. Those who are not recommitting to group prayer should be encouraged to continue their personal prayer life. Let them know you love them, too. And just keep growing!

There are some guidelines to be remembered in small prayer groups:

a. It is better to start small and grow than to start big and flounder half way through.

b. Do not allow long recitals of problems; have them simply explained and pray for them (Acts 4:23-31).

c. Do not allow criticism of others to kill the spirit of the cell; pray *for* others, especially church leaders.

d. Choose a special prayer target for the group: a specific foreign or domestic mission, the salvation of certain people who have not yet accepted Jesus Christ, the growth of leaders and teachers in the church, resolving a local community problem, healing needs of the sick, protection for church families in this anti-family world, personal or family problem resolution, etc.

e. *** KEEP *ALL* PRAYER CONCERNS CONFIDENTIAL, *ESPECIALLY CONFESSIONS OF SIN AND REVELATIONS OF PERSONAL OR FAMILY PROBLEMS.*** Nothing will kill a group more quickly than broken confidences — nothing!

On a more limited basis, any Sunday School class could take ten minutes out of their class opening to break into small prayer groups and intercede for the church and one another. Or perhaps the class could meet together at a separate time once a month for a prayer time. Certainly every class should develop some form of prayer ministry for its members.

Another similar program is to develop a "Prayer Partners" ministry. Rather than a group of three to eight people, Prayer Partners are pairs of Christians who pray for each other and the needs of those about them. Here is one form of this program:

1. Decide you want to invest your time and energy in seeking God's presence with another Christian. Make it a priority in your life.

218

2. Find a partner. Pray for God's help and wisdom, then look for people who need to give and need to receive the blessings of God in prayer.

3. Recruit that person for a three month commitment. Tell him/her: you want him/her to consider being your prayer partner, why you want a prayer partner, why you chose them, and that the commitment is for one hour weekly for three months. Let him/her ask questions and give him/her a day or two to think about their decision. If that person says "No," then thank him/her for his/her honesty and consideration. Then look for another. When you find a willing partner, then:

4. Set a regular weekly meeting time and BE THERE to pray together. Praise and thank God. Intercede for each other and for specific prayer targets you choose. Write down requests and answers. Make giving God glory the purpose of your prayers. KEEP CONFIDENCES.

5. Anticipate the partnership getting stuck somewhere along the line (loss of interest, disruptive situations, even hurt feelings). If one meeting time gets jammed, change it. If feelings get hurt, seek forgiveness and reconciliation. If boredom sets in, you are probably not praying about the concerns that you really feel are important to you. Open up, share the hurt and give it to God.

6. At the end of two and a half months, recruit a new prayer partner and encourage your present partner to do the same. Multiply this ministry.[26]

Prayer Partner programs have also been used by Sunday School classes and women's groups. One approach is for a group to draw names for partners at random and then change partners each quarter. A time is then set aside as the group meets for the partners to pray together.

Another program which incorporates family group prayer with intercession for the lost is the "Prayer Outreach Warrior" ministry.[27] Any person or family who commits themselves to this ministry agrees for one year to do the following:

---

26. This program was presented by Carol Jackson at a North American Christian Convention workshop on "Effective Personal Ministries For Women" on July 7, 1986 at Indianapolis, Indiana.

27. This program was developed by John E. Wasem, Minister of Outreach at East 91st Street Christian Church, Indianapolis.

1. Pray daily as an individual or family for up to ten individuals or families who are prospects for evangelism or membership.

2. Pray daily as an individual or family for the church's evangelism ministry, for one specific evangelistic worker and for one newly established congregation as assigned.

3. Check your P.O.W. [Prayer Outreach Warrior] box for new assignments, updates, personal requests from evangelistic team members, etc. When a person on your list makes a commitment to Christ, you will receive a written notice of this praiseworthy event.

4. Attend annual Outreach Celebration and occasional P.O.W. fellowships.

5. Use "I'm Praying for You" cards to encourage those for whom you are interceding.

6. Consider becoming trained to share in evangelism yourself.

Prayer warrior ministries also can utilize those who are retired, homebound or handicapped who may have more time available to devote themselves to a ministry of prayer. For many people who live alone, such ministries vitally involve them in the work of the family of God on a daily basis. Also, prayer warrior ministries can be set up for a limited time to back a calling campaign, revival calling, area door-to-door survey or other outreach ministry.

One final suggested intercessory ministry for small groups is the prayer chain, a program already used by many congregations. Those who desire to be involved in this ministry are divided into "prayer chain" of five to seven families.[28] The telephone is then used to reach the leaders of each chain when a special prayer need arises. Each leader then sends the request through his/her chain where each family prays for the need. A sample instruction sheet is illustrated on the next page.

Other small group ministries in prayer are being originated daily. So this list is again only suggestive of what you might do in your church.

What are some intercession ideas for congregations?

The most obvious place where we see prayer in the congregational

---

28. Some churches arbitrarily put every church family on a prayer chain. The result is often that some disgruntled member family will break the chain consistently since they did not originally want to be on the chain.

setting is in the worship service. Here are some ideas concerning public prayers and congregational prayers.

Public prayers are by their nature intercessory. They are prayed by a leader who speaks on behalf of the congregation. These prayers are not then to be personal petitions or undercover sermons with three points hiding between an "Our Father" and an "Amen." The public prayers in our services usually include the following: the opening prayer, the prayer for the present congregational needs, the prayer(s) for the Lord's Supper, the prayer(s) for the tithes and offerings and the closing prayer.

Sample Prayer Chain Instruction Sheet

Name _____

You Are A Living Link Of Prayer

What is a Prayer Chain?

A Prayer Chain is a way to communicate urgent prayer needs of those we know to many Christians in a short time. Then we can call to the Father on behalf of those in need together. Your involvement will require making one or two phone calls and praying for the needs involved with your family (if possible).

How does the Prayer Chain work?

1. An urgent need arises. Any person knowing this need calls the Prayer Chain Coordinator (name   ) at (phone number   ).

2. The Coordinator calls the group leaders in our Chain. Your group is shown here. The Leader is the first family listed.

3. Each Leader gets the facts straight and then calls the next family in his group list. [After calling, the Leader family prays for the need.]

4. The Leader explains the need to family #1 carefully. Family # 1 then calls family #2 and relays the need. No answer? Skip to the next family. Later, try to reach those you skipped. [After reaching another family, each family prays.]

5. Each family calls the next until the chain is completed. The last family then calls the Leader. The Leader relays this back to the coordinator.

IF YOU ARE AWARE OF AN URGENT NEED,
CALL (PHONE NUMBER   ) IMMEDIATELY.
LINK OUR CHURCH TO GOD'S POWER IN PRAYER.
THANK YOU FOR LINKING UP.

221

prayer (s) (benediction). Before looking at each of these, consider these general rules for public prayer.

1. *Speak so that you can be heard.* If no one can hear you, it doesn't matter what you say. You are directing the prayers of the congregation, but, if you mumble or whisper, they are left unled (and annoyed). If you have a microphone available, learn to use it to full advantage. If not, lift your head up, speak with a full voice and fully face the congregation. This may not sound reverent if you equate reverence with the style we use for private prayer. But public prayer is irreverent when we ignore the needs of the congregation to share our prayer merely to sustain a personal feeling of sanctity. So speak up and out.

2. *Speak so that you can be understood.* This rule involves both clarity of delivery and message. Our delivery should be clear and crisp, pronounced so that each word is understandable to the last pew.

Also try to rid yourself of annoying cliches and speech patterns. Cliches often come in phrases in public prayers: "each and every," "guide, guard and direct," "the sick and afflicted," "as we gather in Thy house" and "bless all the missionaries at home and on foreign shores." These are lazy ways to pray without thought or involvement. They can be replaced by a little forethought and by slowing down just a little to think about what you are saying.

Speech patterns which annoy are many. One is to say "uh" whenever we pause (I guess out of fear of silence or of people thinking we do not know what to say next). Another is to address the Father in every sentence, like this: "*Lord*, I thank You, *Lord* for being here today with us, *Lord*. And, *Lord*, I ask that You hear us, *Lord*, as we lift our prayers to You, *Lord*." Sadly, those who do this the most often do not even know that they are doing it. They don't hear the "uhs" or extra "Lords." Those words are just stuck in to replace pauses. There are two ways to check to see if *you* are guilty of these (or other) annoying speech habits. One, ask a good honest friend to help you improve your public prayer by listening to your next presentation and give you an honest evaluation. Two, listen to a tape recording of yourself praying (make sure you are sitting down when you do). If the "uhs" don't get you, the "whistling t's" or "nasal twang" may. So make yourself easy to listen to.

But the content should also be understandable. It should be simple. The more flowery we try to get, the more we lose people. Neither God nor most people are impressed by elaborate phrases anyway. If "Thou most holy and ineffable Benefactor, Beloved of multitudes and Supreme Majesty enthroned eternally upon the beatific exaltations of the boundless ages" means "Dear Lord," say "Dear Lord." Strive for simplicity. For help, reread the Lord's Prayer and use it as your model.

If "Thees" and "Thous" just naturally flow into your normal prayers, then perhaps they can be used without major problems. But do not try to use them simply because your grandfather did or because the King James Bible did. The King James Bible used those words because they were the most understandable, common usage of its day, A. D. 1611. If you have a choice, speak in the style your hearers learned in school to be correct usage for today. I doubt if that included "Thee's" and "Thou's."

3. *Speak so that you can be believed.* Some public prayers simply do not feel real. You do not believe the speaker actually believes he is speaking to God. He may be repeating beautiful words from memory or making a good theological point, but he is not praying, not in touch with the Almighty One. This happens when the speaker either prays without thinking or uses his prayer to speak to the congregation. One is praying to himself, the other is praying to the people; but neither is praying to God. Pause before you pray and focus your mind on the eternal Father, revealed in our Lord Jesus Christ. Speak to Him for this group of people that both you and He love, and the congregation will not think to doubt that you have truly prayed for them.

Now, back to the five prayers we use in morning worship; here are a few suggestions on making each effective.

1. *The opening prayer or invocation* — The purpose of this prayer is to prepare the people for worship by recognizing the presence of God and our need to honor and praise Him. It should be short and straight to the point. One or two sentences should do it. Do not give in to temptation to set the mood with warm words; we seek to ask God to prepare hearts, not manipulate men into a set mood.

2. *The prayer for congregational needs or pastoral prayer* — This prayer varies most widely among our churches. It is the prayer that follows the prayer hymn (if there is one) or is simply the major prayer of the services. Of this prayer, the renowned preacher Charles Haddon Spurgeon said:

It is my solemn conviction that the prayer is one of the most weighty, useful and honourable parts of the service, and that it ought to be even more considered than the sermon . . . . if I may have my choice, I will sooner yield up the sermon than the prayer.[29]

For a preacher to give up the sermon for a prayer shows the high value he indeed placed on the pastoral prayer. Of course, this is the same Spurgeon who suggested that this prayer should not be too long but come to an end after ten minutes or so(!).[30] The pastoral prayer usually covers three areas: praise and thanksgiving for the Lord's grace to us, petition for the church and local concerns, and intercession for world concerns and the kingdom of God. An often used form is the "laundry list": "God be with our sick this day; Adam Allen, Betty Burton, Clyde Corker, etc., etc. . . ." This leaves those mentioned without any specific requests on their behalf and also bores the congregation. A printed prayer list could be supplied instead.

Again, this prayer can invite the people to truly approach the Lord with the leader as he prays. But some thought should precede this assignment. Various authors have suggested writing the prayer out or spending half a day in indirect preparation for the prayer. I fear most modern ministers simply do not have the time or interest for such ideas. Instead, in your private devotions on Saturday or Sunday, consider this public prayer, pray about it and perhaps write down a suggestive outline. To this preparation, add final thoughts during the worship service and prepare mentally and spiritually to address God on behalf of His people; it is the most priestly function you may ever undertake.

3. *The prayer(s) for the Lord's Supper or communion prayer* — I say "prayer(s)" due to the varied customs about the communion service. Some churches have two prayers and some one. Those who have two usually designate one for the loaf and one for the cup.[31] The pur-

---

29. *Lectures to My Students* (rpt. Grand Rapids, Michigan: Zondervan Publishing House, 1972), pp. 58-59.

30. *Ibid.*, p. 61. Note: the longest prayer recorded in Scripture can be said in about eight minutes.

31. Biblically, Matthew 26:26-27 and Mark 14:22-24 state that Jesus gave thanks for the loaf and again for the cup. In Luke 22:19-20 and I Corinthians 11:23-25, the second blessing is not specifically mentioned (but implied).

pose for both is to remind the congregation of the meaning of the emblems, to give thanks for what Jesus did for us and to ask God to help prepare us to receive the Lord's Supper as we ought. Preparation for these prayers is also required to keep them fresh, simple and real. Notably, these prayers are NOT to wander over the sicklist again or nuclear disarmament; the focus is strictly on the self-giving of Jesus Christ for our sins and our proper responses to that giving. Dr. James G. Van Buren concludes:

> Finally, Communion prayers should be *brief*. Mostly the emblems speak for themselves . . . . These do not need elaboration. A few words of reminder and dedication should suffice.[32]

In fact, these wise words could also apply equally well to the communion devotions; but I digress.

4. *The prayer(s) for the tithes and offerings or offertory* — Again, "prayer(s)" is used to refer to differing traditions in our churches. Some have a single prayer before *or* after the offering, while others have a prayer before *and* after the offering. Any prayer before the offering should generally ask God on behalf of the people to receive their offerings and the self-dedication those gifts represent. If the prayer follows the receiving of the offering, the theme should be setting these gifts apart to God's service and glory. And here also, no extraneous subjects should be injected in the offertory prayer; center on our gifts given in response to God's vast gracious gifts culminating in our salvation in Jesus Christ.

5. *The closing prayer(s) or benedictions* — Three forms of benedictions are commonly used: the concluding sermonic prayer, the leader's benediction and the volunteer benediction. The concluding sermonic benediction is used by the minister to draw together the point of his preaching and ask God to make it a reality in the lives of the people. It may be said before or after a decision time. Its primary danger is to become a summary of the sermon, seeking to preach at the congregation one last time. Its benefit is to provide a framework for people to make a commitment in prayer to change for the good with His em-

---

32. "Questions and Comments," *The Lookout*, March 16, 1986, p. 9. Italics in the original.

powerment. If used, the preacher would be well advised to plan it as he writes his sermon. This ending prayer is sometimes used with one or both of the other benedictions.

The leader's benediction is usually offered by the minister or worship leader and is a pure intercession, asking for the blessing of God on His people as they go out to serve Him. Biblical blessings include the following:

The "Priestly" Blessing: Numbers 6:24-26.

The "Apostolic" Blessing: II Corinthians 13:14.

The "Covenant" Blessing: Hebrews 13:20-21.

The Pauline Blessings: Romans 15:5-6, 13; Galatians 6:18; Ephesians 6:23-24; II Thessalonians 2:16-17 and 3:16.

Like its Biblical counterparts (which may be used), the leader's blessing should be a solemn and joyful committal of the people to the blessing and service of God.

The volunteer benediction is often used in smaller churches where a member of the congregation closes the service with prayer, normally remaining wherever he was seated. Sometimes the person is asked to so serve in advance, which is good since it gives the person a chance to prepare for the assignment. But too often the preacher or worship leader just looks out, chooses someone and says, "Joe, will you have our closing prayer this morning? Shall we pray?" The first question is rhetorical (Joe *will* have the closing prayer) and the second question is a statement (translate it, "Time to pray; bow your head and be quiet!"). This "fast draw" approach has so many problems that I only have room to mention two: one, eventually only a small handful of agreeable and vocal men will be praying, and two, those who have a hard time with public prayer have a miserable last half of service just worrying if they will get "picked on" this Sunday. If a volunteer benediction is desired, give the person involved as good an advance notice as possible out of courtesy and common sense.

A second area of prayers in the worship service is the area of congregational prayers. At least four main types of congregational prayers are used: silent prayers, directed prayers, requested prayers and "body life" prayers. Very quickly let us review these four types.

Silent congregational prayers occur when a time is intentionally left in a service and announced as a time for silent prayer. Generally the weakness of this approach is that there is no agreement on specific intercessory requests among the believers as they pray. Merely sitting by another person does not make you of one mind with that person (as many spouses know).

Directed congregational prayers take silent prayers one step further. The person leading the service suggests a given topic and directs the congregation in how they might intercede together. For example, he might say, "As John Smith enters the hospital this week, ask the Lord for peace for John and Mary as they face this crisis. Ask that they may be His witnesses in the hospital to the staff and patients." Then the congregation would pray together silently as suggested. Then another prayer need would be announced; and so on, through the prayer time.

Requested congregational prayer has the individual Christian informing the worship leader of prayer needs of which he/she is aware. This can be done by simply asking those who have requests to stand up and share them verbally with the congregation as the leader recognizes them. Other churches have prayer request cards for members and visitors to fill in weekly as needed. These cards are collected early in the service and brought to the worship leader to be shared with the congregation during the pastoral prayer or directed prayer times. One form for these prayer request cards is shown below. Use it to spur your own ideas for such a card.

Prayer Request

Write your request for prayer below:

_____

_____

_____

_____

If your name is here _____ the minister *will* read the request to the congregation.

If your name is here _____ the minister *will not* read the request to the congregation.

If you want us to notify the party involved, by letter, that we are praying for them, write on the reverse side of this card the proper name and full address of the person who should receive such a letter. _____

"Body life" congregational prayer is a concept developed by the ministry of Ray Stedman at Peninsula Bible Church in Palo Alto, California.[33] In this form of worship, personal prayer needs are shared from members of the congregation freely. Then, immediately, another person who can identify with the need goes to the one requesting prayer and, standing with them, leads the congregation in prayer for him/her. Many times needs are met during the service by other members of the church sharing what they have. This kind of free form prayer time requires strong spiritual leadership to keep it on track. Note that this form was used during evening services at Peninsula Bible Church and that the services normally are composed primarily of young people (approximately eighty per cent under twenty-five years old). Much groundwork is required to successfully move toward such a service. Obviously many churches have worship services which incorporate aspects of all four kinds of congregational intercession.

Aside from intercession in worship services, the congregation can establish a variety of ministries to involve its people in this vital task. Here are just a few:

1. *Prayer seminars or classes* — Having taught prayer seminars in several states, I know how such an intensive period of study and experience in prayer can turn a church around in its attitude toward prayer ministry. Classes can provide continuing instruction and motivation about prayer. New Christians especially need education in prayer.

2. *Prayer-backed evangelism* — In the book of Acts, the disciples prayed for ten days and preached one day, Pentecost. Recent "revivals" normally have prayer for one day (perhaps) and preaching for ten days. Perhaps if we followed the prayer to preaching ratio of Pentecost, we would have the results of Pentecost. Every effort in evangelism should be drenched in intercession.

3. *Prayer Vigils* — For special congregational needs, twenty-four hour (or longer) prayer vigils can be established. A sign-up sheet with half-hour segments can be filled in by members and member families who agree to pray for that specific need during that specified time. A prayer room can be set up in the church for those who would choose to come and pray at the church building. An all-church fast may be

---

33. *Body Life* (2d ed.; Glendale, California: Regal Books, 1977), pp. 155-159 and 169-176.

associated with the vigil or held separately.

4. *Printed Prayer Materials* — Aside from books, pamphlets and lessons encouraging intercession, the church may produce and/or distribute many kinds of prayer-oriented materials. Regularly updated prayer lists should be included in bulletins and newsletters (be sure to include praises for answered prayers). Print a year of calendar sheets with different prayer requests given for each day; for member families, for staff, for supported missionaries, for growth of specific Sunday School classes, for the teachers, for each special event, and so on. "Prayer-A-Grams" can be supplied so that those who intercede can inform those they pray for of their prayers and loving concern. "You were remembered" notes can be sent to those who are prayed for during worship services, prayer groups or class meetings.

5. *Regular Prayer Meetings* — Weekly, monthly or quarterly meetings can be set for the specific purpose of praying for the needs of the congregation and the kingdom of God.

6. *Annual Prayer Retreat* — Especially for leadership families, an annual two-day prayer retreat can have life-changing results. Such a retreat is uniquely suited to preparation for long or short-range planning times.

7. *Prayer Room* — A room in the church permanently set aside for prayers says to members and visitors that prayer is important to the life of this congregation. Such a room should be well heated and ventilated and accessible. It should be large enough for a family or prayer cell to use. Furnishings can be simple, from folding chairs to a sofa and kneeling bench. Indirect, soft lighting helps to set a mood of worship. A Bible, hymnbook, prayer list and pen should be laid out. Carpeting, a missions bulletin board and world map are additional ideas. Make it simple, attractive and inviting. Encourage its use regularly.

8. *Prayer Line Call-in Service* — A phone-in service for the congregation and community can be staffed by trained volunteers to share in prayer with those who call in with specific needs. This program can be a great service; it also requires a strong commitment to serving through prayer.

For any of these ministries to get underway, the leadership of the church and specifically the minister must be committed to the need for prayer ministry. They must know how to pray themselves and model this before the congregation (Acts 6:4). The minister and elders should be regularly and systematically praying for the members of their congregation. They also need to pray for each other and their families, since they are prime targets for Satan's attack.[34] Then, prayer must be encouraged in the pulpit and in the classroom. Finally, the leadership is responsible to see that an ongoing ministry of prayer is planned and carried out in their local congregation.

In conclusion, for the process of intercession to function, we need to learn to trust other Christians enough to share our real needs with them and allow them to pray for us. We need to both receive and give intercession's blessings. But, as always, we will find it is more blessed to give.

Thought or Discussion Questions

1. Why would failing to intercede for others be considered a sin (I Samuel 12:23)? How would you explain to a nine-year-old child the reasons why we should pray for others? Why *does* God use our intercession to accomplish tasks that He already desires to do? How does praying for someone change our attitude toward that person? Is there someone toward whom you need to change your attitude? Would you be willing to use intercession as a tool to help your attitude development? Starting when?

2. How can intercession change the members of your church? How does it empower them? Think of a family in your congregation who has gone through a severe crisis recently. How could the concerted intercession of fellow Christians have changed the situation or their reaction to the situation? Is there another family *presently* passing through a fire of stress who could use your intercession? Will you give the time and effort to support them and encourage others to pray as well? How can our prayers affect our society? Who is involved with the ministry of intercession? How?

3. What kinds of aid may we request for others? What can we NOT ask

---

34. A helpful devotional book for ministers is: Terry Muck, *Liberating the Leader's Prayer Life* (Waco, Texas: Word Books, 1985).

for others? What special blessings can we ask for governmental officials? Explain what is meant by the term "confessional intercession"? How do we go about interceding for others by confessing sin on their behalf? How do we support evangelistic efforts with intercession? What is the relationship between intercession, love and unity?

4. What people are your special prayer targets? How do you decide? What are the four basic steps of intercession? How does a written prayer list aid our prayer? How important is it for us to emotionally identify with those we pray for? Why? Should we pray for others without trying to help them? Why? Should we try to help others without praying for them? Why?

5. What are the benefits of praying together as a group for a family? What about as a small group of Christians? What are the six "S's" of conversational prayer? Have you tried conversational prayer? If not, will you? Describe conversational prayer for someone who has never experienced it. If a family member is away from home, what methods can be used to keep close through intercessory prayer?

6. Describe how to start a small prayer group or cell. What are some guide lines for such a group? Do you see a need for one or more of such groups in your church? How would you go about finding and ministering with a Prayer Partner? What other small group intercessory ministries can you think of? What are three general rules for public prayers? How could the prayer in your worship services be improved? What kind of congregational prayer does your church have? Would you like to try any others? If so, which? What prayer ministries does your church have in place right now? Which would you like to change? How? What new ministries of intercession would you like to be involved in? How is your present church leadership encouraging prayer ministry? How will you pray for your leaders to grow in this area?

8

WHAT ARE THE PARTS OF PRAYER?
V. CONFESSION

We sin. God hates sin. Now what?

What do we do about our moral failures? Men have struggled with that essential question since Eden. Basically, two answers have become the most popular. Jesus told us a parable which illustrates these two responses to sin.

> Two men went up into the temple to pray, one a Pharisee, and the other a tax-gatherer. The Pharisee stood and was praying thus to himself, "God, I thank Thee that I am not like other people: swindlers, unjust, adulterers, or even like this tax-gatherer. I fast twice a week; I pay tithes of all I get" (Luke 18:10-12).

Here is the first response to sin: confidence in pride. The Pharisee uses two lines of argument to defend his own (assumed) holiness; one,he compares his life with others, and, two, he points to what he had given up for God. The first argument goes clear back to Adam and Eve. When God confronts Adam with his sin, he points to Eve; when

God turns to Eve, she points at the snake (Genesis 3:11-13). The hope is to get God to concentrate on others we feel are more guilty than ourselves. We console ourselves with lines like, "Well, I may X [my pet public sin], but at least I don't Z [a horrendous sin which I have not committed . . . yet]." We try to reach God by standing on the backs of "worse" sinners than ourselves.

The second argument of the Pharisee is how much he has given up for God. He fasts and pays his tithes faithfully. Essentially, he has paid God off; now that his dues are in he should be free to live life as a paid-up member of the "Beloved of God Club." Men around the world have tried to placate God with gifts and rituals. If we comply with the low standards we set for being "good enough," we then feel free to ignore the rest of our sin. Jesus calls the Pharisee's attitude, "self-exaltation" (Luke 18:14). Or we would call it pride.

Today we are told, "Love yourself," and "Stand up tall," and "Assert yourself." But this pride, this arrogance, does not change the facts. We are not better than anyone else, "for all have turned aside, together they have become useless; there is none who does good, not even one" (Psalm 14:3; Romans 3:12). And our gifts to God are useless when we continue in our evil ways (Isaiah 1:10-17). The confidence in pride of the Pharisee does not remove our sin; it multiplies it.

The second response to sin is seen in the second character in Jesus' parable, the tax-gatherer:

> But the tax-gatherer, standing some distance away, was even unwilling to lift up his eyes to heaven, but was beating his breast, saying, "God, be merciful to me, the sinner!" I tell you, this man went down to his house justified rather than the other, for everyone who exalts himself shall be humbled, but he who humbles himself shall be exalted (Luke 18:13-14).

The response of the tax-gatherer was a confession in humility. To deny our sin is to invite God's judgment to humble us. To admit our sin is to invite God's mercy to exalt us. This admission of who we really are and what we really have done is the fifth part of prayer, confession. There are no arguments to bring before God in confession; no excuses, no "mitigating circumstances." Simply, confession admits I am the "sinner," and yet trusts the love of God sufficiently to ask for His mercy.

CONFESSION: TALKING TO GOD ABOUT OUR SIN

To understand confession, Jesus has given us an image in His most famous parable, the prodigal son. After the son has separated himself from his father both physically and morally, he discovers that the "high" life of sin only leads to the depths of despair. As he decides to return to his father, he composes in his mind words to use when he comes to his home again in shame.

> I will get up and go to my father, and will say to him, "Father, I have sinned against heaven, and in your sight; I am no longer worthy to be called your son; make me as one of your hired men" (Luke 15:18-19).

Imagine his amazement and brokeness when he finds his father running to him, embracing him and kissing him before the son can even get the words of confession out. His wildest dreams are realized; he is not only forgiven, he is a *son* again. Likewise, in confession, we find that, "however far the soul has wandered, the path of prayer is the way home."[1]

Confession of sin has been misunderstood to mean that each sin we commit moves us from being saved to being lost and only by confession can we move back to the state of salvation. This frightful "roller coaster" view of the Christian life leaves many Christians with no assurance of salvation. So many struggle with such questions as, "Did I name *all* my sins last confession?" and "What if I die without being able to confess my last sins?" This is not God's will for us; we are to *know* that we have eternal life, not wonder about it day by day (I John 5:13). But how do we get off the "roller coaster'" and *know* we are saved in Jesus Christ?

We need to understand that our salvation is both a position and a process. Our position is in Jesus Christ (I John 5:20, and many others). In Jesus Christ, "by [the] will [of God], we have been made holy through the sacrifice of the body of Jesus Christ *once for all*" (Hebrews 10:10, NIV). Now how many of our sins did Jesus die for? "The blood

---

1. Gerald Heard quoted in Osborne Miller, comp., *The Path of Prayer* (New York: Harper and Brothers, 1954), p. 111.

of Jesus His Son cleanses us from *all* sin" (I John 1:7). A spiritual exchange has taken place; "[God] made [Christ] who knew no sin to be
sin on our behalf, that we might become the righteousness of God in
Him" (II Corinthians 5:21). This is our present position in Jesus Christ,
clothed in His righteousness in the eyes of God. We are saved from the
wrath of God, for "there is therefore now no condemnation for those
who are in Christ Jesus" (Romans 8:1). In our position, we are certain
of our salvation because it rests entirely in what Christ has done for us.

In the process of salvation, we are *becoming* day by day what we
already *are* spiritually according to our position in Christ. We develop
holiness as we put off sin and put on the character of Christ (II Corinthians 7:1; II Peter 1:5-11). Because this process will not be complete
until death (or the coming of Christ), we are left falling short of the
perfection we desire (Philippians 3:12-14; I John 3:2-3). These sins,
these thoughts, words and deeds falling short of the perfect life of
Christ, we confess to God, but NOT because we have lost our salvation
by being imperfect.

We confess that we have sinned because it is the truth. To deny the
truth would keep us from understanding God's word and having open
fellowship with the Lord (I John 1:6-10). As we hide our sin like Adam
and Eve, we would have to hide ourselves from God. We would still be
His children in Christ; but, like naughty children, not enjoying His love
and fellowship. Confession does not restore to us a salvation we lost by
momentary sins; we never lost it. Rather, confession opens us up to
return to a fellowship with the Father in truth which our momentary sins
had broken.

What is confession? The very word used in the New Testament
describes what it means. The word translated "confess" in our Bibles is
the word *homologeo* in the original language, Greek. This word is a
compound of two other words; *homos*, which means, "the same," and
lego, which means, "to say." So, *homologeo* means "to say the same"
or "to agree in one's statements."[2] Confession, then, means to agree
with God concerning His judgment of our thoughts, words and actions.
We admit what God already knows; we have sinned.

---

2. Dieter Furst, "Confess," *The New International Dictionary of New Testament
Theology,* Colin Brown, ed., I (Grand Rapids, Michigan: Zondervan Publishing House,
1975), p. 344. The intensive prefix *ex-* is added in some cases.

The opposite of confess is to deny (John 1:20; I John 2:23). We can deny our sin as the Pharisee did, by pointing to the sin of others or to our own good deeds. But his does not fool the Lord. He knows our sins whether we admit them or deny them. We deny or contradict God about or sins because it is painful for us to face them. We hate to admit our own failure and weakness. It hurts the proud self-image we build up. But it is the truth, and our growth and spiritual health require we stop denying the facts and accept who we are.

Confession of sins is part of the larger process of repentance. Great crowds accepted the central commandment of the preaching of John the Baptist: to "repent." Part of the process of gaining forgiveness for their sins was that "they confessed their sins" (Matthew 3:2, 5-6 and 11). We will discuss the repentance process later in this chapter.

Two extremes of self-examination are often associated in certain people's minds with repentance, but they are not at all what the Lord calls us to do.[3] One extreme is merciless self-flagellation; such as, "God, what a miserable wretch I am! I am loathsome and unspeakably vile. How can You even stand my existence? Wouldn't it be better if I never was? Yuch! I hate myself!" This is not humility; this is spiritual masochism. The other extreme is casual evasion; such as "Well, Lord, maybe I did become annoyed with John, but I wasn't *really* angry. Anyone would have been hurt with the superior way he talked to me. After all, I've seen him more upset than I was. And Carol agreed that the whole thing was *his* fault, not mine." Here the "confession" is more an attempt to escape responsibility than an honest evaluation of my behavior in the light of God's standards. Neither excoriation nor excusing are the confession God requires.

One of the classic confessional prayers is the fifty-first Psalm, David's confession of his sin with Bathsheba, including the murder of her husband Uriah. A look at the first four verses will show us some basic components of confession.

Verse	Comment
1. Be gracious to me, O God, according to Thy lovingkindness; according to the greatness of Thy compassion blot out my transgressions.	The basis for the forgiveness requested is not David's goodness, but solely the gracious nature of the Lord himself.

---

3. George Arthur Buttrick, *Prayer* (New York: Pillar Books, 1942), p. 296-297.

2. Wash me thoroughly from my iniquity, and cleanse me from my sin.	David admits his moral uncleanness, and only God can cleanse him, not any good work or sacrifice or other ritual.
3. For I know my transgressions, and my sin is ever before me.	David fully and honestly faces what he has done and does not turn away or ignore it.
4. Against Thee, Thee only, I have sinned, and done evil in Thy sight,	David realizes that sin hurts God more than even Uriah, whom he killed. God is always the principal offended Party. Also God saw every sin as it was being done; He is always a witness against our sins.
So that Thou art justified when Thou dost speak, and blameless when Thou dost judge.	David admits that he deserves God's judgment, not His forgiveness; yet he does ask that he be renewed and restored as he comes with a "broken and a contrite heart" (verse 17).

Confession is the fifth part of prayer in our analysis (even though some see it as a specialized form of petition). We are going to see why we are to confess our sins and how we go about it.

WHY DO WE CONFESS OUR SIN?

The Bible suggests four reasons why we should accept the difficult assignment of regular confession in prayer.

Confession is commanded by the Lord.

One of the lines of the model prayer which we are to imitate reads, "Forgive us our debts, as we also have forgiven our debtors" (Matthew 6:12). The debts here are clearly moral debts, obedience we have not paid to God as we ought (Matthew 6:14-15). Asking for forgiveness of our sins requires we confess those sins exist and that we are guilty of them and thus need God's forgiveness.

John writes the clearest passage about confession in his first epistle:

238

If we say that we have fellowship with [God] and yet walk in the darkness, we lie and do not practice the truth; but if we walk in the light as He Himself is in the light, we have fellowship with one another, and the blood of Jesus His Son cleanses us from all sin. If we say that we have no sin, we are deceiving ourselves, and the truth is not in us. If we confess our sins, He is faithful and righteous to forgive us our sins and to cleanse us from all unrighteousness. If we say that we have not sinned, we make Him a liar, and His word is not in us (I John 1:6-10).

Surrounding it with stern warnings not to deny the sin in us, John wrote a great promise of forgiveness and cleansing based firmly on the faithfulness and righteousness of God Himself. But there is a prerequisite to receiving these blessings; we must confess our sins. Any attempt to receiving these blessings; we must confess our sins. Any attempt to deny that we have any sins to confess would give evidence to four dreadful facts: we are self-deceived, we do not have the truth, we make God a liar and we do not have His word.

As we noted earlier, confession is a part of the greater process of repentance. Commands to repent run through the New Testament. It was the command of John the Baptist (Matthew 3:2). It was the initial command of Christ's ministry (Mark 1:14-15). It was the command of Christ in the midst of His ministry (Matthew 11:20; Luke 13:2-3). It was the command Christ sent out at the end of His earthly ministry (Luke 24:46-47). It was the fist command of the preaching of the early church (Acts 2:38; 3:19 and 26:20). It is God's command to all men everywhere (Acts 17:30).

Examples of confession also run through all the Scriptures. Confession was specifically commanded to Israel in the law of Moses (Numbers 5:5-7). Aaron was told to confess the sins of Israel on the Day of Atonement (Leviticus 16:21). Achan was commanded to confess after he stole treasure from the destruction of Jericho (Joshua 7:19-21). Jeremiah called for Israel to confess her sins (Jeremiah 3:12-14). Ezra told those who had married foreign wives to make confession of what they had done (Ezra 10:11). Among those who confessed their sin, we hear Balaam, Saul, David, and Peter (Numbers 22:34; I Samuel 15:24; II Samuel 12:13 and Luke 5:8). Confession is well attested to as God's will for sinners by command and example. "Take words with you and return to the Lord. Say to Him, 'Take away all iniquity, and receive us graciously' " (Hosea 14:2).

Confession makes effective prayer possible.

A major reason for us to incorporate confession regularly into our prayerlife is the fact that our sin blocks our prayers. "No one can both sin and pray. True prayer will prevent us from sinning, or sin will prevent us from praying."[4] The Lord confirms this is Isaiah's writings:

Behold, the Lord's hand is not so short that it cannot save; neither is His ear so dull that it cannot hear. But your iniquities have made a separation between you and your God, and your sins have hidden His face from you, so that He does not hear (Isaiah 59:1-2).

And the Scripture also indicates that our awareness of our sins prevents our prayers from being effective. "If I regard wickedness in my heart, the Lord will not hear" (Psalm 66:18). For this among other reasons, Charles Spurgeon wrote, "For a successful season of prayer the best beginning is confession."[5]

Confession relieves the pressure of guilt and fear.

Guilt is a burden beyond the strength of anyone to bear for long. Slowing but surely it will crush us. Even physical discomfort and insomnia follow us around until we deal with our guilt. David knew this truth all too well. Hear his testimony in the Psalms:

How blessed is he whose transgression is forgiven, whose sin is covered! How blessed is the man to whom the Lord does not impute iniquity, and in whose spirit there is no deceit!

---

4. Lehman Strauss, *Sense and Nonsense about Prayer* (Chicago: Moody Press, 1974), p. 24.
5. *Twelve Sermons on Prayer* (Grand Rapids, Michigan: Baker Book House, 1971), p. 49.

When I kept silent about my sin, my body wasted away through my groaning all day long. For day and night Thy hand was heavy upon me; my vitality was drained away as with the fever heat of summer (Psalm 32:1-4).

Ouch! That description is far too familiar for my comfort. I have been that miserable with the plague of guilt; haven't you? And David even notes that this is the result of God's direct (and gracious) pressure, His heavy hand on us. Obviously, if we sinned and then felt great about it and life went by wonderfully, what motivation would we have to change? But guilt is a great motivator. That's why the Internal Revenue Service gets thousands of dollars every year from anonymous citizens who have cheated on their taxes. The guilt gets so great that they break down and send in some or all of the money they owe. But I wonder if they really are free from their guilt. For David goes on to prescribe the antidote for guilt.

I acknowledged my sin to Thee, and my iniquity I did not hide; I said, "I will confess my transgressions to the Lord"; and Thou didst forgive the guilt of my sin (Psalm 32:5).

Have you ever considered why people would willingly continue under the weight of guilt? Why doesn't everyone repent, confess their sins and find forgiveness? Let me suggest three reasons why people experience continuing quilt.

Guilt continues because forgiveness is undesired. Some people simply do not seek forgiveness from God because they intend to continue their sin. These people include those outside of Christ but, sadly, also includes those who had once claimed Him as Savior and Lord. The latter fell away to pursue their desires and now "it is impossible to renew them again to repentance" (Hebrews 6:4-8). They are like those in Israel described by Jeremiah.

Thus says the Lord, "Stand by the ways and see and ask for the ancient paths, where the good way is and walk in it; and you shall find rest for your souls. But they said, 'We will not walk in it.' And I set watchmen over you, saying, 'Listen to the sound of the trumpet!' But they said, 'We will not listen' " (Jeremiah 6:16-17).

Here is a stiff-necked people asking for disaster. They know they are guilty but remain on the path of sin and destruction anyway. For them, the "passing pleasures of sin" are enough and they want to be their own master, not the Lord. So they pay the price of guilt and judgment and death.

Guilt continues because forgiveness is unasked for. Sometimes we do not feel the weight of guilt as heavily as we might. Then we convince ourselves that the sin was not really wrong, just thoughtless or ill advised. Or we think that the sin is "too small" to bother God with it. Our pride prevents our proper admission of guilt and helplessness in the struggle with temptation. Consider this Old Testament example.

King Hezekiah was considered a godly king in Israel. God protected his life miraculously more than once. But in his latter years, he foolishly took emissaries from Babylon on a detailed tour of his treasure house and armory. In his pride, he disclosed all the secrets of the wealth of God's people. The prophet Isaiah brought word from God that, as a result of his sin, the treasures would all be carried off to Babylon along with some of Hezekiah's sons after they were grown. What was Hezekiah's response to the terrible prophecy? Did he repent of his sin, confess his guilt and beg the Lord's mercy? Hardly.

Then Hezekiah said to Isaiah, "The word of the Lord which you have spoken is good." For he thought, "Is it not so, if there shall be peace and truth in my days?" (II Kings 20:19).

The old king just figured out that, if his sons would have to pay for his sins in the future, that meant his reign would be undisturbed. "So much the better for me," he thought. And he wore his guilt lightly. He did not receive forgiveness since he never thought to ask for it.

Guilt continues because forgiveness is unaccepted. Let us assume that we have felt remorse for our sins and confessed them and asked God for forgiveness. We can *still* miss having our guilt lifted away. For the promise Jesus offers concerning prayer is, "all things for which you pray and ask, *believe that you have received them*, and they shall be granted you" (Mark 11:24). We often refuse to believe in, to accept, the forgiveness we have requested and God has offered. For "prayer is

242

more than asking; prayer is *taking*. Prayer is more than pleading; prayer is *believing*."[6]

God may forgive us but is seems *we* will not forgive us. We listen to our feelings, instead of His promises. We may want to continue to feel guilty for several reasons. We may still find it hard to believe such wonderful persons as we obviously are could have done such a despicable thing; that is, our unrealistic perfectionistic view of ourselves refuses to accept the fact of our sin.

Or perhaps we look into our hearts and realize that nothing has changed; put into a similar situation with a similar temptation, we know we would sin just like we did last time. We have not truly turned away from the sin and drawn on the power of God to change. In fact, we still may cherish the sin and accepting forgiveness might force us to let it go.

Or, finally, perhaps we still see the results of our sin continuing and feel too guilty to allow ourselves to accept forgiveness. The man who used to physically abuse his family still sees fear come into their eyes every time he raises his hand to scratch his head. The ex-gambler looks around at his impoverished home left deep in debt from his past sins. The spouse who has given up the affair still must rebuild the shattered trust within his/her home. The glutton is left pounds of proof of his/her lack of self-control. As long as the results of our sins continue, we may be tempted to take the role of judge away from God and punish ourselves with continuing guilt.

Only full repentance and confession can relieve this guilt. It may hurt to heal these wounds for confession is like a scalpel which must reopen an infected wound with sharp incision to get the infection out and allow it to heal from the bottom up. Our hearts heal from the inside out. We cannot seal over our sin with a lazy, "God has forgiven me; I'm OK now." We have to fully face and fully admit what we have done before God before we can be free of it.

All our excuses for clinging to guilt must be abandoned as we see God extending His hand through Jesus Christ to save us. We reject His love at our own peril, for we are refusing our only true means of gaining peace.

---

6. Ray Stedman, *Jesus Teaches on Prayer* (Waco, Texas: Word Books, Publisher, 1975), p. 35. Emphasis in the original.

God . . . casts all our sins into the deepest sea, the sea of His forgetfulness. Corrie Ten Boom, author and speaker, says, "And we should put up a sign, *no fishing!*" This means also, *no diving*, because once God has forgive us it is a sin against His love for us to either bring up our own or the sins of others.[7]

Aside from guilt, confession also relieves our fears. "Fear has to do with punishment," John tells us (I John 4:18, NIV). Certainly the fear that confession relieves has a great deal to do with both temporal and eternal punishment. While the fear of eternal punishment is obvious to most Christians, our temporal fears are more pressing and somehow harder to handle. The punishment we face for our sin here and now may involve being shown for what we really are, fallible human beings saved by grace alone. But we are afraid to face even the chance of others discovering our faults and weaknesses. And so we deny them.

Fear is the motivating power behind all repressions and suppressions. Guilty fears, the fear of being found out or exposed, of being humiliated, commonly called an "anxiety neurosis" are tremendously damaging and the need here, as with all fear, is to bring the object of dread into the full light and face it. If confession or private examination of conscience can be candid enough, then suppression and repression are overcome.[8]

We are glad to confess the truth of who we are to escape this kind of fear, which is obviously unhealthy and destructive. Yet confession also cooperates with a fear which is healthy.

"The fear of the Lord is the beginning of wisdom" (Psalm 111:10; Proverbs 1:7). Fearing God is wise because He has the ultimate power and judgment. We should not fear the passing persecutions of this life half so much as we totally respect the One who decides who enters eternal life and eternal damnation (Matthew 10:28). Yet, with confession, even this fear is changed into a joyful security that we are loved and forgiven by the Almighty Who is also our Father.

---

7. Rosalind Rinker, *Communicating Love Through Prayer* (Grand Rapids, Michigan: Zondervan Books, 1966), pp. 24-25.
   8. William R. Parker and Elaine St. Johns, *Prayer Can Change Your Life* (Englewood Cliffs, New Jersey: Prentice-Hall, Inc., 1957), p. 65.

Confession allows honest communication with God.

If I were to paste a fake mustache under my nose and pull a hat down over my eyes and then pray, "Hi, God. You know me; I'm Billy Graham," you would have every right to think I was a nut. It would be ridiculous to pretend to be someone else to the Lord God of the universe.

But, oddly enough, that's what many of us try to do. Oh, we do not put on false hair or a costume, but we do hide our true feelings and motives. We "put our best foot forward." Perhaps you have heard someone pray aloud and be surprised to hear them speaking in a totally different voice and style than their normal ones. Do we think that God prefers a mask to who we really are? In our prayer relationship with God, as well as many other areas, we must learn that it is the truth which can make us free; free to be ourselves with our Father without fear (John 8:31-32).

John Powell describes five levels of communication at which we all communicate.[9] Starting with the most superficial level, each additional level reveals a little more of who we really are and is therefore more threatening to us. The more we reveal of ourselves the greater the anguish when what we reveal is rejected by those to whom we disclose ourselves. Consider these levels carefully and ask yourself, "On what level do I normally communicate with God?" and "How open do I *want* to be with my Father?"

FIVE LEVELS OF COMMUNICATION?

[ ] 5. *Cliche Conversation* — In prayer, this consists of phrases which have become so standardized a part of our personal "prayer language" that they have essentially lost all real meaning. "In fact, there is no communication here at all, unless by accident."[10]

[ ] 4. *Reporting the facts about others* — Here is the level of gossip

---

9. John Powell, *Why Am I Afraid To Tell You Who I Am?* (Niles, Illinois: Argus Communications, 1969), pp. 54-62. These were taken from the work of psychologist A. H. Maslow.

10. Ibid., p. 54.

and idle conversation, telling God what's going on with all the involvement of a housewife making out a shopping list. "And I'll need a pound of daily bread . . . . and did I mention my brother is coming in Tuesday? Give him safe travel, of course, and do try to get him to lose a few pounds. Oh, and about my sins, I just haven't been feeling up to holiness lately, what with all we have going on. So You'll understand, won't You?" This describes far too many of our prayers, perhaps not this silly, but with as little thought or involvement.

[ ]   3. *My ideas and my judgments* — At this point we begin to crack the door and reveal a little of who we are. I will tell what I think to some extent, though I will still tend to say things I think God wants me to say. I can grow quite a bit at this level and eventually open my whole mind to God, all that I am thinking (but this is not all there is to communicate). Most mature prayer starts at this level.

[ ]   2. *My feelings or emotions* — These are my deeply personal reactions to what I think and know. I may tell God at level three that I know I need to be a better witness for Him and ask Him to help me. But at level two I add that I am scared stiff that I will freeze up and look stupid and the person I try to witness to will get angry at me and hit me. At level two I tell God how it feels to be me, good, bad or boring. Most of the motives for our words and actions hide at this level; if we never get here, they may remain untouched and we will remain unchanged.

[ ]   1. *Peak communication* — This relatively rare level of communication occurs when two persons trust each other enough and care for each other enough to be totally "in sync." We experience "complete and total personal communion," receiving and giving unqualified acceptance and intimacy. These are the spiritual mountaintops where we feel real oneness with the Lord. Words may even feel unnecessary as we simply enjoy being together with Him, in His presence. This level of communication cannot be programmed; we just grow into it.

The key to moving up to the higher levels of communication is to risk making prayer an exercise in honesty.[11] One of the greatest blocks to such honesty is our self-image; how we see ourselves. We can go to one of two extremes here and miss the truth.

1. *I am fine.* This is the attitude of the Pharisee in the parable we

---

11. Parker and St. Johns, p. 51.

looked at earlier. "Lord, I'm in pretty good shape, don't you think?" Actually, if the Pharisee had not been a member of the religious elite, he probably would not have prayed at all. He had the "Laodicean Languor" mentioned in chapter two of this book. He was comfortable with himself and his life. He had no felt need for God and His forgiveness. We need to re-educate our conscience by a stricter Scripture study and prayerlife. As we examine ourselves in the mirror of the Word and focus our attention upon the Lord in His perfection in prayer, our conscience will learn the true standard against which we are to judge ourselves and the need for repentance will motivate our confessions.

2. *I am nothing.* This attitude also can leave us not praying at all. Some people feel unworthy to pray. They see the church like an airliner with three classes of seating; up front, close to the Pilot (God), are the first class passengers (preachers and missionaries). Then, in second class, where they see movies about the Pilot, are the second class passengers (elders, some deacons and Sunday School teachers). Finally, stuck back in the tail, is tourist class ("just" members, "laymen"). Once a week, someone in first class gets on the PA System to tell the tourists how great it is to know the Pilot (whom they have never seen). Obviously, the feelings this (overstated) illustration represent would leave the "tourists" feeling less than open to share with the Pilot on an intimate basis. But God keeps no such classification system; all who come before Him in prayer can come boldly through the blood of Jesus Christ shed for them (Hebrews 10:19-22).

There is a spiritual danger here. We can too easily accept the self-description that we are "no good" because that means we have "no responsibility" to even try. Or we can babble on to God about being such terrible sinners when we secretly hope this will impress God (and others) with our humility. Such tactics are a sign of a subtle pride and not real repentance or confession at all.

First, we should stop comparing ourselves with others; only God looks upon the heart and is qualified to judge (Galatians 6:4-5). Second, we should listen to the Bible and approach the Lord in prayer. The Word has many promises to lift us up and in prayer we will find a Father Whose love for us is always "first class."

3. *I am God's child.* As a Christian, I am called to be a child of God,

247

in fellowship with Him, indwelt by His Spirit, a citizen of His kingdom, the salt and light of the earth, a member of the living temple of the Lord God Almighty. The right to be His child has been *given* me; I have not and cannot earn it (John 1:12-13). I can be open with Him because I know this; He really does care about me.

> God is opposed to the proud, but gives grace to the humble. Humble yourselves, therefore, under the mighty hand of God, that He may exalt you at the proper time, casting all your anxiety upon him, because He cares for you (I Peter 5:5b-7).

I know that pride makes God my enemy; I know that continuing remorse rots the soul and my soul is too precious to God to allow it to rot.[12] I know my God has called me to enter into His eternal glory in Christ and that He "will Himself perfect, confirm, strengthen and establish" me (I Peter 5:10). I can trust Him, trust Him enough to be open and honest with Him to the highest levels of communication. I can confess my sins without fearing I will lose His love. He knows me full well AND He loves me still. I confess my sins to continue honest communication with my Father Who is in heaven.

HOW DO WE CONFESS OUR SIN?

The process of confession is not as simple as it may look at first glance. We are trying to be honest with ourselves and with God about who we are without becoming so self-absorbed it becomes a sin in itself. Yet the struggle is worth the peace it brings. Here are ten steps of confession.

1. See yourself as you really are.

The only way to know yourself honestly is to ask someone else. Frankly, we have too much invested in our egos to be objective about

---

12. Hope MacDonald, *Discovering How To Pray* (New York: Pillar Books, 1976), p. 75.

the very sins which condemn us. Only a faithful witness can show us what we are really like. And the best witness for this process is God Himself. The one hundred and thirty-ninth Psalm begins by stating, "O, Lord, Thou hast searched me and known me," and ends with this request:

> Search me, O God, and know my heart; try me and know my anxious thoughts; and see if there be any hurtful way in me, and lead me in the everlasting way (Psalm 139:23-24).

It is beyond doubt that the Lord alone knows us fully and can lead us the way we should be heading to arrive at everlasting life (Psalm 19:12-14). So we begin by asking Him in prayer to show us our sins.

What is the actual process God uses to reveal what He knows about us? He has given us a spiritual mirror; the Holy Bible (James 1:22-26). The Scriptures are designed by God to fulfill five functions: (II Timothy 3:14-17)

a. They make us wise unto salvation.

b. They teach us basic truth by which we can determine truth and error.

c. They reprove us by pointing out what is pleasing to God and what is sin in His sight.

d. They correct us by showing us how to recover when we have sinned.

e. They train us in righteousness so that we do not just stop sinning; we replace sin with virtuous thoughts, words and actions "that the man of God may be adequate, equipped for every good work."

As we prepare to confess our sins, it is in the functions of reproof and correction that God may best use the Scriptures to show us the truth about ourselves. Three types of Scripture are especially suited to helping us see the sin we need to confess: the gospels, the positive standards and the negative standards.

The gospels show us Jesus Christ, the reflection of both the ideal Man and God in the flesh. As the perfect Man, Jesus provides a model to which we can compare ourselves; as "the exact representation of [God's] nature,"[13] Jesus reveals God as we can best understand Him.

---

13. Hebrews 1:1-4.

And whenever men are confronted with the presence of God, they tend to quickly become aware of their sin (Job 42:1-6; Isaiah 6:1-5; Luke 5:1-11).

The positive standards of the Bible are those passages which summarize the kind of life man ought to live on planet earth. Four such passages are:

a. the call to love (Mark 12:28-31; I Corinthians 13 and others).

b. the beatitudes (Matthew 5:1-12).

c. the fruit of the spirit (Galatians 5:22-23).

d. the eight qualities of Christian growth (II Peter 1:5-11).

The negative standards of the Bible are those passages which define sin and its practices which we are to confess. The general definitions of sin include:

a. The sin of commission — doing what God has commanded us not to do (I John 3:4).

b. The sin of omission — not doing what God has commanded us to do (James 4:17).

c. The sin of unbelief — not acting in accordance with faith in Jesus Christ (Romans 14:23).

d. The sin of selfishness — the choice of self over God; going our way rather than His way (Isaiah 53:6; Luke 12:16-21).

Individual lists of sin may also be used, though not effectively since we can often convince ourselves we did not do any particular sin in any given case. Our minds can be particularly devious in this area.

At this point, God provides a second major tool for self-understanding; a spiritually mature older brother or sister in Christ. Like Saul, we need a Samuel; like David, we need a Nathan, someone we allow to be perfectly frank with us and show us the sins we blind ourselves to see. Such a friend is worth more than his weight in microchips. This kind of honesty is bitter to take; we need to choose someone strong and wise enough to cut through all our blusters and self-defense and nail us where we need to be nailed. Nailing down hurts, but "faithful are the wounds of a friend" (Proverbs 27:6).

Pray for such a person right now; seek for one today; make an appointment to talk this week; tell them at the top of the conversation that you want them to help you see yourself in your spiritual blind spots and commit to meet and share with them regularly. Sometimes this sharing will be mutual, but not always or even normally. Find an honest and loving prophet to whom you can give permission to "set you straight" every now and then. This person is not your God or guru; but he/she is a Paul to your Timothy, listen and evaluate with care.

When we begin to see ourselves in reality by prayer, study of the Bible and godly counsel, then we have to take the next step: to admit to ourselves who we are, what we have done and what the results have been. We see that much of the pain in our lives is the simple reaping of what we have sown (Galatians 6:7). But there is hope here as well; for , if we sow more good from now on, we shall also reap more good. As we admit who we are, we again must avoid either exaggerating our sinfulness or excusing it.

Exaggeration of our sin tends to make repentance look hopeless. The disciples of Jesus grew up in a culture that saw sin behind every negative event in life. If you stubbed your toe, they would have blamed your sin. Once when they encountered a blind man, their first question to Jesus was, "Rabbi, who sinned, this man or his parents,that he should be born blind?" (John 9:2). Jesus' reply was that sin was not involved here. We also need to be careful not to load ourselves down with guilt for every negative event that goes on around us. We are responsible only for the consequences of our own thoughts, words and actions.

On the other hand, our sins should not be excused away by diminishing their importance or blaming others. Diminishing occurs when we use phrases like, "I *only* did so and so" or "What's so wrong with such and such?" These are attempts to make our sins seem unimportant. But stumbling in one little transgression makes us guilty before all of God's law (James 2:10-11).

Another excuse pattern is to blame others for "causing" us to sin; as in, "He *made* me mad, so it's all his fault!" If we really mean that the people and conditions around us control us to the extent that we are forced to sin, then life becomes hopeless. We would not then have enough control of our lives to change. But God's view of life is hope-filled; we *can* change because our sins are our choices to sin, not anyone else's. When He empowers us to change our choices, we will be able to change.

This personal inventory in preparation for confession may have to begin with a one-time intensive investigation; a full-scale spiritual bath complete with commandment shampoo and godliness body scrub. But preferably, this will come down to a daily "hand-washing" of the conscience. Many spiritual giants have suggested to "keep short accounts with God." In practice, this usually means a regular time to review the day with the Lord just before bed; to check yourself against His Word, confess your sins and find forgiveness. You want a clean heart to greet the new day. In addition, some include a weekly review at a regular time on Saturday to prepare for congregational worship the next day.

While recommending this, I must also warn you of two dangers of self-examination. One is to become so absorbed in our search for internal evil that we get obsessed with a "witch hunt" mentality, seeing evil in all we do and think. We then end up thinking about sin more than serving the Lord or our brothers and sisters. The other danger is to "lose our sense of perspective 'straining out a gnat and swallowing a camel.' "[14] We can become like the Pharisees, who refused to risk ceremonial uncleanness by entering Pilate's palace as they demanded Christ's execution. They kept their petty self-made rules but lost sight of the overriding principles of God (Matthew 23:23-24). So examine yourself without getting hooked by the examination process. With God's help, see yourself as you really are.

2. Repent of your sins.

Seeing your sins leaves you with this question, "Do I choose to keep on pursuing these or do I choose to reject them in favor of obeying the Lord?" We should experience some sorrow over displeasing our Father and failing to follow Christ which has resulted in hurting ourselves and others. But that sorrow is useless if it does not lead to a resolve to change, to crucify this part of our flesh, to commit our members to obedience instead; that is, to a full repentance without any regrets for what we are rejecting (II Corinthians 7:10-11).

To repent simply means to turn around; to turn back from following evil (Ezekiel 33:11) and turn forward to following God in obedience (Acts 26:20). When this decision is made then we are ready to seek God's forgiveness in prayer (Acts 8:22).

---

14. Stephen Winward, *How to Talk with God/the Dynamics of Prayer* (Wheaton, Illinois: Harold Shaw Publishers, 1961), p. 68-69.

3. Confess your sins to God in prayer.

In final preparation, I suggest write down a list of the specific sins you need to confess. This will force you to be definite about each one. Do be specific. If you are too general, first, you may not be telling the whole truth to God about what you have done. Second, general confessions leave one hardpressed to know exactly what to do to repair sins of commission or fulfill sins of omission. How do you change, "I've been bad"? Third, we may miss fully realizing God's forgiveness.[15] So specifically name the sins in your listing.

Then, generally, confess these sins to God. He knows all the details on the list and we do not need to go through them again. In fact, there is often a danger in going over the details in prayer.

Do not repeat them. Particularly does this seem wise when emotional centers have been concerned and anger or envy or jealousy or sex feelings or difficulty in forgiving injuries are involved . . . . Unless our penitence is very complete and our will very resolute, the repetition of those evils in detail even to God is apt to bring a reliving of the occasion and the emotion. In the colder thought which precedes the prayer, and when we are judges of our own selves, this is not so apt to occur.[16]

The wording of the confession will vary to some extent but may contain the following type of elements: Admission: "Lord, I admit that I have sinned against You . . ." (Psalm 51:3-4); Attitude: "I have been [basic attitude; greedy, selfish, fearful, ungrateful, etc.] . . ." (I Samuel 15:24); and Action: "I have [name specific sin] . . ." (Joshua 7:20-21).

While this confession is to be made primarily to God alone, the Scripture also lays the basis for confessing sin to another believer (who may share his confession also) so that you may then pray for one another (James 5:16). The process benefits us in that we hear our sins

---

15. George S. Stewart, *The Lower Levels of Prayer* (New York: Abingdon-Cokesbury Press, 1940), pp. 100-101.
16. Ibid., p. 102.

being accepted and prayed for by a brother in Christ. Somehow we take comfort in the fact that our sins can be accepted without undue shock or contempt by another Christian and that he/she can approach God on our behalf and reassure us of the promises of forgiveness which God has given us. This mutual confession is not necessary in every case, but it can be of particular value in getting past a particularly difficult sin pattern. There are some practical limits to be considered here.

In general, secret sins should be confessed secretly to God; private sins against a brother should be confessed to the brother; sins of a public nature should be confessed publicly.[17]

But one may use the support of a brother or sister in Christ in the confession process without setting up a confessional booth or violating the will of God.

4. Request God's forgiveness through the blood of Christ.

Recently, it has been suggested that we need not ever again ask forgiveness after our initial acceptance of Jesus Christ.[18] We may agree with God in confession that we have sinned, but we have already been forgiven. It is asserted that "a Christian lives in a continual state of forgiveness."[19] Ye the logical extension of this idea would be the doctrine of eternal security, in that a Christian is rather "pre-forgiven" for all sins. But I doubt the author so intends. What does the Bible say?

Jesus Christ taught that asking forgiveness was a part of the standard model prayer (Matthew 6:9-13). Are we to dispense with the Lord's Prayer because it comes before the cross and is under the old covenant? Such a blanket sweeping away of all the teachings of our Lord's earthly ministry seems without warrant. I can think of no other reason to dismiss such an obvious statement of Scripture.

Also the verse quoted in the work referred to, I John 1:9, to support

---

17. Harold Lindsell, *When You Pray* (Grand Rapids, Michigan: Baker Book House, 19969), p. 43.

18. John Hendee, *A Peace Treaty with God* (Cincinnati, Ohio: The Standard Publishing Company, 1984), p. [16].

19. *Ibid.*

confessing our sins, actually also supports the idea that forgiveness is contingent upon confession and not "a continual state." The open clause of this verse, "*If* we confess our sins," implies a condition on the rest of the sentence, that is, that God "is faithful and righteous to forgive us our sins and to cleanse us from all unrighteousness" *when* we confess our sins.[20] I believe this indicates we are indeed to request forgiveness of the sins we confess.

We ask forgiveness based on the blood of Christ alone. We cannot be forgiven on any other basis (Hebrews 9:11-14, 22). Our request does not earn us forgiveness any more than our confession does. After all, we are only agreeing with the Lord's analysis of our actions and seeking forgiveness according to His promises. That does not earn us anything. The forgiveness is a gift of God and we can only receive it, not earn it. Yet, because He has faithfully promised to forgive and cleanse us, we do not need to beg and plead our Father as if He were loath to pardon us. We ask believing His promise and receive.

5. *Receive God's forgiveness.*

It is one thing to ask for forgiveness and another to accept delivery of that forgiveness. We must believe our Lord God's promises to forgive the penitent (Isaiah 55:6-7). We need to make this real to ourselves. We can picture in our minds the image of Isaiah 61:10:

> I will rejoice greatly in the Lord, my soul will exalt in my God; for He has clothed me with the garments of salvation, He has wrapped me with a robe of righteousness, as a bridegroom decks himself with a garland, and as a bride adorns herself with her jewels.

Some have suggested that the confession and request for forgiveness be offered while kneeling and that the believer then stand

---

20. The clause is shown to be a conditional relative clause by the use of the subjunctive mood with *ean*, as is also used in the verses immediately before and after verse nine. See H.P.V. Nunn, *A Short Syntax of New Testament Greek* (Cambridge: University Press, 1965), p. 121.

"as a token of our acceptance of God's pardon."[21] However you con-firm your forgiveness to yourself, do so.

We need then to agree with God and forgive ourselves. This does not mean that we are *satisfied* with ourselves or happy with the results of our past sins. Indeed, such discomfort should motivate the changes our repentance intends.[22] But we are not going to mentally continue to punish ourselves for our past iniquities; we will agree with our Father and "let ourselves off the hook."

6. Give thanks for forgiveness.

Aside from fulfilling the command to "in everything give thanks" (I Thessalonians 5:18), thanksgiving reassures us of both God's forgiveness and cleansing according to His promises (Isaiah 43:25). It turns the sorrow of our confession into the joy of our renewed purity before the Lord. It also provides a *positive* motivation to change: gratitude.

7. Ask for help to avoid the confessed sins in the future.

I believe this is included in the Lord's Prayer request to "not lead us into temptation, but deliver us from evil" (Matthew 6:13). Be sure you have memorized I Corinthians 10:13 as a spiritual bulwark against future temptations. For the same Lord Who is "faithful" to forgive you and cleanse you is also "faithful" to not allow temptations to be greater than your ability to resist them in Him.

8. Put off the things of the flesh.

Begin immediately to act upon your resolve to change your life for the good. Lay aside the parts of the "old self" that got you into trouble

---

21. Buttrick, pp. 297-298.
22. Jay E. Adams, *Matters of Concern to Christian Counselors* (Grand Rapids, Michigan: Baker Book House, 1977), pp. 8-9.

last time (Ephesians 4:20-24; Colossians 3:5-11). Determine to trust God to "go now and leave your life of sin" (John 8:11, NIV).

"Make no provision for the flesh in regard to its lust" (Romans 13:14b). So don't feed your weakness. If you have fallen before in sins of sensuality, get rid of the pornography, cable TV or whatever may help trigger those desires. If you have a problem with gossip, take the phone out for a couple of weeks; survival without it is possible! If greed is your problem, throw away your catalogues and turn off the commercials. If an affair tempts you, break off ALL contact and burn the letters. Cooperate with God in cleansing your home of "all unrighteousness" (I John 1:9).

9. Put on the things of the Spirit.

The universe abhors a vacuum. Simply stopping sin-oriented activities is only half a repentance. Go on to replace the sin-centered activity with God-centered activity. An excellent list of examples occurs in Ephesians 4:25-32. The chart below shows the "put off" and "put on" pairs.

Put Off	Put On
Falsehood	Speaking truth with your neighbor
Sinful, prolonged anger	Sinless anger quickly resolved
Stealing	Laboring at a good job to have enough to share with others
Unwholesome, destructive speech	Words good for edification to give grace to those who hear
Grieving the Holy Spirit with bitterness, wrath, anger, clamor or slander with all malice	Being king to one another, tenderhearted, forgiving one another as God in Christ has forgiven you

Recommit yourself to do these things regardless of whether you like it or not (Psalm 31:5, 24; Proverbs 16:3). Delay reacting on your old habitual responses and begin responding by choice, not by feeling.[23]

---

23. Parker and St. Johns, p. 148.

257

Sow new seeds and you will reap a new and better harvest soon.

10. Make restitution and ask forgiveness of others as needed.

Sinning has been paralleled to driving a nail in a door. The nail may be removed (the sin forgiven by God) but the hole still remains. There are lingering after affects of our sins; debts unpaid and relationships unresolved. While all temporal consequences cannot be stopped, any restitution possible should be attempted. Pray that those consequences which cannot be erased will be borne by those involved with God-given grace. Even where restitution cannot be made, forgiveness may be sought by us from those injured by our sin. This is often harder than facing God concerning our sin, but it is often also the only way to heal relationships (Matthew 5:23-24).

Confession has a power to do that which is otherwise impossible. By confession and receiving forgiveness, we can change our past. Imagine: the power to change the past. We can start today to begin wiping away the sins and healing the hurts of the past, here and now. Praise God!

Thought or Discussion Questions

1. Is the idea of "roller coaster" Christianity held by a majority or minority of the people in your church? What made them this way? How would you explain confidence in our salvation to someone who held this idea? How does the concept of our salvation being both a position and a process help avoid the "roller coaster?"

2. How would you define "confession?" What is the opposite of confession? What are the two extremes of self-examination? Read the fifty-first Psalm. Underline the verses where David confesses his sin. Circle the verses where David requests forgiveness and reconciliation to the Lord. Put a star by the verse where David recommits himself to the service of God. How does this Psalm reassure us?

3. Explain four general reasons why we should consistently confess our sins. Give three reasons why people experience continuing guilt. Which

do you think is the most common reason? Why do people find it hard to forgive themselves for their sin? What kind of fear is bad for us? Why? What kind of fear is good for us? Why?

4. Which of the five levels of communication is the most common in the prayers you hear in your church? Why? Which is most common in your own prayers? Why? What three general self-images can we have? Which is your "normal" self-image? Why? How would you try to help someone have a more honest self-image? Can you think of someone among your family or friends whom you could help in this area?

5. How can we go about seeing ourselves as we really are? How do the Scriptures help in this process? How can another Christian help? Why seek out a Christian and not just any good friend? What dangers exist in sharing our confessions with another Christian? What opportunities exist in sharing our confessions with another Christian? What are the benefits of consistent regular confession? What does it mean to repent of your sins? How do you balance being specific and general in confession? Do you believe we need to ask forgiveness for our sins as we confess them? Why or why not? How can you make receiving God's forgiveness more real to you?

6. How does thanksgiving for forgiveness help us? What channels can God use to help us avoid sin in the future? How can we cooperate in this avoidance of sin? Why is the conscious choice to put off the things of the flesh necessary? Why is putting off the old man alone an insufficient response to our sin? What else do we need to do? How? How do we handle the consequences of our sin which we have no power to change? What are we responsible to do toward those hurt by our sins? Is confession worth it? Explain your answer.

9

WHAT ARE THE COMMON PROBLEMS OF PRAYER?

Prayer is simple, but it is not easy. The practice of prayer has its problems. You and I "struggle" in our prayers against the sin within us and the enemies without, like the early Christians (Romans 15:30; Colossians 4:12).

Are you suffering from one of the prayer problems we are going to discuss? Check if you have one of the eight danger signs listed below.[1]

[ ] I am getting irritable with other people. (I am impatient, easily angered and yet insensitive to the needs of those around me.)

[ ] I am being molded by the opinions of those around me more than I am being transformed into Christ's image. (I worry more about what people think of me than what God thinks of me.)

[ ] I feel no urgency to pray. (I do not experience the spiritual warfare against Satan as real.)

---

1. These are adapted from the answers given by a cross section of ministers to Terry Muck concerning "red flags" they noted when their personal prayer lives were in trouble. See *Liberating the Leader's Prayer Life* (Waco, Texas: Word Books, 1985), pp. 175-184.

[ ] I feel like God is not listening to me when I pray. (My prayers are not answered as I desire and I am experiencing failure for no apparent reason.)

[ ] I am spiritually dry, empty, with nothing to share with others who are hurting. (I cannot think of anything to say at church and Bible study bores me.)

[ ] I seem to have lost control of my life; I am unable to handle decisions and getting anything done. (I cannot seem to get things in order or set priorities; I get depressed easily.)

[ ] I have no desire to pray or read the Bible or go to church or do anything "spiritual." (I am losing touch with God and the world around me; I am "burned out.")

[ ] *I feel that I am doing great things for God; I am proud of my* spiritual progress. (I am blind to my sins and faults and less aware of my utter dependence on God.)

These danger signs may indicate the presence of one or more of the prayer problems listed below. Also your prayers themselves can tell you if you have a problem. If you do not pray or pray bad prayers or pray very irregularly, something is wrong in your prayerlife. Obviously, we realize we have problems spiritually when we quit praying. But we can still be praying but praying "bad" prayers; prayers which are meaningless forms or full of doubt or selfish "shopping lists." Again, we should realize we are suffering from a spiritual problem. Finally, if we pray on an "on again/off again" pattern, we are not making much effort to weave prayer into the pattern of our lives and get to know God better each day. Something is going wrong.

Below are ten categories of common problems people like us experience in praying. Look through the list and check on your own prayerlife. You will notice that the first three are related in that they each deal with a particular lack of faith. Since "the righteous man shall live by faith," doubt in any spiritual discipline disrupts our life with Christ. Any prayer offered under the shadow of doubt has no hope that God will grant what is requested (Matthew 21:22; James 1:6-8).

SOME PEOPLE STRUGGLE WITH UNBELIEF ABOUT PRAYER.

Stanley Plunkett said it simply; "If we believe in prayer, we pray. If we do not believe in it, we do not pray."[2] There are several reasons why some people have difficulty in believing that prayer "works."

Why people struggle with unbelief about prayer.

Some have been influenced by an idea which says, "All that exists is what we can see; there is no 'unseen force' available to us." This materialistic worldview denies the reality of prayer for anybody, including ourselves.

Others do not believe in prayer because they have been taught that God has already given us all we need for life and now it is our job to work it out. If you are sick, call the doctor and take your medicine; why pray? If someone is lost, tell them the gospel and let them decide; why pray? If a flood is coming, find a boat or prepare to die; why pray? Actually this way of life leaves us at the mercy of our own weaknesses. If we cannot handle life, we are left with nowhere else to go, no final court of appeal.

Some people do not trust prayer because they cannot fully understand it. Prayer is a spiritual mystery, at least in part. We do not understand why God uses it to bless us, but He does. For some people that is not enough. First, they want their every question answered and only then will they try this strange procedure. However, spiritual mysteries cannot be solved; they can only be accepted and held in awe. Those who would limit God to operating only on a level they can comprehend would bring the world to a speedy end ; for a man as a whole race understands very little of how God has structured our universe. If I could only use what I understood, I would be back to using just rocks and leaves (and I do not understand *them* very well either).

Finally, many do not trust prayer because they think prayer has "failed" them in the past. "My mother was terribly ill and I prayed for her the best I knew how for three months. But she died anyway." Any time the Lord answers any of our requests "No," we have the option of refusing to accept His answer. That choice would mean we hold

---

2. Quoted in Paul D. Lowder, comp., *Let Us Pray/A Minister's Prayer Book* (Nashville, Tennessee: The Upper Room, 1963), p. 9.

ourselves to be wiser than God and that we question His desire or ability to do good for us. But such an attitude clouds all future prayers with doubt. Whatever the reason, doubting prayer's reality leads to sad results.

Results when people struggle with unbelief about prayer.

If people really cease to believe that prayer is effective in changing things, the logical result would be to become more irregular in our praying or just stop altogether. Why pretend if it is meaningless to "talk to God"? If we felt some duty to continue praying (even though we are not sure we are accomplishing anything), our prayers become empty forms, ritual without faith. We would do what many Christians in fact do now: we would bring our requests to God and act as if *we* had to supply our own needs through ourselves and our friends. So I piously pray for the Lord to supply a needed new winter coat. But then I carefully make it a point to *casually* mention to my relatives that my old coat is wearing out, "and so close to my birthday, too." Who do I really expect to supply my need?

Since I do not expect God to help me, my prayers can become dreary whines, complaints about all my troubles. God becomes like a convenient neighbor to Whom I can tell my troubles. I do not really expect Him to help, but He does have to put up with hearing how rough my life is going. And, since I have only prayed about negatives and only receive negatives (in my eyes), I feel reassured that not even God can help me. People can actually become smug in their wretchedness. How can we overcome this unbelief about prayer?

Help for people struggling with unbelief about prayer.

In building faith in anything, we look at sufficient testimony and evidence to convict us of the faithfulness or truthfulness of the object we are examining. In the case of prayer, we have testimony from at least four sources: the Holy Bible, Christian History, other modern Christians and personal experience. The Bible contains the promises of God upon which our charter to pray to the Lord is based. Also in the Bible are many accounts of the faithfulness of God to respond in mercy and justice to the prayers of men and nations. The character of God Himself is exposed through the life and teaching of Jesus Christ. And the Lord is the faithful One Whose promises we accept when we pray. Reread and meditate on the history of Abraham, Moses, Samuel or Daniel. Memorize some of the many promises. Dwell on the life of Christ. And faith will come "from hearing, and hearing by the word of Christ" (Romans 10:17).

Through the centuries, the writings, histories and biographies of the great men and women of faith are filled with testimonies to the efficacy of prayer (and the continued faithfulness of the God of the Bible). Read these works from time to time. Let your church leaders recommend some good works for you. The voices of the past and near present combine to give evidence that our Father is trustworthy to respond to our prayers.

Today, many Christians in every community agree that they too have found the Almighty open to their petitions and responsive to their pleas. Find some more mature brother or sister who is a "prayer warrior," that is, who believes in the value and consistent practice of prayer. Ask the warrior to share with you how the Lord has worked in his/her life. By all means, have a time of prayer with the warrior. Your faith in God's call to pray will probably grow through such fellowship.

Finally, consider your own prayerlife. Think back over the prayers which you have prayed and which God has answered. The answer probably was not always, "Yes." Yet, from the vantage point of today, can you begin to see the wisdom of each of God's answers? And if there were any troubling answers, tragedies from our viewpoint, can you look at all the evidence from all the saints from all the centuries and open your heart to believe that God is faithful even in His actions which we do not understand?

Prayer itself is always a part of dealing with problems with prayer. Ask the Lord to strengthen your faith in His promise to answer prayer. Begin to keep a daily prayer journal and gather your own evidence of answered prayer to encourage others as well as yourself. Log in your requests by date and leave space to log in the answers as they come. Include your "common" requests as well as the "extraordinary" (from our viewpoint). The Lord does not need to prove Himself, but it always encourages us to "watch" Him at work.

Finally, realize that to question prayer is essentially to question the trustworthiness of God, for His "signature" is signed to the promises concerning answered prayer (Psalm 34:1-22). Indeed, what you believe about prayer reveals the kind of God in Whom you believe. Jesus told us that *His* Father would never trick us by giving us evil gifts when we asked for good (Matthew 7:7-11). We will talk more about faith in God just a little later. For now, open your heart to accept the wondrous gift of prayer; an open line to the heart of the Creator.

SOME PEOPLE STRUGGLE WITH UNBELIEF ABOUT THEMSELVES.

We talked about this in the last chapter but let us summarize what we said there in a different way here.

Why people struggle with unbelief about themselves.

Some of us lack humility; we think of ourselves as self-made individuals. We need the warning of Deuteronomy 8:11-14, 17-18:

Beware lest you forget the Lord your God by not keeping His commandments . . . lest, when you have eaten and are satisfied, and have built good homes and lived in them, and when your herds and your flocks multiply, and your silver and gold multiply, and all that you have multiplies, then your heart becomes proud, and you forget the Lord . . . . Otherwise, you may say in your heart, "My power and the strength of my hand made me this wealth." But you shall remember the Lord your God, for it is He who is giving you the power to make wealth . . . .

The proud or "self-made" person sees little need to pray to a God for Whom the person has never before felt a need. Such a person does not believe the Biblical teaching that he/she is a sinner desperately in need of all that God is willing to give.

Another group of us are lacking in self-acceptance. They know they are sinners; terrible, wretched, loathsome sinners. They grovel before

266

God. They not only humble themselves; they seek humiliation. I know a person who never misses expounding in prayer on how unworthy we are and how we are all great sinners who deserve God's wrath. This truth becomes a lie when it overshadows what we have become through the grace of God. Such people rarely are sure of their salvation and feel unworthy to pray. They do not believe the good news of the gospel of what Jesus has done for us and the results His death and resurrection bring us right now.

Results when people struggle with unbelief about themselves.

Those unsure of their need of God or their right to approach Him tend to avoid the Lord in prayer. They may not pray at all or only irregularly. They may only use empty forms for their prayers, indicating either their self-assurance or self-deprecation before God. Either way, their prayer life is useless as they try to play someone they are not before God. They can be helped if they are willing to take the difficult but essential step of facing who they really are.

Help for people struggling with unbelief about themselves.

As noted in the last chapter, we need to gain a proper self-image by looking into the Word of God and taking an honest look at ourselves through God's eyes. As C. S. Lewis has told us, "we must lay before [God] what is in us, not what ought to be in us."[3] In confession, we find both the humbling of our pride and the love of God which is the basis of our self-acceptance. We see that we are in fact God's children, not through personal purity but through divine grace.

We need to understand ourselves in light of who we are in Christ.

I am convinced that the most outstanding enemy in prayer is the lack of knowledge of what we are in Christ, and of what He is in

---

3. *Letters To Malcolm: Chiefly On Prayer* (New York: Harcourt Brace Jovanovich, Inc., 1964), p. 22.

us, and what He did for us, and our standing and legal rights before the throne.[4]

Read through Ephesians 1:3-14 slowly, underlining everything we have in Christ. The inescapable conclusion is that we are important to the Almighty God through our relationship to Him in His Son. Yet we are as we are as a gift, not a personal achievement.

Pray that you might understand and accept who you are in God's sight. Again, realize that our faith in our need to and ability to pray rest upon our faith in truthfulness of God in His Word. If we do not believe God, we will not accept His analysis of who we are. The problem of unbelief about God Himself is our next subject.

SOME PEOPLE STRUGGLE WITH UNBELIEF ABOUT GOD.

This problem is certainly the most serious of all problems with prayer. Lack of faith in God is at the base of most of the other problems we have with our spiritual lives. As we trust God, we come to know Him through Christ. "And this is eternal life, that [we] may know Thee, the only true God, and Jesus Christ whom Thou hast sent" (John 17:3). To miss faith in God is to miss eternal life. The stakes are staggering.

Why people struggle with unbelief about God.

To believe in God means to step down from the throne of our lives and to ask Him to take control. To believe in God means to admit our sinfulness and our dependency on Him. To believe in God means to open our lives for total renovation; every habit, every possession, every relationship must be exposed to His examination for possible alterations. To believe in God upsets the status quo of our sinful comfort. And many people resist accepting the Lordship of God in Christ to avoid these painful changes. But these minor sufferings are by far overshadowed by the magnificent gifts we receive by faith in God through

---

4. E. W. Kenyon, *In His Presence* (Lynnwood, Washington: Kenyon's Gospel Publishing Society, 1969), p. 141.

Jesus Christ (Romans 8:18).

One of these gifts is the privilege of prayer (John 14:6). Those who have made no commitment to Jesus Christ have no promise that God will hear their cries. And people avoid the commitment to the Lord in faith because they are unwilling to accept His will as the standard for their lives. They will *not* choose to live by the prayer, "Thy will be done." Actually, their view of life is better summarized as, "Not Thy will but mine be done."

Unbelievers do not trust God to fulfill His promises concerning prayer either. They are the antithesis of Paul's description of Abraham that,

> with respect to the promise of God, he did not waver in unbelief, but grew strong in faith, giving glory to God, and being fully assured that what He had promised, He was able also to perform (Romans 4:20-21).

Unbelievers are neither willing to give glory to God nor to trust His promises would be fulfilled. Obviously, if they will not trust God to rule their lives, they are not interested in honoring Him with glory or in becoming dependent upon His promised blessings.

Like believers, unbelievers sometimes encourage one another to a consistent lifestyle. However, where as believers encourage one another to growth in faith and love of God, unbelievers encourage each other to trust themselves and love themselves more. "Do not be deceived: 'Bad company corrupts good morals' " (I Corinthians 15:33).

Results when people struggle with unbelief about God.

A primary result of unbelief in God is indifference to the things of God. Among the activities chiefly affected are church attendance, Bible study, evangelism and prayer. Why attend church regularly if you do not wish to worship the Lord the rest of your life? Why study the Bible to know His will if you do not plan to do His will? Why try to share with others a faith you do not possess? Why pray regularly to a God you do not trust? One can claim a faith he/she does not possess and may still act out these activities. But, without faith in God, such works are not simply meaningless, they are sin (Romans 14:23).

A second result of unbelief toward the Father is worry, fear and anxiety. Whatever he tells himself, man was created a dependent creature, needing the fellowship and support of God to live a fulfilled life. As we turn from the faith relationship which God intended, we have to depend on ourselves — a very shaky foundation indeed. We cannot support ourselves. Each day becomes a balancing act on a precarious perch, juggling our responsibilities and bearing our loads. Also, a fear of God's judgment is added to the natural pressures of life. The Christian can fearlessly bring his cares in faith to his Father to lift the burden. Where can an unbeliever go?

Finally, a third result of rejecting the worship of God is acceptance of the worship of idols. "Idols" need not be stone or metal images, but may be any person, possession, principle or idea which a man sets up in the place of God. Paul describes the spiritual fall of man as the rejection of God as Lord only to turn around and set up some lesser thing to be worshipped (Romans 1:21-23). Even such organizations as Alcoholics Anonymous recognize that each man needs to acknowledge a "higher power" if he is to adequately handle life. Sadly, many have chosen to live in a fantasy world with the imagined idols of their hearts rather than to accept reality where there is only one true God, the Father of our Lord Jesus Christ. And the end of the delusion of idols is eternal death (I Corinthians 6:9-10).

Help for people struggling with unbelief about God.

What can be done for those caught in unbelief? We said earlier that faith is based upon sufficient evidence and testimony to assure us of that which we do not know directly (through our senses). (See Hebrews 11:1 ff.) The Bible is our primary source for our basic knowledge about God. If you doubt the reliability of the Word, there are many excellent books which clearly present the case for the divine inspiration of the Holy Bible.[5] Or you may want to check with a Christian leader in your area

---

5. Two of the best are F.F. Bruce, *The New Testament Documents: Are They Reliable?* (Downers Grove, Illinois: Inter-Varsity Press, 1960) and Josh McDowell, comp., *Evidence That Demands A Verdict* (San Bernardino, California: Here's Life Publishers, Inc., 1979).

for references or just a conversation on the trustworthy nature of the Bible.

To learn more about God, then, study the life of Jesus Christ. He reveals the Father in whom we can have faith (John 1:18). Study the Scriptures to see how this Lord worked with men and women in history. Hear the testimonies of Abraham and Joshua, of Peter and Paul. Join a group studying the Word directly and examine the evidence. You will find a firm foundation for your faith.

If you have never committed your life to Jesus Christ, do so today. Place your faith in Jesus to be Lord of your life and to pay the punishment for your sins. Repent of your taking charge of your life; reject it and all the wrong habits you have developed; ask God to take charge instead. Find a Christian and confess your faith in Jesus Christ and ask to be baptized (immersed in water) as an act of commitment to the Lord, accepting His gift of the Holy Spirit to live in you. As you are buried in the water for a moment, picture the truth that your old lifestyle is dead and has been buried. As you are raised up from the water, picture the truth that you are a new creature spiritually, born anew by the power of God: you are child of God. Read the Word and pray daily to promote your growth into Christlikeness. Meet weekly with other Christians in church to worship the Lord, encourage one another, learn more of His will and prepare for service in His kingdom. And start your conversation with your Father which will last eternally.

If you are already a Christian who has fallen into doubt about your Father, repent and confess your sin of doubt to the Lord. Thank Him for His forgiveness and patience with you. Ask Him to help you to trust Him in more areas of your life each day (Mark 9:23-24). Use the faith you have now; pray and serve to the limits of your faith. Multiply praise in your prayers and in your conversation with others. We showed in another chapter how praise and thanksgiving can encourage our faith in the Lord; try it! Read through Psalm 145 slowly and carefully. Fill your heart filled with its praises. Be a grateful, praise-filled Christian and any lack of faith in the Lord will fade before long.

SOME PEOPLE STRUGGLE WITH UNRELIEVED GUILT.

Since we spent so long on this in the chapter on confession, I will summarize very quickly what was said there.

Why people struggle with unrelieved guilt.

Guilt arises from sin and from not fully accepting God's forgiveness for that sin. For whatever reason, we get comfortable enough with our sin to accept it. But this separates us from fellowship with God (Psalm 66:18-20; Isaiah 59:1-2). A special temptation for the Christian is presumption on God's grace.

This happens when you presume of the love and grace of God and dare to commit sin, "God is loving," you say, "and since I am a Christian, he must forgive me of this sin. Therefore, I will commit it and settle with God later."[6]

Such thinking can become an automatic excuse for habitual sin. We have not repented of a sin we are still committing. So such "Christianized sinning" is just plain old sinning with a religious conscience soother tacked on. Real repentance is needed.

Results when people struggle with unrelieved guilt.

When our guilt is unrelieved, we tend to hide from God for fear of His wrath (Genesis 3:8-11). Rather than repent and confess as God has instructed us, we often try one of four useless strategies to relieve our guilt.[7]

1. We try to kill our conscience by arguments and rebuttals against God's standards. It does not work; we are still guilty before God.

2. We try to avoid our guilt by clouding our minds with alcohol, drugs, overeating, overwork, promiscuity and, tragically, by suicide. It does not work; we are still guilty before God.

---

6. Thomas D. Elliff, *Praying For Others* (Nashville, Tennessee: Broadman Press, 1979), p. 68.

7. Suggested by J. Moulton Thomas in *Prayer Power* (Waco, Texas: Word Books, Publisher, 1976), pp. 65-71.

3. We try to balance the scales within us by doing good deeds to offset our sins. It does not work; we are still guilty before God.

4. We carry the burden of our guilt and punish ourselves in a variety of subtle ways to atone for our sins. It does not work; we are still guilty before God.

Guilt relentlessly drives us. Until we are ready to repent and confess our sin, guilt keeps us far from God. So our prayers are distant, irregular or just nonexistent. Yet, when we are willing to change, our guilt brings us back to God for cleansing.

Help for people struggling with unrelieved guilt.

The relief of guilt requires receiving God's forgiveness and cleansing for our sins. To receive His forgiveness, we turn back to God, rejecting the sin which separated us from Him (repentance). Then we agree with God in prayer that we have sinned against Him and we ask His forgiveness (confession). We now thank the Lord for our cleansing. Finally, we ask the Lord to help us to avoid that same sin in the future and to replace it with some godly virtue or action (deliverance). And remember: the Lord said, "I will be merciful to their iniquities, and I will remember their sins no more" (Hebrews 8:12). We should put behind us what the Lord has forgotten.

SOME PEOPLE STRUGGLE WITH UNLOVING RELATIONSHIPS.

Our relationship with God in prayer is directly connected to our relationship with people day by day. The apostle John binds the two together with this principle:

If someone says, "I love God," and hates his brother, he is a liar; for the one who does not love his brother whom he has seen, cannot love God whom he has not seen (I John 4:20).

Without love relationships with people, we cannot enjoy a loving relationship with God in prayer.

Why people struggle with unloving relationships.

The source of division is sin; as the Lord unifies, sin divides. Primarily, the sins of "the lust of the flesh and the lust of the eyes and the boastful pride of life" divide us (I John 2:16). Lust of the flesh has us using other people to fulfill our personal desires. Especially in the marriage relationship, this sin of using people has divided many couples. For example, one person is interested in romance, while the other wants to catch a nap. If either demands to get what they want, the other will say, "You're just using me!" And love is divided. Peter warns his readers that husbands and wives should fulfill their roles for one another or their prayers *will* be hindered (I Peter 3:1-12).

Lust of the eyes has us fighting with others over the possession of that which we see. James describes the source of our many quarrels.

What is the source of quarrels and conflicts among you? Is not the source your pleasures that wage war in your members? You lust and do not have; so you commit murder. And you are envious and cannot obtain; so you fight and quarrel. You do not have because you do not ask. You ask and do not receive, because you ask with wrong motives, so that you may spend it on your pleasures (James 4:1-3).

Our sinful desires divide us against each other and hinder our prayers to God again.

The boastful pride of life has us "putting people down" to build ourselves up. In our pride, we become angry when someone interferes with *our* plans or infringes upon *our* rights. Such anger with its name-calling and personal attacks is equated with murder by Jesus Christ (Matthew 5:21-24). The Lord goes on to say that we should settle all such differences before attempting to approach God in prayer. In this sin as well, we are divided from those around us and from God in prayer. And what happens as a consequence?

Results when people struggle with unloving relationships.

When we either create or experience unloving relationships, our prayers can be hindered. As we create broken connections with others, our sin interrupts our conversations with God. But when we are the object of attack, our bitterness at the one who sins against us can break our intimacy with God, especially if we return evil for evil. By trying to take our own revenge, we usurp the place of God as Judge and Righter of wrongs (Romans 12:14-21). We are not to overcome evil with more evil but with good. Otherwise, we become as evil as those we judge.

The results of unloving relationships are broken communions with both God and people. We must find how to mend what has been broken if we do not want to live very lonely lives.

Help for people struggling with unloving relationships.

How can we change the past, the sins we have committed against God and people? Would you like the power to wipe out the errors, to restore that which has been broken? We *have* that power! The power to change the past is called, "forgiveness."[8]

The process of forgiveness can be practically laid out in the following steps:

Forgiving Others:

1. Write down those people who have been disloyal to the relationship you shared or have betrayed you to others. Other slights and pains can be overlooked (Proverbs 19:11), but not disloyalty and betrayal. These must be forgiven.

2. One by one, consider what each person did. Remember how it felt to have someone you trusted to let you down so. Do not minimize the emotions or excuse the person. Feel the rage that shouts, "Unfair!" in your heart. Understand what it feels like to be betrayed. You will need to know this.

3. Do not try to explain away what was done. Unless you are

---

8. An excellent discussion of the use of forgiveness to heal broken relationships appears in Lewis B. Smedes, *Forgive and Forget* (San Francisco: Harper and Row, Publishers, 1984).

deceiving yourself about what happened, if the person was disloyal, do not "let him off the hook." "But," you say, "I'm sure they didn't *mean* to hurt me." Perhaps not; but then, hardly anyone really sets out with the primary intent of hurting a companion. It is by our selfish choices that others are hurt. And we must be held accountable for that. The only person who can be forgiven is one who is truly guilty (all others are found innocent and exonerated).

4. In your heart, cut apart the sin from the sinner. This is a crucial step in the process of forgiveness. God does this with us; our sins are going to be swept away but not us (Isaiah 44:22). He can hate the sin and love the sinner, as the cliche runs. We have to do the same. Be able to see that sin apart from the person and picture that person without remembering that sin.

5. Now go to God in prayer. Forgive them in His presence (II Corinthians 2:10-11). Ask Him to forgive them, as your Lord did before you (Luke 23:34). Ask the Lord to bless them for Christ's sake; this is a part of your healing, too (Luke 6:27-28; Job 42:8-10). Thank the Lord for forgiving you and them, and for working even through the painful events to make you more like Christ (I Peter 4:1-2).

6. Sometimes the previous step is as far as you can go. But, many times, the Lord may allow for a full restoring of the relationship. Joseph's brothers may sell him into slavery and still return to his love; Peter may deny the Christ and still be a rock for His church. The daughter may disgrace the family and still have her family. A husband may break his vows with adultery and still retain his wife. It can even be better afterwards. But for this wondrous healing to occur, someone must cross the gulf and reach out his/her hand and say, "I want us to be together again. Let us make a peace." You, will *you* try to be the peacemaker? (Matthew 5:9)

Seeking Forgiveness From Others:

1. Write down those from whom you feel alienated who were at one time close to you, those you have hurt. You may believe their reason for being hurt is "silly" or that "they have to take some of the blame, too." But put their names down anyway.

2. Ask God to open your heart to understand how your words and

actions appeared to the other person, how they were hurt by what you did and how you are responsible for what you do. They may indeed have been partially to blame; but, if you are in *any* way to blame, *you* bear the responsibility of seeking forgiveness for what *you* have done.

3. Seek forgiveness from God, if you have not already done so. Repent, confess your sin and ask for strength and wisdom both not to repeat the sin and to seek forgiveness from the person, if you should. Some individuals may be hurt worse by your attempt to ask forgiveness than they would be healed by releasing you (and themselves) from the painful memory. Seek wisdom and godly counsel on this, if you are in doubt.

4. Go to the person and ask his/her forgiveness (Matthew 5:23-24). A *short* personal visit is best; a telephone call is second best; and any written communication is not good at all. Letters and so on just document your "crime" and do not provide opportunity for forgiveness to be granted or reconciliation begun. Plan in advance exactly what you want to say (like the prodigal son, Luke 15:18-19). Your confession should contain these elements: a true admission of wrongdoing without excuses or accusations, a statement of regret or sorrow for the pain you caused and a simple request for forgiveness. The whole thing should run well under one minute (do not prolong the agony for either of you). A sample statement would be like this: "John, I was wrong in my unloving attitude toward you. I know now how I hurt you in what I did and I deeply regret doing so. I have come today to ask you: will you forgive me for what I did?" The specific sin is not named to prevent reopening old wounds; rather, the underlying attitude is stated (ungrateful, selfish, disrespectful, disloyal, etc.).

5. Wait respectfully for an answer. The choice to forgive is fully theirs; you cannot and should not try to force them to forgive you. If the person says, "Yes, I forgive you," thank him/her sincerely, express a desire to make restitution (if appropriate) and take your leave. A long introduction or closing statement is unnecessary and painful for both of you; keep it short. Get to the point, seek forgiveness and leave shortly thereafter. If the person decides not to forgive you, thank him/her for hearing you out and express a desire to make restitution (if appropriate). Take your leave or say goodbye if you phoned. Leave the responsibility for making peace with them; you have begun the process. Whatever their response, make sure your actions and words from that

277

point on reflect true repentance on your part. Love them for Christ's sake.

Another whole book could be written to detail how we should live in loving relationships with others after we have been reconciled by confession and forgiveness. That book is already in print; and its title is *The Holy Bible.* Incidentally, you will be amazed how your prayer life will improve after you have sought peace with those about you.

SOME PEOPLE STRUGGLE WITH UNHOLY FORCES.

A sixth problem with prayer is the simple fact of our spiritual warfare against Satan and his forces. While we spoke of this earlier, a brief review is contained here.

Why people struggle with unholy forces.

You cannot avoid a fight if you are being consistently attacked by another person. Like the bully who pushes you every day, Satan and his demonic horde are always prodding us toward sin. Either we give in and surrender or we fight back. Christians are called to battle by the Lord against the foes of the souls of men (Ephesians 6:11-20).

Not only does Satan use his spiritual minions to oppose the kingdom of God, but people given to evil also do the bidding of the evil one. Their opposition to the Christian may be direct, such as the Jews who followed Paul around stirring up the crowds against him (II Timothy 3:10-13). Or their opposition may be more secretive and sinister as they come with smiles and hugs to lure us away from the truth into the doctrine of demons (II Corinthians 11:13-15; II Peter 3:17). Whatever their style of attack we must oppose them in the strength of Christ and also attempt to win them over to the cause of Christ. For men caught in sin are to be pitied as well as opposed, loved as well as resisted.

Results when people struggle with unholy forces.

Spiritual opposition was shown in Daniel's day to delay God's answers to the prayers of His people (Daniel 10:12-13). We may experience similar slowed responses in our lives as we become more involved in the war around us. If we are not aware of the struggle involved, we might mistake the silence of waiting for a denial by God of our requests for help under fire.

Struggling with the principalities of darkness is also exhausting. When Jesus faced His greatest spiritual opposition in His wilderness temptations and in His prayers at Gethsemane, He was left so drained that angels had to come to strengthen Him on both occasions (Mark 1:13; Luke 22:43). The drain for us sometimes comes through such intense periods of spiritual struggle, but more often seems to result from the attrition of energy that comes from our daily skirmishes with evil. We get tired of waiting for the final victory which awaits the coming of Christ. We grow weary in well doing (Galatians 6:9).

When we are not alert in prayer, we may find ourselves becoming irregular in our prayer closet warfare or shallow in what we say to the Lord. Most of us have experienced the jolting realization that, as we begin to pray at Sunday worship, the last time we purposefully prayed was at *last* Sunday's service. Tired soldiers make mistakes, even letting their guns be stolen while they try to sleep. We must not allow our prayer and Bible study to be taken from us while we try to rest from the battle (Ephesians 6:18; I Peter 3:7).

Help for people struggling with unholy forces.

In Ephesians chapter six, Paul describes our spiritual warfare in some detail. First, he tells us the source of our strength: "Be strong *in the Lord*, and in the strength of *His* might" (Ephesians 6:10). Second, he introduces our foes:

> Put on the full armor of God, that you may be able to stand firm against the schemes of *the devil*. For our struggle is not against the flesh and blood, but against *the rulers*, against *the powers*, against *the world forces of this darkness*, against *the spiritual forces of wickedness in the heavenly places* (Ephesians 6:11-12).

Third, he describes the armor which protects us in battle: truth, righteousness, the gospel of peace, faith (as the shield against Satan's attacks), salvation and the word of God (which is the offensive weapon of the set; the "sword of the Spirit") (Ephesians 6:13-17). Lastly, Paul describes our plan of attack: PRAYER! We oppose evil by our intense petitions before the Lord, calling upon Him to gain the victories so the glory goes to Him.

Each of those armor segments make our prayers more invulnerable to attack by the forces of darkness. Our understanding of God's *truth* defeats the enemies attempts to deceive us. The *righteousness* we have in Christ gives the enemy no handle of sin to pull us down. Our readiness to share *the gospel of peace* implies both our willingness to serve God, not Satan, and our commitment to free those bound in the kingdom of darkness. By *the shield of faith* we turn back each temptation and assault. Sure of our *salvation* we have no doubts about our relationship to God which the enemy could exploit. And, in our prayers, we wield *the word of God* to fight back against the enemy with the commands and promises of God, even as Jesus did in the wilderness (Matthew 4:2-11).

Three other weapons are suggested in the book of Revelation. Satan, "the accuser of our brethren," is described as being overcome because of: "the blood of the Lamb," "the word of their testimony" and the fact that "they did not love their life even to death" (Revelation 12:10-11). "The blood of the Lamb" refers to what Jesus did for us on Golgotha, saving us from the wrath of God for our sins and overcoming the devil forever. The "blood" proclaims that we are fighting a foe who has already been defeated. "The word of their testimony" refers to the confession of the Christians that they had accepted what Jesus did for them personally, each of them was washed in the blood of the Lamb. Satan has no right to clutch them or command them; they are free from his dark realm. And, since "they did not love their life even to death," their commitment to Christ is complete and unchangeable; Satan cannot even use death to frighten them into recanting their faith in Christ. God in us will always finally overcome the forces of this world (I John 4:2-4; 5:4-5). So don't give up; fight on to victory in Jesus Christ!

SOME PEOPLE STRUGGLE WITH UNGRACIOUS MOTIVES.

God does not just look at the length and content of our prayers; He weighs the motives and intents behind the words. And sometimes our selfish motives defeat our prayers. God is not going to encourage our greed or ingratitude by rewarding them with His grace.

Why people struggle with ungracious motives.

At the base of all ungracious motives to pray is selfishness (James 4:3). We want what we request for *our* pleasure, for *our* comfort, for *our* enjoyment. Our request might be perfectly good, viewed by itself.

For example, a man requests a Sunday School class to pray that his son will accept Christ. "Fine," we think, "what a concerned Christian parent," until we ask why he requests these prayers right now. "Well," the father replies, "John has been coming in late each night for the last week. My wife keeps worrying about him and we get into fights with him all the time. I figure, if John straightens up and accepts Jesus, we'll have a lot nicer home to live in and I can get some peace." Now the request for prayer looks a little different. Dad is not primarily fretting over the eternal life of his son or desiring that the Lord's will be done in his child's life; he just wants some peace and quiet. His prayer is essentially self-serving.

"Just a second there," you say, "wouldn't that mean that all petitions would be wrong since they all ask something for us personally?" Not at all. We can ask for something for ourselves without being selfish in the asking. The difference lies again in the motives behind our request. Am I asking something to meet my basic needs or to aid my growth in Christ or to increase my service in God's kingdom? All of these prayer motives God approves. But am I asking to simply add to my personal pleasure and comfort? This is the selfish motive that James warns us about: "You ask and do not receive, because you ask with wrong motives, so that you may spend it on your pleasures" (James 4:3). When I only want things to make me happy, I am desiring to make myself more important than others and to adapt the world around me to my design. This petty idol-making is what God cannot and will not encourage.

Results when people struggle with ungracious motives.

One of the results of selfish motives in prayer is an increase in ingratitude. The greedy person never has enough and therefore is never satisfied with what he receives. "He who loves money will not be satisfied with money, nor he who loves abundance with its income. This too is vanity" (Ecclesiastes 5:10). How can we truly be thankful as we should be for what we receive when our hearts are grumbling, "I wish there'd been a little more"?

A second result of ungracious prayers can be a marked reduction in intercession for others. We tend to focus our prayers on what we care about, and, if our happiness is uppermost in our minds, prayers for others will take a distant second place. We may even use praise or thanksgiving or intercession as bargaining chips with God. We can think, "Now I know God doesn't like me to be greedy, so I'll praise and thank Him first and pray about other people (He'll like that) and put my petitions (the IMPORTANT prayers) last. Won't He think I'm humble?" Stated in black and white, that sounds silly; but the thought has crossed too many Christian minds to be funny.

A third result of a self-centered prayerlife is stinginess toward those in need around us and toward God. If I pray to receive for myself, I am hardly going to give away all the good stuff I prayed so hard to get for me. I may take some token gift out of my abundance because it makes me feel good, but that is about all. I only tithe when I can afford it (rarely) and I only give to those who are in need more than I am (and who needs more than I?). With such attitudes come further judgments from God. Solomon warned, "He who shuts his ear to the cry of the poor will also cry himself and not be answered" (Proverbs 21:13). And Malachi warns that those who rob from God by not bringing their tithes and offerings to Him will not avoid a "devourer" who will destroy the increase they sought to keep (Malachi 3:7-12). How does one escape this fascination with oneself?

Help for people struggling with ungracious motives.

First, the selfish person has to come to accept that he *is* selfish and confess this sin to God. As he finds forgiveness, he must take active steps to change. The move to selflessness and loving God and others first can begin in prayer. We can ask God for a heart to love as Christ loves. We can consciously choose to spend more time in praise to God and in intercession for others while limiting our petitions to real needs for ourselves.

Another way to become more selfless is suggested by Paul to those who are trying to stop being thieves (a selfish occupation).

> Let him who steals steal no longer; but rather let him labor, performing with his own hands what is good, in order that he may have something to share with him who has need (Ephesians 4:28).

Not only must the one who steals stop stealing, he must replace the self-centered activity of stealing with the other-centered activity of working to share with the needy. To simplify, stop taking and start giving. Giving focuses our attention on others and their needs, if done correctly. Giving also brings with it spiritual blessings: we find more happiness in giving than in receiving and God responds to our giving by giving us more to give. (See Acts 20:35; Luke 6:38; II Corinthians 9:6-15.)

Giving does not limit itself to monetary gifts, but includes sharing possessions, sharing labor, giving time to talk and listen. Intercession is a form of giving, as are appreciation and encouragement. The secret of all giving is demanding nothing to be given back and, in fact, "expecting nothing in return" (Luke 6:30, 34-38). Do not turn giving into selfishness by making it a manipulation to put others in your debt. Give for the simple joyful obedience of living like your generous heavenly Father (Luke 6:35-36).

SOME PEOPLE STRUGGLE WITH UNEMOTIONAL PRAYERS.

John Bunyon once said, "In prayer it is better to have a heart without words than words without a heart."[9] While every prayer need not be a "Gethsemane agonizing," a steady habit of unemotional prayers may be a developing spiritual problem.

Why people struggle with unemotional prayers.

A consistent lack of emotion in our prayers *may* indicate a lack of

---

9. Source unknown.

commitment or personal involvement in the prayer process. Everyone has times when prayer is a dry chore to be done rather than a spontaneous act of joy. That is our nature and may be influenced greatly by our natural temperment. Some people are given to easy displays of emotion while others are by nature reserved and not very demonstrative. But neither temporary "dry spells" nor natural inclinations are the problem we are discussing here.

The unemotional problem in prayer arises when we are holding ourselves back from becoming fully involved with our communication with God. We sometimes stand aloof because we really are not interested in praying and only do so out of duty or habit. There may be a little resentment in our lack of enthusiasm. Also we may be sheltering an unconfessed sin and so we are far from eager to get too close to the Lord. We may be hurt by God's denial of a previous request and spiritually pouting. Finally, our coolness may be the result of a rationalistic approach to life which denies any validity to our emotions. This view of life is not as intellectually defensible as it seems at first glance.

> . . . we can use our reason to the exclusion of all other means of obtaining knowledge. Nothing is more unreasonable than the effort to be exclusively cerebral about anything that pertains to the mystery of God or even to the mystery of human life. Those persons whose pretended knowledge of God or humanity rests entirely on what they see with their observing minds can know nothing at all of either mystery.[10]

Purely logical prayer is rather like computer generated music; the notes are right but the heart is missing. The computer does not care, even if the notes are right or not. It just plays as it is programmed. When we just pray because that is the way we are "programmed," our prayers do not care and that is not the way we are to pray.

---

10. Carroll E. Simcox, *Prayer/The Divine Dialog* (Downers Grove, Illinois: Inter Varsity Press, 1985), pp. 49-50.

Results when people struggle with unemotional prayers.

The first step back in regaining feeling in prayer is self-honesty. Ask the Lord to help you find what you are trying to hide in the freezer compartment of your heart. It is often a sinful attitude or desire which we have been unwilling to face. A man or woman playing with the idea of an affair may hide that away, both shocked at the thought and intrigued by it. We know that to admit it to God would require giving up the little morsel and we are not ready to do so yet. So we hide it instead and try to keep God at arm's length, lest He "find out." Of course, God already knows what we have thought and is hardly shocked by it. But, we must surrender both the sinful desire and our attempt to hide it to God to restore openness to our relationship with Him.

When we pray, we should pray about what matters to us. It does no good to state "nice" polite requests when we want to blurt out, "God, I'm furious with You! How could You have let me be humiliated like that? Don't You care about me at all? I wonder if You are even listening to me!" Before you throw this book down in shock and disgust at even suggesting you talk that way to the God of glory, may I suggest you read through some of the things Job said to God? Or look at the Psalms Jesus quoted from the cross:

My God, My God, why hast Thou forsaken Me? Far from my deliverance are the words of my groaning. O my God, I cry by day, but Thou dost not answer; and by night, but I have found no rest (Psalm 22:1-2).

The book of Psalms contains many "psalms of complaint." Again I remind you that you are not going to shock God with what is in your heart; He already knows it. If you are angry with Him, tell Him so. If you feel abandoned and helpless, let Him hear about it. Pray about what really matters to you and your prayers will not lack for emotional involvement.

Men, I need to talk with you for a moment. We live in a society where many of us were raised to hide our emotions, to remain "cool" at all times. Certainly Jesus is the epitome of manhood, yet see how His prayerlife is described in Scripture:

And being in agony He was praying very fervently; and His sweat became like drops of blood, falling down upon the ground (Luke 22:44). In the days of His flesh, He offered up both prayers and supplications with loud crying and tears to the One able to save Him from death, and He was heard because of His piety (Hebrews 5:7).

You may recall that the shortest verse in the Bible is the simple declaration, "Jesus wept" (John 11:35). True manhood does not mask its feelings, but admits them and deals with the situations causing them. Men, pray with fervency and not with shame but with joy that you care as Christ does.

A last barrier to be removed to bringing our emotions back into our prayerlife is a commitment to act when God desires it. Many times we can remain distant from our prayers because emotional involvement would lead to total involvement in answering our prayers. I may just avoid prayer too often if I know a truthful confrontation with the Lord will lead to me trying to give up a pampered bad habit. But whatever the action I know will be required, I must either face it or give up on a relationship with God in prayer. His call to holiness will not change; my sinful opposition to His will must go. And what I cannot imagine myself doing, He will enable me to do for Him.

SOME PEOPLE STRUGGLE WITH UNREASONING PRAYERS.

The opposite problem to unemotional prayer is prayer which is unreasoning, controlled by emotionalism. The domination of our prayerlife by our feelings can be as harmful as cold formalism.

There are two perils to be avoided. One is emotional unreality and the other is intellectual preoccupation. There must be truth as well as spirit in worship, and nowhere is the combination more necessary than in the secret place of prayer.[11]

---

11. Samuel Chadwick quoted in Muck, p. 173.

Why people struggle with unreasoning prayers.

Jesus spoke of a type of person who seemed dominated by his/her emotions, immediately following Him with joy and immediately leaving Him when faced with opposition (Mark 4:16-17). He says of them that "they have no firm root in themselves." Feelings-oriented people are exactly so; unstable and changeable, irresolute and never fully committed. Now they *feel* fully committed, but feelings have a way of changing.

When applied to our prayers, feelings are indeed a part of our devotion; but emotions are neither the whole nor the most important part of prayer.

Feelings are fickle, easily influenced by health, morale, weather, and mood. Prayer is too important to be put at the mercy of our feelings.[12]

Yet there is a move afoot in Christendom to make our emotions the channel by which the Holy Spirit expresses His direction to us. We saw the fallacy of this theory in an earlier chapter, but many still await the proper feeling to direct their prayers. The results of such an emotional dependency are sad.

Results when people struggle with unreasoning prayers.

One of the first fatalities of an unreasoning emotional prayerlife is regularity in prayer. We cannot pray "when we feel like it" or "feel the Spirit moving in our hearts" and expect much in terms of a disciplined prayerlife. We know not to make any other major decisions of life on the basis of sheer emotion. Even when I wake up in the morning, all of *my* emotions are shouting, "Turn off the sun! Roll over! Back to sleep!" (I am not a "morning person.") But no one would applaud me for following my feelings in that case. Why should I follow them in deciding

---

12. David A. Hubbard, *The Problem with Prayer Is . . .* (Wheaton, Illinois: Tyndale House Publishers, 1972), p. 60.

when to pray? The only result for me would be to know for sure that I would never be "led" by my emotions to pray early in the morning. Praying by feeling leaves prayer irregular at best. If we are in fact in a spiritual dry time, we may not "feel" like praying at all, and so, following our emotions, we would just stop.

Another result of unreasonable prayer would be to leave us at the mercy of our anger and fear. Anger is opposed to the love God intends for us and fear is opposed to the faith we are to hold. Yet, if our emotions have sway in us, anger will cause cursing to be coming out of the same mouth that prays for blessing, which should not be happening (James 3:9-10). If we listen to our fears, our confidence before God in prayer is lost. Emotionally, we tend to react to our problems with fear rather than to stay focused on the faithfulness of the Father.

Directed by our feelings, we tend to make ourselves the judges of truth. Is this action right or wrong? God may say it is wrong in the Bible, but what if my "sanctified" feelings disagree? How often I have heard, "I can't obey that until I know it is right for me." What they mean is "until I *feel* it is right for me." Such a way of life puts our emotions in the place of judging the correctness of God's Word, instead of the Word judging whether our emotions are correct. The spiritual danger to such people should be obvious, but it is not, if they do not feel that they are in danger.

Help for people struggling with unreasoning prayers.

Emotions are a wonderful gift from God if they are kept under the control of our will which is instructed by the Word of God. Self-control is a fruit of the Spirit we should constantly be praying to develop. We need to cooperate in this development by consistently doing what we know to be God's will *regardless of how we feel*. When it is time to pray, pray, with or without a burning heart. The proper emotions will respond to our choice to pray as we ought, but there is no guarantee that following our emotions will lead us to pray as we ought.

When your emotions are running counter to the will of God, admit this to Him and ask Him to give you thoughts to meditate upon which will alter your emotions. Certainly, as I begin to concentrate upon the love of God, for example, my feelings of helplessness and loneliness are replaced by joy, love and peace. Paul said that as we bring our burdens to God, thanking Him for His blessings, and as we think on the positive things of God and obey Him, the result will be that both the peace of God and the God of peace will be with us (Philippians 4:6-9).

When anger or fear try to take control, immediately call to God for help and He will free you as you concentrate on His mercy and greatness. If you fall into sin by following your feelings, repent and confess and ask God to help you focus on His Word and not your feelings.

Emotions are physical reactions to the way we perceive our situation at any given moment. They help us be physically prepared to run or fight or sing with power and joy. They were never intended to be our masters but our servants. Actually, our feelings can only serve us well when they are under the control of our wills which are in turn under the control of the will of God. Then we are free to feel and to speak and to act and to pray as our Lord desires for us.

SOME PEOPLE STRUGGLE WITH UNDISCIPLINED PRAYERS.

"I want to pray regularly, but I don't know how to start." "I keep having weird thoughts come into my head when I try to pray; am I weird myself?" "I try to talk to God whenever I can, but I never seem to have enough time." Sound familiar? Many people struggle with getting a regular quiet time just because they cannot discipline themselves. How about you?

Why people struggle with undisciplined prayers.

Many people do not have a regular quiet time with God because they just do not know how to go about it. They are "afraid of doing it wrong" or "think they will look stupid if anyone saw them." Even the apostles asked Jesus, "Lord, teach us to pray just as John also taught his disciples" (Luke 11:1). So it is not unusual for people to need instruction on regulating their prayer habits.

Other Christians are "quiet time dropouts." They have tried to start a quiet time on many different occasions. For some reason, they always falter before the devotional habit is set. Then, each new attempt creates a greater fear of renewed failure until some just give up on ever meeting regularly with God.

Some of us have to admit to being lazy. A daily prayer regimen is opposed by Satan's forces and is therefore not easy. And it sure feels better just to stay in that warm bed. So we need the admonition:

> We do not want you to become lazy, but to imitate those who through faith and patience inherit what has been promised (Hebrews 6:12, NIV).

Some of us have never learned to manage our time well. We just go where the press of events pushes us. We are controlled by urgent messages from others rather than by priorities set in cooperation with our Father in heaven. We do not know how to say "No" to others and so we cannot say "Yes" to the Lord to get away each day to talk with Him. The British New Testament scholar William Barclay observed:

> In an age that believes in incessant action, silent waiting is an unpalatable prescription. For a man whose every waking moment is occupied—who even steals time from the hours of sleep—there may be necessary a complete reorganization of life, if he is to find time for this silent waiting on the Spirit. It is hard to find time for that apparent "doing nothing" which means everything.[13]

Results when people struggle with undisciplined prayers.

Without discipline and planning, we will have no regular place for prayer, no regular time to meet God and no regular order to follow in our quiet time. We will be at the mercy of wandering thoughts which distract us in the very midst of talking with God. Our prayerlife will become irregular and triggered only by one crisis or another (for which we are never spiritually prepared). Careless preparation for communing with the Lord God leaves us repeating comfortable phrases until they have all the meaning worn out of them. How can we change all this?

---

13. *The Promise of the Spirit* (London: Wyvern Books, 1964), p. 125.

Help for people struggling with undisciplined prayers.

Every good habit begins with a commitment to act and is sustained by consistent repetition and starting over immediately if a break should occur. To begin the discipline of a daily quiet time with God, you must decide when you are going to have it, where you are going to be and how you are going to go about it. Here are some suggestions about each.

When are you going to have your daily quiet time with God? Each person has to make a personal decision here. My schedule is no doubt different than yours and so the time for your devotional period and its length will probably be different, too. Some prefer the morning hours and there is considerable Biblical basis for that (Psalm 5:3; Mark 1:35, etc.). The morning devotion starts the day with God and brings Him to mind as we wake and plan our day. It is probably the favorite choice of most people. Early hours are usually quiet times around most homes when solitary devotions may be uninterrupted by others. Scriptures studied in the morning may provide guidance for the day ahead.

Some prefer evening devotions. Again, the Scriptures give examples of those who chose the night to approach the throne of the Almighty (Psalm 4:4; 63:6, etc.). The night is a good time to review the day to give thanks and confess sins; then petitions and intercessions may be offered for the day ahead. The Scriptures studies just before bed have the opportunity to fill the mind through the night and send us into a comfortable sleep. Again the night is a time when many households settle down and a truly "quiet" time may be had. Those who are "night people" may be more alert in the evening than in the morning.

There is no "right" or "wrong" time here. Find the best time in your schedule. Some mothers of young children like to wait for nap time or after the children leave for school to have their devotions. Some business people use part of their lunch hour or break time. Those with more time available may have more than one quiet time each day. Some have a morning watch where they read their Bible and have a time of praise, petition and intercession with the Lord for the day ahead; they then close the day with an evening watch in which they review their Scripture reading and end the day with thanksgiving and confession to prepare their hearts for rest. Still others pray three times a day as Daniel did (Daniel 6:10). How often and when you pray is determined by your situation and schedule.

Now how long should your devotions be? Again there is no fixed rule. Some spend as little as five minutes while others spend an hour or more. Regardless of what you may have heard, I find no indication in the Bible that God is particularly impressed by long prayers. The only long prayers mentioned in the New Testament are those of the scribes and Pharisees who are condemned for making these long prayers only "for a pretense" and "for appearance's sake" (Matthew 23:14; Mark 12:40; Luke 20:47). Special needs may lengthen your prayer time, but it would seen best to begin with a modest target and lengthen it as you have need. Some have started with five minutes of Scripture reading and five minutes of prayer. It is better to start small and grow than to try for an hour and fail.

Where are you going to have your daily quiet time with God? Find a place which is quiet, private and comfortable, *if possible*. I realize this will be easier for some than for others. A chair in your bedroom, a corner of the basement, a nearby church or library which is open when you need it; wherever you choose, find a place where you can concentrate on God. Be creative. Use ear plugs to provide quiet if none exists. Susanna Wesley with her many children was said to just pull her long apron up over her head when she needed to get away with the Lord (she had trained her children not to bother Mother when her apron was on her head). Look around and find a place.

How are you going to go about your daily quiet time with God? First, clarify what you are trying to do during your quiet time. This is NOT the time to work on a Sunday School lesson or prepare a communion devotion. This is a time to prepare your heart to hear the Word of God for your life today. This is a time for your own personal spiritual growth. So, if you want to have family devotions, great! But have them at another time. Quiet time is a private conference between you and the Lord.

Second, take a minute or so at the beginning of each devotional period to prepare your heart to meet with your Father, the Lord God Almighty, Creator of all things great and small and the King of kings over all the universe. If you were invited to a private interview with the President of the United States, you would want a minute to prepare your thoughts before being ushered into the President's office. Here each day you have the high privilege of meeting with Someone infinitely greater; still the rushing of your thoughts and focus on Him as you enter His presence. A verse to focus on at this time might be, "Cease striving and know that I am God" (Psalm 46:10).

Third, after a sentence or two of praise to the Lord, ask for His wisdom as you read His Word. Then begin your daily Bible reading. The point here is not to study the Bible in depth. That should be done with a Bible study group or Sunday School class or, if private, at a separate time. Here we are reading His Word to receive encouragement and direction for this day. Those who have committed themselves to regular Bible reading have often testified how the Lord speaks through a particular passage to meet their specific needs for that specific day.

There are many Bible reading plans available. Just make sure you do not try to read too much for the time you have. Otherwise you can get depressed by being constantly rushed to finish the reading and more depressed as you get behind on your readings, to the point that many give up on their devotions. Instead of trying for distance, try reading for understanding. Simply ask, as you read, "Lord, what do I need to know to become more like Christ and please you today?" Read and reread major sections of the Bible until they become a part of your thought patterns, like the following (just a sample):

the creation (Genesis 1-2), the fall of man (Genesis 3), the faith of Abraham (Genesis 22:1-19), the ten commandments (Exodus 20:1-21), the great commandment (Deuteronomy 6), Joshua's call to leadership (Joshua 1), the life of Gideon (Judges 6-8), the life of Samson (Judges 13-16), Ruth's story (Ruth), David's sin and repentance (II Samuel 11-12 and Psalm 51), the life of Elijah (I Kings 17-19 and II Kings 2), Joash repairs the temple (II Kings 12), Nehemiah rebuilds Jerusalem's walls (Nehemiah 1-6), Esther's story (Esther), any of the Psalms, any chapter of Proverbs, the folly of worldly living (Ecclesiastes), the beauty of marital love (Song of Solomon), the charge against Israel (Isaiah 1), Isaiah's commission (Isaiah 6), the suffering Servant (Isaiah 52:13-53:12), call to the thirsty (Isaiah 55), true fasting (Isaiah 58), Lamentations, the soul who sins (Ezekiel 18), Daniel's life (Daniel), Hosea and his wife (Hosea 1-3), Jonah's story (Jonah), true and false worship (Malachi), the sermon on the mount (Matthew 5-7), the prologue to John's gospel (John 1:1-18), Jesus' high priestly prayer (John 17), any chapter of the gospels, the beginning of the church (Acts 2), Paul's textbook on basic theology (Romans), the source of unity (Ephesians), the source of joy (Philippians), stand firm until Christ returns (I Thessalonians), three lessons on leading the church (I and II Timothy and Titus), the superiority of Christ (Hebrews), practical Christian living (James), signs of salvation (I John), letters to seven churches (Revelation 2-3), heavenly worship (Revelation 4-5), and the last judgment and the new Jerusalem (Revelation 20-22).

You may want to use simple markings in your Bible's margin to note verses you especially want to act on. Here is one such marking system.

Use " + " to mark positive commands, principles or examples you want to add to your life.
Use "-" to mark negative commands, principles or examples you want to remove from your life.
Use "P" to mark promises of God you want to claim for your life.
Use "?" to mark verses which you do not understand and want to investigate further at a later time.

Be sure to use a translation of the Bible which is both easy for you to understand and an accurate rendering of the Scriptures in english. My personal choices would include the New American Standard Version and the New International Version. If you were raised on the King James Version and can mentally translate it into modern english, by all means use it. But you might want to keep a modern translation nearby to help you update some of the phrases.

Fourth, begin your prayer time. Here are some suggestions. Try to keep your prayer generally balanced between time spent on praise, thanksgiving, petition, intercession and confession. The order may vary, though it is often good to begin with praise and thanksgiving, turn to confession and petitions and close with a period of intercession for others. Use a prayer notebook to keep a record of your requests and God's answers and to list those for whom you have committed yourself to pray regularly.

What position should your body be in when you pray? The Bible has people praying standing, sitting, kneeling and lying down. While kneeling is more of a posture of humility, it is not the best if you have a tendency to drop off to sleep. Vary your position to stay comfortable but not too comfortable. Perhaps this poem by Sam Walker will make my point.

> The proper way for a man to pray, said Deacon Herman Pease
> And the only proper attitude is down upon his knees;
> Now I should say the way to pray, said Reverend Doctor Wise
> Is standing straight with outstretched arms, enrapt and upturned eyes.
> Oh, no, no, no! said Elder Snow, such posture is too proud,
> A man should pray with eyes fast closed and head contritely bow-ed;
> It seems to me his hands should be ostensibly clasped in front,
> With thumbs a-pointing toward the ground, said Reverend Doctor Blunt;
> Last year I fell in Hutson's well head first, said Cyrus Brown,
> With both my heels a-stickin' up, my head a-pointin' down;
> And I made a prayer right then and there, best prayer I ever said—
> The prayin'st prayer I ever prayed, was standin' on my head![14]

I suggest you try praying aloud in a natural but quiet tone of voice. This will help us in several ways: audible prayer helps us feel the reality of talking to another Person; audible prayer helps prepare us for praying aloud with others; and audible prayer helps us to concentrate and choose our words wisely. Use words which come to you naturally without using coarse words or foul language. God will understand you just fine.

If you experience the common problem of wandering thoughts, when you realize you are off beam, *do not let your embarrassment stop your prayer.* Simply acknowledge to God that you got sidetracked and pray about the thoughts you wandered into (apparently they are something that interest you right now, so talk to God about them). Again, praying aloud and having a prayer list to follow can also help to keep you on track.

---

14. Source unknown.

Vary your devotional time to keep it fresh. Do not allow boredom to keep you from your daily appointment with God. Use devotional readings occasionally (but do not allow these to replace direct reading from the Bible). Try memorizing Scriptures regularly. Keep a hymnal nearby and sing softly as a part of your personal worship. Plan a period of quiet to meditate on your Scripture reading to seek how to apply it in your life. Read inspirational poetry. Have your devotions outside (weather permitting) or, better yet, have your prayer time as you take a walk in the country (my favorite). Try fasting and prayer as an occasional change. Work to make your quiet time with the Lord a special time you look forward to instead of dread.

Now, what about when you have skipped one or more days for some reason (good or not)? Again, *do not let your embarrassment cause you to give up your quiet time.* Just tell God what happened and recommit yourself to meet with Him regularly. If you miss a morning watch, nothing says you cannot have your devotions in the evening this once. If you have been following a reading schedule, do not put yourself under pressure trying to catch up. Just begin with the reading for this day and go on from there.

Most important, get started! Below is a sample commitment sheet you may want to fill in right not (even if you are already involved with personal devotions). Why not now?

MY QUIET TIME COMMITMENT

Following the example of my Lord Jesus, I commit myself to strive to draw apart each day to meet with God in Bible reading and prayer. I plan to begin each day at _____ and meet with Him at
                                                      (time)
_____. I am beginning this commitment on _____. May the
(place)   (date)
Lord use this devotional time to His eternal glory through Jesus Christ.

Signed,

_____

(your name)

A good test of the reality of our prayer is the spirit in which we come from it and turn to our ordinary duties. If we feel little or no connection between the two sides of our life there must be some mistake somewhere. A good prayer is not tested by our feelings or fervor at the time but by our behavior afterwards.[15]

Prayer should change us steadily and day by day to conform more closely to the image of the lifestyle of Jesus Christ. If our prayers do not change us, they have failed at a basic level. For prayer is to be a self offering to God, presented with the request, "Thy will be done in me."

A Closing Warning.

A book on prayer has certain inherent dangers. First, we may become a spectator of our own prayers, listening to see if we are "doing it right." This is rather like a beginning golfer. He tries to keep so many different rules and pointers in his head as he swings that he cannot relax, hit the ball and enjoy the game. Remember that God is not expecting perfect prayers or perfect pray-ers, but the words of children, His children. He delights in our most miserable attempts. Relax and pray.

The only way to pray is to pray, and the way to pray well is to pray much. If one has no time for this, then one must at least pray regularly. But the less one prays the worse it goes.[16]

You will not learn to pray from this or any other book; you will learn to pray by praying.

A second warning; do not seek to say "good prayers." By "good prayer" I mean prayers which sound good, are well balanced and use proper form. Such prayers become an end in themselves; showpieces. Pharisees were experts at such "good prayers" and Jesus said that the only reward they got for such prayers was the recognition people gave

---

15. Olive Wyon quoted in Osborne T. Miller, comp., *The Path of Prayer* (New York: Harper and Brothers Publishers, 1954), p. 140.

16. Anonymous quoted in Lowder, p. 7.

them. God was neither impressed nor moved to grant such model works (Matthew 6:5).

And a final warning and challenge from the pen of Olive Wyon; "It is dangerous to read a great deal *about* prayer, unless at the same time we are doing all we can to practice it."[17] Over the door of an eastern college library is this statement: "He who reads and reads and never does is like the farmer who plows and plows and never sows. " May this book have planted some seeds which will grow into a flourishing prayer ministry in your life and church. May you reach out each day and touch the love and power of God through Jesus Christ and be changed. Amen.

Thought or Discussion Questions

1. Why do some people have a hard time believing that prayer "works"? What are some results of doubting the effectiveness of prayer? What four sources provide evidence to believe that prayer is a reality? What testimony could you give as to how prayer has worked in your life? What does it really mean when we question the reality of prayer?

2. How can we not believe about ourselves in relation to prayer? What results from such unbelief? How would you help someone who felt they were unworthy to pray? How would you help someone who felt that they do not need to pray?

3. Why is unbelief about God the most serious of the problems we can have related to prayer? Why do people refuse to believe in (trust) God? What three results are apparent concerning one who refuses to trust God? How would you lead a non-Christian to accept Jesus Christ as their Lord and Savior? How would you respond to a fellow Christian who is experiencing doubts about God's goodness?

4. What do you mean by "presuming on God's grace"? In what four ways do people try to deal with guilt aside from repentance and confes-

---

17. *The School of Prayer* (London: SCM Press, 1943), p. 126.

sion? How would you lead someone through the steps of repentance and confession to gain a clear conscience?

5. What three sinful desires lie at the base of our unloving relationships? How does each divide us from other people? What happens as a result of unloving relationships to our prayerlife? How do we go about forgiving others? How do we go about seeking forgiveness from others? Are there those you need to forgive or ask for forgiveness today?

6. What unholy forces oppose our prayers? How does the unseen battle affect our prayers? How does each part of our armor strengthen our prayer? What are our five spiritual weapons and how do we use each one against the dark army?

7. What is the basic ungracious motive behind our prayers? Does this mean all my prayers are from the wrong motive? What are three results of selfish prayers? How would you counsel someone trying to be more unselfish in both his/her prayers and lifestyle?

8. What is good about using our emotion in prayer? How does praying without significant feeling affect us? How would you overcome a habit of cold, unfeeling prayer? How honest can we be in our prayers? Explain. What can we say in prayer which would shock God? What could we say which would not please Him?

9. What is not good about using our emotions in prayer? What three negative results come from praying by our feelings? How does someone pull themselves out of a feeling-orientation to life? How could you help such a person?

10. Why do people have trouble having a consistent daily prayer time in their lives? What are the results of a lack of personal discipline? How does one decide when and how long to pray each day? What would you look for in a good place for daily devotions? What are the four steps to an effective quiet time? What is the purpose for daily Bible reading? What would you suggest to someone just starting a daily prayer time? How should you handle wandering thoughts? Why use a variety of approaches for your devotional time? List some variations you can use.

What do you do if you skip a few days? What are the dangers of reading this book? What have you gained from studying through this subject? Will you commit yourself to a life of fellowship with the Father in prayer?

APPENDIXES

APPENDIX A

BIBLICAL WORDS ASSOCIATED WITH PRAYER

In the two charts below, the various words used in the Old and New Testaments for communicating with the Lord are listed and examined. These lists are extensive without presuming to be exhaustive.

The term, "uses," in the first column indicates how often the word is used in the Bible; but not every "use" of the word concerns prayer. Also, words are listed in alphabetical order of the Hebrew alphabet in the first chart and of the Greek alphabet in the second.

I. Old Testament Words Associated With Prayer

Hebrew/ Aramaic Words	Major English Translations	Prayer Emphasis	Meaning (Especially When Used For Prayer)[1]
alah, noun 38 uses	oath, curse	petition	A request for God to witness a covenant or to condemn another (often a covenant-breaker). Ezekiel 17:11-21
amar, verb 5276 uses	say, speak	action	To say, verbally communicate, accent on content rather than activity of speaking. Genesis 32:9
anna, interjection 19 uses	beseech, O	emotion, petition	A strong participle of entreaty. Psalm 116:4
anachah, noun 21 uses	groan, sigh	emotion	A weeping in any sorrow which may be heard by the Lord. Psalm 38:9
bakah, verb 110 uses	weep	emotion, petition	To weep in joy or sorrow, to vocalize strong emotion, often in pleading or complaint. Numbers 11:18-20, Judges 20:23
beki, noun 30 uses	weeping	emotion	A sobbing (often to God). Psalm 6:8

302

bea, verb 12 uses	make petition, request	petition	To search for (favor from God), Aramaic. Daniel 6:12-13
baqash, verb 225 uses	seek	petition, intercession	To seek to receive, earnestly requesting of God according to His instructions. Deuteronomy 4:29, I Chronicles 16:10-11, Ezra 8:21-22
barak, verb 415 uses	bless	petition, intercession, praise	To kneel before God to bless Him, adoration, ask to endue with power for success. Genesis 14:19-20
dabar, verb 1137 uses	speak	action	To arrange words, accents the activity of speech rather than the content. Genesis 18:22-23, Psalm 145:21
dumiyyah, noun 7 uses	silent	action	A waiting in quiet resignation. Psalm 62:1, 65:1
damam, verb 34 uses	be still, be silent	action	To remain in silent meditation while waiting for God to act. Psalm 62:5
darash, verb 164 uses	seek, inquire	peition, action	To search for with care, to seek out God, especially for direction. Psalm 22:26; II Chronicles 7:14, 15:12-15
hadar, verb 10 uses	honor, glorify	praise	To show respect for, adorn with glory, Aramaic/Hebrew. Isaiah 63:1; Daniel 4:34,37; 5:23
hillul, noun 2 uses	praise, festival	praise, action, emotion	A festal jubilation with both merry making and thanksgiving. Leviticus 19:24
halal, verb 206 uses	praise, boast	praise, thanksgiving, emotion, action	To express deep thanksgiving by lauding God through song, music, dance and speaking; source of the word, "Hallelujah" ("Praise the Lord!"). Psalm 22:22-23; 150:1-6
hamah, verb 34 uses	roar, be boisterous	emotion	To make loud noise from unrest and discontent. Psalm 55:17

303

zamar, verb 46 uses	sing praise	action, praise	To make music in praise of God. Psalm 47:6-7
zaaq, verb 74 uses	cry out, cry, call	emotion, petition, intercession	To cry out for help in the time of distress. II Chronicles 20:9; Ezekiel 9:8
chakah, verb 15 uses	wait	action	To wait with earnest expectation and confident hope. Psalm 33:20; Isaiah 8:17, 64:4
chalah, verb 16 uses	entreat	petition	To seek the favor of God, usually for mercy or help. Exodus 32:11; Zechariah 8:21-22
chanan, verb 78 uses	be gracious, make supplication	peition	To ask God to bestow His favor especially in redemption from enemies, evils and sins. I Kings 8:33; Psalm 142:1
yeda, verb 2 uses	give thanks	thanksgiving, praise	To confess in praise, Aramaic. Daniel 2:23; 6:10
yedah, verb 114 uses	give thanks, praise, confess	thanksgiving, praise, confession	To acknowledge or confess the character and works of God or of our sin; there is no separate concept of thanksgiving in the Old Testament; thanks is absorbed into praise, even though scholars translate some words as "thanks" or "thanksgiving."[2] I Chronicles 16:34-35; Psalm 118:28-29
yachal, verb 40 uses	wait, hope	action, emotion	To wait with hope towards God as a solid ground of expectations, linked with trust. Psalm 69:3; Micah 7:7
kabed, verb 111 uses	honor, glorify	praise	To be or make heavy with honor Psalm 22:23; 86:9
kabod, noun 200 uses	glory, honor	praise	The glory seen to be God's due Psalm 29:1-2
lachash, noun 5 uses	whispered prayer	action	A whispering, charming; soft prayers in response to God's chastening. Isaiah 26:16

maseth, noun 14 uses	gift, portion, lifting	action	A lifting up of hands in prayer. Psalm 141:2
na, verb 380 uses	please, now	petition, emotion	To exhort to aid; basis of the word, "Hosanna" ("O Lord, save us!") in Psalm 118:25 Amos 7:2; Jonah 4:2-3
neaqah, noun 4 uses	groaning	emotion	The groans of the wounded or oppressed. Exodus 2:24; 6:5; Judges 2:18
nagad, verb 364 uses	tell, declare	action, praise, confession	To make conspicuous, to place a matter high. Deuteronomy 26:3; Psalm 38:18; 79:13; 142:2
nasa, verb 655 uses	lift, take, carry	action	To lift up or bear; of prayer, to lift the hands, voice, eyes or soul to God/heaven. Ezra 9:5-6; Psalm 25:1; 28:2; 123:1
paga, verb 44 uses	fall on, reach, intercede	intercession	To make contact with God on behalf of another. Numbers 21:7; Isaiah 53:12; 59:16
palal, verb 84 uses	pray	intercession, petition	To entreat, normally on behalf of another; most common Old Testament verb translated as "to pray." I Samuel 12:19; I Kings 8:26, 29-30
tsahal, verb 8 uses	cry aloud, shout	emotion, action	To cry out shrilly in distress or joy. Isaiah 12:5-6
tsela, verb 2 uses	pray	petition	To bow in prayer, Aramaic. Ezra 6:10; Daniel 6:10
tsaaq, verb 54 uses	cry out	petition, emotion	To call out for help under great distress. Exodus 8:12; 14:10; Psalm 107:6; Lamentations 2:18
tseaqah. noun 21 uses	cry, outcry	action	A cry of distress. Exodus 3:7, 9; 22:23

qarah, verb 46 uses	wait for, hope for	action	To wait for with eager anticipation in faith. Psalm 25:3, 5, 21; 27:14; 130:5
qol, noun 496 uses	voice, sound	action	A sound of voice. Genesis 30:6; Numbers 21:3; Psalm 27:7; 66:19; 77:1
qara, verb 733 uses	call, name, proclaim	action	To enunciate a specific message, often inviting a response; calling on the name of the Lord. Genesis 2:19; Deuteronomy 4:7; Psalm 116:2, 13, 17
rua, verb 45 uses	shout, sound	action, emotion	To raise a noise; war cry, shouts of joy, complaint or distress. Psalm 47:1;66:1; 81:1; 95:1-2
rub, verb 66 uses	contend, plead	petition	To strive or contend with. Job 23:3-6
rib, noun 62 uses	strife, case dispute	petition	A strife or lawsuit; a verbal contention. Job 9:1-3; Jeremiah 12:1
rinnah, noun 32 uses	shout of joy, cry	emotion, action	A ringing cry of joy or sorrow. Psalm 126:2, 5-6
ranan, verb 52 uses	sing for joy, shout for joy	emotion, action	To express jubilation in many forms, denoting the prominence of joy as the attitude of Old Testament worship. Psalm 81:1; 95:1
shaal, verb 176 uses	ask, inquire	petition	To ask someone to give something; especially to "inquire of the Lord" for guidance. Judges 20:18, 23; Psalm 2:8
shelah, noun 14 uses	petition, request	petition	A request of any kind. I Samuel 1:17, 27
shebuah, noun 30 uses	oath	petition	A swearing before God, often conditional. Exodus 22:10-11; Deuteronomy 29:14-15
shabach, verb 8 uses	praise	praise	To commend God for His mighty acts and deeds. Psalm 63:3; 145:4; 147:12

shebach, verb 5 uses	praise	praise	To give praise, to laud, Aramaic. Daniel 4:34
shaba, verb 184 uses	swear	petition	To bind oneself by invoking God as judge and witness to hold parties accountable. Genesis 21:23-24
shava, verb 22 uses	cry for help	petition, emotion	To cry out for help, unknown if God will answer. Psalm 18:6; 30:2; Jonah 2:2
shavah, noun 11 uses	cry for help	petition, emotion	A cry of despair for aid. II Samuel 22:7; Psalm 18:6
shachar, verb 16 uses	seek diligently	petition, action	To rise at dawn to seek after God earnestly. Psalm 63:1; Hosea 5:15
siach, verb 20 uses	meditate	praise, action	To go over a matter inwardly, especially God and His Word. Psalm 119:27, 48, 78
siach, noun 13 uses	complaint	petition	A repeating of a painful matter before God. Psalm 64:1; 142:2
sichah, noun 3 uses	meditation	praise, action	A deliberation of God and His Word in one's mind. Job 15:4; Psalm 119:97, 99
shir, verb 82 uses	sing, singers	praise, petition, emotion	To sing in praise or lament to God. Exodus 15:1, 21; Psalm 21:13
shir, noun 47 uses	song	praise, petition	A song offered to God. I Chronicles 6:31-32; Psalm 28:7; 69:30
shirah, noun 12 uses	song	praise,	A song offered to God. Exodus 15:1; Deuteronomy 31:19, 21
tehillah, noun 55 uses	praise	praise	The hymns or praises resulting from considering God and His divine actions. Psalm 34:1; 51:15; 66:2; 67:3
todah, noun 31 uses	thanksgiving	thanksgiving, praise	Praise in offerings and acknowledging and abandoning sin and worship. Psalm 50:14; 69:30; 95:2

techinnah, noun 25 uses	supplication	petition	A request for God's grace and mercy; especially, when one has sinned. I Kings 8:28, 30, 33, 38, 45, 47, 49, 52, 54, 59
tachanun, noun 18 uses	supplication	petition	The outpourings of troubled souls, always plural. Psalm 28:2; Daniel 9:3
tephillah, noun 72 uses	prayer	intercession, petition	A request to God, often on behalf of another; most common noun for "prayer" in the Old Testament. II Samuel 7:27; II Chronicles 6:19; Psalm 55:1

II. New Testament Words Associated With Prayer

Greek Words	Major English Translations	Prayer Emphasis	Meaning (Especially When Used For Prayer)[4]
adō, verb 5 uses	sing	action	To sing and ode, glorifying God's acts and praising Him. Ephesians 5:19; Colossians 3:16; Revelation 5:9; 14:3; 15:3
aineō, verb 8 uses	praise	praise	To glorify God. Luke 2:13, 20; 19:37; 24:53; Acts 2:47; 3:8-9; Romans 15:11; Revelation 19:5
ainesis, noun 1 use	praise	praise	A lifting up of God. Hebrews 13:15
ainos, noun 2 uses	praise	praise	Glory given to God. Matthew 21:16; Luke 18:43

airō, verb 101 uses	take away, raise	action	To lift the eyes, voice or hand in prayer. John 11:41; Acts 4:24; Revelation 10:5
aiteō, verb 70 uses	ask	petition	To make a specific request of God, primarily for oneself. John 15:7; James 1:5-6
aitēma, noun 3 uses	requests	petition	An asking of one's desires. Philippians 4:6; I John 5:15
anaideia, noun 1 use	persistence	action	Shameless insistence. Luke 11:8
anthomo- logeomai, verb 1 use	give thanks	thanksgiving	To publicly acknowledge the actions and nature of God. Luke 2:38
boaō, verb 12 uses	cry, shout	emotion, action, petition	To call out with strong emotion, often an anguished cry for help. Mark 15:34; Luke 18:7-8
boē, noun 1 use	outcry	emotion	A cry of the oppressed, arising out of need for help. James 5:4
deēsis, noun 18 uses	prayer	petition, intercession	A fervent request for specific aid from God. Romans 10:1; II Corinthians 1:11; 9:14
deomai, verb 22 uses	beg, pray	petition, intercession	To request specific aid out of a real need and expecting definite help. Matthew 9:38; Luke 22:32
doxa, noun 167 uses	glory	praise, intercession	The honor given one for one's actions or character. Luke 2:14; Romans 4:20; Ephesians 3:21
doxazō, verb 61 uses	glorify	praise	To honor and magnify; to clothe with splendor. Mark 2:12; Acts 21:20
ekzēteō, verb 7 uses	seek for	action	To seek out or search for, as for the Lord. Acts 15:17; Hebrews 11:6

enteuxis, noun 2 uses	prayer, petition	intercession, thanksgiving, petition	A request for oneself or for another; thanksgiving. I Timothy 2:1; 4:5
entug-chanō, verb 5 uses	intercede	intercession	To plead concerning another, used especially of Jesus and the Spirit interceding for us. Romans 8:27, 34
exomo-logeō, verb 10 uses	confess	confession	To acknowledge one's true acts (confess sins) and God's true nature (praise Him). Matthew 3:6; Romans 14:11; 15:9; James 5:16
epaineō, verb 6 uses	praise	praise	To applaud, laud, usually of a man, occasionally God. Romans 15:11
epainos, noun 11 uses	praise	praise	Approval or recognition, rare to be used of God. Ephesians 1:6, 12, 14
epairō, verb 20 uses	lift, raise	action	To lift up, as raise eyes or hands in prayer. Luke 18:13; 24:50; John 17:1; I Timothy 2:8
epikaleō, verb 31 uses	call upon	petition	To call out to God for aid. Acts 2:21; Romans 10:12-14
erōtaō, verb 67 uses	ask	petition, intercession	To ask, often for another; an intimate conversational word, used often of Christ's prayers. John 14:16; 17:9, 15, 20
eulogeō, verb 40 uses	bless	praise, thanksgiving	To speak well of or call down God's gracious power upon. Matthew 26:26; Luke 6:28; James 3:9
eucha-risteō, verb 38 uses	give thanks	thanksgiving	To render thanks, normally to God. Matthew 15:36; Romans 1:21
eucha-ristia, noun 15 uses	thanksgiving	thanksgiving	The expression of gratitude; technically used for the Lord's Supper. II Corinthians 9:10-12

310

euchē, noun 3 uses	vow, prayer	petition	A wish, supplication. James 5:15
euchomai, verb 6 uses	pray, wish	petition	To ask of, to desire. II Corinthians 13:7, 9; James 5:16; III John 2
zēteō, verb 117 uses	seek	action	To search for out of need or desire; to seek God. Matthew 7:7-8; Acts 17:27
hiketē-rios, noun 1 use	supplication	petition	The seeking of a request from God. Hebrews 5:7
krazō, verb 54 uses.	cry out	petition, emotion	To scream for help or need, or for joy. Matthew 14:30; 21:9; 27:50; Revelation 6:10; 7:10
kraugē, noun 6 uses	crying	emotion, petition	A loud shout of excitement, grief, pain or anxiety; fervent prayer. Luke 1:42; Hebrews 5:7
krouō, verb 9 uses	knock	action, petition	To pound (at a door), used as a metaphor for seeking access to God. Matthew 7:7-8; Revelation 3:20
homo-logeō, verb	confess	confession, praise	To say the same thing, confess both of sin and praise. Matthew 10:32; I John 1:9
parakaleō, verb 109 uses	entreat, exhort, encourage	petition	To call to one's side to aid; to implore. Matthew 26:53; II Corinthians 12:8
pro-seuchē, noun 37 uses	prayer	petition	A request to God. Luke 6:12; Acts 2:42
pro-seucho-mai, verb 87 uses	pray	petition, intercession	To pray, a comprehensive term for prayer in general. Matthew 6:7; Luke 22:44

stenag-mos, 2 uses	groan, groaning	emotion, petition	A deep sigh or groan of deep emotion or distress. Acts 7:34; Romans 8:26
humneō, verb 5 uses	sing a hymn, praise	action, praise	To sing a hymn of praise to God. Matthew 26:30; Acts 16:25
huperentugchanō verb 1 use	intercede	intercession	To meet with on behalf of another. Romans 8:26
charis noun 155 uses	grace, thanks	thanksgiving	For men, the expression of the gratitude we owe to God. Romans 6:17; 7:25; I Timothy 1:12; II Timothy 1:3
psallō, verb 5 uses	sing, sing praise	action, praise	To sing praise with a musical instrument. Romans 15:9; Ephesians 5:19

---

1. Primary reference works used for this chart are: Robert L. Thomas, ed., *New American Standard Exhaustive Concordance of the Bible* (Nashville: Holman, 1981); Francis Brown, S.R. Driver and Charles A. Briggs, ed., *The New Brown, Driver, and Briggs Hebrew and English Lexicon of the Old Testament* (Lafayette, Indiana: Associated Publishers and Authors, Inc., 1907); and R. Laird Harris, ed., *Theological Wordbook of the Old Testament,* 2 vols. (Chicago: Moody Press, 1980).

2. Claus Westermann, *The Praise of God in the Psalms* (Richmond: John Knox Press, 1965), pp. 26-27.

3. Primary reference works used for this chart are: Robert L. Thomas, ed., *New American Standard Exhaustive Concordance of the Bible* (Nashville: Holman, 1981); William F. Arndt and F. Wilbur Gingrich, *A Greek-English Lexicon of the New Testament and Other Early Christian Literature* (Chicago: University of Chicago Press, 1957); and Colin Brown, ed., *The New International Dictionary of New Testament Theology,* 3 vols. (Grand Rapids, Michigan: Zondervan Publishing House, 1975).

APPENDIX B

QUESTIONS AND ANSWERS ABOUT PRAYER

I hope that many questions about prayer's theory and practice have already been answered for you in the text of this book. This appendix contains a few questions the answers to which did not fall neatly into the text outline. So consider this a "catch-all" to pick up topics that we would have otherwise missed discussing.

What is the connection between prayer and fasting?

Another book in this series is entirely devoted to the subject of fasting and so I will only share a summary of my understanding of this subject.[1] Fasting is generally defined as the act of abstaining from food for spiritual purposes.[2] There is no "normal" length for a fast. Fasts may take one of the three forms listed below.

Forms of Fasting

Form	Characteristics
Normal Fast	Abstaining from all food in solid or liquid form, but not from water (Matthew 4:2).
Absolute Fast	Abstaining from all food *and* water, never more than three days and often caused by a desperate situation (Ezra 10:6; Esther 4:16; Acts 9:9).
Partial Fast	Restriction of diet (normally to simple foods) (Daniel 1:15; 10:2-3).

A normal fast is a choice of an *individual* to refrain from eating for some spiritual purpose. Occasionally, groups or nations are called to a

---

1. Don DeWelt and James Baird, *What The Bible Says About Fasting* (Joplin, Missouri: College Press, 1984).
2. This differs from involuntary fasting caused by lack of food or emotional distress (Daniel 6:18; Matthew 15:32).

fast for some particular purpose. Only the Day of Atonement was set aside as a regular national fast day for Israel in the law of Moses (Leviticus 23:27). Four additional fast days were added after the Babylonian captivity to recall the four major events of the destruction of Jerusalem.[3] Under extraordinary conditions, national fasts were also called to deal one time with some pressing emergency conditions (II Chronicles 20:1-4). But there were no regular weekly or monthly fast days for the people in the Old Testament.

In the New Testament, the Pharisees and the disciples of John the Baptist apparently did have regular weekly fasts (Mark 2:18). The Pharisees normally fasted on Mondays and Thursdays which were market days when many people could see and admire their "commitment to God" in fasting.[4] Yet, there is no commandment for Christians to fast on a regular basis. We are free to fast as often or as little as we have need.

And why do we fast? Fasting is a way of serving God (Luke 2:37; Acts 13:2). To fast is to humble oneself, to subdue the lusts of the flesh and to discipline the body to focus on God rather than our appetites (Psalm 35:13; 65:10; I Corinthians 9:27). While fasting may be practiced alone as an act of contrition, prayer and fasting are intricately connected.

> Prayer is the one hand with which we grasp the invisible; fasting, the other, with which we let loose and cast away the visible . . . fasting helps to express, to deepen, and to confirm the resolution that we are ready to sacrifice anything, to sacrifice ourselves, to attain what we seek for the kingdom of God.[5]

---

3. The month of each fast and the event it recalled were as follows: tenth month — the beginning of the siege of the city (II Kings 25:1); fourth month — the fall of the city (Jeremiah 39:2); fifth month — destruction of the city and the temple (II Kings 25:8-9); and seventh month — the murder of the Jewish governor Gedaliah (II Kings 25:25). From Arthur Wallis, *God's Chosen Fast* (Fort Washington, Pennsylvania: Christian Literature Crusade, 1968), p. 31. Wallis has written one of the best modern treatments of this subject.

4. Richard J. Foster, *Celebration of Discipline: the Path to Spiritual Growth* (San Francisco: Harper and Row, Publishers, 1978), p. 44.

5. Andrew Murray, *With Christ in the School of Prayer* (Old Tappan, New Jersey: Fleming H. Revell Company, 1953), p. 74.

The time of prayer with fasting may be conducted for a variety of reasons as seen in the chart below.

Biblical Purposes for Prayer and Fasting

Purpose	Scripture	Person(s)
To be instructed by God	Exodus 34:28	Moses
To be victorious in battle	Judges 20:24-28	Israel
To seek granting of prayer	I Samuel 1:7	Hannah
To overcome fear	I Kings 19:8	Elijah
To have physical safety	Ezra 8:21-23	Ezra
To express mourning	Nehemiah 1:4	Nehemiah
To express repentance	Jonah 3:4-10 Acts 9:8-9	Nineveh Paul
To overcome temptation	Matthew 4:1-11	Jesus
To set aside one to service	Acts 13:3; 14:23	Paul and others; and elders

Fasting and prayer are not a way of forcing God to grant our requests. (See II Samuel 12:16-23.) Rather, fasting and prayer prepare us to accept the will of God. We wrestle with God in prayer and fasting that we might be defeated by Him and so gain the victory. Dietrich Bonhoeffer puts it in these terms:

Jesus takes it for granted that his disciples will observe the pious custom of fasting. Strict exercise of self-control is an essential feature of the Christian's life. Such customs have only one purpose — to make the disciples more ready and cheerful to accomplish those things which God would have done. Fasting helps to discipline the self-indulgent and slothful will which is so reluc-

315

tant to serve the Lord, and it helps to humiliate and chasten the flesh.[6]

Here are some practical suggestions about fasting, should you choose to add this to your spiritual discipline.

1. Enter into your fast with faith that the Father will recognize and reward this action (Matthew 6:17-18).

2. Do not wait for an emergency to force you to pray and fast. Begin soon to try this experience. Set a definite objective for the fast, such as a specific prayer objective.

3. Start slowly with a one or two MEAL fast. For any fast beyond one meal, check with your doctor. Such people as diabetics and expectant mothers should not fast. And do not "pig out" in the last meals before the fast to "store up" for the mealless period. Otherwise, you are still feeding your appetites and you will also be more miserable as your body reacts to the heavy eating followed by nothing.

4. Do not be surprised by such initial discomforts as bad breath, headaches or abdominal discomfort.

5. Read a lot of Scripture to feed your spirit as your body does without (Matthew 4:4). Use the time once used for meals to pray and meditate on God's Word.

6. Drink plenty of water. When your stomach "growls," remember that your "hunger" is largely a matter of habit and not a true reflection of your body's needs.

7. Beware of pride in your fast and of boasting to others what you are doing. Only those who need to know of your fast should be informed (such as the one who prepares your meals or the family members with whom you normally eat). (Matthew 6:16-18; Luke 17:10).

8. Break your fast gradually, especially a longer fast of twenty-four hours or more. Begin with fruit or vegetable juices (fresh if possible and not chilled). Then add green vegetables and whole fruits. Then bring in bread and cheeses or eggs the next meal, and, finally, meat and fish. Eat slowly and chew your food

---

6. *The Cost of Discipline* (New York: Macmillan Publishing Co., Inc., 1963), p. 188.

well. At the first sign of fullness, stop eating. Do not go hog wild to make up for lost meals.

The primary thing to watch in your fast is whether your motives are what God desires. The classic passage which describes the kind of fast God chooses to bless and the fast which He rejects is found in Isaiah 58:1-12. In part, the Lord says this to Isaiah and to us:

> Is not this the fast which I choose, to loosen the bonds of wickedness, to undo the bands of the yoke, and to let the oppressed go free, and break every yoke? Is it not to divide your bread with the hungry, and bring the homeless poor into the house; when you see the naked, to cover him; and not to hide yourself from your own flesh? Then your light will break out like the dawn, and your recovery will speedily spring forth; and your righteousness will go before you; the glory of the Lord will be your rear guard. Then you will call, and the Lord will answer; you will cry, and He will say, "Here I am" (Isaiah 58:6-9a).

In summary, this passage says that God prefers for us to withhold our selfishness more than for us to withhold our food; our fasting is meaningless if our hearts are not set on doing His will during and after the fast. We are not to focus on ourselves and our needs but to see the needs of others and meet them as God empowers us. Our danger in fasting is to become so spiritual that we forget to obey the Lord in the practical daily ways of life. Fasting which pleases God is prayer in action, giving to the needy. Then God can answer our prayers with justice and mercy, since we have treated others with justice and mercy.

What is watching with prayer?

"Watchings" are times when we abstain from sleep to pray. Jesus prayed through the night before selecting His apostles (Luke 6:12-13). He also encouraged Peter, James and John to "watch and pray" with Him in Gethsemane, though, in their weakness of flesh, they could not "watch with [Christ] for one hour" (Matthew 26:40-41). Such late-night prayers are not chosen, but the result of our earnest desires to seek the Lord which *compel* us to lay aside rest in order to continue before God's presence. So, "devote yourselves to prayer, *keeping alert* in it with an attitude of thanksgiving" (Colossians 4:2).

What is the relationship of healing to prayer today?

Many claims are being made today by those claiming to be channels of healing from God to others. They pray and men are healed, or such is claimed. Sometimes they lay hands on the sick. Their claims are based on the following arguments.[7]

1. Claim: " 'Jesus Christ is the same yesterday and today, yes, and forever' (Hebrews 13:8). So, since He healed all those who came to Him when He was on the earth, He will heal *all* those who believe in Him to do so today (Matthew 8:16-17)." Answer: Of course, Jesus Christ still can heal as He did in the first century. But the healings of His public ministry had a specific purpose: to give evidence that He was the One God sent (Matthew 11:2-6; John 14:11). The question is, "Is it in fact always God's will to heal everyone every time?" Certainly, "it is appointed for men to die once" (Hebrews 9:27). If every sickness is to always be healed, why is the record length of life in the United States a mere one hundred and thirteen years?[8] Does it fit some purpose of God for us to continue in comfort and health forever in this sin-sick earth? Our faith is to be based upon the actions of Christ on the cross, not upon our experiences with healing (I Corinthians 15:1-8).

2. Claim: "The salvation bought by the blood of Jesus Christ saves both the soul *and* the body (Romans 8:12). There is therefore healing for our bodies in the atonement of Christ (Isaiah 53:4-5)." Answer: True, Christ did acquire the redemption of our bodies as well as our souls on the cross. But when will this promised redemption take place? We will be given renewed, eternal and perfect bodies at the resurrection from the dead, not before (I Corinthians 15:12-58; Philippians 3:20-21). The verses often used to claim present healing through Christ's atonement are from Isaiah.

---

7. James I. Packer, "Poor Health May Be The Best Remedy," *Christianity Today,* May 21, 1982, p. 14-16.

8. Jerry Bergman, "The Psychological Dilemma of Faith Healing," *The Restoration Herald,* July, 1978, pp. 3-5.

Surely our [sickness] He Himself bore, and our [pains] He carried; Yet we ourselves esteemed Him stricken, smitten by God, and afflicted. But He was pierced through for our transfressions, He was crushed for our iniquities; the chastening for our well-being fell upon Him, and by His scourging we are healed (Isaiah 53:4-5).[9]

Now when will Jesus bear our sickness and carry our pains? The New Testament says this prophecy was fulfilled in Christ's healing ministry while He was alive on the earth, not when He died for us (Matthew 8:16-17).[10] The atonement of Christ was to redeem our bodies at the resurrection, not for bodily healing today.

3. Claim: "We miss our healing because we do not have faith that God will hear; we do not really ask (James 1:6-7; 4:3). If we are not healed, it is not because God has not been able or willing to heal but that you have not believed 'enough'." Answer: This wicked lie has left many a Christian in grief and depression as they think themselves second class citizens of the Kingdom, unable to conjure enough faith to be healed. The fact is that God does *not* always choose to heal. Timothy had frequent ailments for which Paul simply suggested medicinal wine (I Timothy 5:23). Paul had left Trophimus "ill at Miletus" (II Timothy 4:20). Epaphroditus became so sick while visiting Paul that he was close to dying. Only by God's mercy was he returned to health (Philippians 2:25-27). If close companions of Paul the apostle did not receive healing with Paul there to teach them and lay on *his* hands, we can only presume that God did not desire them to be healed at that time.

Paul himself spoke of a "thorn in the flesh" which he had sought God to remove through prayer. The reply of the Lord was not, "You don't have enough faith; try again when you believe more." Rather, Paul was told, "My grace is sufficient for you, for power is perfected in weakness" (II Corinthians 12:7-10). Paul was then prepared to be content with his pain; in his humility, Christ was able to demonstrate a greater power than simple healing. The Lord was able to show His power through Paul's stand-

---

9. The words "sickness" and "pains" are the marginal readings in the N.A.S.V. and most other versions. The translations in the text read "griefs" and "sorrows."

10. May Wybern, *The Healing Delusion* (New York: Loizeaux Brothers, Inc., n.d.), pp. 17-26.

ing under the pain, and, by Paul's ability to serve Christ even while weak in his flesh, the world could know that it was Christ and not Paul who deserved the credit. Indeed, some of the finest testimonies I have seen lived were those given by men and women in hospital beds or wheelchairs. The joy and grace of their spirit won more hearts than any "miracle of healing" could ever have done. Their faith was evident; they had each asked for healing at some point with devotion and fervency. But, God had graciously said, "No, My grace is sufficient for you; grow among the rocks and you will grow far stronger." And they did.

To summarize thus far, the arguments of the "faith healers" are not based on a sound understanding of the Bible. They begin with the assumption that God wills that all people be physically well all the years of their lives. This is simply not so. God allows accidents and illness to enter our lives for our greater good. At the resurrection, however, all such pain and sorrow shall cease. So these pains continue only for the short time of our "training" before we enter eternity with perfect bodies beyond sickness and death.

Does this mean God never heals anyone of sickness in response to prayer? Not at all; God heals in answer to prayer commonly, but not always. The classic text on prayer for healing is found in the letter of James.

Is anyone among you suffering? Let him pray. Is anyone cheerful? Let him sing praises. Is anyone among you sick? Let him call for the elders of the church, and let them pray over him, anointing him with oil in the name of the Lord; and the prayer offered in faith will restore the one who is sick, and the Lord will raise him up, and if he has committed sins, they will be forgiven him. Therefore, confess your sins to one another, and pray for one another, so that you may be healed. The effective prayer of a righteous man can accomplish much (James 5:13-16).

The following general steps are noted in these verses:

1. The one suffering from any cause should himself pray to God for help.

2. When times are better or grace is given us to indeed "consider it all joy" in our trial, we may sing praises to the Lord.

3. The sick person is one here who has not the strength or

ability to leave his/her home. He or she is to call for the elders of the church, not someone with a "gift" or a "faith healer." Attendance at a "healing service" is not required.

4. The elders are to anoint the sick person with oil and pray over the person. The oil has been seen by commentators as using medicine, as a symbol of the Holy Spirit or as a channel of God's grace like the cup in the communion service or the waters of baptism.[11] Perhaps there is some truth in each. Also be it noted that anointing also symbolizes the dedication to the Lord of that which is anointed (Leviticus 8:10-12).[12] The sick person is being turned over to the care of God and his Spirit.

5. The elders' prayer is to be offered in faith in the Lord who can heal and forgive. This is not a prayer of great or unusual faith, but a prayer which simply has no doubt in the ability of God to heal. (See James 1:6-8)

6. The sick person may then be healed. The promise is stated in general terms as many of those of Christ are (Matthew 17:20; Mark 11:24). The limitations of the promise are seen in other Scriptures, like I John 5:14-15 where we are to ask only in God's will. So, the sick person may indeed by healed.

7. Sin may cause illness (Psalm 32; I Corinthians 11:30). In order for healing to be completed, the sin of the sick person may have to be dealt with (especially if the sin caused the illness). Confession of the sin and intercession for each other are given as the steps to forgiveness and total healing.

Not every case of sickness may require all these steps. Perhaps only private confession and prayer will be needed at times. At other times, the calling of the elders for confession, anointing and prayer may be required. But, rest assured that our loving Father does indeed still heal His people as they pray.

Must we pray to be saved?

The "decision page" of the widely used evangelistic booklet, the

---

11. Grayson H. Engisn, "Let's Restore the Procedure for Healing to the Church," *Christian Standard,* October 4, 1981, pp. 14-15.

12. R.A. Torrey, *Divine Healing* (Grand Rapids, Michigan: Baker Book House, 1974), p. 21.

"Four Spiritual Laws," reads as follows:

YOU CAN RECEIVE CHRIST RIGHT NOW BY FAITH THROUGH PRAYER

(Prayer is talking with God)

God knows your heart and is not so concerned with your words as He is with the attitude of your heart. The following is a suggested prayer:

"Lord Jesus, I need You. Thank You for dying on the cross for my sins. I open the door of my life and receive You as my Savior and Lord. Thank You for forgiving my sins and giving me eternal life. Take control of the throne of my life. Make me the kind of person You want me to be."

Does this prayer express the desire of your heart?

If it does, pray this prayer right now, and Christ will come into your life, as He promised.[13]

The saying of a prayer invites Christ into our life? Certainly this is an idea which is widespread; but is it Biblical? If so, we would expect to find at least these three items in the Word of God:
   a. Commands for men to pray and ask Jesus into their lives.
   b. Examples of men accepting Christ by praying a prayer.
   c. A sample wording for a prayer asking Jesus into one's heart.
First, are there commands to pray for salvation? The Scripture quoted in the *Four Spiritual Laws* is Revelation 3:20.

Behold, I stand at the door and knock; if anyone hears My voice and opens the door, I will come in to him, and I will dine with him, and he with me.

---

13. Bill Bright, *Have You Heard of the Four Spiritual Laws?* (San Bernardino, California: Campus Crusade for Christ, Inc., 1965), p. 10. Note also that the prayer is addressed to Jesus; see our comments on this in Chapter Three.

322

The problem of using this passage as a command to pray for salvation is that this is not addressed to non-Christians at all but to a church grown lukewarm in its concern for God's kingdom. The Laodiceans addressed are told to "be zealous therefore, and repent," not to pray a prayer to ask Christ in (Revelation 3:19). This verse is quite unsatisfactory for a basis for so important a doctrine (dealing as it does with the salvation of mankind). So are there others?

The other Scriptures tend to center around the need for faith to receive God's gift (John 1:12-13; Ephesians 2:8-9). To this is added the assumption that prayer is the preferred way to demonstrate that "saving faith." Or, since confession of Christ is required by the Lord, prayer is used as a means to confess His name (Matthew 10:32-33; Romans 10:9-10). One other Scripture often pointed to is Romans 10:12-13.

For there is no distinction between Jew and Greek; for the same Lord is Lord of all, abounding in riches for all who call upon Him; for "Whoever will call upon the name of the Lord will be saved."

How are we to "call upon the name of the Lord"? This phrase which Paul quotes comes from Joel 2:32. This same verse is quoted by Peter in his great sermon on the day of Pentecost. But what did Peter instruct the crowd on that day to do? He said, "Repent, and let each of you be baptized in the name of Jesus Christ for the forgiveness of your sins" (Acts 2:38). Later, when Paul relates how he was instructed by Ananias to accept Jesus Christ, he reported that Ananias told him, "And now why do you delay? Arise, and be baptized, and wash away your sins, *calling on His name.*" (Acts 22:16) These two sections from the book of Acts are the only accounts of what people actually *did* when they "called upon the name of the Lord" to be saved. In both, it appears that more is involved than a simple prayer, spoken or unspoken. Indeed, no specific prayer is indicated in either case; even though Paul had been earnestly praying and fasting for three days before he met Ananias, he was still told to be baptized, "calling on [Jesus'] name." (See Acts 9:9-11.) If "calling on His name" for salvation simply means prayer, would not three days of prayer have been sufficient to wash away his sins? In commenting on Romans 10:13, an early scholar of the Restoration Movement, Moses E. Lard said:

But the person here, who calls upon the name of the Lord, is not he who merely says to him, Lord, Lord, and does no more. . . . the calling is of the kind enjoined upon Saul by Ananias (Acts xxii:16) when he said to him: "Arise, and be baptized and wash away your sins, *calling on the name of the Lord*." That is, after belief, every act of obedience, as repentance, confession, baptism, is to be performed calling on the name of the Lord. From the moment we believe on him, we are thenceforward never to ignore his name. He is to be recognized in every act, and his guidance and blessing constantly invoked.[14]

In summary, there are no Biblical commands merely to pray to receive salvation.

Are there any Biblical examples of people praying to "invite Jesus in their hearts"? From the day of Pentecost when the preaching of the gospel with the promise of the Holy Spirit began to the end of the New Testament, we do not have *one* example of someone praying for salvation.

If this prayer to accept Christ is so important (one could hardly think of a more important prayer), do we have a sample prayer to follow? No, we do not. The only passages normally cited are these: the "prayer" of the prodigal son (Luke 15:18-19), the prayer of the publican (Luke 18:13) and the request of the thief on the cross (Luke 23:42). The prodigal's "prayer" is not a prayer, does not ask for salvation, was quoted before Christ died on the cross for our sins and sent the Holy Spirit, and is not even close to the sample prayers printed in many evangelistic tools. The publican's prayer is a wonderful prayer of repentance but it does not ask for salvation, was quoted before Christ died on the cross for our sins and sent the Holy Spirit, and is not even close to the sample prayers printed in many evangelistic tools. The requests of the thief on the cross does indicate his faith in Christ but it does not ask for salvation, was quoted before Christ died on the cross for our sins and sent the Holy Spirit, and is not even close to the sample prayers printed in many evangelistic tools.

---

14. *Commentary on Paul's Letter to Romans with a Revised Greek Text, Compiled from the Best Recent Authors and a New Translation* (1875; rpt., Delight, Arkansas: Gospel Light Publishing Company, n.d.), p. 335.

Interestingly, the suggested prayers in the evangelistic tools I have reviewed are all different.[15] They differ in who is addressed, whether repentance is involved, what is believed and what God is doing! In follow-up, one mentions public confession and baptism while the other two do not. There seems to be some confusion concerning just how one accepts Jesus Christ, but we are grateful that the Bible is not so confused.

While prayer is not wrong during the process of accepting Christ and is to be encouraged, prayer is *not* the Biblically designated act of faith by which one accepts Jesus Christ as Lord and Savior. Baptism by immersion in the name of Jesus Christ is that act. Prayer may and should accompany that baptism.

Should I always bow my head and close my eyes when I pray?

In searching the Scriptures, I have not found anyone who is said to have shut his/her eyes to pray. Jesus lifted His eyes to heaven when He prayed, and the publican in Jesus' parable was too humbled to raise his eyes, but none are said to close their eyes (John 17:1; Luke 18:13). There is nothing wrong with closing one's eyes in prayer as far as I know. It can aid in concentration, to shut out the sights of the world around you. When people are praying together, closed eyes can help prevent the embarrassment of eye contact.

Yet I do see more good reasons to pray with your eyes open. First, as you look at the world as you pray, prayer is not separated from reality but connected to it. Praise and thanksgiving are easier as we can find reasons for praise and thanks just by looking around. Prayer lists can be studied instead of trying to remember for whom you should be praying. Sleep is much easier to avoid with open eyes. In prayer groups, praying with eyes open draws you together in honesty, once you get used to it. No, you do not *have* to pray with your eyes open. But just try it. And, please, do not try to drive your car and pray with your eyes closed!

---

15. Compare the prayer in the *Four Spiritual Laws* with the prayers in D. James Kennedy, *Evangelism Explosion*, 2d ed. (Wheaton, Illinois: Tyndale House Publishers, 1983), p. 43, and *Life's Most Important Question* . . . (Winona Lake, Indiana: BMH Tracts, 1975, p. 13.

As to bowing your head, only one person I can find bowed his head in Scripture and that was Jesus Christ as He accepted death (John 19:30). Many bowed down their whole bodies in worship. In Psalm 95:6, the Psalmist says, "Come, let us worship and bow down; let us kneel before the Lord our Maker." Such a position was a sign of reverence, of putting yourself down to lift God up (Psalm 5:7). Bowing down was significant when: it was the true God alone to whom you bowed (II Kings 17:35-36), it was a sign of humble obedience toward God (Micah 6:6-8), and it was a sign that we love those whom God loves and serve them (Isaiah 58:5-7). If bowing your head is a small way of bowing yourself before God in truth, then by all means do so.[16]

Should I end every prayer with, "In Jesus' name Amen"?

To begin with, no prayer recorded in the Bible ends with this phrase (including the Lord's Prayer). Many take Jesus' command to pray "in His name" in a legalistic sense which requires the inclusion of this phrase somewhere in their prayers (John 14:13-14; 15:16; 16:23-24). Since neither James nor John nor Peter nor Paul includes this phrase in any of their prayers, it seems unlikely that this is the meaning of Christ's command.

We are commanded through Paul to do everything we do in the name of the Lord Jesus Christ (Colossians 3:17). Surely, Paul is not saying we are to continuously repeat the phrase "in the name of the Lord Jesus" every moment of every day. Rather, he is commanding that we speak and act according to Jesus' will and by His authority. Likewise, we pray "in Jesus' name" when our prayers are according to His will and based on our position in Him. The present "standardized" use of the phrase is a tradition which we have developed. It is not bad if it *reminds* us of the attitude in which we are to pray and does not *replace* the attitude with mere words. I still say the phrase in public

---

16. Regretfully, physically kneeling down or bowing down in worship is widely considered to be too "fanatical" for us. We tend to smile smugly at the Moslem prostrate on his prayer rug; yet, though his faith is in error, his humility and his willingness to demonstrate it are proper attitudes before God. You may notice that the pews of the majority of churches are not even designed to allow for kneeling.

prayer since I have found that, if I leave it out, the congregation will not hear the cue to move on from joint prayer and remain with heads bowed and eyes closed. It makes it very difficult to preach with them like that!

As for the use of "amen," the word is used often in the Old and New Testaments, but not consistently, to end prayers. Two thirds of the time *amen* is used in the New Testament it is translated, "truly."[17] When used to end a prayer, "amen" means "so let it be,"[18] said in order to confirm the content of the prayer and establish a formal close to that statement.[19] Not every prayer in the Bible ends with "amen." For example, Luke's version of the model prayer does not end this way (Luke 11:4).[20] In fact, not one of the prayers of Jesus Christ recorded in the gospels ends with "amen." The majority of Paul's recorded prayers do not end with "amen."

So, while we *may* so end a prayer, it is not *necessary* to do so according to the Bible. Certainly there is no command to that effect. Again, our *custom* has been to end any public prayer with "amen." In doing so, we make it possible for the congregation to agree with the prayer and confirm it personally with their own "amen;" also it lets them know when to look up or sit down. So let it be.

---

17. Robert L. Thomas, ed., *New American Standard Exhaustive Concordance of the Bible* (Nashville, Tennessee: Holman, 1981), p. 1630. *Amen* is translated "amen" 31 times and "truly" 99 times in the N.A.S.V.

18. *Amen,* William F. Arndt and F. Wilbur Gingrich, *A Greek-English Lexicon of the New Testament and Other Early Christian Literature* (Chicago: The University of Chicago Press, 1957), p. 45.

19. Hans Bietenhard, "Amen," *The New International Dictionary of New Testament Theology,* ed. Colin Brown (Grand Rapids, Michigan: Zondervan Publishing House, 1979), I, 97-99.

20. Neither does the model prayer in Matthew's account according to the best manuscripts (Matthew 6:13).

Index of Topics

As arranged in *Monser's Topical Index and Digest of the Bible* edited by Harold E. Monser with A.T. Robertson, D.R. Dungan and others.

Abba, ab'ba. Emphatic form of Aramaic for "father"—Mk. 14:36; Rom. 8:15; Gal. 4:6.

Accept. Acts 24:3; II Cor. 8:12 (A.V.). David accepted — I Sam. 8:5 (A.V.). *Accepts Abigail's offering* — I Sam. 25:35. Deliverance — Heb. 11:35. Esau may accept — Gen. 32:20. Exhortation — II Cor. 8:17. God accepts — Gen. 19:21. Offering — Lev. 1:4; 7:18; 10:19 (A.V.); 22:21; 23:11; I Sam. 26:19; Ps. 20:3; 119:108; Is. 56:7; 60:3; Jer. 14:12; Hos. 8:13; Amos 5:22; Mal. 1:10,13. Persons — Gen. 4:7; 11:3; Amos 24:23; Job 13:8,10 (A.V.); 32:21 (A.V.); 34:19 (A.V.); 42:8,9; Ps. 82:2 (A.V.); Jer. 14:10,12; Ez. 20:40,41; 43:27; Hos. 8:13; Mal. 1:8,9; Acts 10:35 (A.V.); II Cor. 5:9 (A.V.); Gal. 2:6; Eph. 1:6 (A.V.). Work — Deut. 33:11; Eccl. 9:7. See Lu. 20:21. Mordecai — Esth. 10:3. Petition — Jer. 37:20 (A.V.); 42:2 (A.V.). Punishment — Lev. 26:41,43. Saints — Rom. 15:31 (A.V.). Saying — I Tim. 1:15; 4:9. Time — II Cor. 6:2 (A.V.). Words — Deut. 33:11; Eccl. 9:7.

Access. Rom. 5:2; Eph. 2:18; 3:12.

Accursed. Persons. — Deut. 21:23; Josh. 6:18; 7:12; Is. 65:20; John 7:49; Rom. 9:3 (A.V.); I Cor. 12:3 (A.V.); Gal. 1:8,9 (A.V.). Things. — Josh. 6:17,18 (A.V.); 7:1, 11, 13, 15 (A.V.).

Acknowledge. Gen. 38:26; Is. 61:9; 63:16; I Cor. 14:37 (A.V.); Col. 2:2; Philemon 6. Brethren — Deut. 33:9; I Cor. 16:18; II Cor. 1:13,14. God — Pr. 3:6; Is. 33:13; Dan. 11:39. Sin — Ps. 32:5; 51:3 (A.V.); Jer. 3:13; 14:20. Truth — II Tim. 2:25 (A.V.); Tit. 1:1 (A.V.).

Agree. Lu. 5:30; Rev. 17:17 (A.V.). Adversary, with thine — Mt. 5:25. Ananias and Sapphira — Acts 5:9. Gamaliel, with — Acts 5:40. Householder — Mt. 20:2,13. Jews — John 9:22. One, In — I John 5:8. Two — Amos 3:3; Mt. 18:19. Witnesses — Mk. 14:56,59. Words of the prophets — Acts 15:15.

Amen. Num. 5:22; Deut. 27:15,26; Ps. 41:13; I Cor. 14:16; II Cor. 1:20; Rev. 1:6,7; 3:14; 19:4.

Anxiety. Casting all your — I Pet. 5:7. For all the churches — II Cor. 11:28.

Ascribe. David, Unto — I Sam. 18:8. Jehovah, Unto — Deut. 32:3; I Chr. 16:28; Job 36:3; Ps. 68:34.

Ask. Alms — Acts 3:2. See Alms, Beggars. Amiss — Jas 4:2,3. Before you ask him — Mt. 6:8. Do above all that ye — Eph. 3:20. Faith, In — Jas. 1:6. Give to him that — Mt. 5:42; Lu. 6:30. Know not what ye — Mt. 20:22; Mk. 10:38. One thing — Ps. 27:4. Signs, For — Mt. 16:1; I Cor. 1:22. Whatsoever ye ask — Mt. 7:7-11; 21:22; Mk. 11:24; Lu. 11:13; John 11:22; 14:13,14; 15:7,16,23-26; I John 3:22; 5:14-16. See Prayer.

Attend. Job 32:12. Altar — Heb. 7:13. Cry (prayer) — Ps. 17:1; 55:2; 61:1; 66:19; 86:6 (A.V.); 142:6. Know understanding, To — Pr. 4:1. Lord, Upon the — I Cor. 7:35. Reading — I Tim. 4:13 (A.V.). Things — Acts 16:14 (A.V.); Rom. 13:6. Wisdom — Pr. 5:1. Words — Pr. 4:20; 7:24.

Beseech. Elijah — II Ki. 1:13. Esther 8:3. Fellow-servant — Mt. 18,29. Festus — Acts 25:2. God — Ex. 32:11; Deut. 3:23; II Sam. 12:16; I

Ki. 13:6; II Ki. 13:4; 20:3; II Chr. 33:12; Ezra 8:23; Neh. 1:5, 11; Ps. 116:4; 118:25; Is. 38:3; Jer. 26:19; Jonah 1:14; Mal. 1:9. See Prayer. Jesus — Mt. 8:5,31,34; 14:36; 15:23; Mk. 1:40; 5:10,12,23; 6:56; 7:26,32; 8:22; Lu. 4:38; 5:12; 7:3,4; 8:31,32,37,38,41; 9:38,40; 11:37; John 4:40,47; 19:31,38.

Blessings: Old Testament. — Blessings from God. — Creatures of air and sea — Gen. 1:20-22. Adam and Eve — Gen. 1:28; 5:2. The sabbath — Gen. 2:3; Ex. 20:11. Noah and sons — Gen. 9:1.
Abrahamic blessing. — Gen. 12:2,3; 18:18; 22:17,18; Acts 3:25; Gal. 3:8,9,16. Sarah — Gen. 17:16. Isaac — Gen. 26:3,4. Jacob — Gen. 28:14; 48:3,4. Prophesied — Is. 51:1-3; 61:9; Ez. 34:25-31; Zech. 8:11-13; Mal. 3:10-12. Fulfilled in apostle's day — Acts 3:25; Gal. 3:8,13. Jacob wrestles — Gen. 32:26-29; 35:9.
Children of Israel. — Ex. 20:24; Deut. 12:5,12,18; 14:26. Bless their bread and water — Ex. 23:25. Their crops — Lev. 25:18-22. Blessing through Balaam — Num. 22:12; 23:11,12; Deut. 23:5. The work of their hands — Deut. 2:7; 12:7,12. Because of liberality — II Chr. 31:10; Lu. 6:38. Being blessed, must bless others — Deut. 15:14; 16:10; I Pet. 3:9. Many blessing catalogued — Deut. 11:8-25; 28:1-14; 30:15-20. Samson — Ju. 13:24. Obed-edom protects ark — II Sam. 6:10-12; I Chr. 13:14; 26:5. David's prayer for blessing — I Chr. 17:26,27. Job — Job 1:10; 42:12. Egypt blessed — Is. 19:25. Sacrifice to be blessed — I Sam. 9:13. Children a blessing — Gen. 5:29; Ps. 113:9; 127:3-5; Pr. 10:1; 15:20; 17:6; 23:24; 27:11; 29:3.
New Testament — The Beatitudes. — Mt. 5:3-12; Lu. 6:20-23. The seeing

eye — Mt. 13:16-17; Lu. 10:23,24. Blessing bread — Mt. 14:19; 15:36; 26:26; Mk. 6:41; 8:7; 14:22; Lu. 24:30; Acts 27:35; Rom. 14:6. Simon Bar-Jonah at Caesarea Philippi — Mt. 16:17. Faithful servant — Mt. 24:45-47. Those on right hand — Mt. 25:34. Little children — Mk. 9:36,37; 10:16. Hearers of word preferred — Lu. 11:27,28. Watchful servants — Lu. 12:37,38. Those who feed the poor — Lu. 14:13,14. Referring to John the Baptist — Mt. 11:6; Lu. 7:23. Jesus' departure — Lu. 24:50-51. Referring to Thomas — John 21:29. The forgiven — Rom. 4:7,8. Saints blessed — Eph. 1:3. The earth — Heb. 6:6,7. The tested man — Mt. 5:10; Lu. 6:22; Jas. 1:12; 5:11; I Pet. 3:14; 4:14. The obedient person — Lu. 11:28; John 13:17; Jas. 1:25. Called to inherit blessing — Gal. 3:14; Heb. 12:17; I Pet. 3:9. The Lamb worthy — Rev. 5:12,13.

Bow, v. Job 31:10; Ps. 145:14; 146:8; Eccl. 12:3; Is. 2:9,11,17; 10:4; 46:1,2; 49:23; 60:14; 65:12. Angels, Before — Gen. 18:2; 19:1. Back, The — Rom. 11:10. Ear, Down the — II Ki. 19:16 (A.V.); Ps. 17:6; 34:2; 86:1; Pr. 52:17 (A.V.). Everlasting hills — Hab. 3:6. Evil before good — Pr. 14:19. Faces — I Sam. 25:41; 28:14; Lu. 24:5. Head, The — Heavens — II Sam. 22:10; Ps. 18:9; 144:5. Knees — Gen. 41:43; Ju 7:5,6; I Ki. 19:18; Is. 45:23; Mt. 27:29; Mk. 15:19; Rom. 11:4; 14:11; Eph. 3:14; Phil. 2:10,11. Mourning, In — Ps. 35:14; 38:6; 57:6. Shoulder — Gen. 49:15. Soul — Ps. 44:25; 57:6. Together — Lu. 13:11. Worship, In — Ex. 20:5; 23:24; Deut. 5:9; Josh. 23:7,16; Ju. 2:12; II Ki. 5:18; 17:35; II Chr. 7:3; 20:18; 25:14; 29:29,30; Ps. 22:29; 95:6; Mic. 6:6.

330

Care, *n.* Casting care on God — Ps. 9:9; 23:1; 62:1; I Pet. 5:7 (A.V.). Churches, For the — II Cor. 8:16, 11:28 (A.V.); Phil. 2:20; I Tim. 3:5. Disciples for each other — I Cor. 12:25. Earnest — II Cor. 7:11; Elisha, For — II Ki. 4:13. Free from — I Cor. 7:32. Life, Of this — Lu. 8:14; 21:34. See World. Paul, For — II Cor. 7:12; Phil. 4:10. Without — Jer. 49:31. World, Of this — Mt. 13:22; Mk. 4:19; Lu. 8:14; 12:22; John 6:27; I Cor. 7:32,34; Phil. 4:6; I Tim. 6:8; Deut. 11:12. No man, For — Mt. 22:16; Mk. 12:14. Oxen, For — I Cor. 9:9. Perish, That we — Mk. 4:38. Poor, For the — John 12:6. Samaritan, Parable of the good — Lu. 10:20-27. Sheep, For the — John 10:13. Soul, My — Ps. 142:4.

Censer. Incense burned in — Lev. 10:5; 16:12; Num. 16:6,17,18,46; II Chr. 26:19; Ez. 8:11; Rev. 8:3,5. Tabernacle, In — Num. 9:4 (marg.)

Continually, Continue. Apostles teaching, In — Acts 2:42. Bread — Num. 4:7; Neh. 10:33. Burnt offering — Ex. 29:42; Num. 28:3,4,10,15,23, 24,31; 29:11,14,16,22,25,28,31,34, 38. Covenant — Not in my — Heb. 8:9. Faith, In the — Acts 14:22. Col. 1:23. Fasting — Acts 27:33. Feast — Pr. 15:15. Gates shall be open — Is. 60:11. Grace of God, In the — Acts 13:43. Hope, I will — Ps. 71;14. Jehovah will guide thee — Is. 5:8-11 (A.V.). Kingdom shall not — I Sam. 13:14. Lamp, To burn — Lev. 24:2. Love, Let — Heb. 13:1. Lovingkindness — Ps. 36:10. Memorial, For a — Ex. 28:29. Name, His — Ps. 72:17. Name blasphemed — Is. 52:15. Not — Job 14:2. People provoke me — Is. 65:3. Prayer, In — Acts 1:14; Col. 4:2; Rom. 12:12; I Tim. 5:5. Praise shall be — Ps. 34:1. Priest, Abideth a — Heb. 7:3.

Cry. Unto Jehovah. — Deut. 15:9; I Sam. 7:8; Ps. 40:1; 57:2; 61:1; 86:3; 88:2. Of David — II Sam. 22:7; Ps. 89:26. In affliction — II Chr. 20:9.
For help. — Ps. 28:1; 107:19,28; 119:169; 141:1; 142:6. From Israel — Ps. 106:44; Joel 1:14,19,20. From Nineveh — Jonah 3:8.
Cry of. — Supplication — Esau — Gen. 27:34. *To God* — I Ki. 8:28; II Chr. 6:19; Job 19:7; Ps 5:2; 17:1; 18:6; 27:7; 28:2; 39:12. Job — Job 30:20,24; Heb. 5:7. *To king* — II Ki. 8:3. Israel at Red Sea — Neh. 9:9. Blind men — Mt. 9:27. Affliction — Zion — Ps. 102:1; Lam. 2:19; 3:8,56; Ez. 9:4; 21:12. Anguish — Ps. 22:2. Mordecai — Esth. 4:1. Blind beggar — Mk. 10:47. Children in the temple — Mt. 21:15. Complaints — I Sam. 8:18; 9:16; Neh. 5:1,6; Job 16:18. Demoniac — Mk. 5:5; Lu. 4:41. Egyptians — Ex. 11:6; 12:30. Widow and fatherless heard by Jehovah — Ex. 22:23. City — I Sam. 5:12. Fools — Eccl. 9:17. Grief — Heard by Eli — I Sam. 4:14. Tamar — II Sam. 13:19. David — Ps. 69:3. Horonaim — Jer. 48:3. Joy — Is. 12:6; 54:1; Gal. 4:27. Leper — Lev. 13:45. Midnight, At — Mt. 25:6. Oppressed — Job 35:9,12; Is. 5:7. Israel in bondage — Ex. 2:23; 3:7,9; 5:8. Those overcome — Ex. 32:18. The perishing — Num. 16:3,4. Pity — Is. 15:5. Poor — Job 34:28; Ps. 9:12; Pr. 21:13. Righteous — Ps. 34:15,17. The elect — Lu. 18:7. Streets, In — Is 23:11. Two daughters of the horseleach — Pr. 30:15. Unclean —

Acts 8:7. Warning — Is. 58:1; Jer. 2:2; 4:5; Jonah 1:2; Zech. 1:14,17. By Paul and Barnabas — Acts 14:14. Wicked — Job 27:9. To idols — Ju. 10:14; I Ki. 18:17; Job 36:13; Is. 46:7. Sodom and Gomorrah — Gen. 18:20,21; 19:3. Wisdom — Pr. 8:1. Not heard of Jehovah — Ez. 8:18; Mic. 3:4; Hab. 1:2.

Curses. In Old Testament. — Upon the serpent — Gen. 3:14-15. Upon the ground — Gen. 3:17-19; 5:29; 6:7,13. The curse removed — Gen. 8:21,22. Upon Cain — Gen. 4:11. Upon Canaan — Gen. 9:25. Upon the disobedient — Lev. 26:14-39; Deut. 11:26-29; 27:13-26; 28:15-46; 29:19-21; Josh 8:34,35; Pr. 3:23; Mal. 2:2. Upon Meroz — Ju. 5:23. Upon Shimei — II Sam. 16:5-13. Upon Gehazi — II Ki. 5:27. Upon robbers of tithes — Mal. 3:9. Upon persecutors of the poor — Ps. 10:2; 109:9-16. Cursing the name of Jehovah — Lev. 24:10-16,23. Cursing father and mother forbidden — Ex. 21:17; Lev. 20:9; Ps. 109:17; Pr. 20:20; 30:11; Mt. 15:4; Mk. 7:10. In New Testament. — Fig tree — Mk. 11:21. Upon those ignorant of the law — John 7:49; Gal. 3:10. Upon those who preach another gospel — Gal. 1:8,9. Upon those who love not Christ — I Cor. 16:22.
Curses uttered by men. — II Pet. 2:14. By Noah — Gen. 29:26. By Jotham — Ju. 9:20,57. By Job — Job 3:1-10. By Jeremiah — Jer. 20:14. By Peter -Mt. 26:74; Mk. 14:71. From the tongue — Jas. 3:9,10.
Infirmities considered by the Jews as curses from God. — John 9:2. Bless them that curse you. — Lu. 6:28; Rom. 21:14. Christ redeems from the curse. — Rom. 3:10; Gal. 3:10; Rev. 22:3.

Daily. Bread — Mt. 6:11; Lu. 11:3.

Cross — Lu. 9:23. Offering — Num. 28:24; Ezra 3:4; Ez. 45:23; 46:13; Heb. 7:27. Prayer — Ps. 88:9. Scriptures read — Acts 17:11. Tasks — Ex. 5:13,19. Teaching — Mt. 26:55; Mk. 14:49; Lu. 19:47; 22:53; Acts 5:42; 17:17; 19:9. Worship — Ps. 61:8.

Delight. Abominations — Is. 66:3. Almighty, In — Blessing, Not in — Ps. 109:17. Blood — Is. 1:11. Burnt offerings, In — I Sam. 15:22. Commandments — Ps. 112:1. Fatness — Is. 55:2. God, With — Job 34:9. Gold, Not — Is. 13:17. Goodness — Neh. 9:25. Honor, To — Esth. 6:6,7,9,11. Law, In — Ps. 1:2 (A.V.); Ps. 119:70. Lies, In — Ps. 62:4. Lovingkindness — Mic. 7:18 (A.V.). Men, Sons of — Eccl. 2:8. Scoffing — Pr. 1:22 (A.V.); Son, In — Pr. 3:12. Soul, Unto — Pr. 29:17. Statues, In — Ps. 119:16. Strength — Ps. 147:10. Truly, Deal — Pr. 12:22. Understanding, In — Pr. 18:2. Way, In his — Ps. 37:23. Weight is, A just — Pr. 11:1. Will, To do — Ps. 40:8.

Draw Nigh. Is. 41:5; Ex. 3:5; Ps. 119:150. Abraham — Gen. 18:23. Bethphage, Unto — Lu. 19:29 Counsel of Holy One — Is. 5:19. David, To meet — I Sam. 17:48. Day — Ez. 7:12; 22:4. Decree — Esth. 5:2. Feast of unleavened bread — Lu. 22:1. Fruit, Time of — Mt. 21:34. Gates of death — Ps. 107:18. God, Unto — I Sam. 14:36; Ps. 73:28; Jas. 4:8. Heart, With — Heb. 10:22. Jerusalem, Unto — Mt. 21:1. Jesus, Unto — Lu. 22:47. Philistine — I Sam. 17:41. Pharaoh — Ex. 14:10. Promise, Time of — Acts 7:17. Publicans — Lu. 15:1. Redemption — Lu. 21:28. Sheol, Unto — Ps. 88:3. Soul — Ps. 69:18. Time — Gen. 47:29. Years — Eccl. 12:1.

Enemy. Personal. — Saul — I Sam.

18:29; 19:17. Haman — Esth. 8:1. Job's — Job 16:9,10. Opponent at law — Mt. 5:25; Lu. 12:58.

Spiritual enemies. — God's — II Sam. 12:14; Ps. 8:2; 37:20; 68:1; 83:2; 89:10,51; 92:9; 139:20,22; Is. 42:13; 59:18; 66:6,14; Rom. 5:10; Col. 1:21. Of Christ: *The devil* — Mt. 13:39. *The wicked* — Mt. 13:36; 21:46; 26:4; Mk. 11:18; 12:12; 14:1,2,10,11,55,56,65; 15:3,10,11, 29,30; Lu. 19:47; 20:19,43; 22:2-6, 52,53; 23:2; John 5:16,18; 7:1,19, 25; 8:37,40; 11:53; I Cor. 15:25,26; Phil. 3:18; Heb. 1:13; 10:13. Of Holy Spirit — Mt. 12:24,31,32; Mk. 3:22, 28-30; Lu. 12:10. Of saints: *The accuser* — Job 1:9-11; 2:3-4; I Pet. 5-8; Rev. 12:10. *The wicked* — Mt. 10:16,17,25; Lu. 22:35-38; Acts 4:21,26,29; 5:17,18,33,40; 6:9-14; 7:59; 8:1,3; 12:1-3; 14:19; 21:30, 31; 23:14. *Own household* — Mic. 7:6; Mt. 10:21,35,36.

Become enemy by speaking the truth. — Gal. 4:16.

Treatment of personal enemies. — I Sam. 24:4-6,11,19; 26:8,9; Pr. 24:17,18; 25:21,22; Mt. 5:25,43,44; Lu. 6:27,35; 22:50,51; 23:34; Acts 7:60; 9:3-6; 13:9-11; 16:28,27.

Entreat. Acts 28:20. Corinthians — II Cor. 9:5; 10:1. Courteously — Acts 27:3 (A.V.). Evil — Ex. 5:22 (A.V.); Deut. 26:6; Job 24:21 (A.V.); Acts 7:6. Jehovah — I Ki. 13:6. Shamefully — Lu. 20:1 (A.V.); I Thess. 2:2 (A.V.). Spitefully — Mt. 22:6 (A.V.); Lu. 18:32 (A.V.). Two men — Acts 9:38. Well — Jer. 15:11.

Face: Faces mentioned. — Face of Jehovah — Ex. 33:23; Ps. 17:15; 89:14; Jer. 16:17; 21:10; 32:31; Lam. 2:19; 3:35; Ez. 7:22; 14:3,4,6,7; 15:7. Hid his face — Deut. 31:18; 32:20; Mic. 3:4; Lu. 1:76. Will not turn away his face — II Chr. 30:9. Declare to — Job

21:31. Against — Ez. 14:18. Turned away — Jer. 18:17. Set his face against — Lev. 17:10; 20:3,5,6; 26:17. Fled from the face of Jehovah — II Chr. 29:6.

Obeisance to God. — Abraham talked with God — Gen. 17:3,17. Balaam — Num. 22:31. Jehoshaphat — II Cor. 20:18. Ezekiel fell on — Ez. 3:23; 1:28; 9:8; 11:13; 43:3; 44:4. Daniel — Dan. 8:17,18. Jesus prays — Mt. 26:39. Dagon — I Sam. 5:3,4. David and elders — I Chr. 21:16. Elijah — I Ki. 18:42. Joshua — Josh. 5:14; 7:6,10. Lot — Gen. 19:1. Moses and Aaron — Num. 14:5; 16:4. Moses — Num. 16:4,22,45; 20:6. Manoah and wife — Ju. 13:20. People at Mount Carmel — I Ki. 18:39. People at burnt-offering — Lev. 9:24. Unbelievers — I Cor. 14:25. Turned face from Jehovah — II Chr. 35:22. Renounced to Jehovah's face — Job 1:11; 2:5.

Face to face. — Gen. 32:30; Ju. 6:22; II Ki. 14:8; II Chr. 25:17,21; Ez. 20:35; Acts 25:16; I Cor. 13:12.

Seeking the face of the Lord. — I Chr. 16:11; II Chr. 7:14; Ps. 27:8; 105:4; Pr. 7:15; Hos. 5:15.

Faith. *Pisteuo*, to believe. A union of assurance and conviction — Heb. 11:1. See Hab. 2:4; Mt. 6:25-34; Lu. 12:22-31; 18:8; Heb. 13:7.

Given by God. — Lu. 17:5,6; Rom. 12:3; I Cor. 2:4,5; 12:8,9.

Comes by hearing the Word of God. — Acts 15:7; Rom. 10:13-17; I Cor. 1:21; Gal. 3:1,2; I Thess. 2:13.

In God. — Lu. 1:38-55; Acts 27:25; Heb. 6:1; I Pet. 1:21; 4:19; I John 3:21.

Facts produce feeling. — Mt. 23:37-38; 27:3-5,54; Lu. 15:4-10,16-20; John 11:8,16,32-33; 21:15-17; Acts 2:22-23,37; 5:27-28; 7:51-54; II Cor. 5:14-15.

Testimony produces faith. — John 1:7;

3:11-12; Acts 2:40-42; 8:4-8; 10:39-43; 26:16-18; Rom. 10:13-17; I John 1:1-3; 5:8-10.

Faith as a grain of mustard seed. — Mt. 17:19,20; Lu. 17:5,6. Faith of Abraham — Rom. 4:18-22. In quenching fiery darts — Eph. 6:16. The prayer of faith — Jas. 5:15. (See also Heb. Ch. 11.)

Prayer without faith is vain. — Pr. 28:9; Mt. 21:22; Acts 10:31-33; Eph. 6:16-18; Heb. 10:21,22; 11:6; Jas. 1:5-7; 5:15-18.

Faithfulness. Consistency with expressed or known character.

God's faithfulness. — Deut. 7:9; Ps. 143:1; 119:86,138; Is. 49:7; Jer. 42:5; I Cor. 1:9; 10:13; I Pet. 4:19; Heb. 10:23. Extent of — Ps. 36:5; 40:10; 88:11; 119:75,90. Exalted — Ps. 89:1,2,5,8,24,33; 92:2; Is. 25:1; Lam. 3:23.

God's promise to the faithful. — I Sam. 2:35; Ps. 31:23; 101:6; Pr. 28:20.

Of Christ. — Is. 11:5; I Thess. 5:24; II Thess. 3:3; II Tim. 2:13; Heb. 2:17; 3:2; 10:23; I John 1:9; Rev. 1:5; 19:11.

Of followers of Christ. — Eph. 1:1; Col. 1:2,7; Rev. 17:14. Required — I Cor. 4:2; Rev. 2:10.

Fasting. Fast proclaimed. — Lev. 23:27; II Chr. 20:3; Ezra 8:21; Neh. 9:1; Esth. 4:3,16; Joel 2:12,16; Jonah 3:5. Recommended — II Cor. 6:5.

Spirit of prayer. — Ez. 8:21-23; Dan. 9:3. Confession. — I Sam. 7:6; Neh. 9:1,2. Mourning. — Joel 2:12. Humiliation — Deut. 9:18; Neh. 9:1; Ps. 35:13; 69:10.

Manner of. — Esth. 9:31; Mt. 6:17.

Kinds of. — False — Is. 58:4; Jer. 14:12; Mt. 6:16; Lu. 18:12. True — I Sam. 31:13; I Chr. 10:12; Neh. 1:4; Is. 58:6; Acts 13:2,3; 14:23; 27:33.

Time. — Neh. 9:1; Jer. 36:6; Mk. 2:19. Length of — Forty days and forty nights: Moses — Ex. 34:28; Deut. 9:9,18. Elijah — I Ki. 19:8. Our Lord — Mt. 4:2. Fourteen days — Acts 27:33. Effects of — Ps. 109:24; Mt. 15:32; Mk. 8:3. Promises connected with — Is. 58:8-12; Mt. 6:18.

How often. — Lu. 18:12; II Cor. 11:27.

Recommended. — II Cor. 6:5.

Examples of. — Moses — Ex. 24:18; 34:28; Deut. 9:9,18. David — II Sam. 1:12; 3:35; 12:16. Elijah — I Ki. 19:8. Children of Israel — Ju. 20:26; I Sam. 7:6; 14:24-30; I Chr. 10:12. Men of Jabesh-Gilead — I Sam. 31:13. Ahab — I Ki. 21:27. Jehoshaphat — II Cor. 20:3. Ninevites — Jonah 3:5-10. Darius — Dan 6:18. People of Judah — Jer. 36:9. Daniel — Dan. 9:3; 10:1-3. Ezra — Ez. 11:6; 8:21-23. Nehemiah — Neh. 1:4. Disciples of John — Mt. 9:14; Mk. 2:19. Anna — Lu. 2:37. Pharisee — Lu. 18:12. Apostles — II Cor. 6:5. Christ — Mt. 4:2. Barnabas and Saul — Acts 14:23. Saul — Acts 9:9. Paul — II Cor. 11:27. Disciples of Chirst — John 21:12,15.

Christ defends his disciples for not. — Mt. 9:14,15; Mk. 2:19; Lu. 5:33-35.

Fellowship: With Christ (I Cor. 1:9; I John 1:3). — Life — John 14:19; II Tim. 2:11. In sufferings — Rom. 8:17; Phil. 3:10; Col. 1:24. Death — Rom. 6:3f.,10,11; Col. 2:12; II Tim. 2:11. Resurrection — Rom. 6:5f; Col. 2:12; Eph. 2:6. Sonship — I John 3:2. Heirship — Rom. 8:17. Fruitfulness — John 15:1-5. Power — John 14:12; Phil. 4:13. Authority — I Cor. 6:2,3; II Tim. 2:12; Rev. 2:26,27. Possession — John 16:15; I Cor. 3:21-23. Baptism — Rom. 6:1,3-10; Col. 2:12.

Fellowship of Jesus with us. — II Cor. 8:9; Heb. 2:10,18.

With the saints. — Standing and responsibility — Rom. 11:17-21; I Cor. 14:20; Eph. 2:19-22; 4:17-24; Tit. 3:1,2. Unity — Ps. 133:1-3; Eph.

29:15; 37:28; 66:18; Jer. 32:19; Amos 9:2-4; Mt. 10:29,30; I Cor. 8:3.

Foreknowledge. — Gen. 41:25-32; I Sam. 23:10-12; Ps. 139:15,16; Is. 41:26; 42:9; 44:7; 45:11,21; 46:10; 48:3,5; Jer. 1:5; Dan. 2:28-45; 10:14; Mt. 6:8,32; 24:36; 26:24; Lu. 22:22; 24:27,44; Acts 2:23; 3:18; 4:28; 15:18; Rom. 8:29; 11:2; Gal. 1:15,16; II Tim. 1:9; I Pet. 1:2,20.

He is immutable. — Num. 23:19,20; I Sam. 15:29; Job 23:13; Ps. 33:11; 102:27; Is. 40:28; Mal. 3:6; Rom. 11:29; Tit. 1:2; Heb. 6:17,18; Jas. 1:17.

He is omnipresent. — Gen. 28:16; Deut. 4:35-39; I Ki. 8:27; II Chr. 2:6; Ps. 34:18; 139:7-10; Pr. 15:3; Is. 57:15; 66:1; Jonah 1:3,4; Jer. 23:23,24; Acts 7:48,49; 17:24-28.

Love of. — Deut. 10:15,18; 23:5; II Sam. 12:24; Ps. 103:13; 146:8; Jer. 31:3; Mal. 1:2; John 3:16; 14:21,23; 16:27; 17:10,23,26; Rom. 5:8; 9:13; II Cor. 9:7; 13:11; Eph. 2:4; II Thess. 2:15; Heb. 12:6; I John 3:1; 4:8,9,10,16,19; Jude 21. Love manifested — Ex. 6:7; 19:4; Lev. 25:42; 26:12; Deut. 28:9; 32:9-12; Ps. 31:19,21; 90:1; 114:2; Is. 49:16; 54:5,6,10; Mal. 3:16,17; Mt. 18:11-14; Rom. 5:8; 8:31,32,39; Eph. 3:1-6; Heb. 11:16; Jas. 1:18.

Mercy of God a further exemplification of His love. — Ex. 20:2,6,22; 22:27; II Chr. 30:9; Ezra 9:9; Neh. 1:10; 9:17,27-31; Is. 54:9; 57:11; 65:2; Jer. 2:9; 3:12; 4:27; Hos. 2:14,23; Lu. 6:36; Acts 26:16-18; Rom. 10:10-13.

Sovereignty. — Ex. 15:18; I Chr. 29:11,12; II Chr. 20:6; Job. 9:2-12; 25:2; 33:12,13; Ps. 59:13; 82:1,8; 89:11-14; 93:1,2; 97:1-6,9; 103:19; 105:7; 113:3-5; 135:5-21; 145:11-13; Is. 40:12-31; 66:1; Lam. 3:27; 5:19; Dan. 6:26; Mic. 4:7,13; Mt. 6:10; 11:25; Lu. 10:21; John

10:29; 19:11; Acts 7:48-50; 17:24-31; Rom. 9:19-33; 11:33-36; Heb. 1:1-14; Rev. 4:11; 19:6.

God is a jealous God. — Ex. 20:5; 34:14; Deut. 4:24; 5:9; 6:15; 29:20; 32:15-27; Josh. 24:19,20; I Ki. 14:22; II Chr. 16:7-9; Ps. 78:58; Is. 30:1-3; Ez. 8:17,18; 23:25; 36:5,6; 38:19; 39:25; Joel 2:18; Nah. 1:2; Zeph. 1:18; 3:8; Zech. 1:14; 8:2; I Cor. 10:22.

Access to God. — Very desirable — Deut. 4:7; Ps. 27:4; 43:2; 65:4; I John 2:1. We must be pure in heart — Ps. 1:1-6; 24:3,4; 51:10-12; 145:18; Is. 55:3; Mt. 5:8. Only through Christ can we come to the Father — John 10:7,9; 14:6; Rom. 5:1; Col. 1:21,22; Eph. 2:13,18; 3:12; Heb. 2:17; 4:16; 7:19,25; 9:15; 10:19,22; I Pet. 3:18; I Tim. 2:4,5,6. He will welcome all — Mt. 11:28-30; Acts 2:21; Rom. 10:12,13. See Salvation. The Father draws men to Christ — John 6:44,45. Calls them by the Gospel — Mk. 1:17; Rom. 9:11; I Cor. 1:17; 4:15; Gal. 1:6; I Thess. 2:12; 5:24; II Thess. 2:14; II Tim. 1:9; Jas. 1:18; I Pet. 1:15.

Grant. Apostles, To — Mk. 10:37. Deliverance — II Chr. 22:7; Lu. 1:74. Jehovah — Ruth 1:9; I Sam. 1:17; I Chr. 4:10; II Chr. 22:7; Job 6:8; Acts 14:3; Rom. 15:5; Eph. 3:16. King — Ez. 7:6; Neh. 2:8. Knowledge — II Chr. 1:12. Life — Job 10:12. Loving kindness — Job 10:12. Mercy — Neh. 1:11; II Tim. 1:16,18. Petition — Esth. 5:6; 7:2, 5:8; 8:11; 9:12,13; Ps. 20:4. Redemption of land — Lev. 25:24. Salvation — Ps. 85:7; Acts 11:18. Wisdom — II Chr. 1:12.

Hand. Necessary member of the body. — I Cor. 12:21.

Prayer. — Hands lifted in — Ps. 28:2; 134:2; 141:2; Lam. 2:19; 3:41; I Tim. 2:8. Spread out in — Ex. 9:29;

Ezra 9:5; Job 11:13; Ps. 88:9; 143:6.

Healing. Healing was considered by the Hebrews as a token of forgiveness — Ex. 15:26. The connection of priest with physician was very close. Medical knowledge of their day was quite defective. Such a thing as a science of medicine was then unknown, but there were physicians. From II Chr. 16:12 it would seem that the writer considered it a sin to consult physicians. Priests had the supervision in cases of leprosy — Lev. Chs. 13,14; and prophets, even, were applied to for medical advice — I Ki. 14:2; II Ki. 4:22-25.

God the healer. — Deut. 32:39; Ps. 6:2; 30:2; 103:3. Abimelech and his family — Gen. 20:17,18; Jer. 3:22; 17:14; 30:17; Hos. 14:4.

In answer to prayer. — Miriam — Num. 12:12-15. Jeroboam — I Ki. 13:4-6. Hezekiah — II Ki. 20:1-7.

Manners of healing. — Strange remedies — Num. 21:9; II Ki. 5:10; John 3:14; 9:6,7.

Provision for. — Ex. 21:19. Gradual healing — Mk. 8:23-25. Failure in — Jer. 46:11. Threefold healing — Mt. 12:22. Gratitude for — Lu. 4:38,39. Physicians — II Chr. 16:12; Jer. 8:22; Mt. 9:12; Lu. 4:23; Col. 4:14.

Medical treatment. — II Chr. 16:12; II Ki. 8:29; Lu. 10:34.

Medicines. — A cheerful heart — Pr. 17:22. Leaves for healing — Ez. 47:12; Rev. 22:2. No healing medicines at hand — Jer. 30:13; Ez. 30:21. Vain medicines — Jer. 46:11.

Remedies. — Balm (for pain) — Jer. 8:22; 46:11; 51:8. Caperberry (for desire) — Eccl. 12:5 (marg.). Mint, anise, cummin (for carminatives) — Mt. 23:23; Lu. 11:42. Salt (to purify water) — II Ki. 2:20,21. Oil (for wounds) — Is. 1:6; Lu. 10:34; (for sickness) — Jas. 5:14. Poultices of figs (for boils) — II Ki. 20:7; Is. 38:21.

Wine (for exhaustion) — Lu. 10:34; (for infirmities) — I Tim. 5:23; (for narcotics) — Mt. 27:34; Mk. 15:23. (Figurative use for healing) applied to troubled soul — Ps. 6:2. To impure and wronged nations — Jer. 8:22; 30:17. The capturer needs it — Jer. 51:8,9. False healing — Jer. 6:14; 8:11.

Holy Spirit. The Spirit of God in the Old Testament: Ruach — Ps. 51:11,12; 139:7; 143:10; Is. 40:7-13; 59:19, 21; Ez. 36:27; 37:14; Mic. 2:7; Hag. 2:5; Zech. 4:6; 7:12.

Christians are temples of the Holy Spirit. — John 14:17; Rom. 8:9-17; I Cor. 3:16,17; 6:19; Eph. 2:21,22; 3:16,17; II Tim. 1:14.

Communion of the Holy Spirit. — II Cor. 3:6-18; 11:4; 12:18; 13:14; Phil. 2:1; Col. 1:8.

Inspires. — Num. 12:6,8; II Ki. 17:13; Neh. 9:20-30; Is. 59:21; Zech. 7:12; Mt. 10:20; Mk. 13:11; Lu. 1:70; 12:11,12; Acts 3:18; 4:8; 11:28; 20:23; 21:10,11; Rom. 1:1,2; 3:21; 16:26; I Cor. 2:4,9-14; 7:40; 12:3; Eph. 3:5,6; II Tim. 3:16; Heb. 1:1; 3:7,8; 9:8; 10:15,16; I Pet. 1:10-12; II Pet. 1:21; Rev. 2:7; 22:6.

Convinces the world of sin. — Gen. 3:6; John 6:44,45; 16:7-9; Acts 7:51,52; Gal. 5:16-23; Eph. 6:17.

Commissions. — Acts 13:2-4; 20:28.

Baptism in the name of the Father, Son, and Holy Spirit. — Mt. 28:19.

Invites to salvation. — Rev. 22:17.

Makes intercession. — Rom. 8:26; Eph. 2:18; 6:18; Jude 20.

Sanctifies. — Rom. 15:16; I Cor. 6:11; II Thess. 2:13; I Pet. 1:2.

Incense: Sweet incense. — Ex. 25:6. Its composition — Ex. 30:34-35. Altar to burn on — Ex. 30:1-8; 40:5,27; II Chr. 2:4; 32:12. Aaron offers it — Lev. 16:12-13. Unlawfully offered by Nadab and Abihu — Lev. 10:1. By

Korah and others — Num. 16:6. 250 men offer it — Num. 16:35. Example of rebellion — Num. 16:36-40. Bezalel made it — Ex. 37:29. Offered morning and evening — Ex. 30:7-8; II Chr. 13:11. Prayer goes forth as — Ps. 141:2. Indication of praise — Mal. 1:11. Of approved service — Eph. 5:2. Presented by wise men to Jesus — Mt. 2:11.

Ingratitude: Of those benefited. — Absalom — II Sam. 15:1-6. Hezekiah — II Chr. 32:25. Israel — Ps. 78:16,17,42. Nebuchadnezzar — Dan. 5:18-20. The nine lepers — Lu. 17:15-17.

Ingratitude punished. — Israel — Deut. 28:47-57. King Baasha — I Ki. 16:1-4. Hezekiah — II Chr. 32:35.

Gratitude commanded by Jesus. — Lu. 17:17-19. Practised by Jesus — John 11:41,42.

Exhorted by Paul. — Phil. 4:6.

Practised by Paul. — Phil. 1:3-7.

Intercession. Is. 53:12; 59:16; Jer. 27:18; Rom. 8:26,34; Heb. 7:25.

Intreat. Heb. 12:19; Jas. 3:17. Abraham, By — Gen. 23:21. Christian, By — I Cor. 4:13. Father, By — Lu. 15:28. Favor — Ps. 45:12; 119:58; Pr. 19:6. Jehovah — Gen. 25:21; Ex. 8:8,9,28-30; 9:28; 10; 17:8; Ju. 13:8; I Sam. 2:25; II Sam. 21:14; 24:25; I Ki. 13:6; I Chr. 5:20; II Chr. 33:13,19; Ezra 8:23; Ps. 45:12; 119:58; Is. 19:20; I Cor. 4:13. See Prayer. Land, For — II Sam. 21:14; 24:25. Moses, By — Ex. 8:9,28-30; 9:28; 10:17,18. Peter — Acts 9:38. Pharaoh, For — Ex. 8:9,28-30; 9:28; 10:17,18. Ruth, By — Ruth 1:16. Sinner, For — I Sam. 2:25.

Jesus Christ. — Teaching concerning: Glorifying God. — Mt. 5:16; John 11:4;

12:28; 13:31,32; 14:13; 15:8; 21:19. Importunity in prayer. — Lu. 11:5-8; 18:1,8.

Prayer. — Jesus set example: *Praying before or during baptism* — Lu. Ch. 3. *On preaching tour* — Mk. 1:35; Lu. 5:16. *Choosing apostles* — Lu. 6:12. *Feeding five thousand* — Mt. 14:19, 23; Mk. 6:41,46; Lu. 9:16; John 6:11,23. *Feeding four thousand* — Mt. 15:36; Mk. 8:6. *Revelation of Messiahship* — Lu. 9:18-21. *Transfiguration* — Lu. 9:28,29. *Report of the seventy* — Mt. 11:25,26; Lu. 10:21. *Teaching Lord's prayer* — Lu. 11:1. *Raising Lazarus* — John 11:41,42. *Blessing children* — Mt. 19:13; Mk. 10:16. *Sending the Holy Spirit* — John 14:16. *Last Supper* — Mt. 26:26,27; Mk. 14:22,23; Lu. 22:17,19,32; I Cor. 11:23-25. *Betrayal* — John Ch. 17. *Gethsemane* — Mt. 26:36,39,42,44; Mk. 14:32, 35,36,39; Lu. 22:41-44. *On the cross* — Mt. 27:46; Mk. 15:34; Lu. 23:34,46. *For Simon Peter* — Lu. 22:32. *For disciples* — John 17:9,11,15,17,20,21. *All night* — Lu. 6:12. *He commends the man who prays* — Lu. 12:37; Acts 9:11. *Men need to be taught* — Lu. 11:1,2.

Teaches how to pray: *Not as the hypocrites* — Mt. 6:5. *Not with vain repetitions* — Mt. 6:7; Mk. 12:40; Lu. 20:47. *In the chamber* — Mt. 6:6. *In temple* — Lu. 18:10. *Kneeling or standing* — Mk. 11:25; Lu. 22:41.

God's relation to: *As a Father* — Mt. 6:9,14,15; 7:11; Lu. 11:13; John 14:16; 16:23. *Knowing before* — Mt. 6:8. *Able and willing to give* — Mt. 6:26,30,33; 7:11. *Seeking true worshippers* — John 4:23. *Duty to pray* — Mt. 7:7; 9:38; 26:41; Mk. 14:38.

How: (a) *Faith in God* — Mt. 17:20; 11:21,22; Mk. 11:22,23,24. *In Christ, pray in His name* — John 14:13,14; 15:16; 16:23,24,26. (b) *Abiding in Christ* — John 15:7,16. (c)

Words of Christ abiding in us — John 15:7. (d) *Heartfelt* — Mt. 15:8,9; Lu. 11:5-10; John 4:23,24. (e) *Forgiving enemies* — Mt. 6:14,15; 18:21,22, 35; Mk. 11:25. (f) *According to will of God* — Mt. 6:10; 26:39; Lu. 22:32. *Unselfish* — 18:19,20. *For others* — Mt. 6:12,14,15; 9:38. *Humble* — Lu. 18:13,14. (g) *Like the Lord's prayer* — Mt. 6:9; Lu. 11:2.

What to pray for: *Persecutors* — Mt. 5:44. *Ministers* — Mt. 9:38; Lu. 10:2. *Deliverance from misfortune* — Mt. 24:20; Lu. 21:36. *To avoid temptation* Mt. 6:13; Lu. 22:40. *Hallowing God's name* — Mt. 6:9; Lu. 11:2. *Triumph of kingdom* — Mt. 6:10; Lu. 11:2. *Will of God over the earth* — Mt. 6:10. *Food and raiment* — Mt. 6:11,33; Lu. 11:3. *Forgiveness* — Mt. 6:14. *Mercy* — Lu. 18:13.

What blessings follow: *Good things* — Mt. 7:11. *What we need* — Mt. 6:8,32,33. *The Holy Spirit* — Lu. 11:13. *Power over evil* — Mk. 9:29. *Forgiveness* — Mt. 6:12,14; Lu. 18:14. *Deliverance* — Mk. 18:18. *Recompense* — Mt. 6:6. *Justice* — Lu. 18:7,8. *What asked for* — Mt. 18:19; John 14:13,14; 15:7; 16:23.

Jesus prayed: *Not for world* — John 17:9. *For apostles* — John 17:9,11, 15,17,24. *Believers* — John 17:20,21.

Receive. — Mt. 10:8; 11:14; 19:12; 20:10; 21:34; 25:27; Mk. 12:2; Lu. 6:24,34; 16:4,9,25; John 3:27,32, 33; 4:36; 5:34,41,44; 7:23,39. Receiving a child — Mt. 18:5; Mk. 9:37; Lu. 9:48. Receiving Christ — Mt. 18:5; Mk. 9:37; John 5:43; 13:20. Greater condemnation — Mk. 12:40; Lu. 20:47. Receive a hundredfold — Mt. 19:29; Mk. 10:30. See Lu. 18:30. Receiving a prophet — Mt. 10:41. Receiving a righteous man — Mt. 10:41. Receiving what we ask in prayer — Mt. 7:8; 21:22; Mk. 11:24; Lu. 11:10; John 16:24. Receiving the word — Mt. 13:20; 19:11; Mk. 4:16,20; Lu. 8:13; John 12:48; 17:8. Whosoever shall receive you — Mt. 10:40; Lu. 10:8; John 13:20. Whosoever shall not receive you — Mt. 10:14,15; Mk. 6:11; Lu. 9:5; 10:10.

Repentance. — Mt. 4:17; 21:28-32; Mk. 1:15; Lu. 13:3-5; 15:4-32: 16:30; 17:3,4; 24:47. Calls sinners to repentance — Lu. 5:30-32. Compares ancient cities with the cities of His day and condemns those of His time — Mt. 11:20-24; 12:41; Lu. 10:11-15; 11:29-32.

Joy And Rejoicing: Wicked find joy in folly. — Pr. 15:21. In unrighteousness — II Thess. 2:12. In death — I Tim. 5:6. In carnal pleasures — Eccl. 2:10,26. Deceptive — Eccl 7:6; Is. 22:13. Faces the judgement day — Eccl. 11:9. Momentary — Job 8:19; 20:5. Fool gives none — Pr. 17:21.

Duty of righteous to rejoice. — It is strength — Ezra 6:22; Neh. 8:10; Ps. 42:4; Col. 1:11; 2:5. Commanded — Deut. 12:18; Ps. 43:4; Rom. 12:12; Phil. 3:1; 4:4; I Thess. 5:16; I Pet. 4:13.

Reasons for rejoicing. — Grace — Lu. 1:47; Acts. 2:28. Indwelling in Christ — John 15:10,11. Answer to prayer — John 16:24. Fellowship of saints — II Tim. 1:4; I John 1:3,5; II John 12. Care — Ps. 5:11; 16:89; 105:43. By faith — Ps. 89:16; 149:2; Heb. 3:8; Rom. 5:11. In hope — Rom. 5:2; Heb. 3:6. In the truth — II Cor. 2:3. In the Lord — Phil. 4:10. Even in persecutions, sorrow, trials, or calamities — Mt. 5:11,12; Lu. 6:23; Heb. 10:34; II Chr. 6:10; Jas. 1:2; I Pet. 1:6; Heb. 3:17,18; Rom. 8:28. Unspeakably great — Ps. 21:6; 32:1; 68:3; Zech. 9:9; Lu. 6:23; Acts 8:8; I Cor. 8:2. Abides forever — John 15:11; I Thess. 5:16. Joy follows affliction — Job 29:13; Ps. 30:5; 126:5;

Is. 35:10; John 16:20,33; I Pet. 4:13.
Presence of Christ gives — John 3:29;
17:13.

Gratitude for food and raiment. — Deut.
28:47; Ps. 65:13; Eccl. 5:19,20; Mt.
6:11,31-33; 7:11; Lu. 11:3; Acts
14:17. For goodness — II Chr. 7:10;
Ps. 67:4. For promises — Ps. 132:16;
Is. 35:10; 55:12; 56:7; Jer. 31:13;
33:9-11; Zech. 8:19; Heb. 6:18; I
Pet. 1:4. For good preaching — Neh.
8:12; Jer. 15:16; Lu. 8:13; Acts 8:8;
13:48. For Zion — Ezra 6:16; Neh.
12:43; Ps. 48:2; Lam. 2:15; Gal.
4:26,27; Heb. 12:22.

Joy of the gospel. — The very name,
good tidings of great joy — Lu. 2:10.
Abraham saw — John 8:56; Gal. 3:4.
Prophets and angels desire to know —
Mt. 13:17; I Pet. 1:10-12. Salvation
— I Sam. 2:1; Ps. 9:14; 13:5; 20:5;
21:1; 35:9; 51:12; Is. 12:3; 25:9;
61:10; II Cor. 1:6. Better than lands
— Ps. 4:7; Mt. 10:42; Lu. 12:15,21.
Future joy — Ps. 16:11; Mt. 25:21,
23; I Pet. 4:13; Jude 24.

Joy is to. — The just and upright — Ps.
32:11; 97:11; Pr. 21:15.
Peacemakers — Pr. 12:20; Mt. 5:9.
The meek — Is. 29:19; Mt. 5:5. The
wise — Pr. 15:23. Parents of the good
— Pr. 23:24; Ps. 113:9. Believers —
Lu. 24:52; Acts 2:46; 8:8,39; 13:52;
15:3.

Ministers count converts as. — II Cor.
7:4; Phil. 2:2; 4:1; I Thess. 2:20; 3:9;
Philemon 20; II John 4. Help — II
Cor. 1:24; Phil. 1:25. Pray for —
Rom. 15:13. Live in — Ps. 100:2;
Rom. 15:32. Die in — Acts 20:24.
Render account in — Phil 2:16; Heb.
13:17.

God rejoices over His people. — Zeph.
3:17; Ps. 149:4. For fidelity: Enoch —
Heb. 11:5. Fear — Ps. 147:11. Prayer
— Pr. 15:8. Uprightness — I Chr.
29:17; Pr. 11:20. Repentance — Lu.
15:7,10. Obedience — II Chr. 30:26.
To do them good — Num. 14:8;

Deut. 30:9,10; Jer. 32:41; II Sam.
22:20; II Chr. 20:27; Is. 49:13;
51:3,11; 52:9; 60:15; 65:19.

Christ anointed to preach. — Is. 61:1,3;
Lu. 4:18. Holy Spirit's fruit is — Gal.
5:22. Kingdom of heaven is — Rom.
14:17. Shout for — Ezra 3:11-13.

Figurative. — Stars rejoice — Job 38:7.
Trees — Ps. 96:12.

Results of. — Strength — Neh. 8:10;
Phil. 4:10,13. Sacrifice — Ps. 27:6.
Liberality — I Chr. 29:9,17; II Cor.
8:2.

Meditation. Ps. 104:34. All thy doings,
On — Ps. 143:5. Beforehand — Lu.
21:14. Consider my — Ps. 5:1. Day
and night — Josh. 1:8. Heart, Of —
Ps. 19:14; 49:3. Isaac, Of — Gen.
24:63. Law, On — Ps. 1:2; 119:97.
Night watches, In — Ps. 63:6. On
God's word — Josh. 1:8; Ps. 1:2;
119:15,23,48,97,99,148; 139:17,
18; 143:5; Pr. 4:20,22. Peoples —
Ps. 2:1. Precepts, On — Ps. 119:15.
Testimonies are my — Ps. 119:99.
Work, Upon — Ps. 77:12; 119:27.

Name: Import of names. — Gen.
2:19,20; 4:25; 17:5; 32:28; Dan.
1:7; Mt. 1:21; Lu. 1:13,59-63. Saul's
name changed — Acts 13:9. Simon's
name changed — Mt. 16:18; John
1:42.

Name as reputation and standing. — I
Sam. 18:30; Ju. 13:17,18; Pr. 22:1;
Eccl. 7:1; Eph. 1:20,21. What is due
to God's — Ps. 29:2; 86:9,12; 103:1.

Symbol of power. — Gen. 11:4; 12:2;
Ex. 15:3; Num. 6:27; II Sam. 8:13; I
Chr. 17:8,21; Ps. 52:9; 54:1; 63:4;
Jas. 5:14.

Symbol of authority. — Ex. 9:16; 23:21;
Mt. 7:22; 18:20; 21:9; 23:39; 24:5;
Mk. 9:37; Lu. 9:49; 10:17; Acts
4:7,10,12; Phil. 2:10.

Rallying force. — Gen. 48:16; Deut.
12:5,11,21; 14:23,24; 16:2,6,11; II
Sam. 7:13; Neh. 1:9; Is. 26:8; Mt.

garment of praise for spirit of heaviness — Is. 61:3. Bringing sacrifices of thanksgiving — Jer. 17:26. Earth full of His — Hab. 3:3.
From New Testament. — Out of mouth of babes Thou has perfected — Mt. 21:6. Give God the praise — John 9:24 Whose praise is not of men — Rom. 2:29. Do that which is good and thou shalt have — Rom. 13:3. Brother whose praise is in gospel — II Cor. 8:18. In this I praise you not — I Cor. 11:17.

Prayer. What is prayer? It is the soul's desire for God — Ps. 42:1,2; 63:1-3; 84:2; 143:6-9.
It is as universal as man — Ps. 65:2; 86:9; Is. 66:23. Began with Seth — Gen. 4:23.
It is a cry — a supplication — Ex. 22:23,27; Job 23:3,4; Ps. 34:15,17; 86:3; 88:1,2,9,13; Is. 19:20; 30:19; 58:9.
It is an instinct that must have utterance. — Ps. 51:1-3; Is. 44:17; 45:20; Mt. 27:46; Mk. 15:34; Lu. 18:7,13.
It is an appeal from the child to the father — Hos. 14:3; Mt. 6:6-13; Lu. 11:2-4.
It is a necessity — Hos. 14:1-3; Amos 5:6; Heb. 4:16.
Enjoined. — I Chr. 16:11,35; 28:9; II Chr. 7:14,15; Ps. 35:6; 62:8; 105:3,4; Is. 55:6; 58:9; 65:24; Jer. 29:12,13; 33:3; Lam. 2:10; 3:41; Ez. 36:37; Hos. 14:2; Zeph. 2:3; Zech. 10:1,6; Mt. 7:7; 24:20; 26:41; Mk. 13:33; 14:38; Lu. 11:5-13; 18:1; 21:36; John 16:24-27; Acts 8:22; Rom. 12:12; Eph. 6:17,18; Phil. 4:6; Col. 4:2; I Thess. 5:17; I Tim. 2:1,8; Heb. 4:16; Jas. 1:5-7; 5:13; I Pet. 4:7.
Confession. — Duty of — Lev. 5:5; Num. 5:6,7; Jer. 3:13; Mt. 10:32; Lu. 12:18; 15:21; John 9:22; Rom. 10:9; 14:11; Phil. 2:11; Jas. 5:16. Blessedness of — Lev. 26:40-42; Job 33:27,28; Pr. 28:13; I John 1:9. In-

dividual — Gen. 32:9,10; II Sam. 24:17; I Chr. 21:8; Job 40:4,5; Ps. 32:5; 38:4; 40:11,12; 41:4; 51:3,4; 69:5; 119:176; 130:3; Is. 6:5; Dan. 9:20; Lu. 18:13.
National — Num. 14:40; Ju. 10:10,15; I Sam. 7:6; 12:10; Neh. 9:2,33-35; Ps. 106:6,7; Jer. 3:25; 14:7,20; Lam. 5:16; Dan. 9:5-15. *Moses* for Israel — Ex. 32:31,32; 34:9; Num. 14:19. *Ezra* for Israel — Ezra 9:5-15; 10:1. *Nehemiah* for Judah — Neh. 1:4-11. *Isaiah* for Judah — Is. 64:6,7. *Daniel* for Israel — Dan. 9:7-23. *Daniel* for Judah — Dan. 9:3-19.
Intercession. — Gen. 20:7; Jer. 27:18; 29:7; II Cor. 9:14; Eph. 6:18; I Tim. 2:1; II Tim. 4:16; Heb. 13:18-21; Jas. 5:14-16; I John 5:16. Priestly — Ex. 28:9-12,29,30,38.
Instances of — Old Testament: *Abraham* for Abimelech — Gen. 20:7,17,18. For Ishmael — Gen. 17:18. For Sodom and Gomorrah — Gen. 18:23-32. *Boaz* for Ruth — Ruth 2:12. *Daniel* for Israel and Judah — Dan. 9:3-23. *David* for the Child of Bathsheba — II Sam. 12:16. For Israel — II Sam. 24:17; I Chr. 29:10-19; Ps. 25:22; 28:9. For the righteous — Ps. 7:9; 36:10. For Solomon — I Chr. 29:19. *Eli* for Hannah — I Sam. 1:17. *Elisha* for the Shunammite's son — II Ki. 4:33. *Ezekiel* for Israel — Ez. 9:8. *Ezra* for Israel — Ezra 8:21-23; 9:5-15. *Hezekiah* for Judah — II Ki. 19:14-20. For those who had cleansed themselves for the passover — II Chr. 30:18-20. *Isaiah* — Is. 37:4; 63:16-19; 64:1-12. *Job* in behalf of his friends — Job 42:8-10. *Joshua* for Israel — Josh. 7:6-9. *Moses* for Israel — Ex. 32:11-14,31,32; 34:9; Num. 11:1,2; 14:13-24; 21:7; Deut. 1:11; 9:18-20,25-29; 10:10; Ps. 106:23. God's model for Moses — Num. 6:22-27. *Moses* for Aaron — Deut. 9:20. For Miriam — Num. 12:13. For Pharaoh — Ex. 8:12,30,31; 9:33,34;

10:18,19. *Naomi* for Ruth — Ruth 1:8,9. *Nehemiah* for Judah — Neh. 1:4-11. *Samuel* for Israel — I Sam. 7:5-8; 12:19-23. *Solomon* for Israel — I Sam. 7:5-8; 12:19-23. *Solomon* for Israel — I Ki. 8:22-54; II Chr. 6:12-42. New Testament; *Jesus:* For Peter — Lu. 22:32. For His disciples — John 17:9-24. For those who crucified Him — Lu. 23:34. *Epaphras* for the Colossians — Col. 4:12. *Paul* for Israel — Rom. 10:1. For Christians of Rome — Rom. 1:9. For Ephesians — Eph. 1:16-21; 3:14-21. For Philippians — Phil. 1:3-7,9. For Colossians — Col. 1:3,9. For Thessalonians — I Thess. 1:2; 3:10-13; 5:23; II Thess. 1:11,12; 2:16,17; 3:5,16. For Onesiphorus — II Tim. 1:16,18. For Philemon — Philemon 4-6. *Philemon* for Paul — Philemon 22. *The Church in Jerusalem* for Peter — Acts 12:5. For the Sick — Jas. 5:14,15. Paul asks for prayers of disciples — Rom. 15:30; II Cor. 1:11; Eph. 6:19; Col. 4:3; I Thess. 5:25; II Thess. 3:1; Heb. 13:18. See Phil. 1:19,20. Forbidden to pray for — Jer. 7:13-16; 14:10-12.

Imprecation. — (Note that *every* instance belongs to Old Testament except three) — Commands to curse — Deut. 11:29-30; 26:11-13; Josh. 8:33; II Sam. 16:11-12. Commands not to curse — Num. 22:12; 23:25. Curses requested — Num. 22:6-11; 23:7-8; 24:10; Josh. 24:9-10. *Upon one's self* — II Sam. 24:17; I Chr. 21:17; Job 3:1-10; Ps. 7:3-5. *Upon persecutors of poor* — Ps. 10:2; 109:9-16. *Upon enemies and transgressors* — Num. 16:15; Deut. 33:11; Ju. 16:28; I Sam. 26:19; Neh. 4:4-5; 5:13; Job 27:7; Ps. 5:10; 6:10; 9:20; 10:15; 28:4; 31:17-18; 35:4,8,9,26; 40:14-15; 55:9,15; 58:7; 59:5-15; 68:1,2; 69:23-28; 70:2-3; 79:10-12; 83:13-17; 109:17-29; 119:78,84; 129:5; 140:9,10; 145:12; 144:6; Jer. 11:20;

12:3; 15:15; 17:18; 18:21-23; 20:12; Lam. 3:64-66.

New Testament: Upon preachers of another gospel — Gal. 1:8-9. Upon Alexander the coppersmith — II Tim. 4:14. Upon those who love not Christ — I Cor. 16:22.

Praise. — Ps. 30:4; 59:16; 63:3; 92:1-2; 95:2; 106:1; 107:8,21,31; 147:7; Is. 12:5; 63:7; Jer. 20:13; Dan. 2:23; Lu. 1:64; 2:13,28; 18:43; 19:37; Acts 2:47; 3:8; 16:25; Heb. 13:15; Rev. 4:9-11; 5:12.

Supplication. — Ex. 33:12-16,18; I Ki. 8:22-53; II Ki. 20:3; II Chr. 6:12-42; Ezra 8:21-23; Job 8:5; Ps. 6:9; 22:19,21; 28:2; 40:11-17; 69:1,2,13-18,29; 70:5; 88:1-18; Jer. 36:7; Dan. 6:11; Jonah 1:14; Rom. 10:1; II Cor. 1:11; 9:14; Eph. 6:18; Phil. 1:4,19; 4:6; I Tim. 5:5; II Tim. 1:3.

Thanksgiving. — Gen. 24:27; Ex. 18:10; I Sam. 2:1; I Ki. 8:15,56; I Chr. 16:8; II Chr. 20:21-28; Neh. 12:31-40; Ps. 18:17-49; 75:1; 118:1-4; 140:13; Dan. 2:19,23; Rom. 1:8; I Cor. 15:57; II Cor. 2:14,15; 9:15; Eph. 1:3; Phil. 1:3-7; Col. 1:3,12,13; I Thess. 1:2; I Pet. 1:3.

How Shall We Pray? Should be offered to God. — Deut. 6:13; Ps. 5:2. As to a Father. — Mt. 6:9-13; Lu. 11:2-4. To Jesus. — Acts 7:59.

In the name of Jesus. — Mt. 18:19-20; 28:18-20; John 14:13,14; 15:16; 16:23-26; Eph. 2:18; 5:20; Col. 3:17; I Pet. 2:5. See Lu. 23:42.

Continually — Ps. 55:17; 88:1; Rom. 12:12; I Thess. 5:17. Faith, In — Ps. 56:9; 86:7; Mt. 21:21,22; Mk. 11:24; Heb. 10:22; Jas. 1:6; I John 5:14. Fasting, With — Neh. 1:4; Dan. 9:3; Acts 13:3. Forgiving spirit, With — Mt. 6:11-15; 18:21-35; Mk. 11:25. Hasty, Not — Eccl. 5:2. Heart, With the — Lam. 3:41. Heart, With the whole

— II Chr. 22:9; Ps. 119:58,145; Jer. 24:7; 29:12,13. Heart, With preparation of — Job 11:13; Heb. 10:22. Humility — II Chr. 7:14; 33:12. Importunity — Gen. 32:26-28; Mt. 7:7-11; Lu. 11:8; 18:1-7. Model — Mt. 6:9-13; Lu. 11:2-4. Repetitions, Avoid vain — Mt. 6:7. Righteous, must be — Ps. 34:15,17,18; John 15:7,16. Secret, In — Mt. 6:6. Sincerity — Mt. 6:5; Heb. 10:22. Spirit and understanding, With — John 4:22-24; I Cor. 14:14-19. Truth, In — Ps. 145:18; John 4:24. Unfeigned lips, With — Ps. 17:1. Watch and pray — Neh. 4:9; Ps. 5:3; Mt. 26:41; Lu. 21:36; Eph. 6:18; Col. 4:2,3; I Pet. 4:7. Will of God, According to — I John 5:14-16. *Jesus in Gethsemane* — Mt. 26:39; Lu. 22:32. Described as: Beseeching the Lord — Ex. 32:11. Calling on the Lord — Acts 7:59; Rom. 10:12-14; II Tim. 2:22. Calling on the name of the Lord — Gen. 4:26; 12:8; Ps. 116:4; Acts 22:16; I Cor. 1:2. Crying unto God. See "What is Prayer?" Drawing near to God — Ps. 73:28; Heb. 10:22. Lifting up the heart — Lam. 3:41. Lifting up the soul — Ps. 25:1. Pouring out the heart — Ps. 62:8. Pouring out the soul — I Sam. 1:15. Seeking the face of the Lord — Ps. 27:8. Seeking unto God — Job. 8:5.
Postures in prayer. — Bowing down — Gen. 24:52; Ps. 95:6. Bowing the knees — Is. 45:23; Rom. 14:11; Eph. 3:14; Phil. 2:10. Bowing the head — Gen. 24:26,48; Ex. 4:31; 12:27; II Chr. 20:18. Falling on face — Num. 16:22,45: 20:6; Josh. 5:14; 7:6; I Chr. 21:16; II Chr. 20:18; Ez. 9:8; Mt. 26:39; Mk. 14:35. Kneeling — I Ki. 8:54; II Chr. 6:13; Ezra 9:5; Ps. 95:6; Dan. 6:10; Lu. 22:41; Acts 7:60; 9:40; 20:36; 21:5. Looking up — Ps. 5:3. Standing — I Sam. 1:26; I Ki. 8:14,22,55; II Chr. 20:9; Mk. 11:25; Lu. 18:11-13. Toward the

temple in Jerusalem — I Ki. 8:35,48,49; II Chr. 6:38; Ps. 5:7; Dan. 6:10; Jonah 2:4. Lifting up the hands — Neh. 8:6; Ps. 28:2; 134:2; 141:2; Lam. 2:19; 3:41; I Tim. 2:8. Spreading out the hands — Ex. 9:29; I Ki. 8:22,38,54; Ezra 9:5; Job 11:13; Ps. 28:2; 63:4; 88:9; 143:6; Is. 1:15; Lam. 1:17.
Answers to prayer. — Ex. 22:23,27; II Chr. 7:14; Job 12:4; 33:26; 34:28; Ps. 21:2,4; 34:15,17; 38:15; 55:16,17; 56:9; 65:2,5; 69:33; 86:5; 91:15; 99:6; 102:17,18; 118:5; 138:3; 145:18,19; Pr. 15:8,29; Is. 19:20; 30:19; 55:6,7; 58:9; 65:24; Jer. 29:12,13; Lam. 3:57; Ez. 36:37; Dan. 9:20-23; 10:12; Joel 2:32; Jonah 2:2; Zech. 13:9; Mt. 6:6; 18:19; Lu. 11:13; 18:7; John 15:7; 16:23-27; Acts 4:31; II Cor. 12:8; Jas. 5:16-18; I John 3:22; 5:14,15. Christ received answer — John 11:42; Heb. 5:7. Christ answers — John 14:13,14.
Examples: Abraham — Gen. 15:1-20; 17:20. Lot — Gen. 19:19-21. Abraham's servant — Gen. 24:12-21. Isaac — Gen. 25:21. Jacob — Gen. 32:24-30. Israelites — Ex. 2:23,24; 14:10; Ju. 3:9,15; 4:3,23; 6:7-14; 10:10,15,16; I Sam. 12:10,11; II Chr. 15:4,15; Neh. 9:27; Ps. 106:15. Gideon — Ju. 6:36-40; Manoah — Ju. 13:8,9. Samson — Ju. 15:18,19; 16:28-30. Hannah — I Sam. 1:10-17,27. Samuel — I Sam. 7:9. David — I Sam. 23:10-12; Ps. 18:6. Solomon — I Ki. 3:1-13; 9:2,3. Man of God — I Ki. 13:6. Elijah — I Ki. 18:36-39; Jas. 5:17,18. Elisha — II Ki. 4:33-35; 6:18,19. Jehoahaz — II Ki. 13:4. Hezekiah and Isaiah — II Ki. 19:14-20; 20:1-6,10,11; II Chr. 32:20,21, 24. Jabez — I Chr. 4:10. Abijah's army — II Chr. 13:14-18. Asa — II Chr. 14:11-15; 15:16. Jehoshaphat — II Chr. 18:31; 20:6-27. Levites — II Chr. 30:27.

Manasseh — II Chr. 33:13,19. Ezra — Ezra 8:21-23. Nehemiah — Neh. 4:9,15. Job — Job 42:10. Jeremiah — Lam. 3:55,56. Daniel — Dan. 9:20-23. Jonah — Jonah 2:2,10. Reubenites — I Chr. 5:20. Jews — Ezra 8:21,23; Zech. 7:1-4. Zacharias — Lu. 1:13. Apostles — Acts 4:29-31. Ananias — Acts 10:4. Cornelius — Acts 10:4,21. Disciples — Acts 12:5,7. Paul — Acts 28:8. Paul and Silas — Acts 16:25,26.

Prayer of wicked not answered. — Deut. 1:45; II Sam. 22:42; Job 35:12,13; Ps. 18:41; 34:16; 66:18; Pr. 1:24-28; 15:8,29; 21:13,27; 28:9; Is. 1:15; 59:2; Jer. 11:11; 14:12; 15:1; 18:17; Ez. 8:18; 20:3,31; Hos. 5:6; Mic. 3:4; Zech. 7:12,13; Mal. 2:11-13; Lu. 18:11-14; John 9:31; Jas. 1:6-8; 4:3.

Christ as a mediator. — Rom. 8:34; Eph. 2:18; 3:12; I Tim. 2:5; Heb. 4:14-16; 13:15.

Aid of Holy Spirit. — Zech. 12:10; Rom. 8:26; Eph. 2:18; 6:18; Jude 20.

Assurances. — Is. 37:4; 81:10; Is. 65:24; Jer. 33:3; Mt. 9:29; Mk. 11:24; John 14:14; 15:7,16; Eph. 3:20; Jas. 5:16; I John 3:20.

Private prayer. — Job. 22:27. Commanded — Mt. 6:6.

Examples of: Lot — Gen. 19:20. Abraham's servant — Gen. 24:12. Jacob — Gen. 32:9-12. Moses — Deut. 9:18-20. Gideon — Ju. 6:22,36,39. Hannah — I Sam. 1:9-15. David — II Sam. 7:18-29. Hezekiah — II Ki. 20:2,5. Isaiah — II Ki. 20:11. Manasseh — II Chr. 33:12,13. Ezra 9:5,6. Nehemiah — Neh. 1:4; 2:4. Jeremiah — Jer. 32:16-25. Daniel — Dan. 9:3,17-20. Daniel and companions — Dan. 2:17-23. Jonah — Jonah 2:1. Anna — Lu. 2:37.

Public prayer. — God hears — II Chr. 7:14,16. God accepts — Is. 56:7. Christ sanctions — Mt. 18:20. Form of prayer — Mt. 6:9-13; Lu. 11:2-4.

Should be understood — I Cor. 14:14-16. Examples — Joshua — Josh. 7:6-9. David — I Chr. 29:10-19. Solomon — II Chr. Ch. 6. Jehoshaphat — II Chr. 20:5-13. Levites — Neh. Ch. 9. Jews — Lu. 1:10. Disciples — Acts 2:46; 4:24; 12:5,12; 13:3; 16:16.

Prayers in Old Testament. — *Aaron and priests,* for blessing — Num. 6:22-26. *Abraham,* for a son — Gen. 15:2. For Ishmael — Gen. 17:17,18. For Sodom — Gen. 18:22-23. *Asa,* for victory — II Chr. 14:11. *Daniel,* for Jerusalem — Dan. 9:4-19. Toward Jerusalem — Dan. 6:10. *David,* for his house — II Sam. 7:18-29. For forgiveness and peace — Ps. 51. For Israel — II Sam. 24:17. At the end of his life — I Chr. 29:10-19. *Eliezer,* for success — Gen. 24:12-14,27. *Elijah,* for widow's son — I Ki. 17:20. At Carmel — I Ki. 18:36,37. To die — I Ki. 19:4. *Elisha,* for opening inner eyes — II Ki. 16:17. For blinding the army — II Ki. 6:18. *Ezekiel,* for people — Ez. 9:8. *Ezra,* confession — Ezra 9:5-15. For protection — Ezra 8:21-23. *Gideon,* colloquy with an angel — Ju. Ch. 6. *Habakkuk,* for a revival — Hab. 3:1-16. *Hannah,* for a son — I Sam. 1:11. In thanksgiving — I Sam. 2:1-10. *Hezekiah,* for his protection — II Ki. 19:15-19; 20:3; Is. 38:3. In the temple — Is. 37:16-20. For the uncleansed — II Chr. 30:18. *Isaiah,* a prayer, praise and thanksgiving — Is. 63:7; 64:12. *Israel,* for expiation — Deut. 21:6-8. Confession — Deut. 26:5-10. Tithing prayer — Deut. 26:13-15. *Jabez,* for blessing — I Chr. 4:10. *Jacob,* before Esau — Gen. 32:9-12. In a vow — Gen. 28:20. While wrestling with an angel — Gen. 32:24 (*cf.* Hos. 12:3,4). *Jehoshaphat,* for deliverance — II Chr. 20:6-13. *Jeremiah,* in famine — Jer. 14:7-9. For comfort — Jer. 15:15-18. *Jonah,* for freedom —

345

Jonah 2:2-9. At Nineveh — Jonah 4:2. *Joshua,* for mercy — Josh. 7:7-9. Against enemies — Josh. 10:12-14. *Levites,* confession — Neh. 9:5-38. *Manoah,* for guidance — Ju. 13:8,9. *Men in general* — Gen. 4:26. *Moses,* in a colloquy with God — Ex. Chs.3 and 4. Appeals to God — Ex. 5:22. Calls for relief for Pharaoh — Ex. 8:12,29,30; 9:33; 10:17,18. For the people — Ex. 32:11-13. For guidance — Ex. 33:12-16. For God's presence — Num. 10:35,36. For help — Num. 11:11-15. For Miriam — Num. 12:13. For murmurers — Num. 14:13-19. For a successor — Num. 27:15-17. To enter Canaan — Deut. 3:24. *Nehemiah,* for captives — Neh. 1:5-11. For protection — Neh. 4:4,5. Levites' prayer — Neh. 9:5-38. *Psalmist,* in a large number of Psalms. *Samson,* for vengeance — Ju. 16:28. *Samuel,* for Israel — I Sam. 7:5-12. Regarding Israel's desire for king — I Sam. Chs. 8 and 12. Attitude for Israel — I Sam. 12:23. *Solomon,* for wisdom — I Ki. 3:5-9. Temple dedication — I Ki. 8:23-61; II Chr. 6:14-42. Titles of Psalms — 17: 86; 90; 102; 142.

Prayers of Jesus. — Mt. 19:13; Lu. 3:21; 11:1; John 12:27,28; Heb. 5:7. Of thanksgiving — Mt. 11:25,26; 14:19; 15:36; 26:27; Mk. 6:41; 14:22; Lu. 22:17; John 11:41,42; I Cor. 11:24. In a mountain — Mt. 14:23; Mk. 6:46; Lu. 6:12. In the upper room — John 17:1-26. For Peter — Lu. 22:32. In Gethsemane — Mt. 26:36-42; Mk. 14:32-39; Lu. 22:41-45. On the cross — Mt. 27:46; Lu. 23:34,46.

Paul's prayers. — Rom 1:3; 10:1; I Cor. 1:3; II Cor. 13:7; Eph. 1:16-19; 3:14-19: Phil. 1:3-10; Col. 1:3,9; I Thess. 1:2; 3:10-13; 5:23; II Thess. 1:11; 2:16,17; 3:5,16; II Tim. 1:3,18; Philemon 4-6; Heb. 13:20,21.

Promises. *Promissum,* from *promittere,* to send, or put forward. Commands involved in promises — Ex. 19:5-8; 23: 20-33; II Cor. 7:1; Gal. 3:21,22; Heb. 3:14-19.

Promises founded upon five pillars — (1) God's justice — Gen. 18:25; Job 8:3-7; Is. 9:7. (2) God's goodness — Deut. 11:31-32; Is. 49:15,16; Heb. 6:10. (3) God's truth — Num. 23:19; Ps. 102:24-28; Mal. 3:6; Heb. 1:10-12. (4) God's power — II Chr. 20:6,7; 25:7-9; Dan. 3:17; 6:20-22; Mt. 9:27-30; Acts 20:32; Rom. 4:20,22; 11:23; 14:4; I Cor. 10:13; II Cor. 9:8-11; Eph. 3:20; Phil. 3:20,21; II Tim. 1:12; Heb. 2:18; 7:25; Jude 24,25. (5) God's oath — Deut. 7:8; Ps. 89:3,4; 105:9; Jer. 11:6; Heb. 6:13-20.

Receive. Abundance — Rom. 5:17. Adoption of sons — Gal. 4:5. Almighty, From — Job. 27:13. Blessing — Ps. 24:5; Heb. 6:7. Brother's blood — Gen. 4:11. See Cain. Burnt offerings — I Ki. 8:64; II Chr. 7:7. Commandments — Pr. 10:8. Correction — Jer. 5:3. Corruptible crown — I Cor. 9:25. Crown of glory — I Pet. 5:4. Crown of life — Jas. 1:12. Edifying — I Cor. 14:5. See Edification. Good, Evil — Job 2:10. Grace — Rom. 1:5. Holy Spirit — Acts 2:38; 8:17,19. Inheritance — Num. 34:14; Josh. 13:8; 18:7. Instruction — Pr. 1:3; 8:10. Interest — Ez. 18:17. Law — Job 22:23; Acts 7:53. Me to glory — Ps. 73:21. Money — II Ki. 5:26. More blessed to give than — Acts 20:35. Plagues, Of — Rev. 18:4. Pledge — Gen. 38:20. Power — Acts 1:8. Prayer, My — Ps. 6:9. Prize — I Cor. 9:24. See Prayer. Present — Gen. 33:10. Promise — Gal. 3:14; Heb. 11:17. Recompence — Rom. 1:27; Col. 3:24. Remission of sins — Acts 26:18. Reward — II John 8; I Cor. 3:8. Sayings — Pr. 4:10. Shame

— Hos. 10:6. Stripes — I Cor. 11:24. Testimony — Acts 2:18. Tithes — Heb. 7:18. Words, My — Pr. 2:1. Ye one another — Rom. 15:7.

Repentance. Gr. *Metanoia,* Complete "Change of mind." A state of feeling — Gen. 6:6,7; Ju. 2:18; 21:6,15; I Sam. 15:11,35; Job 42:6; Ps. 106:45; Jer. 8:6; 20:16; 31:19; Mt. 27:3; Rom. 2:4,5; II Cor. 7:8-10; Heb. 6:1-6.
A change of purpose. — Ex. 13:17; 32:12-14; Num. 23:19; Deut. 32:36; I Sam. 15:29; II Sam. 24:16; I Ki. 8:47; I Chr. 21:15; Ps. 90:13; 110:4; 135:14; Jer. 4:28; 18:7-10; Ez. 24:14; Joel 2:12-14; Amos 7:3-6; Jonah 3:9,10; 4:2; Mt. 3:1,2; 9:13; 41;29-32; Mk. 1:4,15; 6:12; Lu. 5:32; 16:30; 17:3,4; Acts 2:38; 3:19; 13:24; 17:30; 19:4; 26:20; II Cor. 12:21; Rev. 2:5,16; 3:3,19-21; 16:9.
Essential to salvation. — I Ki. 8:47; Jer. 20:16; Mt. 11:20-22; 12:41; Mk. 1:4; Lu. 3:3; 5:37; 10:13,14; 11:32; 13:3-5; 15:7-10; 24:47; Acts 2:38; 3:19; 8:22; 11:18; 17:30; II Cor. 7:10; II Tim. 2:25,26; II Pet. 3:9.
Should lead to reformation of life. — Mt. 3:8-11; 21:29; Lu. 3:8; 5:32; 15:7; Acts 26:20.

Restitution. Guilt, For — Num. 5:7,8. Law of — Lev. 24:18-21; Pr. 6:31; Lu. 19:8. Make — Ex. 22:3; Lev. 5:16. Times of — Mt. 19:28; Acts 3:21.

Reverence. Ps. 45:11; Heb. 12:9. Demeanor, In — Tit. 2:3. God — Ps. 111:9; Eccl. 5:2. Haman, To — Esth. 3:2,5. House of God — Eccl. 5:1. My son — Mt. 21:27; Mk. 12:6; 20:13. Offer service with — Heb. 12:28. Sanctuary — Lev. 19:30; 26:2.

Seeking. God and His Christ seek men. — Sent messengers early — II Chr. 36:15,16; Jer. 25:4. All day — Is. 65:2; Rom. 10:21. Seeks true worshippers — John 4:23. As a shepherd — Lu. 15:3-7; John 10:11,15,16. As a redeemer — Mt. 20:28; Mk. 10:45; Lu. 19:10.
Men sought to see Jesus. — Shepherds —Lu. 2:15,16. Wise Men — Mt. 2:1,2,10,11. John's disciples — John 1:37,38,41,45. Nicodemus — John 3:1,2. Galileans — John 6:24. Zaccheus — Lu. 19:3. Greeks — John 12:20,21.
Exhortations to seek God: Because — God requires it — Deut. 10:12,13; Mic. 6:8; Acts 17:26,27. He will punish — Deut. 11:16,17; Josh. 24:19,20,23; I Sam. 12:14,15; Amos 4:12; Zeph. 2:3; I Chr. 28:9; II Chr. 15:2; Jer. 29:13; Lam. 3:25,26. He can be found — Deut. 4:29; Mt. 7:7,8; Acts 17:27,28. It glorifies His name — I Ki. 8:60,61. Man always seeks a god — Is. 8:19,20. Now is the time — Eccl. 12:1; Is. 55:3,6,7. God is good — Lam. 3:25,26. Of what God has done — I Chr. 22:18,19; Ps. 65:9-13; Ez. 34:26,27; Acts 14:17. Of what God will do — Ezra 8:22; Ps. 1:3; 34:10; 37:4,7,9,34; 69:32; 70:4; 105:4; 119:2; Heb. 6:11,12,17-20; 11:6.
Seeking knowledge of God is seeking God. — Pr. 2:3-5; John 17:3. It is blessed — Is. 30:18; Mt. 5:6. It is the step to strength — I Chr. 16:10,11; Is. 40:29-31. It leads to honor — I Sam. 2:30; Is. 49:23; Rom. 2:7-10. It is the track to all things — Mt. 7:11; Rom 8:16,17,28,32. It is the path to mercy — Hos. 10:12; 12:6; Joel 2:12,13.

Shouting: Occasions for. — Appointing of king — I Sam. 10:24. Bringing of ark to camp — I Sam. 4:5,6. To Jerusalem — II Sam. 6:15; I Chr. 15:28. Fall of Jericho — Josh. 6:10,16,20. War — Ju. 15:14; I Sam. 17:20,52; II Chr. 13:15; Job 30:25;

Amos 1:14; 2:2.

Thanksgiving to Jehovah. — II Chr. 15:14; Ps. 41:15; Pr. 11:10; Is. 12:6; 42:11; 44:23 (fig.); Jer. 31:7; Zeph. 3:14; Zech. 9:9. Joy — Ezra 3:11,12,13; Job 38:7; Ps. 6:11; 32:9,16.

Sin. Heb. *"Going astray;"* Guilt, Iniquity. *Gr.* Missing the mark; failure.

Forgiveness of. — Acts 8:22; Rom. 4:7; Col. 2:13; I John 1:9.

God is forgiving. — Ex. 34:6,7; Num. 14:18-20; II Sam. 12:13; Ps. 85:2; 99:8; 130:4; Is. 1:18; 6:6; 43:25; 44:21; 55:6; Jer. 31:34; 33:38; Dan. 9:9; Heb. 8:12; 10:17; Jas. 5:15; I John 1:9.

The sin and trespass offerings in order to forgiveness. — Lev. 4:1-35; 5:1-19; 6:1-7,24-30; 7:1-10; 19:21-22.

Forgiveness conditional. — Man must repent — Ez. 18:21-32; 33:10-16. See Repentance.

Man must forgive his fellow man — Mt. 6:14,15; 18:21,22; Mk. 11:25; Lu. 11:4; 17:3,4; Eph. 4:32.

Parable of the unmerciful servant — Mt. 18:23-35. Of the two debtors — Lu. 7:41-50.

Forgiveness is in Christ. — Eph. 1:17; Col. 1:14. Christ forgave the paralytic — Mt. 9:2-6; Mk. 2:1-12; Lu. 5:18-25. The woman in the Pharisee's house — Lu. 7:36-50. Fallen woman — John 8:1-11. Apostolic forgiveness — John 20:23.

The unpardonable sin. — Num. 15:30; Mt. 12:31; Mk. 3:29; Lu. 12:10; Heb. 6:4,6; 10:26-29; I John 5:16-17.

The pleasure of sin. — Job 20:12-15; Lu. 8:14; Heb. 11:25.

Sing. Idle songs — Amos 6:5. Jehovah, To — Ex. 15:21; Ps. 57:7; 87:7. Joy, For — Ps. 96:12. New song — Rev. 5:9.

Supplication. Jas. 5:16. Continueth in

— I Tim. 5:6. Hearken to — I Ki. 8:30; Ps. 6:9; 28:2. Helping by — II Cor. 1:11. Make — II Chr. 6:37; Dan. 6:11; Phil. 1:4. Thanksgiving, With — Phil. 4:6. See Prayer.

Thanksgiving: Offered to God. — Ps. 69:30; 95:2; 100:4.

Occasion for. — II Cor. 4:15; 9:11,12; Col. 2:7.

Through Christ. — Rom. 1:8; Col. 3:17. In the name of — Eph. 5:20; Heb. 13:15.

Reasons for. — Gifts from God — I Tim. 4:3,4. God's nearness — Ps. 75:1,9. Supply of bodily needs — John 6:11; Acts 27:35; Rom. 14:6,7; I Tim. 2:1. Conversion — Rom. 6:17. Victory over death — I Cor. 15:57. Divine guidance — II Cor. 2:14. Under all circumstances — Phil 4:6.

Forms of. — Sacrifices — Lev. 7:12,13,15; 22:29; Ps. 50:14; 107:22; 116:17; Amos 4:5. Prayer — Neh. 11:17; Phil. 4:6; Col. 4:2. See prayer. Song — Neh. 13:8,46; Ps. 147:7. See songs. Ministers appointed to lead in — I Chr. 16:4,7; 23:30; II Chr. 31:2.

Occasions for. In worship — Ps. 35:18; Dan. 6:10. Dedication — Neh. 12:27.

Prophecies concerning. — Is. 51:3; Jer. 30:19.

Christ sets example of. — Mt. 11:25; 26:27-29; Mk. 14:22; Lu. 22:19; John 6:11; 11:41.

Upright. I Sam. 29:6; Job 1:1; Ps. 19:13; 112:4; Mic. 7:4. Cut off — Job 4:7. Friendship of — Pr. 3:32. Good will of — Pr. 14:9. Jehovah is — Ps. 25:8. Man made — Eccl. 7:29. Might reason — Job 23:7. Path of — Pr. 15:19. Praise for — Ps. 33:1. Prayer of — Pr. 15:8. Soul — Hab. 2:4. Wisdom for — Pr. 2:7.

Vow. A promise to God to do His pleasure on condition of receiving a

blessing from Him. — Gen. 28:20;
Num. 21:2; Ps. 65:1; Is. 19:21.
Two kinds of vows: The ordinary or
lesser vow — Num. 30:2 ff.; the
Nazirite or greater vow — Num. 6:2 ff.
Law regulating (governing) vows. —
Num. 30:2-13. No compulsion to take
vows — Deut. 23:22; Eccl. 5:5. But
must be fulfilled if taken — Deut.
23:21; Eccl. 5:4; Num. 30:2; John
2:9. Women's vows, to be approved
by father or husband — Num.
30:3,6-16. But widows and divorced
women may vow for themselves —
Num. 30:9. Sacrifice as vow offering
— Lev. 7:16; 22:21,23; Num.
16:3,8; Deut. 12:11.
Nazirite vow. — Num. 6:2-21. Prohibi-
tions pertaining to strong drink —
Num. 6:3. Shaving hair — Num. 6:5.
Touching dead bodies — Num. 6:6.
Sacrifice for the redemption of —
Num. 6:10 ff. Ceremonial of redemption — Num. 6:13-21.
Notable vows in history. — Jacob's —
Gen. 28:20; 31:13. Jephthah's — Ju.
11:30,39. Hannah's — I Sam.
1:11,21. Absalom's — II Sam.
15:7,8. Paul's — Acts 18:18. Of the
four whom he took into the temple
with him — Acts 21:23.

Wait. Job 6:11,19; 14:14; 17:13;
29:23; 32:4; 35:14; Ps. 39:7;
119:95; Jer. 9:8; Dan. 12:12. Altar,
At the — I Cor. 9:13. Consolation of
Israel, For — Lu. 2:25. Cornelius —
Acts 10:24. Fowlers lie in wait — Jer.
5:26. Fruit, For — Jas. 5:7. Gates of
wisdom, At — Pr. 8:34. God — Is.
30:18. For God. — II Ki. 6:33; Ps.
25:3,5,21; 27:14; 33:20; 37:7,9,34;
40:1; 62:1,5; 65:1; 69:36; 104:27;
106:13; 130:5; 145:15; Pr. 20:22; Is.
8:17; 25:9; 26:8; 33:2; 40:31; 49:23;
51:5; 60:9; 64:4; Jer. 14:22; Lam.
3:25; Hos. 12:6; Mic. 7:7; Zeph. 3:8.
Longsuffering of. — I Pet. 3:20. Hope
of righteousness, For the — Gal. 5:5.

Israel — Ez. 19:5. Jesus, For — Lu.
2:25; 8:40; I Cor. 1:7; Phil 3:20; I
Thess. 1:10; II Thess. 3:5; Heb. 9:28.
King, On the — II Chr. 17:19.
Kingdom, For the — Mk. 15:43; Lu.
23:51. Law of God, For the — Is.
42:4. One for another — I Cor.
11:33. Patience, With — Ps. 37:7;
40:1; Rom. 8:25. Paul — Acts 17:16.
Priests, On — I Chr. 23:28. Promise,
For the — Acts 1:7. Revealing of sons
of God — Rom. 8:19-25. Robbers for
a man — Hos. 6:9. Service, Upon the
— Num. 3:10; 4:23; 8:24,25; I Chr.
6:32,35; Neh. 12:44; I Cor. 9:13.
Soldier of Cornelius, Devout — Acts
10:7. Sons of men. For — Mic. 5:7.
Soul, For my — Ps. 56:6. Sword, For,
of the — Job 15:22. Twilight, For —
Job 24:15. Vision, For — Hab. 2:3.
Words, For — Job 32:11,16.

Worship: Of Jehovah. — Ex. 20:3; I
Chr. 29:30; II Chr. 7:3; Neh. 8:6;
9:3; Job 1:20; Is. 27:13; John 12:20;
Acts 24:11; I Cor. 14:25; Heb. 1:6;
Rev. Ch. 4.
Of Jesus. — Mt. 2:2,8,11; 8:2; 9:18;
14:33; 15:25; 28:9,17; Mk. 5:6; Lu.
24:52; John 9:38; Rev. 7:9,10.
With an offering. — Gen. 22:5; Ex.
24:1,5; Deut. 26:10. Before one altar
— II Chr. 32:12; Ps. 95:6; 99:5;
132:7; Jer. 7:2; 26:2.
Toward the temple. — Ps. 5:7; 138:2;
Ez. 46:2,3.
In the beauty of holiness. — I Chr.
16:29; Ps. 27:4; 29:2; 96:9.
With song and music. — Ps. 66:4;
100:1-4; II Chr. 5:12-14; 29:27-30;
Ezra 3:10,11; Is. 30:29; Rev. 5:8-14;
15:2-4.
In spirit. — John 4:23,24; Phil. 3:3.
Universal. — Ps. 22:27-29; 86:9; Is.
49:7; 66:23; John 4:20-24; Phil.
2:10,11. From the gods — Ps. 97:7.

Zion, zi'on. Called — City of David — II
Sam. 5:7-9; I Ki. 8:1; I Chr. 11:5,7; II

Chr. 5:2. Holy Hill — Ps. 2:6; 78:68. Mountain of Jehovah — Mic. 4:2. Zion, of the Holy One of Israel — Is. 60:14. Mountains of — Ps. 133:3.

Description of. — Beauty — Ps. 48:2; 50:2. Glory — Ps. 48:11. Towers of — Ps. 48:12. Gates of — Ps. 87:2. Palaces of — Ps. 48:3,13.

Chosen by Jehovah. — Ps. 132:13; Is. 51:16.

Ark brought from. — II Chr. 5:2.

Prayer for. — Ps. 51:18.

Dwelling of Jehovah. — Ps. 9:11; 65:1; 74:2; 76:2; 84:7; 99:2; 128:5; 134:3; 135:21; Is. 8:18; 24:23; 31:9; Joel 3:16,17,21; Zech. 2:10.

Source of strength. — Ps. 20:2; 110:2; Is. 52:1.

Songs of. — Ps. 137:3.

Lament over. — Ps. 14:7; 53:6; Is. 10:24; 49:14; Lam. 1:4,17; 2:6; 4:2,11,22; 5:11,18.

Seat of worship. — Ps. 102:21; Jer. 51:10.

Captives return. — Ps. 126:1.

Zion's praise to Jehovah. — Ps. 146:10; 147:12; 149:2; Is. 12:6.

Index of Subjects

Index of Scriptures